Twenty-First-Century Gothic

Edinburgh Companions to the Gothic

Series Editors
Andrew Smith, University of Sheffield
William Hughes, Bath Spa University

This series provides a comprehensive overview of the Gothic from the eighteenth century to the present day. Each volume takes either a period, place or theme and explores their diverse attributes, contexts and texts via completely original essays. The volumes provide an authoritative critical tool for both scholars and students of the Gothic.

Volumes in the series are edited by leading scholars in their field and make a cutting-edge contribution to the field of Gothic studies.

Each volume:
- Presents an innovative and critically challenging exploration of the historical, thematic and theoretical understandings of the Gothic from the eighteenth century to the present day
- Provides a critical forum in which ideas about Gothic history and established Gothic themes are challenged
- Supports the teaching of the Gothic at an advanced undergraduate level and at masters level
- Helps readers to rethink ideas concerning periodisation and to question the critical approaches which have been taken to the Gothic

Published Titles
The Victorian Gothic: An Edinburgh Companion
  Andrew Smith and William Hughes
Romantic Gothic: An Edinburgh Companion
  Angela Wright and Dale Townshend
American Gothic Culture: An Edinburgh Companion
  Joel Faflak and Jason Haslam
Women and the Gothic: An Edinburgh Companion
  Avril Horner and Sue Zlosnik
Scottish Gothic: An Edinburgh Companion
  Carol Margaret Davison and Monica Germanà
The Gothic and Theory: An Edinburgh Companion
  Jerrold E. Hogle and Robert Miles
Twenty-First-Century Gothic: An Edinburgh Companion
  Maisha Wester and Xavier Aldana Reyes

Visit the Edinburgh Companions to the Gothic website at:
www.edinburghuniversitypress.com/series/EDCG

Twenty-First-Century Gothic

An Edinburgh Companion

Edited by
Maisha Wester and
Xavier Aldana Reyes

EDINBURGH
University Press

Edinburgh University Press is one of the leading university presses in the UK. We publish academic books and journals in our selected subject areas across the humanities and social sciences, combining cutting-edge scholarship with high editorial and production values to produce academic works of lasting importance. For more information visit our website: edinburghuniversitypress.com

© editorial matter and organisation Maisha Wester and Xavier Aldana Reyes, 2019, 2021
© the chapters their several authors, 2019, 2021

Edinburgh University Press Ltd
The Tun – Holyrood Road, 12(2f) Jackson's Entry, Edinburgh EH8 8PJ

First published in hardback by Edinburgh University Press 2019

Typeset in 10.5/13 Sabon by
Servis Filmsetting Ltd, Stockport, Cheshire

A CIP record for this book is available from the British Library

ISBN 978 1 4744 4092 9 (hardback)
ISBN 978 1 4744 4093 6 (paperback)
ISBN 978 1 4744 4094 3 (webready PDF)
ISBN 978 1 4744 4095 0 (epub)

The right of the contributors to be identified as the author of this work has been asserted in accordance with the Copyright, Designs and Patents Act 1988, and the Copyright and Related Rights Regulations 2003 (SI No. 2498).

Contents

Acknowledgements — vii

Introduction: The Gothic in the Twenty-First Century — 1
Maisha Wester and Xavier Aldana Reyes

PART I UPDATING THE TRADITION

1. Postcolonial Gothic — 19
   Sarah Ilott

2. Queer Gothic — 33
   Andrew J. Owens

3. Postfeminist Gothic — 47
   Gina Wisker

4. Neoliberal Gothic — 60
   Linnie Blake

5. Gothic Digital Technologies — 72
   Joseph Crawford

PART II CONTEMPORARY MONSTERS

6. Contemporary Zombies — 89
   Xavier Aldana Reyes

7. Contemporary Vampires — 102
   Sorcha Ní Fhlainn

8. Contemporary Serial Killers — 117
   Bernice M. Murphy

9. Contemporary Ghosts 131
   Murray Leeder

10. Contemporary Werewolves 144
    Kaja Franck and Sam George

PART III CONTEMPORARY SUBGENRES

11. The New Weird 161
    Carl H. Sederholm

12. Ecogothic 174
    Sharae Deckard

13. Gothic Comedy 189
    Catherine Spooner

14. Steampunk 203
    Claire Nally

15. Posthuman Gothic 218
    Anya Heise-von der Lippe

PART IV ETHNOGOTHIC

16. South African Gothic 233
    Rebecca Duncan

17. Asian Gothic 249
    Katarzyna Ancuta

18. Latin American Gothic 263
    Enrique Ajuria Ibarra

19. Aboriginal Gothic 276
    Katrin Althans

20. Black Diasporic Gothic 289
    Maisha Wester

Notes on Contributors 304
Index 309

Acknowledgements

We would like to thank the editors of the Edinburgh Companions to the Gothic, Andrew Smith and William Hughes, for their guidance with, and enthusiasm for, this book, especially during its initial stages. We would also like to thank Jackie Jones and Ersev Ersoy at Edinburgh University Press for their help and support and Nick James for the preparation of the index.

This collection would not exist without the time, effort and dedication of its contributors. A huge thank you to them for their cooperation and professionalism. It has been an utter pleasure working with them.

We would also like to thank the external reviewers for their suggestions on the first draft of the book. They made this collection stronger and more thorough.

Our respective Gothic students have shaped the contents and direction of this collection, and it is largely for the benefit of future generations that we have put it together. We are indebted to them for their passion and inspiration.

Finally, we would like to thank our partners and families for their understanding and love. We could not do this without them.

Maisha would like to dedicate this book to her loving partner, Jess Turner, and her wonderful parents, James Wester and Gail Leverett.

Xavier would like to dedicate this book to his grandparents, Victoriano Aldana Moruno and Trinidad Ribeiro Centeno.

In memoriam

Introduction: The Gothic in the Twenty-First Century

Maisha Wester and Xavier Aldana Reyes

The establishment of the Gothic as one of the prevalent artistic modes of the post-millennial period is not something that could have been easily foreseen in the mid-twentieth century. For a long time relegated to specialist university units on Romanticism and Enlightenment literature, still heavily associated with medieval and revival architecture and certainly not in wide circulation as a term through which to describe contemporary cultural products, the Gothic underwent a seismic change during the 1980s and 1990s. The astounding effect of scholarly work, especially the pioneering books by David Pirie (1973), David Punter (1980), Chris Baldick (1992), Fred Botting (1996), Victor Sage and Andrew Lloyd Smith (1996) and Catherine Spooner (2006), which argued for either the endless recycling or else the persistence of the Gothic in modern and contemporary times, alongside a sustained wave of interest from students, authors, associations and readers/viewers/gamers, brought about a re-evaluation of both the epistemological value of this artistic category and its notional limits. Although definitions of the Gothic in modern times have continued to be loose and hazy, going as far as characterising the nature of the mode as inherently transgeneric and category-resistant, it is now associated with the dark side of culture. By the 2010s, the Gothic no longer refers to a historically specific strand of 'terrorist' and/or romance writing in the late eighteenth and early nineteenth centuries. It no longer demarcates simply a fantastic retrojection to barbaric pasts either, although this is still the one area where the Gothic manifests in a clearer manner. In the Anglo-American world and, increasingly, the global sphere, the Gothic has become a wider term to designate non-realistic modes of writing and now encompasses horror, certain strands of science fiction and speculative fiction, especially the weird tradition, magical realism, the supernatural more widely (even fairy tales) and all generic hybrids that contain elements traditionally associated with the Gothic (such as monstrous figures like the ghost and the vampire or grotesque and macabre tableaus). Whereas in some areas of the continent, such as France and Spain, other umbrella terms – 'le fantastique', 'le roman noir', 'lo fantástico' – have prevailed, the Gothic, as a mode no longer constrained by fixed settings, time or characters, has freely materialised beyond the borders of generic ascription or emotion-generation in the English-speaking world.[1]

Significant cultural bodies and organisations in countries like the UK, where the Gothic has been celebrated and seen as linked to important notions of national identity, have contributed to the legitimisation of the Gothic in the twenty-first century and turned the term, once the preserve of the academic community, into public currency through talks, workshops and exhibitions. For example, the British Film Institute ran an enormous thematised film season, *Gothic: The Dark Heart of Film* (October 2013–January 2014), which included dozens of screenings throughout the UK and public sessions on the value of the Gothic. Similarly, the British Library ran another major exhibition, *Terror and Wonder: The Gothic Imagination* (October 2014–January 2015), which led to the biggest display of Gothic literature and associated media ever (paintings, film scripts and even real vampire-killing kits). Both exhibitions included large numbers of modern and post-millennial texts. The foundation of the International Gothic Association (which unites teachers, scholars and students across the world), of its biennial conference in the early 1990s, and of its main associated journal, *Gothic Studies*, in 1999, were all key to the institutionalisation of the Gothic. This flurry of activity has been followed in the twenty-first century by the further entrenchment of the Gothic in university undergraduate and postgraduate curricula and by the foundation of research centres such as the Manchester Centre for Gothic Studies, the Centre for the History of the Gothic at Sheffield University and the International Centre for Gothic Studies at Stirling. The term 'Gothic' is now readily used to refer to the work of many contemporary authors, such as Sarah Waters, Patrick McGrath, Neil Gaiman, Kate Mosse and Sarah Perry, and used to market the work of international authors such as Spanish writer Carlos Ruiz Zafón and Mexican director Guillermo del Toro. The Gothic has moved beyond initial debates about its respectability, anachronistic nature and staying power and is now firmly rooted in the imaginations of readers and those responsible for marketing campaigns and education programmes.[2] The only price the Gothic has had to pay for its longevity has been a loss of specificity. What exactly does it mean to call something 'Gothic' in the twenty-first century, and how does such a polysemantic marker continue be of critical value? Any attempt at collecting all forms of Gothic manifestations is bound, by the mode's very nature, to prioritise some elements and historical points of origin over others. Although we remain wary of unqualified generalisations, it is necessary for us to offer an approximation to the Gothic today and, most importantly, to its use in this collection. After all, it is only by demarcating the limits of any cultural manifestation that its inner operations can be duly scrutinised.

Delimiting the Gothic in the Twenty-First Century

It is important to acknowledge that the meanings ascribed to the term 'Gothic' were already quite varied in the eighteenth century, even if 'barbaric' and 'medieval' were the two most predominant associations for readers (Longueil 1923; Sage 1990: 17).[3] Broadly speaking, the Gothic still retains some of these 'original' connotations. Gothic fictions, whichever the medium, are often set in an imaginary version of the 'barbarous' past; the main difference is that the 'Gothic cusp' – the 'transitional phase, when the Gothic epoch came to an end, and the modern one began' (Miles 1995: 87) – is increasingly positioned in the Victorian period, as this era best allows for the articulation of the struggle between modern sensibilities and the 'unenlightened past' for twenty-first-century audiences (Spooner 2007: 42). Sometimes the archaic past may be confined to a building, for example in the trope of the haunted manor house or asylum, where space and place are inseparable. When Gothic texts are set in the present, they tend to stage some type of return of either repressed or forgotten deeds in the form of a curse, ancestrally or magically imposed, an obsession or a haunting. Certain locations, due to their recurring appearances and formulaic rehashing, have come to metonymically stand in for the Gothic: ruins, in particular those of abbeys and monasteries, medieval castles, cemeteries and moonlit cliffs are only some of the most typical. In the American context, forests, wild, dangerous and potentially magical, are also stalwarts of the Gothic as championed by Charles Brockden Brown and Nathaniel Hawthorne. The specificity of setting, although not a crucial Gothic element for some critics, may ultimately prove invaluable in separating the Gothic – which we see as strongly marked by time, characters and place – from horror, largely defined by the emotion it aims to generate.[4] As we show below, however, since the Gothic is important in terms of the type of cultural work it enables, it is possible to overlook its older formulae and prioritise individual characters or tropes (the double, the monster) because they open up texts to a series of socially-significant readings.

The Gothic's richness has grown exponentially, and part of the difficulty involved in delimiting it is that the mode has evolved into an artistic palimpsest with tendrils reaching out into virtually every connected genre and subgenre. Firstly, the characteristics of subsequent periods (the urban mise-en-scène of the Victorian and Edwardian Gothic, the parodic and metatextual play of modern and postmodern Gothic) and of a number of later artistic manifestations (the penny dreadful, the ghost story, the decadent novel) that are perceived to have a strong emotional or representational affinity with 'first wave Gothic' have joined the melting pot.[5] This means that later additions, such as monsters like the serial killer, the werewolf and the zombie, may be retroactively read as part of a generative canon of the Gothic which, in itself, becomes indexical. In other words, as the Gothic accrues additional tropes and scenarios in hindsight, both its history and reach expand. Secondly, as the Gothic turns more and more self-referential and intertextual, drawing on, when not continuing, key texts like Mary Shelley's *Frankenstein* (1818), Bram Stoker's *Dracula* (1897), Robert Louis Stevenson's *The Strange Case of Dr Jekyll and Mr Hyde* (1886) and Henry James's *The Turn of the Screw* (1898), critics begin to look back for earlier prototypes and re-inscribe them as Gothic. The legacy and impact of horror film to the creation of a coherent set of visual Gothic cues cannot be understated either. The monster cycles of early German cinema, Universal and Hammer, as well as the old dark house mysteries of the 1910s, 1920s and 1930s, were foundational in building strong bonds between monsters and the Gothic, and between the Gothic and the Victorian period melodrama's spatial accoutrements. As a result of the constant and all-inclusive revision and rewriting of the history of the Gothic, it is now possible to find antecedents for virtually any horrific trope in the Gothic tradition. Yet, we still maintain that the Gothic is more marked by aesthetics than by affect, especially where images connote the past, decay and death.[6] Now more than ever, the Gothic is not created in a vacuum, it is in direct alignment with its artistic past (especially the twentieth century, many trends of which it borrows from and develops) and contemporary developments (generic hybridity). For this reason, many of the chapters in this collection begin with, or reach out to, the twentieth century too. In order to discern the particularities of the Gothic in the present, it is necessary to explore its recent history. We also accept that the contemporary Gothic exceeds the literary, so our approach, like those of others in recent years (Byron and Townshend 2013; Hogle 2014), is eminently transmedia. While we do not cover every artistic development, we do focus on those that have been most studied in the humanities: literature, film and television.

The widening of the artistic canon has run alongside a perspectival shift that has seen the Gothic, once understood as a genre (Varma 1957), evolve into an artistic mode (Warwick 2007; Chaplin 2011) less delineated by plot, tropes and technique than by ethos. In short, the Gothic in the new millennium designates a dark form of cultural engagement, rather than a form of fiction constrained by a number of narrative coordinates. This has had both positive and negative effects. On the one hand, understanding the Gothic as mode has allowed for its cultural explosion, as well as its last transformation into a reading tool or methodology (offering a 'Gothic reading' of a text). On the other, it has led to confusion not just about the limits of artistic genres and modes, but to the work the Gothic does. One may well ask if anything, read under a given angle, may escape the conceptual clutches of the Gothic. Regardless of our own personal position vis-à-vis the lack of specificity of the post-millennial Gothic, it is undeniable that the mode has moved forward to embrace a number of new horrific scenarios more pertinent to the reality of contemporary audiences. It has also furthered postmodernism's rejection of the division between high art and low art and its preference for eclecticism. The collection's third part, 'Contemporary Subgenres', analyses these changes in some detail by focusing on thematic pockets that we consider particularly post-millennial. As the chapters by Sharae Deckard and Anya Heise-von der Lippe on the Ecogothic and the posthuman Gothic evince, the Gothic has adapted to modern settings and preoccupations such as climate change and the role of digital communications on human subjectivity. The Gothic's dark scenarios prove a great barometer for our environmental and technological anxieties. Claire Nally's chapter shows that, like neo-Victorian fiction, but stemming from a different tradition closer to cyberpunk, the contemporary artistic practices labelled 'steampunk' relate to, and perform, the past in an important Gothic fashion. Finally, the chapters by Carl H. Sederholm and Catherine Spooner on the new weird and Gothic comedy demonstrate the transmodal nature of the post-millennial Gothic. Whether through speculative fiction or comedy (not restricted to parody), the Gothic may operate in ways that are not ultimately defined by the emotions associated with horror. As the Gothic has fragmented, it may become more difficult, even pointless, to maintain a position that privileges an artificial sense of 'Gothic' purity. It is, indeed, a commonly-held stance to theorise the Gothic, not only in the contemporary period, as a highly hybridised form.[7]

Monstrosity, defined according to corporeal and supernatural parameters was not a predominant trope of the early Gothic novel up until *Frankenstein*, but it is arguably one of its most important markers in the twenty-first century.[8] In order to acknowledge the role that these beings play in the negotiation of both what the Gothic is and what it does, we dedicate an entire section 'Contemporary Monsters', Part II of the collection, to their study. Nowadays, monsters no longer have to remain the direct (and problematic) catalysts for horror and disgust, the repositories of discriminatory discourses around disability and eugenics, they once were (Smith 2011). They are likely to be 'sympathetic' and embody the socially disenfranchised, and they have even attained a certain degree of 'cool', as the chapters by Xavier Aldana Reyes, Sorcha Ní Flainn, and Kaja Franck and Sam George argue with regards to zombies, vampires and werewolves. This is partly because difference is celebrated in contemporary culture. It is not a coincidence that someone like Lady Gaga, once venerated for her iconoclasm, used to refer to her fans as 'little monsters'. The evolution of monsters has also been influenced by a distinct rejection of 'evil' as an innate concept. As post-millennial films like *Maleficent* (Robert Stromberg, 2014) and *Wicked* (Stephen Daldry, 2019) show, contemporary audiences are more likely to believe that 'evil' is a consequence of traumatic upbringing, social inequality and poor decision-making, and be more interested in the personal histories behind characters' 'bad' behaviour. In the case of serial killers, as Bernice M. Murphy shows, these fascinating real monsters can even become social heroes, especially when pitted against worse or 'inhumane' killers. This collection also proposes that the Gothic monsters of the twenty-first century, tied as they are to the past and to a long representational tradition, are necessarily inflected by modern technological developments. The ubiquitous analogue and digital ghosts that have populated countless Gothic fictions in the twenty-first century, as explored by Murray Leeder in his chapter, are the best case in point. As he argues, 'the glitch ghost is a logical digital-age continuation of that centuries-old association of the supernatural and technological' (134).

Part II of this book focuses upon the five most prevalent figurations of monstrosity, the ones most debated and played upon at the dawn of the millennium.[9] The contemporary preference for, and revisions of, monsters such as zombies and serial killers illustrates anxiety over the destructive excesses engendered, in part, by the failures of current economic policies and social structures inherited from the twentieth century. Thus, when Linnie Blake speaks in the first part of this book about a Neoliberal Gothic strand, we may also understand it as intimately connected to the anxieties embodied by the modern zombie in the second part. Although we separate the manifestations of the Gothic into convenient thematic and methodological categories, this does not mean that they do not mingle and cross-pollinate. In fact, since contemporary monsters, due to our overfamiliarity with them and their narrative formulae, are potentially less scary than they once were, the messages in their stories gain significance. We even go further than this to suggest that the Gothic has not just become a social and political arena for writers (it always was), but that its socio-political work, namely its capacity to channel historic, economic and national discourses of exclusion and oppression, as well as those of the repression of minorities, has actually become an indicator of the Gothic in itself. In academic circles, for a Gothic text to be worthy of scholarly consideration it needs to engage with its cultural context meaningfully. This drive, partly encouraged by changes to the humanities in academia (Spooner 2017: 15–16), is transforming the ways in which we perceive the mode, as its borders gradually become dialectical and defined by transgression and intellectual value, rather than by strict aesthetic or narrative allegiances.

Technological, Global and (Trans)National Changes

In considering how and when the Gothic arises in various cultures, we must remain cognisant of its origins as a genre that grew out of, and in opposition to, the Enlightenment. The Gothic proclaimed the hollowness of Enlightenment ideals of rationality, order and progress. It highlighted the fears of atavism which accompanied theories of evolution, and authors such as Oscar Wilde and Karl Marx and Friedrich Engels (who notably utilised Gothic tropes in their socio-economic theories) indicted Enlightenment's hypocritical and alienating elements. Consequently, the genre's reinvention of the feudal past served as a mirror for 'the hidden ugliness and corruption at the heart of Western modernity in the late Victorian present' (Lah 2012: 119). As has been argued, eras of progress are invariably also eras of profound instability and they are therefore prone to witness eruptions of the Gothic. Quoting Elizabeth Kerr, Martin and Savoy emphasise that '[t]he revival of the Gothic in the twentieth century, the age of technology, is parallel to its birth in the eighteenth century, the age of reason' and that, accordingly, 'postmoderns inscribe their mixed fascination and horror at the effects [. . .] of the technological somehow installed in the bedrooms of the suburbs and no longer simply in Transylvania' (2009: x–xi). Although Martin and Savoy position technological progress as the point of haunting and terror, Kerr sees technological advancement as a modern variation of the intellectual and social progress defining the Enlightenment era. These periods of seemingly profound cultural, political, social and scientific progress prove haunted, as they are invariably shadowed by repressed questions of human frailty and failure. As a consequence, in the twentieth and twenty-first centuries, 'the gothic may be said to appear everywhere' while also seeming 'to cohere *nowhere in particular*. There are sites, there are moments. There is no All' (ix). Although the two specifically speak to the mode's insidious manifestations in the US – appearing even outside of fiction to function amid socio-political discourses around immigration and race, for example – globalisation forces us to consider how the mode's pervasiveness proves true for many cultures.

In fact, the growth of global capitalism as a by-product of globalisation in the twentieth century has proven valuable terrain for Gothic nightmares in the twenty-first century, giving rise to the Neoliberal Gothic thematic strand which, as Linnie Black notes in her chapter on the subject, iterates the ways the workings of capital in a world espousing the lie of free trade make modern subjects monstrous. Thus, Neoliberal Gothic articulates the nightmares of global economic progress by privileging capitalism's dehumanising potential. Further, Rebecca Duncan notably clarifies in her essay for this collection on 'South African Gothic' how the 'Gothic has thus proliferated [...] at those moments in the history of the capitalist world-system when one phase of accumulation gives way to another: periods when the shape of reality shifts to disorientating and widely injurious effect' (242). Thus, in many ways, the very origins of the Gothic can be traced to moments of economic shift and progress, in addition to the variety of other social upheavals witnessed in the eighteenth century.

A variety of essays in this collection address the question of progress associated with modern global industry, technology and economy. Joseph Crawford's chapter on 'Gothic Digital Technologies' particularly enunciates the relationship between (technological) progress and the Gothic as it appears in various locations. Charting the ways internet sites such as alt.folklore.urban and Creepypasta enable the rise of new, horrifying urban legends, Crawford reveals how technology has changed the nature of the Gothic, displacing its geographic specificity with a virtual(ly endless) field of play, and enabling technology itself to become a point of horror. Indeed, Crawford explains how the postmillennial Slenderman mythos is rooted in anxieties around progress in information technologies given that its pursuit of victims echoes the trauma of cyberstalking, online harassment and internet surveillance. Further, Slenderman himself proliferates virally, much like computer viruses, online pornography and propaganda. Similarly, Enrique Ajuria Ibarra's discussion of the Charlie Charlie challenge in his chapter 'Latin American Gothic' defines how the shift from analogue play to digital phenomenon revitalised and disseminated the challenge across borders far beyond its Central American origins. Originally a game of spiritual invocation played by children with pencil and paper, the shift to internet play means that much of the summoning occurs independently of human action. Invoking such spirits through the digital medium notably registers the Gothic's terror of animism as we wonder if the technology meant to serve as a mere channel for information and images can itself become haunted.

The very fact of globalisation at the turn of the millennium – when various Western populations claim to have achieved postmodern and postcolonial states – produces various tensions, collisions and traumas which speak to Gothic plots. Their consequences are the new monsters and subgenres discussed in Parts II and III of this collection, as well as changes to the tradition itself. Thus, the first part of this collection, 'Updating the Tradition', is devoted to exploring the ways in which the pressures of a global world produce anxieties around, for example, the fact and nature of postcolonialism and the entrenchment of capitalism alongside the rise of a global economy. In the chapters 'Queer Gothic', 'Postfeminist Gothic' and Neoliberal Gothic', Andrew J. Owens, Gina Wisker and Linnie Blake portray the ways contemporary Gothic texts in Western societies respond to the seismic shifts in national politics surrounding issues of sexuality, gender and political economy. Similarly, Crawford's essay on 'Gothic Digital Technologies', as previously noted, explores the horrors arising out of a modern technology that both connects people beyond the borders of their communities and nations and threatens to possess them – especially as social technologies change and develop at exponential rates and seem to assume lives of their own. Sarah Ilott's chapter, 'Postcolonial Gothic', explores a similar, if not inverted, fear in the works under discussion there. Her chapter details the ways in which twenty-first-century postcolonial texts are haunted by the sense of a history that insists on returning in the spectres of (neo-) imperial violence.

The Gothic became a lucrative business in the twentieth century and continues as such into the twenty-first thanks, in part, to the processes of globalisation. The proliferation of new national, regional and ethnic forms and subgenres are as much expressions of the trauma of modernity and encounters with the (post)colonial as they are the products of globalisation's social and cultural impact. The modern mode not only registers the easy fluidity of people across borders and the rapid exchange of products among nations, but also the changes in response to the various cultural and socio-economic shifts wrought by these various migrations. Consequently, Glennis Byron argues that one can detect the spectre of globalisation in contemporary Gothic motifs even as the mode reminds us that our anxious responses are nothing new:

The conditions of globalization call up familiar Gothic motifs of hauntings, of monsters, of pasts that refuse to lie still and which draw sustenance from the sweep of globalizing forces, emerging with renewed vigor. But the contemporary emergence of these motifs is provoked by new kinds of disturbances to identities and borders, and these motifs are familiar and yet unfamiliar, simultaneously global and local. Increasingly detached from any specific historical, social, or cultural 'origins,' Gothic as it travels nevertheless inevitably incorporates, and necessitates attention to, different historical, social, and cultural specificities at the same time as it produces figures of collective fears and traces the outlines of a growing global darkness. (2012: 376)

While we can observe these developments in a number of locations, Ethnogothic particularly records the tensions outlined above. Typically produced by a population prey to the collision of non-Western traditions and beliefs with colonising/imperial systems, these texts register the terror of history and prove suspicious of the promises of globalisation. Japanese Gothic, for instance, expresses the ambivalence of contemporary Japanese identity, conveying 'the split in the Japanese "Self" between the endless striving for the ideal of "Western" modernity and the nationalistic affirmation of an empowered "Japanese" (post)modernity' (Lah 2012: 112). As Katarzyna Ancuta shows in her chapter on 'Asian Gothic', the split manifests itself, in part, through the mobilisation of non-Western Japanese and Asian monsters – which predate the Gothic even as they fit within the mode – alongside very contemporary anxieties, such as shifting gender dynamics. Significantly, while Ancuta explains that Gothic is still a contested (sub)genre in a variety of Asian countries, the 'poetic violence of the Gothic mode and its propensity for the grotesque is often attractive to Asian authors working under authoritarian governments and battling censorship, as social and political criticism rarely invites repercussions when perceived as "magical realism" or a ghost story'.

Appropriating the Gothic is a complex project for non-Western (postcolonial) populations, given that the mode is fraught with problematic racial and ethnic representations and discourses. Indeed, numerous scholars, such as Jack Halberstam, H. L. Malchow and Teresa Goddu, have noted the myriad ways Gothic tropes contain racial and ethnic discourses. The black devils of texts like Matthew Lewis's *The Monk* (1796) and Charlotte Dacre's *Zofloya: or, The Moor* (1806) easily metaphorised the difficult but, at the time, persistent question of racial difference alongside issues of humanity and freedom. Consequently, when Mary Shelley's novel *Frankenstein* appeared, its imagery was quickly appropriated in socio-political discourses about slavery and the possibility of emancipation. Likewise, Dracula's peculiar features drew from stereotypes of Jews while his threat harkened to anxieties about rising immigration rates from Eastern Europe. As we can see, ethnic and minority authors writing in the mode face a number of peculiar traps and pitfalls amid the mode's tropes. Recognising a global Gothic is equally fraught with concerns. One is that identifying non-Western texts as Gothic can be read as a form of colonial imposition. While regionally specific forms of the Gothic in nations such as Canada, Australia and New Zealand can be 'viewed as outgrowths of an imported Anglo-European genre that, while restaging established Gothic tropes for a new world, subsequently develops distinctively local characteristics' (Byron 2012: 369), defining Gothic narratives in (post)colonial contexts cannot as readily restage the tradition. As Byron, *pace* Robert Mighall, explains, '"[e]pochs, institutions, places, and people are Gothicized, have the Gothic thrust upon them" [. . .] and so, one might add, do texts. Indeed, the very naming of a global Gothic could be seen as complicit in such a process' (370). Katarzyna Ancuta's essay notably alludes to this issue; Gothic still registers 'as a foreign category and a denominator of paperback literature of questionable quality' (249) in the Asian Gothic.

Yet identifying a non-Western Gothic may be understood as 'part of an attempt to overcome modernity's Eurocentrism by rescuing the otherwise suppressed voices, experiences and cultural legacies of others, thus positing alternate and/or multiple modernities. In this case, the term "Gothic" may be read as claimed rather than imposed' (Byron 2012: 370, 371). Hence, narratives which once conflated globalisation with Westernisation and/or Americanisation are being challenged as postcolonial and Ethnogothic texts uncover new multidirectional and transnational approaches to the Gothic. Further, postcolonial and Ethnogothic texts disrupt the idealisation of the West as the heart of modernity by 'contest[ing] the more optimistic foundational narratives of new worlds' (369). In the twentieth and twenty-first centuries, authors writing in this vein give voice to the 'lingering traumas produced by colonial life, with buried pasts resurfacing in horrific form to disturb the present' (369). In fact, they reveal the trauma of globalisation itself, using tropes of haunting and ghosts to depict the 'unprecedented movement and dislocation of people across the globe associated' with capitalism's proliferation (Goldman and Saul 2006: 648). Through such texts, authors remind readers of the ways global encounter produces the colonial subject while also signalling back to the mode's origins as the product of cultural exchange between Britain, France and Germany. As Byron notes, acknowledging the global Gothic in the twenty-first century, and its diverse writers, means not only recognising the power and movements of modernity, but acknowledging that transnational flow reinvigorates the mode by 'opening up multiple new fields of play [as] the literature and film of different countries feed off each other to produce new forms of Gothic that reveal the increasing cross-cultural dynamics' of the modern world (2012: 373).

The Gothic's destabilisation of Enlightenment notions of humanity and civilisation has proven useful to postcolonial and non-Western authors interrogating the brutalities of (a haunting) colonialism throughout the twentieth century. Such writers reveal how the experience and history of postcolonial populations 'reeks of the elements of horror: silencing, hauntings of repressed past histories, ghosts, abjection and the split self, [and] colluding with the ruler' (Wisker 2005: 174). More broadly, the mode has proven a way of indicting the West and its neo-colonialist and imperialist regimes throughout and at the close of the twentieth century. Thus, contemporary postcolonial and Ethnogothic authors utilise tropes of monstrosity, decay and contamination to cast the West as an alien devouring Other while they anxiously worry over the ways global economy reproduces the brutalities of colonialism for new nation states. As Emily S. Davis argues, such texts, 'written [. . .] from the perspective of the abject, the monster, the unheimlich of a new global economic and cultural order, [. . .] build upon versions of the gothic as a reaction against an emerging capitalist system by deploying gothic tropes to represent imperialism, neocolonialism, and globalization' (2013: 104).

Although the anxiety stemming from the processes of globalisation is evident in the works of Western writers, the trauma it offers is especially evident in the works of non-Western populations typically not associated with Gothic writing even as their historical encounters with the West lend themselves to such narratives. While Gothic texts addressing globalisation point towards the destabilisation of traditional identities and cultures, Gothic subgenres like the postcolonial Gothic, discussed in the first part of this book, and the Ethnogothic in particular, reveal other aspects of globalisation's dark underbelly, such as the ways global capitalism is rife with Gothic excess 'as a system that demands surplus, produces ghosts, turns people into objects, disrupts linear time, and offers extravagant pleasures with high costs' (Davis 2013: 105). Globalisation, in such narratives, proves a force of 'material and psychic invasion, a force of contamination and dominance' (Byron 2012: 372) as the new world order threatens to reproduce old colonial systems. Yet globalisation also provides non-Western authors access to a mode through which they can articulate and critique the pressures of the new world order and the traumas of national history. Appropriation of the mode does not necessarily signify assimilation to Western ideals or even betray a Western-focused literacy. Rather importation of the Gothic into non-

Western regions produces texts which trouble the very notion of a stable field of cultural production. Instead, Ethnogothic texts are defined by fluid exchanges between the Gothic and specific regional forms, such as magical realism and the fantastic (in the case of Latin American Gothic), and folk traditions and beliefs, such as blues figurations and motifs (in the case of Black Diasporic Gothic).

This collection explores the area of Ethnogothic writing and representation in depth in its fourth part. Essays by Rebecca Duncan, Katarzyna Ancuta and Enrique Ajuria Ibarra interrogate the ways in which the very process of globalisation in the late twentieth and early twenty-first centuries manifests the kinds of abjecting behaviours that drive Gothic plots. Essays by Katrin Althans and Maisha Wester in this section also illustrate how various non-Western and minority populations, such as Australian Aboriginals and Black Diasporic writers, use the mode to portray the complex social contradictions arising out of globalisation, 'including a fundamental contradiction between a seemingly irresistible modernity, and past legacies that not only refuse to go away but draw renewed vitality from the very globalizing process' (Dirlik 2016: 49–50). Indeed, as Rebecca Duncan proposes in her chapter on the South African Gothic, so similar is the reproduction of old colonial regimes in the new world order that contemporary Ethnogothic artists challenge whether the colonial is dead at all.

The essays in this collection demonstrate that, far from exhausted, the Gothic has continued to adapt to contemporary times, to new voices and traditions, opening up and hybridising further to the point where an engagement with the tradition's origins has been complicated by the postmodern simulacral recuperation of the mode and its multifarious monsters. As it travels across genres, nations and imagined versions of the past, present and future, the Gothic becomes polyvocal and intertextual, rather than redundant and diffuse, adapting to the zeitgeist and to well-versed, canny audiences. Our aim is to showcase not just the multiplicity of ways in which the Gothic has manifested in the twenty-first century, a notable 'boom' period, but also how, as a mode intrinsically connected to the repressed, the oppressed and the forgotten, the Gothic is in a perfect position to critique lasting notions of convention, propriety and discrimination. The Gothic has become a methodological mode in itself, a critical tool connected to various artistic, philosophical and theoretical concepts (such as the uncanny, the sublime, hauntology and abjection) which allows critics and students to perform specific readings that concentrate on the gaps and suppressions of older texts and on the more explicit socio-political messages of contemporary ones. For us and the various contributors to this volume, the Gothic, as an artistic language of liberation and denunciation, is actually *the* cultural mode of a historical period fraught with occlusions, demagogy, violence and radicalisms. With *Twenty-First-Century Gothic*, we leave behind ossified notions of cultural legitimacy and generic ascription in order to focus on and further debates that preoccupy contemporary readers, academics and students: where the Gothic is, where it is going and what it still does for us.

Notes

1. We are very specifically alluding to the fact that some genres are strongly determined by setting, time and characters (the Western) and others by the emotions they aim to generate (horror).
2. We refer to uses of the word 'Gothic' in book reviews in websites like goodreads.com, in marketing campaigns like those for writer Laura Purcell and as part of educational events and courses in the UK like those run by the English and Media Centre (their Teaching the Gothic and the Supernatural for A Level course, on 9 June 2016) and the Higher Education Academy (their third annual conference, 'Heroes and Monsters: Extra-Ordinary Tales of Learning and Teaching in the Arts and Humanities', which took place on 2–4 June 2015).
3. The word 'Gothic' was used to describe the 'Goths', the East Germanic tribes responsible for the Sack of Rome (410 AD). The Renaissance view connected medieval times with these 'uncivilised' peoples.
4. This is why it is possible to speak of 'Gothic horror', a type of horror fiction inflected by specific Gothic formulae and archetypes.
5. 'First wave Gothic' is a phrase used to refer to the period between 1764 and 1820, bookended by the publications of Horace Walpole's *The Castle of Otranto* and Charles Robert Maturin's *Melmoth the Wanderer* in those respective years.
6. This is not to say that affect is not key to the experience of the Gothic (see Aldana Reyes 2015). Unless the Gothic is parodic or metatextual, the Gothic's aesthetics tend to be connected to negative emotions.
7. Anecdotally, the fourteenth conference of the International Gothic Association, run in 2018, was named 'Gothic Hybridities: Interdisciplinary, Multimodal and Transhistorical Approaches'.
8. Fred Botting explains that '[i]n eighteenth century aesthetic and moral criticism the word "monster" signified ugliness, irrationality and unnaturalness' (2009: 204). Of course, aristocratic and monastic villains, as well as the devil, in first wave Gothic novels are 'morally' monstrous.
9. Witches and mummies are also important contemporary Gothic monsters, but less ubiquitous in Gothic academia, perhaps because of their connection to specific historical periods.

References

Aldana Reyes, Xavier (2015), 'Gothic Affect: An Alternative Approach to Critical Models of the Contemporary Gothic', in Lorna Piatti-Farnell and Donna Lee Brien (eds), *New Directions in 21st Century Gothic: The Gothic Compass*, Abingdon and New York: Routledge, pp. 11–23.
Baldick, Chris (ed.) (1992), *The Oxford Book of Gothic Tales*, Oxford: Oxford University Press.
Botting, Fred (1996), *Gothic*, London and New York: Routledge.
— (2009), 'Monstrosity', in Marie Mulvey-Roberts (ed.), *The Handbook of the Gothic*, 2nd edn, New York: New York University Press, pp. 204–5.
Byron, Glennis (2012), 'Global Gothic', in David Punter (ed.), *A New Companion to the Gothic*, Blackwell Publishing, pp. 369–78.
Byron, Glennis, and Dale Townshend (eds) (2013), *The Gothic World*, London and New York: Routledge.
Chaplin, Sue (2011), *Gothic Literature: Texts, Contexts, Connections*, London: York Press.
Davis, Emily S. (2013), *Rethinking the Romance Genre: Global Intimacies in Contemporary Literature and Visual Culture*, Basingstoke and New York: Palgrave.
Dirlik, Arif (2016) [2007], *Global Modernity: Modernity in the Age of Global Capitalism*, Abingdon and New York: Routledge.
Goldman, Marlene, and Joanne Saul (2006), 'Talking with Ghosts: Haunting in Canadian Cultural Production', *University of Toronto Quarterly*, 75.2, 645–55.
Hogle, Jerrold E. (ed.) (2014), *The Cambridge Companion to the Modern Gothic*, Cambridge: Cambridge University Press.
Lah, Waiyee (2012), 'Superflat and the Postmodern Gothic: Images of Western Modernity in Kuroshitsuji', *Mechademia*, 7, 111–27.
Longueil, Alfred E. (1923), 'The Word "Gothic" in Eighteenth-Century Criticism', *Modern Language Notes*, 38.8, 453–60.
Martin, Robert K., and Eric Savoy (eds) (2009), 'Introduction', in Robert K. Martin and Eric Savoy (eds), *American Gothic: New Interventions in a National Narrative*, Iowa City: University of Iowa Press, pp. vii–xii.
Miles, Robert (1995), *Ann Radcliffe: The Great Enchantress*, Manchester: Manchester University Press.
Pirie, David (1973), *A Heritage of Horror: The English Gothic Cinema 1946–1972*, London: The Gordon Fraser Gallery.
Punter, David (1980), *The Literature of Terror: A History of Gothic Fictions from 1765 to the Present Day*, London and New York: Longman.
Sage, Victor (1990), 'Introduction', in Victor Sage (ed.), *The Gothick Novel*, London: Macmillan.
Sage, Victor, and Allan Lloyd Smith (eds) (1996), *Modern Gothic: A Reader*, Manchester: Manchester University Press.
Smith, Angela S. (2011), *Hideous Progeny: Disability, Eugenics, and Classic Horror Cinema*, New York: Columbia University Press.
Spooner, Catherine (2006), *Contemporary Gothic*, London: Reaktion.
— (2007), 'Gothic in the Twentieth Century', in Catherine Spooner and Emma

McEvoy (eds), *The Routledge Companion to Gothic*, Abingdon and New York: Routledge, pp. 38–47.
— (2017), *Post-Millennial Gothic: Comedy, Romance and the Rise of Happy Gothic*, London: Bloomsbury.
Varma, Devendra P. (1957), *The Gothic Flame: Being a History of the Gothic Novel in England*, London: Arthur Barker.
Warwick, Alexandra (2007), 'Feeling Gothicky?', *Gothic Studies*, 9.1, 5–15.
Wisker, Gina (2005), *Horror Fiction: An Introduction*, New York: Continuum.

Part I

Updating the Tradition

Chapter 1

Postcolonial Gothic
Sarah Ilott

Postcolonial authors have frequently adopted the Gothic as a mode well suited to registering colonial violence and critiquing colonial discourse. It provides a language suited to horror and trauma; it writes back to a body of imperial Gothic literature that supported the colonial project through the othering of colonised peoples; and it recognises the 'boomerang effect' that renders the Frankensteinian monster-makers themselves monstrous. Ashcroft, Griffiths and Tiffin, in *The Empire Writes Back*, describe postcolonial writing as the process of 'seizing the language of the centre and re-placing it in a discourse fully adapted to the colonized place' through a combination of appropriation and abrogation (2002: 37–8). From the outset, postcolonial Gothic has engaged thematically with its colonial counterpart in this manner, exposing and deconstructing the fears inherent in imperial Gothic: 'individual regression or going native; an invasion of civilisation by the forces of barbarianism or demonism; and the diminution of opportunities for adventure and heroism in the modern world' (Brantlinger 1988: 230).

The act of 'writing back' and entering into dialogue with specific Gothic novels is evident in many of the most canonised texts in the body of postcolonial Gothic literature and film. A foundational work, Jean Rhys's *Wide Sargasso Sea* (1966) reimagines Charlotte Brontë's *Jane Eyre* (1847) by placing Rochester's white Creole wife centre stage, as a vehicle for historicising a repressed history of racial hierarchisation, enslavement and colonisation. Following suit, Margaret Atwood's *Surfacing* (1972) reworks a trope from Joseph Conrad's *Heart of Darkness* (1899), J. M. Coetzee's *Waiting for the Barbarians* (1980) reconfigures Bram Stoker's *Dracula* (1897) and Jane Campion's film *The Piano* (1993) is indebted to Emily Brontë's *Wuthering Heights* (1847). Each of these works engages with their source text to critique the underpinning ideologies while appropriating their aesthetics. For James Procter and Angela Smith, '[e]ven in its name, postcolonial Gothic seems to have "written back" to the empire, appropriating the signifier "Gothic" and its literary conventions to resist the work of empire' (2007: 97). As such, postcolonial Gothic simultaneously appropriates the language of the Gothic and abrogates its ideologies, while displacing the central concerns of imperial Gothic by centralising those who were once marginalised and made monstrous.

Imperial Gothic frequently did the work of naturalising structures of otherness and monstrosity crucial to colonial rhetoric in terms of easing the consciences of the colonisers. As Andrew Smith and William Hughes have rightly stated:

> One of the defining ambivalences of the Gothic is that its labelling of otherness is often employed in the service of supporting, rather than questioning the status quo. This is perhaps the central complexity of the form because it debates the existence of otherness and alterity, often in order to demonize such otherness. (2003: 3)

Imperial Gothic made monstrous that which was nationally or racially Other, as in Charlotte Brontë's 'mad' Creole Bertha Mason, Stoker's titular Transylvanian vampire, or the cannibalistic tribes encountered by Conrad's Marlow. Rather than merely reversing such patterns of monstrosity, the work of postcolonial Gothic is often to expose the Hegelian dialectic on which such binary oppositions of good/evil, white/black, centre/margin and self/Other rest. Such a deconstructive bent is evident in Salman Rushdie's postcolonial Gothic novels. In *Midnight's Children* (1981) the doubling of the titular children – Saleem and Shiva, who are both born at the moment of Indian Independence and Partition – registers their interdependence, as they are nevertheless fated to live very different lives driven by opposing forces of creation and destruction. In *Shame* (1983), the monstrous Sufiya Zinobia embodies a number of oppositions, bringing together that which discourse conventionally divides. As Susan Spearey states: 'Rushdie collapses the angel/fiend dichotomy; she is simultaneously Beauty *and* the Beast, she is Hyder and, once married, Shakil, an Eastern and inverted version of the Jekyll/Hyde figure' (2000: 174). In *The Satanic Verses*, the fates of protagonists Gibreel Farishta and Saladin Chamcha are interlocked. Collectively, and without resolution, they negotiate oppositions between the angelic and demonic, the pure and the hybrid, the fixed and the mutable. During a particularly memorable scene, in which Saladin finds himself unhappily metamorphosed into a horned, capric beast, he is informed that the transformation is the result of 'the power of description' (Rushdie 2006: 168) – he is the outworking of colonial stereotype. This darkly comic scene renders visible the mechanisms of colonial racism in a manner exemplary of postcolonial Gothic's negotiations with alterity.

Alongside revealing the ambivalences and incongruities inherent in colonial discourse, the Gothic provides postcolonial authors with a shorthand for articulating repressed histories and recounting past traumas through a language of haunting and spectrality. Demonstrating the compatibility of postcolonialism and the Gothic, Alison Rudd states that the Gothic furnishes postcolonial writers with 'a means, in narrative and idiom, to expose and subvert past and continuing regimes of power and exploitation, and to reinscribe histories that have been both violent and repressed' (2010: 1–2). Described as such, Gothic literature effectively functions as a talking cure for colonial violence. Though often registered through individual or familial loss, shame or trauma, the political subtext of postcolonial Gothic is habitually writ large. Accordingly, in Arundhati Roy's *The God of Small Things* (1997), a novel concerned with the familial guilt following a sequence of traumatic events centred on the family of twins Rahel and Esthappen, personal narratives are largely dictated by the howling 'Big God' of national history, who demands 'obeisance' and overshadows personal turmoil (2004: 19). The 'History House' that is central to Roy's novel and the cause of fascination for her child protagonists illustrates the way that the colonial past hauntingly persists:

> [W]e can't go in [...] because we've been locked out. And when we look in through the windows, all we see are shadows. And when we try and listen, all we hear is a whispering. And we cannot understand the whispering, because our minds have been invaded by a war. A war that we have won and lost. The very worst sort of war. A war that captures dreams and re-dreams them. A war that has made us adore our conquerors and despise ourselves. (199)

The passage depicts the characters excluded from a history that is nevertheless their national inheritance, a 'History House' that bears an uncanny resemblance to the mansions of English Gothic. However, their status as subjects trapped outside history is partly blamed on themselves, as 'a family of anglophiles' (53). The implication is that Anglophilia amounts to a colonisation of the mind that displaces their sense of native Indian history; they have been possessed by an 'English' manner of thinking.

With any literary subgenre, there are continuities and ruptures as the contexts of production and reception change. Postcolonial Gothic of the twentieth century rejected the ideology of imperial Gothic while borrowing from its aesthetic, vocabulary and dominant tropes, with absent fathers, awful inheritances, acts of possession and dispossession and unhomely experiences providing a ready shorthand for the traumas wrought by colonisation. If twentieth-century postcolonial Gothic was defined by its negotiation with epistemic violence (how to speak the unspeakable; how to uncover repressed histories; how to challenge structures of knowledge that fix the colonised as monstrously Other), then twenty-first-century postcolonial Gothic might be conceived as taking a more materialist turn in its focus on actual (continuing) and systemic colonial violence. This appears both in a literary oeuvre more attuned to the lingering material effects of empire (how to engage with the lived realities of racial hierarchisation, economic disenfranchisement, environmental disaster and warfare that are the persistent legacies of colonialism) and in a newly materialist turn in postcolonial studies that rejects the postmodern postcolonialism concomitant with the likes of Homi Bhabha and Salman Rushdie (cf. Lazarus 2011). Twenty-first-century postcolonial Gothic retains the anti-colonial politics and the problematisation of the 'post' in postcolonialism central to its twentieth-century forebears. But as the effects of (neo)imperial violence continue to manifest in the present day, modes of expression and forms of criticism take a more materialist approach.

Contemporary postcolonial Gothic provides a language for re-engaging with the political realities of the post/neo-colonial present, speaking truths that are structurally repressed elsewhere. Voicing a common anxiety about the Gothic as 'unrealistic and frivolous', Teresa Goddu notes that its 'apparent lack of connection to reality and intellectual purpose has made it troubling to use in conjunction with African-American writers' (1997: 140). Yet what we might understand, with Michael Löwy, as the 'critical irrealism' of the Gothic, actually endows it with subversive critical potential. Challenging the Lukácsian notion that only realist artwork can function to critique contemporary society, Löwy argues that irrealist (fantasy, Gothic, surreal) works can 'help us understand and transform reality' (2007: 206). Taking this further, the Warwick Research Collective (WReC) suggest that irrealist writing is a pervasive feature of world literature produced at moments of systemic crisis, which they suggest is due to its 'in-mixing of the imaginary and the factual' that is 'more sensitive' to registering 'specific circumstances of combined and uneven development' (2015: 70). Understood as such, the Gothic is not a means of escape, but a means of re-engagement with the lived realities of twenty-first-century postcolonial societies in the face of systemic violence and the structural exclusion of minority voices. In what follows, I explore how the irrealist aesthetics of twenty-first-century postcolonial Gothic function as critical commentary on the systemic failings of the contemporary moment, linking these failings to a history of colonisation, yet going further than the critique of colonial discourse or epistemology that predominated in twentieth-century postcolonial Gothic literature and criticism. The subgenre of postcolonial Gothic has evolved to encounter new contexts wrought by environmental disaster and resurgent nationalism that require action in the present in order to create a usable future, to address new racisms emerging from neo-imperial and nationalistic movements, and to repurpose new monsters suited to systemic critique.

New Contexts

Much recent postcolonial Gothic literature bears witness to the changing world of the twenty-first century by registering the distinctive aftershocks of European colonialism on the contemporary moment. These aftershocks have included, but are not limited to, the global reach and unequal experience of the financial crisis of 2007–8; the impact of climate change, particularly on the Global South, in generating war and human migrations; 9/11, the consequent 'War on Terror' and increased Islamophobia; and resurgent nationalisms with their literal and ideological fortification of borders and associated 'refugee crises'. These new contexts, while materially and ideologically related to historical periods of colonisation, have engendered new modes of representation. In deference to a more complex understanding of the postcolonial world and the multiple forced and chosen migrations of its inhabitants, the literature and criticism is no longer so indebted to the binaristic 'writing back' model of postcolonial literature, leading to a more multi-valent critique of a world irreparably changed by colonial violence and plundering.

One new subgenre of postcolonial Gothic is 'border Gothic': Gothic texts that are concerned with the impossible resurrection of borders of the self, in which the individual body often functions metonymically for its national counterpart. For example, recent British authors draw on the setting of the Kentish coast and the symbolically overdetermined white cliffs of Dover as the 'literal and metaphorical site at which the borders of Britishness are negotiated' (Ilott 2018: 212). Texts such as Helen Oyeyemi's *White Is for Witching* (2009) appropriate and thereby expose and critique the language and rhetoric of imperial Gothic recurrent in contemporary racisms, in which perceived threats to the national identity or the British adventurer abroad in the colonies are rendered Gothic as the outsider is made monstrous. Bram Stoker's *Dracula* (1897) is a key intertext to Oyeyemi's novel both in terms of the vampirism of the 'goodlady' that animates a xenophobic guesthouse tasked with the torture and expulsion of foreign guests in a transparent analogy for British nationalism, and in the tension between guest and prisoner enacted in Harker's unusual sojourn at the Count's castle and mimicked in black British Ore's stay at the maleficent guesthouse. Ore finds the sanctity of her body under threat. The hatred explicit in the British National Party pamphlets she receives is reflected in the dissolution of her body in the guesthouse. Ore finds shreds of skin in 'black liquid, as dense as paint' on her towel following a shower: 'The black is coming off' and 'Rule Britannia', someone chants from outside the door (Oyeyemi 2009: 214). Although Ore is British, the racist guesthouse expels her, much as the foreign nationals. As such she embodies the contested borders of national identity in a manner rendered Gothic through bodily horror and the violence of possession and expulsion that she is alternatively made to feel.

Contemporary postcolonial Gothic references the continuation of colonial violence and its legacies, rather than its haunting remainder. Increased precarity, poverty and enforced displacement are the inevitable outcomes of the environmental disaster and warfare engendered by the pillaging of natural resources and racial hierarchisation that are the primary effects of colonisation. Concerned with curses, possessions, Gothic inheritances, patriarchal violence and the haunting power of a found manuscript, Nnedi Okorafor's *Who Fears Death* (2010) combines fantasy logistics and locales with a distinctly Gothic register to convey a post-apocalyptic future in which human technological advances have caused environmental disaster and the remaining people eke out a living on a desert landscape in which soil is described in defamiliarising terms as 'a type of fragrant substance' (2010: 277). The past is dimly remembered in stories collectively known as the *Great Book*, which figures as a religious text and incites racial division between the black Okeke and the lighter skinned Nuru. This conflict references the civil war in Sudan, which ended in 2005 and led to the independence of South Sudan in 2011, and it has particular resonances with the genocide that began in Darfur in 2003. The protagonist, Onye, is 'Ewu', a 'child [. . .] of violence' resultant of the rape of an Okeke woman by a Nuru man (21). Her peers distrust and ostracise her as her lighter skin links her to the violence of the Nuru, yet Onye possesses magical powers that enable her to visit the spirit realm where she meets her nemesis, a man who turns out to be her father and who is trying to kill her. The novel details her physical and spiritual journey as she fights to end the 'curse', the genocide of the Okeke. Okorafor adopts the irrealist aesthetics of the fantasy and Gothic modes as a vehicle for re-engagement with legacies of violence, racial hierarchisation and environmental disaster that continue disproportionately to affect postcolonial societies.

The genre hybridity of the novel is related to the nature of its engagement with history, memory and time as it links the violence of the past to an imagined future. Its elision of traumatic histories and fearful inheritances with a post-apocalyptic fantasy allow the past to haunt the future in profoundly material ways. It is notable that despite the violence of her conception, Onye is haunted not so much by the past as by how her actions will determine her future and that of her people. She has premonitions described as 'ghosts of the future' (202), a formulation that is crucial to an understanding of the function of contemporary postcolonial Gothic. In order to attain a post-racial and harmonious future, Onye must do battle with history, as represented by her rapist father and the *Great Book* that preaches racial division. Okorafor's genre-blurring postcolonial text allows the outcomes of the economic, epistemic and ecological violence of colonialism to resound into the future in a manner that calls for a renewed critical engagement with the past and reparations in the present in order to change the course of history.

New Racisms

In 2001, there was a significant shift in modes of discrimination from race to religion. Exploiting an increase in Islamophobia following the terrorist attacks of 9/11, racist discrimination frequently adopted a new discourse centred on Islam while targeting the same minorities as previous racist discourse: Arab Americans, British Asians and Palestinians. Concurrent with this shift in racist discourse was the increased 'framing' of Muslims in mainstream news sources. Peter Morey and Amina Yaqin rightly identify the ways in which there has been a wholesale 'distortion of particular features of Muslim life and custom, reducing the diversity of Muslims and their existence as individuals to a fixed object – a caricature in fact', as 'behavior, the body and dress are treated not as cultural markers but as a kind of moral index, confirming non-Muslim viewers of these images in their sense of superiority and cementing the threatening strangeness of the Muslim Other' (2011: 3). The effect of this combination of discrimination and stereotyping is that Muslims are represented as fixed in their otherness and the language through which Muslim experience can be registered has become circumscribed. What this framing of Muslims attempts to disguise through the language of cultural difference is the neo-imperial effort to control oil in the Middle East: military intervention is then justified as a response to 'their' hatred of 'us', to adopt George W. Bush's terms (2001). As realist representations of Muslims have become overdetermined, this has led to the employment of strategies of postcolonial Gothic both to index the failure of realist representation and to provide a language for the experiences of alienation and abjection of Muslims.

British Pakistani author Nadeem Aslam employs the Gothic mode in *Maps for Lost Lovers* (2004) to render Muslim peoples and places ghostly, demonstrating the impossibility of confronting certain issues, such as the novel's central 'honour' killing, in public for fear of reprisals. The northern English neighbourhood is described in Gothic terms:

> it hoards its secrets, unwilling to let on the pain in its breast. Shame, guilt, honour and fear are like padlocks hanging from mouths. No one makes a sound in case it draws attention. No one speaks. No one breathes. The place is bumpy with buried secrets and problems swept under carpets. (Aslam 2004: 45)

Tabish Khair suggests that '[t]he screams and sulky silences of Gothic fiction do not set out to "represent" the Other; they primarily register the irreducible presence of Otherness' (2009: 173). Works such as Aslam's, however, employ the Gothic mode alternatively to render visible the mechanisms of silencing that cast certain groups as Other. The silence of the town is positioned as an effect of necessary repression in a culture in which *all* Muslims are held responsible for the actions of *individual* Muslims. The town is described in terms of Gothic entrapment, in which '[e]veryone here was imprisoned in the cage of others' thoughts' (118). Though critical of aspects of Muslim belief, the novel's Gothic modality ultimately casts Islamophobia as the villain, ensnaring Muslims in stereotypes from which they cannot break free and effectively silencing Muslims by circumscribing the stories that can be heard.

In an Indian context, Raj Kamal Jha's *Fireproof* (2006) uses instances of abject body horror to convey the ways in which Indian Muslims are not recognised as integral to an increasingly Hindu nationalist self, coupled with a magic realist register that allows for the speaking of the unspeakable. The novel is set amidst the communal violence that flared up across Ahmedabad in the wake of an arson attack that killed fifty-nine Hindu passengers on the Sabarmati Express train near Godhra in 2002. During riots that author and activist Arundhati Roy has described as 'the Gujarat pogrom', Muslim people and properties were targeted in an effort understood 'at best [as] conducted under the benign gaze of the state and, at worst, with active state collusion' (2009: 8). The condoning of anti-Muslim violence reflects the international zeitgeist in the wake of 9/11 and the ongoing Indo-Pak border relations that combined to provide what social anthropologist Arjun Appadurai termed 'golden opportunities' (2006: 93) for the ruling Hindu nationalist Bharatiya

Janata Party and its allies. Jha's novel follows protagonist Mr Jay as he traverses the city on fire with his newborn, heavily disfigured son, whom he names Ithim in deference to the division between 'those who would look at him and see an object and those who would look at him and see my son, my baby' (Jha 2006: 47). The narrative intersperses the voices of the dead, who speak from the prologue and footnotes. The text's dramatic irony means that readers can distinguish between the living and dead characters that Mr Jay encounters where he cannot, a device to reflect the protagonist's repression of his own culpability as one of a gang of men who have tortured and killed a series of Muslims.

Ithim functions as national allegory for the abjection of Indian Muslims. He is associated throughout with abject substances such as blood, faeces and corpses that, for Julia Kristeva (1982), threaten the borders of the self and are rejected by it in a manner that is perennially incomplete. The visceral disgust provoked by a character described variously as 'a vegetable', 'an oversized insect', 'a bird, its feathers plucked', 'a piece of plastic tubing', 'a caterpillar', 'a Thermos flask' and 'a broken toy' (Jha 2006: 74) renders visible the processes by which Indian Muslims are made abject when the final twist reveals that Ithim is one of the city's many Muslim victims, cut from the womb of his mother and subsequently dismembered by Mr Jay and his accomplices. Having repressed his role in the slaughter, Mr Jay is not cognisant of (what he believes to be) his son's Muslim heritage. This means that he is unable to offer a reason for Ithim's imaginative association with blood and faeces, where readers might retrospectively surmise that his attempts at disassociation from Ithim stem from a repressed Islamophobia and a desire to distinguish Hindu (national) self from Muslim Other. While Ithim is represented in physically abject terms, the novel's other dead are graphically abjected, speaking from the footnotes and prologue as a method of rendering visible the horror of their silencing through oral mutilation and murder. Through its Gothic subject matter and irrealist techniques the novel calls to mind the inexistence of realist structures of representation capable of capturing this horror when contemporary discourse does not allow for an understanding of Muslims as victims rather than perpetrators of violence.

New Monsters

For Jennifer Lawn, the ghost offers a productive concept for a postcolonial Gothic reading practice: it 'aligns with models of collective history that emphasise mediating processes of transference and transformation' and 'bears the capacity to enter a sickly, static situation and open avenues to new modes of knowledge' (2006: 149). What is endemic to the figure of the ghost, however, is that it is rooted to a particular space or object. This is typical of twentieth-century postcolonial Gothic, in which, for example, *The God of Small Things* contains a ghost pinned to a tree with a sickle. As such, the ghost is a useful vehicle for unearthing occluded or repressed histories, but its histories are localised, moored or fixed to a specific place in a way that forecloses systemic structural critiques.

In the twenty-first century, the new monster – or rather the newly repurposed monster – is the soucouyant, a shapeshifting, vampiric creature of Caribbean folklore. Although national traditions in the Caribbean regarding the nature of the soucouyant differ, she is generally recognised as taking the form of an elderly woman who sheds her skin at night to travel as a ball of fire in search of victims. Myth has it that she feasts on the blood or souls of her young victims before returning to her own skin in the morning, forced to join her flame to that of the rising sun if she is not reunited with her body by dawn. The monster can only be slain by leaving her without a host at dawn, by treating her skin with salt and pepper and thereby making it too itchy to don, or by scattering rice that the soucouyant will be compelled to pick up, grain by grain, before returning to her skin. If the soucouyant drains her victim too much, they either perish or become its host. The tradition of the soucouyant is believed to have derived from a combination of African and European folkloric traditions and crossed the Atlantic during the slave trade, adopting multiple guises in the Caribbean. As such, the hybrid figure registers through its very existence the horrors of the slave trade and the combination of colonialism and capitalism that birthed it. Following the important work of Giselle Liza Anatol on the figure of the soucouyant, her existence references a 'network', encouraging a reading of 'routes over roots' (2015: 21) that prioritises complex interconnectivity rather than a singular historical or geographical trajectory. Unlike the ghost, it is associated both through its actions and its history with journeys, making it more suited to the registering of an increasingly globalised present and systemic, rather than localised, acts of violence.

Yet the soucouyant is a figure of dispersed and ambivalent monstrosity. Descriptions of the soucouyant alternate between positioning her as witch or as vampire, creatures that 'occupy distinct places in most African cultures'. For Giselle Liza Anatol this is significant for its transgression of us/them binaries: 'the accusation of witchcraft is reserved for people *within* the community [...] while vampires are associated with foreignness' (2015: 17). Furthermore, the nature of the soucouyant's possession makes it difficult to distinguish between monster and victim, as the victim may eventually play host to and thereby embody the monster. Associated with marginalised women and social outsiders, it is also difficult to ascertain whether the soucouyant should be regarded with horror or pity. As such, it turns the gaze upon the monster-makers: the people and systems who associate marginality and difference with deviance and monstrosity. Finally, the figure embodies both movement and stasis – forced to travel in search of food yet tied to a skin that can function as a trap. The forced (micro-)migrations of the soucouyant – in combination with the skin that defines its identity – render the creature a corrective to more utopian notions of hybridity associated with the postmodernist, postcolonial school of thought. Two of the most notable postcolonial Gothic novels of the twenty-first century – David Chariandy's *Soucouyant: A Novel of Forgetting* (2007) and Helen Oyeyemi's *White Is for Witching* – have drawn on the soucouyant as a means of exploring Gothic themes of possession, dispersed monstrosity and frustrated negotiations with occluded or repressed histories.

Chariandy's *Soucouyant* recounts the tale of a young man who returns to his childhood home in Ontario to find his Trinidadian mother suffering from dementia under the care of a mysterious young woman. The novel – and the soucouyant central to its symbolism – offers an alternative engagement with history, memory and haunting to that commonly found in Canadian Gothic fiction. Cynthia Sugars, in a defining work on *Canadian Gothic* (2014), suggests that 'many settler-postcolonial historical fictions' seek to 're-ghost' the colonial period 'as a way of entrenching White settlers into the landscape or national community' (179). While demonstrating the significance of Gothic literature in shaping a sense of national identity, this also highlights ways in which certain histories have become fixed in the national imaginary, to the occlusion of others. The soucouyant as an ambivalently located monster points to the ways in which the various characters, each identified with the soucouyant at different moments through bruising on the skin, exhibit the marks of a traumatic past accompanied by the violence of forgetting associated in the novel with both dislocation and dementia. Dementia and the soucouyant function symbiotically to register both the horror and the necessity of forgetting, allegorised as possession by another and the erasure of one's own history. In *Soucouyant*, the protagonist calls repeatedly on his mother to 'remember', pressing her fingers to the strange bones of her knee to force her to acknowledge him as 'Your son. Your youngest son. Remember, mother?' (Chariandy 2007: 8). The soucouyant is a colonising force – a monster that 'speak[s] a truth about the horror of Gothic invasion' (Sugars 2014: 200) – in its capacity to sever victims from historical memory and familial identification. Yet the soucouyant is also the vehicle *of* historical memory in its challenge to settler-colonial and settler-postcolonial Gothic that has sought to create and fix a national history through its representations.

Oyeyemi's *White Is for Witching* employs the soucouyant as a figure through which to engage questions of national identity, occluded histories and possession. There are no Caribbean characters in Oyeyemi's British-based novel, and the soucouyant – referred to as the 'goodlady' – is nominally associated with Anna Good, protagonist Miri's white British great-grandmother, who was also responsible for animating the xenophobic guesthouse with her hatred. The soucouyant's link to Anna Good associates it with a version of national identity premised on whiteness, xenophobia and biological inheritance – 'She's like tradition [. . .] She's in our blood' (Oyeyemi 2009: 66) – yet its links to Caribbean folklore point to histories that are occluded through exclusionary national narratives, such as Britain's unacknowledged economic reliance on its former colonial endeavours and contemporary migrant labour. The effort required to challenge the dominance of these versions of history is registered through Miri's potentially suicidal battle with the soucouyant as a means of saving her lover from its malign effects. As with Chariandy's novel, what is made monstrous through the soucouyant is the systemic violence wrought by exclusionary nationalism.

Postcolonial Gothic – both as critical reading practice and mode of writing – combines an anti-colonial politics with the Gothic mode to render visible the mechanisms of colonial and neo-imperial violence. In the twenty-first century, postcolonial Gothic critics continue the work of their twentieth-century counterparts, but with a newly materialist focus that disavows the predominance of postmodernist iterations of postcolonialism in order to foreground systemic and economic structures of inequality. Registering both the continuing aftermaths of colonial violence and the new atrocities that accompany neo-imperial ventures and mindsets, contemporary postcolonial Gothic has adapted to new contexts and new modes of racism, while appropriating new monsters sympathetic to the complex relationships of national identity, history and possession in an increasingly globalised present in which the legacies of European colonialism nevertheless mean that access to wealth, power and opportunity is profoundly unequal.

References

Anatol, Giselle Liza (2015), *The Things That Fly in the Night: Female Vampires in Literature of the Circum-Caribbean and African Diaspora*, New Brunswick, NJ: Rutgers University Press.
Appadurai, Arjun (2006), *Fear of Small Numbers: An Essay on the Geography of Anger*, Durham, NC: Duke University Press.
Ashcroft, Bill, Gareth Griffiths, and Helen Tiffin (2002), *The Empire Writes Back: Theory and Practice in Post-Colonial Literatures*, 2nd edn, London: Routledge.
Aslam, Nadeem (2004), *Maps for Lost Lovers*, London: Faber and Faber.
Brantlinger, Patrick (1988), *Rule of Darkness: British Literature and Imperialism, 1830–1914*, Ithaca: Cornell University Press.
Bush, George (2001), 'President Bush Addresses the Nation', *The Washington Post*, 20 September, https://www.washingtonpost.com/wp-srv/nation/specials/attacked/transcripts/bushaddress_092001.html??noredirect=on (accessed 25 July 2018).
Chariandy, David (2007), *Soucouyant: A Novel of Forgetting*, Vancouver: Arsenal Pulp Press.
Goddu, Teresa A. (1997), *Gothic America: Narrative, History and Nation*, Chichester: Columbia University.
Ilott, Sarah (2018), 'Gothic Immigrations: Kentish Gothic and the Borders of Britishness', in William Hughes and Ruth Heholt (eds), *Gothic Britain: Dark Places in the Margins and Provinces of the British Isles*, Cardiff: University of Wales Press, pp. 211–32.
Jha, Raj Kamal (2006), *Fireproof*, London: Picador.
Khair, Tabish (2009), *The Gothic, Postcolonialism and Otherness: Ghosts from Elsewhere*, Basingstoke: Palgrave Macmillan.
Kristeva, Julia (1982), *Powers of Horror: An Essay on Abjection*, New York: Columbia University Press.
Lawn, Jennifer (2006), 'From the Spectral to the Ghostly: Postcolonial Gothic and New Zealand Literature', *Australasian-Canadian Studies: A Journal for the Humanities and Social Sciences*, 24.2, 143–69.
Lazarus, Neil (2011), *The Postcolonial Unconscious*, Cambridge: Cambridge University Press.
Löwy, Michael (2007), 'The Current of Critical Irrealism: "A moonlit enchanted night"', in Matthew Beaumont (ed.), *Adventures in Realism*, Oxford: Blackwell, pp. 193–206.
Morey, Peter, and Amina Yaqin (2011), *Framing Muslims: Stereotyping and Representation after 9/11*, Cambridge, MA: Harvard University Press.
Okorafor, Nnedi (2010), *Who Fears Death*, New York: Daw Books.
Oyeyemi, Helen (2009), *White Is for Witching*, London: Picador.
Procter, James, and Angela Smith (2007), 'Gothic and Empire', in Catherine Spooner and Emma McEvoy (eds), *The Routledge Companion to Gothic*, Abingdon: Routledge, pp. 95–104.
Roy, Arundhati (2004), *The God of Small Things*, London: Harper Perennial.
— (2009), *Listening to Grasshoppers: Field Notes on Democracy*, London: Penguin.

Rudd, Alison (2010), *Postcolonial Gothic Fictions from the Caribbean, Canada, Australia and New Zealand*, Cardiff: University of Wales Press.

Rushdie, Salman (2006), *The Satanic Verses*, London: Vintage.

Smith, Andrew, and William Hughes (2003), 'Introduction: The Enlightenment Gothic and Postcolonialism', in Andrew Smith and William Hughes (eds), *Empire and the Gothic: The Politics of Genre*, Basingstoke: Palgrave Macmillan, pp. 1–11.

Spearey, Susan (2000), 'Dislocation of Culture: Unhousing and the Unhomely in Salman Rushdie's *Shame*', in Rowland Smith (ed.), *Postcolonializing the Commonwealth: Studies in Literature and Culture*, Waterloo, ON: Wilfrid Laurier, pp. 167–80.

Sugars, Cynthia (2014), *Canadian Gothic: Literature, History, and the Spectre of Self-Invention*, Cardiff: University of Wales Press.

WReC (Warwick Research Collective) (2015), *Combined and Uneven Development: Towards a New Theory of World-Literature*, Liverpool: Liverpool University Press.

Chapter 2

Queer Gothic
Andrew J. Owens

Since the mid-1990s, much ink and blood (mostly metaphorical, some literal) has been spilt across the pages of trade journals, entertainment blogs/vlogs, fan sites and the popular press in both the US and UK addressing what appears to be a flourishing yet enigmatic media phenomenon: a fascination with the non-normative sexualities of Gothic horror. On television, series such as *Buffy the Vampire Slayer* (1997–2003), *Being Human* (2008–13), *True Blood* (2008–14), *The Vampire Diaries* (2009–17), *Penny Dreadful* (2014–16) and *American Horror Story* (2011–) have delivered substantial ratings and engendered diehard fan cultures across both the heterosexual and LGBTQ+ spectrums. In cinema, vampires, witches, ghosts and other queerly Gothic things that go bump in the night have seen dynamic success in the *Underworld* (2003–16), *Twilight* (2008–12) and *Brotherhood* (2001–9) franchises, reboots of the 1985 cult classic *Fright Night* (2011, 2013) and around the international art-house circuit vis-à-vis *Låt den rätte komma in* (*Let the Right One In*, Tomas Alfredson, 2008), *Only Lovers Left Alive* (Jim Jarmusch, 2013), *The Neon Demon* (Nicolas Winding Refn, 2016) and the mixed-media oeuvre of Canadian queercore artist Bruce LaBruce. In print, Gothic sexualities have flourished across the fictional work of authors such as Clive Barker, Poppy Z. Brite, Stephen King, Charlie David and Anne Rice, as well as in key fiction anthologies such as the Lambda Literary Award winner *Queer Fear: Gay Horror Fiction* (2000), edited by Michael Rowe, and the Bram Stoker Award winner *Unspeakable Horror: From the Shadows of the Closet* (2008), edited by Vince A. Liaguno and Chad Hedler.

These and other texts have been singled out by both critics and fans as capturing a cultural zeitgeist, wrenching non-normative sexualities from the margins to the mainstream of Anglo-American culture. Scholars have both offered queer readings of the literary canon (Haggerty 2006; Hughes and Smith 2009a; Haefele-Thomas 2012) and mapped out previously neglected areas, such as the lesbian Gothic in fiction (Palmer 1999), contemporary queer Gothic fiction (Palmer 2012, 2018), queer horror in film and television (Elliott-Smith 2016) and trans* Gothic in literature and film (Zigarovich 2017). Yet a strictly teleological gesture from the marginal to the mainstream is misleading when it comes to the sexualities of the Gothic for, as Hughes and Smith have argued, 'Gothic has, in a sense, always been "queer"' (2009b: 1) stylistically, structurally and, of course, sexually. Indeed, the queerness of the genre has always been part of its enduring appeal.

As detailed by Eve Kosofsky Sedgwick, the late queer theorist who began her career writing about the Gothic, certain characteristic preoccupations have always haunted the genre since its inception as a literary mode in the late eighteenth century:

> These include the priesthood and monastic institutions; sleeplike and deathlike states; subterranean spaces and live burial; doubles; the discovery of obscured family ties; affinities between narrative and pictoral art; possibilities of incest; unnatural echoes or silences, unintelligible writings, and the unspeakable; garrulous retainers; the poisonous effects of guilt and shame; nocturnal landscapes and dreams; apparitions from the past; Faust- and Wandering Jew-like figures; civil insurrections and fires; the charnel house and the madhouse. (Sedgwick 1980: 9–10)

Given the latitude of these interests, the Gothic has unfailingly functioned, according to Robert B. Heilman, as a mode consumed with opening horizons beyond normative social patterns, rational decisions and institutionally approved emotions: 'in a word, to enlarge the sense of reality and its impact on the human being. It became then a great liberator of feeling. It acknowledged the non-rational – in the world of things and events, occasionally in the realm of the transcendental, ultimately and most persistently in the depths of the human being' (Heilman 1958: 131).

The Gothic's avowal of the irrational and the non-normative has made queer theory an especially persuasive heuristic through which to approach its contemporary manifestations. Since its instantiation as a legitimated field of academic study in the mid-to-late 1980s, few terms have engendered as much debate and critical handwringing as 'queer'. As Annamarie Jagose observes, queer's 'definitional indeterminacy, its elasticity, is one of its constituent characteristics' (1996: 1). Echoing this malleability, Alexander Doty's formative study *Making Things Perfectly Queer: Interpreting Mass Culture* (1993) suggests that queer embraces

> a range of nonstraight expression in, or in response to, mass culture. This range includes specifically gay, lesbian, and bisexual expressions; but it also

includes all other potential (and potentially unclassifiable) nonstraight positions. [. . .] '[Q]ueer' [marks] a flexible space for the expression of all aspects of non- (anti-, contra-) straight cultural production and reception. (Doty 1993: xvi, 3)

Further, and especially germane to analyses of the Gothic, Harry Benshoff labels queer as a 'stance which negates the oppressive binarisms of the dominant hegemony [. . .] both within culture at large, and within texts of horror and fantasy. [. . .] [Q]ueer suggests death over life by focusing on non-procreative sexual behaviors, making it especially suited to a genre which takes sex and death as central thematic concerns' (1997: 4–5). To be sure, such concerns have been woven into the fabric of the Gothic from its very beginnings, offering what George Haggerty calls a 'testing ground for many unauthorized genders and sexualities, including sodomy, tribadism, romantic friendship (male and female), incest, pedophilia, sadism, masochism, necrophilia, cannibalism, masculinized females, feminized males, miscegenation, and so on' (2006: 2).

This chapter focuses on the key questions about contemporary queer theory through a focus on television, as this is the medium where it has seen most significant developments in the early twenty-first century. In its twenty-first-century adaptations across Anglo-American popular culture, Gothic media continues to corroborate Robin Wood's famous contention that the genre, at least in its decidedly horrific modes, represents a 'return of the repressed' (2002: 29). What returns to wreak havoc across our collective screens and cultural fantasies in the guise of the Gothic monster, according to Wood, is sexuality itself. Indeed, if queer sexualities have been historically repressed in the West, then the Gothic proves a more than suitable bedfellow, as the true subject of the genre is the 'struggle for recognition of all that our civilization represses or oppresses, its re-emergence dramatized, as in our nightmares, as an object of horror, a matter of terror' (Haggerty 2006: 28).

Genres of popular culture are always subject to historical contingency and queer Gothic media has proved no exception in the new millennium. In what follows, my analysis centres on what is perhaps one of the most curious developments for the genre in the twenty-first century: a paradoxical bifurcation, especially on television, between specifically *gay* programming, such as Here!'s *Dante's Cove* (2005–7), and that which is more comprehensively *queer*, like Showtime/Sky's *Penny Dreadful* (2014–16). This division, although seemingly splitting hairs at first glance, has become clearly manifest not only through those bodies and acts represented on screen but, perhaps more importantly, via the reading protocols with which audiences have approached these series.

Gay Gothic is Here!

In the summer of 2003, direct broadcast satellite service DirecTV became the first US distributor to ink a deal to carry Here!, a new pay-per-view channel directed specifically at the interests of gay and lesbian audiences. Founded by Paul Colichman and Stephen P. Jarchow, Here! is a division of their Regent Entertainment Group, which had previously seen success among LGBTQ audiences as a producer of films such as the Academy Award-winning *Gods and Monsters* (Bill Condon, 1998). Charging US$3.99 apiece for a catalogue of independently produced gay feature films that rotated each month, executives at Here! hoped to capitalise upon a lucrative segment of the gay and lesbian marketplace: 'an affluent, underserved niche group with lots of buying power, an estimated $450 million to $600 million in annual disposable income, who have been starving for TV programming relevant to their lives' (Moss 2004a).

If much of the trade press coverage of Here!'s launch as a fully-fledged LGBTQ cable network banged the drum of belatedness, the question still remained as to what kinds of representation the network would programme. As reported by *Daily Variety*'s Stuart Levine, Colichman was adamant that the mission of Here!'s original programming was to

> ensure that the gay characters seen throughout the channel are realistic, not a glossed-over or patronized version often depicted in broadcast television. 'Our battle every day is to make sure we are showing an authentic look at the lives of our viewers. [. . .] We are the gay HBO. We set our sights very high.' (Levine 2006)

Here!'s rhetorical press flourishes on the eve of its twenty-four-hour launch smack continuously of realism, community relevance and appeals to verisimilitude. 'What does it mean to be gay in the twenty-first century?', was the predominant question that the channel seemed to pose. Premiering on 7 October 2005, *Dante's Cove* (2005–7), billed by its stars as 'a blend of *Sex and the City* meets *Dark Shadows* meets *The O.C.* meets *Buffy the Vampire Slayer* with a little bit of *Melrose Place* thrown in there' (*Dantes' Cove: Season 1 Backlot*), began as a two-part miniseries. While anxiously awaiting her marriage to local entrepreneur Ambrosius Vallin (William Gregory Lee) in the year 1840, Grace Neville (Tracy Scoggins) becomes restless and uncertain of her fiancé's fidelity. Impatient to lose her virginity to the man she loves, Ambrosius reminds Grace that they must not spoil their wedding night and assures her that he has absolutely no interest in other women. The irony of this promise is swiftly addressed as, upon Grace's exit, Ambrosius's valet Raymond (Dylan Jordan) enters the drawing room, disrobes and begins to receive oral service from his employer. Recalling that she left her gloves on top of another soon-to-be ironic set piece, Ambrosius's copy of *Dante's Inferno*, Grace arrives back at his home just in time to witness Raymond bending Ambrosius over an armchair while penetrating him from behind. Grace's anger directed toward this gay mise-en-scène is matched only by her indignation that her fiancé would engage in such supposedly emasculating behaviour. As Ambrosius scrambles for a quick explanation, Grace's eyes suddenly turn bright red and the fully nude, semi-erect Raymond begins to convulse uncontrollably on the floor. Unbeknownst to Ambrosius, Grace is one of a long line of witches who practise an ancient magickal art (used in its archaic, religious form to distinguish it from the art of stage magic) known as Tresum. Chaining up her fiancé in the basement of her mother's Gothic estate, Grace gives Ambrosius one final chance: recant his gay ways and come back to her or forever be doomed to rot in his own personal hell on earth. Swearing that he would rather suffer an eternity alone than live a lie with her, Grace places a curse on her beloved: only the kiss of a young man will set him free.

Dante's Cove draws inspiration in its thematic material and soap opera conventions from the frames of one of US television's Gothic series par excellence: *Dark Shadows* (1966–71). Indeed, Grace and Ambrosius are clearly drawn in this series as the Angelique Bouchard (Lara Parker) and Barnabas Collins (Jonathan Frid) for the twenty-first century. As Darren Elliott-Smith contends, spectators must often make the primary leap of reading the '*symbolic* homosexual' (2014: 96) within the Gothic milieu of texts like *Dark Shadows*. And indeed, therein lies the key division that has recently ramped up to detach *queer* Gothic media from *gay* Gothic media. While *Dark Shadows*' queerness comes to the fore as a sort of playful tug-of-war between viewer and text vis-à-vis narrative ellipses, circumlocution and aphoristic misdirection, *Dante's Cove* makes Ambrosius's and other characters' struggles with their own non-normative sexual identities entirely explicit.

From Ambrosius's subterranean imprisonment, *Dante's Cove* fast-forwards over 150 years to present-day Venice Beach, California, where Toby Moraitis (Charlie David) and Kevin Archer (Gregory Michael) enjoy a final lovemaking session during a fading summer fling. Encouraging Kevin to run away from his mother and homophobic stepfather, Toby does not understand why his lover cannot simply be honest with everyone about his sexuality. For Toby, the series' hardworking gentleman with a heart of gold, being gay means being open, authentic and true to oneself without compromise, an outlook the teenage Kevin simply is not ready or willing to embrace. However, when tensions flare later that evening at the Archer home and his stepfather smacks him across the face with an appalled 'faggot' slur, Kevin resolves to catch the next bus out of town and join Toby, who has left for his winter job on the island of Dante's Cove.

Kevin's arrival at the Hotel Dante, a gay male reframing of the canonically feminine Gothic ingénue's entrance into a mysterious new world, is presaged by supernatural visions of both a shirtless and shackled Ambrosius and a magickal tome known as the Book of Tresum. These dreams are quickly overshadowed, however, when Kevin is welcomed into the local fold by Toby's friends: Van (Nadine Nicole Heimann), a local lesbian artist with her own soon-to-be-discovered magickal abilities; Cory (Josh Berresford), the Hotel Dante's 'resident slut'; and Adam (Stephen Amell), would-be straight man whose own repressed love for his high-school best friend Toby eventually bubbles to the surface. Considering the history of minority sexual representation on television, one of the most remarkable elements about *Dante's Cove* and a network like Here! is their gay ubiquity. 'If gays on TV (and in mainstream film) have too often been relegated to the token roles of sidekick, accessory, neighbour, on view for heterosexuals within a largely heterosexual world', Suzanna Danuta Walters argues, 'here gays are the only show in town' (2001: 121). In fact, the only straight character with a speaking part throughout the entire run of *Dante's Cove* is Grace, and nightly parties at the Hotel Dante feature little else than same-sex couples involved in various levels of sexual behaviour set against bass-pumping trance music.

As Lorna Jowett and Stacey Abbott explain of Gothic horror on contemporary television, it is no mistake that such narrative spaces are often set in isolated communities, 'divorced in many ways from the larger world' (2013: 46–7), where common codes of realism, morality and plausibility are replaced by logics (or perhaps illogics) of the supernatural. Indeed, *Dante's Cove* makes a conscious effort to construct clear dichotomies between 'the mainland' and its insulated island setting. According to cast member Charlie David, the thematic outlook of *Dante's Cove* can be described somewhat as a process of Gothic rationalisation: '[o]k, this is where we live. We're in Dante's Cove. It's a little nuts around here. There's [sic] ghost children and warlocks and witches, [...] [a]nd it's more coming to terms with what the reality of living here is like' (*Dante's Cove: Season 2 Backlot*). In the context of the gay Gothic on Here!, we might add sexuality itself to the list of normative codes that are disrupted, as *Dante's Cove* never questions the fact that nearly every resident of this island presents somewhere on the

LGBTQ spectrum. As director Sam Irvin explains, the 'overall theme of our series is that there's just a complete acceptance' (*Dante's Cove: Season 3 Backlot*) of the reality of these alternative lifestyles, both sexual and supernatural.

Since his arrival at the Hotel Dante, Kevin has been presented not only with a plethora of new gay friends, but also various legends and continuing dreams of the island's haunting by a horde of supernatural forces. One evening, following an ethereal voice down into the basement of the hotel, Kevin finds a usually padlocked cellar door inexplicably open. What he finds below is the aging body of Ambrosius Vallin, who is magickally brought back to youthful vitality after stealing a kiss from Kevin in what becomes a prescient milieu of gay Gothic bondage and S&M. Indeed, Ambrosius's release from his subterranean prison is the catalyst that propels the remainder of *Dante's Cove*'s Gothic narrative over a three-year, twelve-episode run, including subplots ranging from Toby and Kevin's struggle to keep their relationship together in the face of Ambrosius's unrelenting advances to woo Kevin at any cost, Grace's own resurrection and plans to enact continued revenge on Ambrosius, and the arrival of a thought-to-be-imprisoned dark magickal force that threatens to kill every resident of the island.

By the time *Dante's Cove* premiered in October 2005, Regent Entertainment was no stranger to supporting the gay Gothic. Indeed, the studio had previously produced the first instalment then distributed the second instalment of the direct-to-video gay vampire/witchcraft franchise *The Brotherhood*, directed by Roger Corman protégé David DeCoteau. When asked why Here! decided to make its first original series a 'sexy show with elements of magic', CEO Colichman provided a revealing response:

> The horror genre has always been an important part of the gay and lesbian community. The reason horror and gay people have always gone hand in hand is that the gay community felt like they were monsters among everyone else. There was a sense of alienation. And really horror deals with alienation [. . .] So what we did was take a very traditional genre, the horror soap, and populated that world with our gay and lesbian characters so that we could combine a genre that was comfortable to people who had been feeling alienated with people who were not alienated from themselves, people who had a strong sense of who they were, and a community that was all about being gay and lesbian. ('The Men of Dante's Cove' featurette, *Dante's Cove: Season 2*)

Yet from coverage in *Variety*, *Multichannel News* and other trades, representatives from Here! made one thing abundantly clear: the channel had every intention to eschew sexually explicit media. 'We want mainstream, middle-of-the-road programming for gays and lesbians from the age of 16 on up', Colichman said; 'if people want porno, let them take it off the Internet' (quoted in Dempsey 2003). In light of the fact that full-frontal male nudity appears within the first five minutes of *Dante's Cove*'s premiere episode, however, representatives from Here! may have simply been protesting too much. 'It's not adult content, it's not erotica', Colichman affirmed, 'but it is designed for a mature audience that pays for it and wants it' (quoted in Moss 2004b).

In a dismissive yet ultimately revealing question posed by Andrea Lafferty, the executive director of the Traditional Values Coalition asked in response to Colichman, '[w]hat are they going to do, have homosexuals knitting?' (quoted in Moss 2004a). According to Thomas Waugh, sexually explicit visual culture has always had to serve not only as 'stroke materials' for gays and lesbians, but also as 'our family snapshots and wedding albums, as our cultural history and political validation' (1996: 5). Such materials have a privileged relationship with gay culture due in no small part to their 'unique blend of indexical (motivated) and iconic qualities [. . .] [resembling] the living flesh of everyday sexual experience (iconic) but also [testifying] to the existence of that flesh (indexical)' (12), thereby unleashing the psychological potential for polymorphous identification, voyeurism and/or fetishism in the spectator. In turn, after the first season success of *Dante's Cove*, Colichman and Here! began to change their representational tune: 'we had to uncensor ourselves, to some extent. To allow us to have the same level of sexuality that other premium cable channels like Showtime and HBO have. And we had to allow that same level for our own community' (*Dante's Cove: Season 1 Backlot*).

Take, for example, the ways in which Ambrosius's modus operandi in *Dante's Cove* becomes solidified by demonstrating how his masculinity and sex appeal to other men are actually enhanced by his command of magickal forces. For instance, one evening Ambrosius returns home, takes off his shirt and stands in front of a full-length mirror while unbuttoning his pants to slowly reach inside and pleasure himself. This magickal masturbatory act not only summons spectral visions of a fully nude Kevin, but also physically beckons Cory, previously enslaved by Ambrosius to do his bidding, who gets down on his knees and provides oral service before both strip and Ambrosius penetrates him from behind. As director Sam Irvin notes, 'Ambrosius in *Dante's Cove* is the Barnabas Collins or Dracula for the new millennium. He's got a very sort of darkly sexual romantic side to him' (*Dante's Cove: Season 1 Backlot*).

As Danuta Walters maintains, two of the principal complaints about gay representation on television – 'that gays are token, isolated from other gay people, and that gays are desexualized, denied the pleasures of the flesh' (1996: 121) – are challenged in a series like *Dante's Cove* that wears its gay sexual identity proudly on its sleeve. Indeed, increasingly explicit flourishes of simulated sex and orgasmic release continue to ramp up throughout the series' third season and only become further tethered to its Gothic milieu. With the arrival of Griffen (Jensen Atwood), the bisexual consort of the Tresum Council who is sent to Dante's Cove in order to make sure that supernatural phenomena on the island do not run amok, Ambrosius is steadily seduced by this newcomer and is introduced to the power that gay sex can have in siphoning off magickal energy between men.

In the final episode of the series' third season, recurrent jockeying for power and magickal supremacy eventually climaxes when Ambrosius, Kevin, Toby, Grace and Griffen prevent a thought-to-be-banished force known as the House of Shadows from taking over Dante's Cove. During an elongated battle sequence, Toby suffers the same fate as his new lover Adam had in the penultimate episode, being pulled into a mystical nether realm from which there is little hope of escape. It is also during this finale mêlée that, on the brink of death, Kevin and Ambrosius reignite their love. In the episode's final scene, Ambrosius and Kevin lay naked in bed discussing everything they have been through. Even though Ambrosius reminds him that he is free to leave at any time, Kevin assures him that there is nowhere else he would rather be. As the couple kisses and begins to make love, the camera pans to a mirror that superimposes Kevin and Ambrosius with Toby and Adam trapped in their magickal prison.

Soon after *Dante's Cove*'s third season finale aired on 21 December 2007, Here! announced that the show would be brought back for a fourth season that has yet to materialise but is currently in the process of being fundraised online through Kickstarter. However, the series did inspire a similarly Gothic spin-off, *The Lair* (2007–9), which follows the goings-on inside the island's local sex club that has been taken over by a coven of gay male vampire witches.

'Do You Really Want to be Normal?'

On 17 May 2015, Showtime/Sky premiered the third episode in the second season of its popular Gothic drama *Penny Dreadful*. Imagining a shadowy, sinister, *fin-de-siècle* London throughout which the lives of both original and famously adapted characters from nineteenth-century

Gothic literature collide, including Dr Victor Frankenstein (Harry Treadaway), Dr Henry Jekyll (Shazad Latif), Dorian Gray (Reeve Carney) and Count Dracula (Christian Camargo), this particular episode dedicated itself exclusively to the backstory of the series' central protagonist, Vanessa Ives (Eva Green). Haunted by demons, both literal and figurative, from her past, Vanessa confides in Ethan Chandler (Josh Hartnett), *Penny Dreadful*'s own bachelor-turned-werewolf whose influences from *Dark Shadows*' Quentin Collins are more than slight. 'It all began several years ago', Vanessa's flashback commences, 'and far from here'.

Seeking answers to exactly who and what she is, Vanessa travels to the farthest reaches of the West Country in search of a 200-year-old witch known only as the Cut-Wife of Ballentree Moor (queer popular culture icon Patti LuPone). Over several days of withstanding wind, rain and lightning at the Cut-Wife's gate, Vanessa proves that she is more than a naive village girl searching for a love potion or the witch's namesake speciality: abortion. And indeed, Vanessa's merit is proved through a most queer introductory encounter, as the Cut-Wife thrusts her hand up Vanessa's skirt in order to 'sense' her person via the most intimate areas of her body. 'I am like no others', Vanessa confesses: 'that's why I'm here'. 'Leave everything you were outside this door', the Cut-Wife responds: 'everything you are, bring with you'.

Once inside the Cut-Wife's cottage, what Vanessa is becomes increasingly clear: a tortured soul with magickal gifts who seeks redemption after failing to save her best friend Mina Harker (Olivia Llewellyn) from capture by a malevolent supernatural force, later revealed as Count Dracula. As Vanessa discovers under the Cut-Wife's tutelage, however, magick is a fickle mistress that rarely rewards even the best of intentions. 'I started thinking about themes', *Penny Dreadful* showrunner John Logan told *The Hollywood Reporter*'s Lesley Goldberg in a January 2014 interview, 'and why almost 200 years after [Mary Shelley's *Frankenstein*] was written, we're still reading [it] [. . .] I think it's because the monsters break my heart. Growing up as a gay man before it was socially acceptable, I knew what it was to feel different, alienated and not like everyone else' (quoted in Goldberg 2014). Indeed, if much of the affectively queer resonance of being a witch, a vampire or any other manner of otherworldly Gothic entity resounds with outlawry, secrecy and living beyond normative borders, then both the Cut-Wife and Vanessa exemplify this inclination. 'Monsters all, are we not?', the Cut-Wife reminds her protégé.

Upon *Penny Dreadful*'s arrival in May 2014, Tim Goodman, also of *The Hollywood Reporter*, began a review of the series' premiere episode by stating unequivocally that 'the world doesn't need another psycho-sexual horror story' (2014). Appearing on the crest of a Gothic media wave that included HBO's *True Blood*, FX's *American Horror Story* and The CW's *The Vampire Diaries*, *Penny Dreadful* struck Goodman as symptomatic of a televisual genre that risked, quite literally, being done to death. Yet the cyclical recurrence of the Gothic's deathly queer eroticism from print to screens – both large and small – is exactly what our contemporary media landscapes have proven themselves to habitually foster. Since the turn of the new millennium, adaptations of the Gothic have continued to provide some of the most fertile grounds for non-normative sexualities to make their mark upon Anglo-American popular culture.

When asked why he chose to write *Penny Dreadful* as a period drama, Logan responded in revealing fashion: 'I chose to set the show [in 1891] not because it would be cool visually but because the Victorian era reminds me of right now [...] They were on the cusp of the modern world [...], grappling with the very elemental question of what it means to be human' (quoted in Goldberg 2014). Furthermore, *Penny Dreadful*'s *fin de siècle* setting also reimagines a time when the Western world was beginning to publicly wrestle with the very question of what it meant to be a sexual outcast, none more infamous than Oscar Wilde, whose own biography is collapsed into the series' depiction of his most notorious protagonist: Dorian Gray.

To be sure, explicitly gay sex and sexualities do pepper all three seasons of *Penny Dreadful*. But the series is often at its best, according to both critics and fans, when it engages viewers in the same class of euphemism, circumlocution and unsaid-ness that seems congruent with its historical context and made predecessors like *Dark Shadows* so popular among queer audiences. As Doty contends, the project of reading queerly is not reducible to '"alternative" readings, wishful or wilful misreadings, or "reading too much into things" readings. [Queer readings] result from the recognition and articulation of the complex range of queerness that has been in popular culture texts and their audiences all along' (1993: 16).

And perhaps no scene is more amenable to this critical heuristic in *Penny Dreadful* than the conclusion of the series' first season finale. Desperately seeking council from a priest, Vanessa is challenged to both articulate *and* reconsider her outcast state.

> Vanessa: Do you believe a soul can be taken over by another? That you can lose yourself to something dark?
> Priest: I believe in the devil... If that's what you mean.

Vanessa: That's what I mean. I believe in *curses*. I believe in demons. I believe in monsters. Do you?

[...]

Priest: Before we say another word, you must look into your heart and you must answer me a question, just one. If you have been *touched* by a demon, it's like being touched by the backhand of God. Makes you sacred in a way, doesn't it? Makes you unique. You're a kind of glory… The glory of *suffering*. Now, here's my question: do you really want to be normal?

While Vanessa's struggles for redemption may amount to just another psychosexual horror story, both the 'queerness' of a series like *Penny Dreadful* and the 'gayness' of a series like *Dante's Cove* are likely to keep on evolving side by side, along with an increased interest in Gothic trans* exploration, as television producers, filmmakers and scriptwriters continue the unfinished business of expanding the socio-political horizons of possibility for LGBTQ individuals and communities. And indeed, the Gothic may continue to provide some of the most fertile ground for this work, as vampires, witches, ghosts and other supernatural figures are no longer drawn exclusively as tragic representatives of repressed sexuality.

Film and Television

American Horror Story (FX, 2011–)
Being Human (BBC Three, 2008–13; Syfy, 2011–14)
Buffy the Vampire Slayer (The WB, 1997–2001; UPN, 2001–3)
Dante's Cove (Here!, 2005–7)
Dark Shadows (ABC, 1966–71)
Låt den rätte komma in (*Let the Right One In*, Tomas Alfredson, Sweden, 2008)
Only Lovers Left Alive (Jim Jarmusch, UK, 2013)
Penny Dreadful (Showtime/Sky, 2014–16)
The Lair (Here!, 2007–9)
The Neon Demon (Nicolas Winding Refn, France/Denmark/USA, 2016)
The Vampire Diaries (The CW, 2009–17)
True Blood (HBO, 2008–14)

References

Benshoff, Harry (1997), *Monsters in the Closet: Homosexuality and the Horror Film*, Manchester: Manchester University Press.
Danuta Walters, Suzanna (2001), *All the Rage: The Story of Gay Visibility in America*, London and Chicago: University of Chicago Press.

Dempsey, John (2003), 'DirecTV Bows PPV for Gay Auds', *Variety*, 7 July, https://variety.com/2003/biz/news/directv-bows-ppv-service-for-gay-auds-1117888946 (accessed 7 July 2018).

Doty, Alexander (1993), *Making Things Perfectly Queer: Interpreting Mass Culture*, Minneapolis: University of Minnesota Press.

Elliott-Smith, Darren (2014), '"Blood, Sugar, Sex, Magik": Unearthing Gay Male Anxieties in Queer Gothic Soaps *Dante's Cove* (2005–2007) and *The Lair* (2007–2009)', in Michael Stewart (ed.), *Melodrama in Contemporary Film and Television*, Basingstoke: Palgrave, pp. 96–113.

— (2016) *Queer Horror Film and Television*, London and New York: I. B. Tauris.

Goldberg, Lesley (2014), 'Showtime's Monster Drama *Penny Dreadful* Will Explore Modern Themes', *The Hollywood Reporter*, 16 January, https://www.hollywoodreporter.com/live-feed/showtimes-monster-drama-penny-dreadful-671676 (accessed 7 July 2018).

Goodman, Tim (2014), '*Penny Dreadful*: TV Review', *Hollywood Reporter*, 8 May, https://www.hollywoodreporter.com/review/tv-review-showtimes-penny-dreadful-702313 (accessed 7 July 2018).

Haefele-Thomas, Ardel (2012) *Queer Others in Victorian Gothic: Transgressing Monstrosity*, Cardiff: University of Wales Press.

Haggerty, George (2006), *Queer Gothic*, Urbana and Chicago: University of Illinois Press.

Heilman, Robert B. (1958), 'Charlotte Brontë's "New" Gothic', in Robert C. Rathburn and Martin Steinmann, Jr. (eds), *From Jane Austen to Joseph Conrad: Essays Collected in Memory of James T. Hillhouse*, Minneapolis: University of Minnesota Press, pp. 118–32.

Hughes, William, and Andrew Smith (eds) (2009a) *Queering the Gothic*, Manchester: Manchester University Press.

— (2009b) 'Introduction: Queering the Gothic', in William Hughes and Andrew Smith (eds), *Queering the Gothic*, Manchester: Manchester University Press, pp. 1–10.

Jagose, Annamarie (1996), *Queer Theory: An Introduction*, New York: New York University.

Jowett, Lorna, and Stacey Abbott (2013), *TV Horror: Investigating the Dark Side of the Small Screen*, London and New York: I. B. Tauris.

Levine, Stuart (2006), 'Cablers Step up to Plate with Original Gay P'gramming', *Variety*, 6 April, https://variety.com/2006/scene/markets-festivals/cablers-step-up-to-plate-with-original-gay-p-gramming-1117941129/ (accessed 7 July 2018).

Moss, Linda (2004a), 'Pushing the Boundaries: Fledging Nets Will Supply a Groundswell for Gay Fare', *Multichannel News*, 18 October, http://www.multichannel.com/news/pushing-the-boundaries (accessed 17 July 2017).

— (2004b), 'Gay-Aimed "Here TV!" Goes Premium', *Multichannel.com*, 3 October, https://www.multichannel.com/news/gay-aimed-here-tv-goes-premium-141349 (accessed 7 July 2018).

Palmer, Paulina (1999) *Lesbian Gothic: Transgressive Fictions*, London: Cassell.

— (2012) *The Queer Uncanny: New Perspectives on the Gothic*, Cardiff: University of Wales Press.

— (2018) *Queering Contemporary Gothic Narrative 1970–2012*, Basingstoke: Palgrave.
Sedgwick, Eve Kosofsky (1980), *The Coherence of Gothic Conventions*, New York: Methuen.
Waugh, Thomas (1996), *Hard to Imagine: Gay Male Eroticism in Photography and Film from Their Beginnings to Stonewall*, New York: Columbia University Press.
Wood, Robin (2002) [1986], 'The American Nightmare: Horror in the 1970s', in Marc Jancovich (ed.), *Horror: The Film Reader*, London and New York: Routledge, pp. 25–32.
Zigarovich, Jolene (ed.) (2017) *TransGothic in Literature and Culture*, London and New York: Routledge.

Chapter 3

Postfeminist Gothic
Gina Wisker

Two troubling, troublesome and nebulous terms, Gothic and postfeminism combine in postfeminist Gothic to disturb comfortable ignorance and blinkered constructions of gender, identity, sexuality, relationships and culture. Despite the energies of feminism, maligned as outdated in some postfeminist texts, the demise of sexism, heterophobia and racism are overstated, and equality is far from our grasp. Complacency is a major target of the Gothic, and postfeminist Gothic texts disturb complacent assumptions of the radical achievements of feminism. They also reassert how very necessary and contemporary the morphed and ever-morphing feminist worldviews and active challenges must be.

Postfeminist Gothic was first defined in mainstream culture around 2007, with Ben Brabon and Stéphanie Genz's book *Postfeminist Gothic* (2007). However, since then claims that feminism is stale and finished have been proven too hasty, and the familiar characters, targets and forms of disturbance of the Gothic have become more complex and diverse. Postfeminist Gothic texts reveal that the issues which concern feminism and feminists are, at best, only undead. Having established debates around intentions and achievements of postfeminism and postfeminist Gothic, this chapter then focuses in the main first on Sarah Waters's novels *The Little Stranger* (2009) and *The Paying Guests* (2014); the short stories 'The Loves of Lady Purple' (1974), by Angela Carter, and 'The Glass Bottle Trick' (2000), by Nalo Hopkinson; with a final debate between forms of postfeminist Gothic in the *Twilight* series (Stephenie Meyer's novels (2005–8) and their film adaptations (2008–12)) and the TV series *Buffy the Vampire Slayer* (1997–2003).

Postfeminism?

The 'post' in postfeminism assumes that all advances that feminism fought for are tired, outdated and achieved (Meyers 2001). However, much postfeminist work in the twenty-first century thus far shows that issues confronting women have become more acute and diverse and that they haunt everyday attempts to eradicate them.

In 2003, Elaine J. Hall and Marnie Salupo Rodriguez established postfeminism's four claims: '1) overall support for the women's movement has dramatically eroded because some women (2) are increasingly antifeminist, (3) believe the movement is irrelevant, and (4) have adopted a "no, but . . . " version of feminism' (2003: 878). 'Post', read as 'after', 'beyond' or even 'anti', seems to signal either a tired failure or that the battles of feminism are won. If we read 'chick lit' (postfeminist) such as Helen Fielding's *Bridget Jones's Diary* (1996) or read and watch the *Twilight* series (postfeminist Gothic), we find these fears confirmed in the focus on self, white, middle-class normativity, commodification, consumer pleasures and the eternal promise of romance. Much postfeminist work, including 'chick lit', eschews the political activism of feminism and substitutes for social values, superficial, purely material ones (Merrick 2006).

Emphasising the role of the media in undermining feminism, Angela McRobbie argues that the 'cool' celebration of sexuality for young women involves a rejection of feminism and a depoliticised stance. As she puts it, '[t]he media has become the key site for defining codes of sexual conduct. It casts judgement and establishes the rules of play. Across these many channels of communication feminism is routinely disparaged' (2009: 258). In *Interrogating Postfeminism*, Negra and Tasker critique the notion of linearity in which something achieved loses its relevance. They cut across popular culture and the media, echoing McRobbie and concentrating on postfeminism's fascination with self-fashioning and makeovers, its complacency, blinkered homogenisation of difference and vacuous consumer orientation:

> [Postfeminism is] defined by class, age, and racial exclusions; it is youth-obsessed and white and middle-class by default. Anchored in consumption as a strategy and leisure as a site for the production of the self, postfeminist mass media assumes that the pleasures and lifestyles with which it is associated are somehow universally shared and [. . .] accessible. (2007: 2)

Simultaneously they dispute that feminism has accomplished its goals.

Very few of the promises of the feminist movement are actually manifest as part of our everyday lives: the equal pay, equal rights, an end to violence against women, control over our own equal bodies, and sexual equalities in culture and religion, to name a few. The liberation and equality that first and second wave feminists agitated for led to some positive change and insights, but much of this, it seems, lies now with small pockets of good behaviour, while neoliberalism and far right activism strip our politics, higher education and organisations of humanity. Consequently sexism, homophobia and racism are ever uglier on the street and in the hearts of power. With the resurgence of sharp inequalities, such as the defunding of Planned Parenthood and a revival of sexual harassment, the arguments and activism of feminism remain very necessary. Beyond 'chick lit', many postfeminist texts resurrect familiar questions and demands with new nuances and enhanced urgency, while pointing accusatory fingers at what has worsened, thus exposing new horrors. Such texts question the commodification of women's lives and values and the achievement of equality in social, political, cultural, personal and economic life, and undercut the utopian element of the feminist vision. The gender equality and sexual liberation apparently won are far from visible in soft- and hardcore pornography, for example, masquerading as 'what women are looking for' in films and texts such as the *Fifty Shades of Grey* series (E. L. James's novels (2011–15) and their film adaptations (2015–18)). If feminism has achieved its goals, one also wonders about reification and the rise of hyper-sexualised female AI robots, from the quite intelligent Sophia (developed by former Disney sculptor Dr David Hanson) to the sex dolls abused in Japan, the UK and the US.

Neither failure nor complacency are honest and safe spaces. Postfeminist Gothic texts emphasise tensions and contradictions. On the one hand, they reveal that many of feminism's ostensible achievements have been overclaimed (equal rights, equal pay) or swept away (Hall and Salupo Rodriguez 2003; Brabon and Genz 2007), so in Sarah Waters's *The Paying Guests* there is darkness, an undermining of sexual freedoms and an emptying out of values of sisterhood and trust, all hard won during second wave feminism. On the other hand, they reveal traces of, and revive, reconsider, re-energise and reimagine new ways of dealing with, the issues feminism addressed. Postfeminist Gothic, including Angela Carter's earlier work and more recent work by Nalo Hopkinson, avoids both feminism's idealistic naiveté and its rejection, reviving its energies and enacting agency, and underscoring the need for new challenges to gender inequalities. In 2007, considering the work of Nalo Hopkinson, I disputed that feminism's arguments had been won, recognising instead a new lease of life around postcolonial women's postfeminist Gothic (Wisker 2007: 117–18).

Rosi Braidotti emphasises that some of the breakthroughs of feminism, queer theory and practice, and some characteristics of the destabilisation and questioning of the Gothic, are now inescapable in text and the popular imaginary: '[p]ost-modern Gothic and post-gender sexualities are haunting the imaginary of post-industrial societies' (2002: 87). The radical changes offered by feminism haunt our texts, largely because their promise has not been realised. In response, postfeminist Gothic consistently problematises complacencies about rights and cultures.

Violence, Hatred, Entrapment

In *Splattered Ink* (2016), Sarah Whitney discusses Alice Sebold's *The Lovely Bones* (2002), and suggests the novel questions that violence against women is a thing of the past:

> Postfeminist Gothic novels [. . .] violently intrude on the well-constructed fantasy of a safe and equitable world. They feature abject protagonists who are socially invisible, physically broken, or speaking from the grave. Emphasising women's *dis*empowerment, they go against the grain of a victim-resistant, empowerment-oriented age [. . .] [They] eschew the therapeutic structures embedded in postfeminist popular culture. (2016: 2)

A young girl murdered by the local paedophile tells her tale and conspires with her father to help capture the man. This is not a safe world; however, her agency beyond the grave helps redress some of the cruelty and negation of her as a living woman.

But violence is not always punished, and lesbian love, another feature of some feminist Gothic, is not always happy ever after. In Waters's *The Paying Guests* nothing is resolved. Rather 'there are continuing, haunting concerns, dark scenarios, where ostensibly improved conditions have in fact worsened, where idealistic hopes for gender and other equality are revealed as fantasies' (Wisker 2018: 143). Violence can be disguised as romance or marriage. Waters's more celebratory Gothic romances of pre-Victorian, Victorian and Second World War periods – *Affinity* (1999), *Fingersmith* (2002) and *The Night Watch* (2006) – offered happily-ever-after alternatives. *The Paying Guests* seems an opportunity for Frances and Lilian to escape the destructive aftermath of the First World War: for Frances, their attraction offers an escape from spinsterhood and the drudgery associated with keeping house for her mother after the death of her brothers and father; for Lilian, it offers escape from her crass husband, Leonard. But the lesbian love story deteriorates into complicity over Leonard's murder, which Lilian engineered, only to leave Frances alone, confused and still dominated by the house and outdated versions of women's roles. There really is no love story here, its death figured in Leonard's murder. *The Paying Guests* participates in postfeminism's exploration of violence, because the two lovers murder the unwanted husband, yet the novel refuses simple resolutions. Leonard's murder is almost pinned on an innocent man, and once the trial is over, the two women go their separate ways, the more street savvy Lilian moving into other relationships.

Sarah Waters's *The Little Stranger*, a ghost story of unfulfilled romance and haunted houses, is situated just after the Second World War, when some women could earn a living, escaping domesticity with a factory or shop job. Like Frances, Caroline Ayres is imprisoned within her home, Hundreds Hall, a great decaying English country house, a relic of empire and wealth. Although striding around the muddy fields approving new council houses, her incarceration in the house and the legacy of her damaged family prevent any escape. Her only way out is ostensibly with grammar-school educated Doctor Faraday, whose sexual disgust at women, and particularly 'masculine', hairy-legged Caroline, hides his very real desire to own the house of his working-class youth. This postfeminist Gothic novel casts the house and the working-class suitor in Gothic roles, one entrapping, the other invading and seeking possession. Caroline is a virtual mad woman in the attic, stuck by her social position, the debts and history of Hundreds Hall. A sour ending and a drab frightening stasis show what postfeminist Gothic can undercut: alternative spaces, love, escape.

Violence and oppression are also an issue in one of the several contemporary texts focusing on controlling heterosexual relationships. Feminism is a touchstone in Helen Dunmore's novel *Birdcage Walk* (2017), where historical feminist pamphleteer Julia Fawkes is only a mark on a gravestone, her radical links with the French Revolution and women's equality forgotten. Her daughter Lizzie's marriage, seen as freedom of choice, becomes one where at any moment we expect to find her body walled into the new building overlooking the Bristol Gorge, from whence her domineering architect husband John Diner Tredevant follows her movements, intending to limit them to the house and immediate environs. The novel opens with a murder, as a man returns to bury a dead woman, out in the wild forest where no one will find her. The detail and care with which the murderer places the grass back over her are a craftsman's skills. Seeing John, architect and builder, we realise he is the murderer, but he does not see it that way. He views his surveillance of Lucie, the first wife, as normal behaviour, and his (mis)reading of her actions as infidelity, punishable by death.

The darkest elements are John's overwhelming need to own second wife Lizzie, her mind, body and all her possessions. His bullying dominance of her life hides behind paternalism. His views are that, as a middle-class woman and wife of the great builder, she does not need to work, but be ornamental, incarcerated, a bird in a cage as part of the showhouse for his overambitious masterpiece, the soaring terrace above the Bristol Gorge. The house is Lizzie's prison, as his body imprisons her, hurting her in their lovemaking, weighing down like the heavy stone of his buildings. John's mind games are worse. There are dark threatening moments in the labyrinthine wine cellar. He intends to murder her as they flee debtors, in the Bristol Channel, but Lizzie fools him and escapes. Psychologically oppressive and silencing, the text is a murder ballad exposing the predatory behaviour hiding behind the everyday respectability of marriage. Husbands treat women as owned objects or playthings, using romance to lure young women to violent deaths. Lizzie's mother's feminism seems powerless, extinguished in life, but in death she warns her daughter of John's deadly intent to kill her.

Undead Women, Dolls, Cyborgs, Ghosts and Duppies

Postfeminist Gothic revitalises feminism's broader issues, including gender equality, inclusivity and diversity. It destabilises complacent certainties of relationships, of identity and wholeness of self, undermining seemingly safe places, revealing false dreams, violence and oppression. It also radically reimagines familiar Gothic figures of fear – the witch, mermaid, puppet/doll, vampire, monster, zombie and werecreature – to expose the objectification and commodification of bodies, unfinished dark business and new threats to women's existence. It troubles what is taken as achieved and settled to scrutinise and rewrite history and everyday narratives. Sometimes, it breaks through the darkness, highlighting change, enhancement and difference as positive ways forward.

With postfeminist Gothic, the restless, troublesome exposure and challenge of the Gothic is accompanied by a complex focus on gender and politics, although it refuses easy celebration of embracing the darkness and freedom, happy endings and transcendence enacted in lesbian vampire collections from the 1990s, such as Victoria A. Brownworth's *Night Bites* (1996) and Pam Keesey's *Dark Angels: Lesbian Vampire Stories* (1996). There are no idealistic, simplistic celebrations of either sisterhood or lesbian love. Coupling postfeminism with Gothic results in the querying of established, comfortable constructions of identity, love, romance, domesticity, family, inheritance, heredity, safety and health.

It navigates contradictions, darknesses and possibilities, simultaneously questioning complacencies of feminism concerning sisterhood and the power to make substantial changes to improve equality and women's lives. Familiar feminist issues concerning gender and power, bodies and the inseparable interaction between the political and the personal remain but are replayed differently. There are also many new issues of gender and sexuality to tackle since the early days of second wave feminism, including transgender recognition and celebration, AI, cyborgs and posthumanism. In texts considered here, postfeminism and the Gothic can offer speculative possibilities of change largely through diversity and hybridity. To do so, they often splice with post-apocalyptic fiction, Ecogothic and Afrofuturism. Postfeminist Gothic can display potential developments for bodies and gender, giving voice and body to the Other and radicalising representations of gender and gender-based identities, particularly in relation to (the horror of) heteronormativity (Halberstam 2007). It emphasises contestation through the haunting and morphing of familiar Gothic concerns and the figures which articulate them: vampires, ghosts, werewolves, zombies, cyborgs and serial killers.

Postfeminist Gothic has a lively interest in questions of the posthuman, in the constructed performed body. In *Gothic Pathologies* (1998), David Punter defines the cyborg/posthuman as gestures towards transcendence, incarnation, the sublime (220), while Anya Heise-von der Lippe recognises posthuman Gothic as a part of our construction of self: 'the posthuman Gothic makes us aware that the monstrous Other is not only lodged within, but an essential part of our (human) identity construction' (2017: 6). In 'Inventing, Revising, and Reinventing Women' (2015), Katherine Weese uses Laura Mulvey's work to reveal how such 'transcendence' is impacted by gender difference, and explores how Steven Millhauser's novellas create female cyborgs or automata, arguing that his characters respond to notions of the perfect in woman, but have no idea of real skin and body texture. An example is Olivia in *August Eschenburg* (1986), a construction reminiscent of Olimpia, the doll in E. T. A. Hoffmann's 'The Sandman' ('Der Sandmann', 1816), idolised by Nikolas. Hoffmann's Olimpia was followed by the makeover of a poor girl into an object of desire: Trilby in George du Maurier's 1894 novel of the same title. Postfeminist Gothic considers and questions cyborg bodies, performativity, sexuality, the posthuman and the fluid (lesbian) continuum, as defined by Adrienne Rich (1980), along which gender and sexual choices lie.

Postfeminist Gothic's undermining of repressive myths of women as manipulated objects of desire and disgust, the toys and waste of society's reliance on oppressive hierarchies, probably begins with Angela

Carter's exposure of woman as manipulated whorish puppet in 'The Loves of Lady Purple'. Carter's tale of Lady Purple exposes the patriarchal control of women and sexual freedom. Constructed and manipulated by an Asiatic professor, a powerful but gimcrack figure, to play out whorish scenarios for male audiences, Lady Purple is punished to restore their sense of order, ensuring double satisfaction: voyeuristic pleasure followed by punishment and packing away. Carter writes that

> she could not escape the tautological paradox in which she was trapped; had the marionette all the time parodied the living or was she, now living, to parody her own performance as a marionette? Although she was now manifestly a woman, young and beautiful, the leprous whiteness of her face gave her the appearance of a corpse animated solely by demonic will. (1974: 39)

Carter's early postfeminist Gothic tale and later *Nights at the Circus* (1987), with liberated bird-woman protagonist Fevvers, built upon feminist theories related to performance and violence. These include Judith Butler's exposure of performativity in *Gender Trouble: Feminism and the Subversion of Identity* (1990), Andrea Dworkin's exposure of violence against women in *Pornography: Men Possessing Women* (1981) and Julia Kristeva's psychoanalytical clarification of how women have been developed as objects of desire and disgust, the receptacles and victims of abjection in *Powers of Horror: An Essay on Abjection* (1982). Lady Purple is vampiric and self-aware, coming alive like Sophia the AI robot and stalking off into the village to earn her own money in a brothel.

Carter exposes gender inequalities based on economics and constraining, socially and mythically rooted expectations, opportunities and behaviours. However, she neither idealises nor idolises women as perfections of sisterhood. Carter's women are articulate, aggressive, larger than life, carnivalesque figures splicing horror and the comic, exposing dehumanising manipulations. Fevvers, in *Nights at the Circus*, retains secrets about her real/fantastic hybridity as bird/woman, refusing to be trapped as a love object or an imprisoned art object, a golden bird in a golden cage in a Fabergé egg. In the brothel, a winged Venus, Fevvers debunks romantic relationships:

> Sealed in this artificial egg, this sarcophagus of beauty, I waited, I waited ... although I could not have told you for what it was I waited. Except, I assure you, I did not await the kiss of a magic prince, sir! With my two eyes I nightly saw how such a kiss would seal me up in my appearance forever. (Carter 1987: 39)

Carter's work exemplifies critiques of the idolisation of cyborgs, dolls as performed, dehumanised versions of male fantasies of desirably compliant and depraved, guilty women.

Holly Black's Young Adult (YA) Gothic novel *The Coldest Girl in Coldtown* (2013) also problematises some of the characteristics of powerful feminist heroines who question love, romance and body image. Black's balance is different. With Tana, she both expresses YAs interest in looks (what to wear, how others judge you) and exposes the dangers of investment in artifice at the expense of valuing one's own life and that of others. The performative vampire cult operating within the 'coldtowns' constructed to incarcerate the vampire infected might seem party heaven, but they rely on trickery, gullibility, slavery and ultimately slaughter of those sucked in. The teenagers are vulnerable consumers/consumed: '[e]ven from the beginning, that was a problem. People liked pretty things. People even liked pretty things that wanted to kill and eat them' (2013: 107).

There are homosexual and lesbian as well as heterosexual relationships, but the text neither insists on nor reverts to compulsory behaviours, emphasising celebration of diversity, first seen in Tana's rescue of Aidan, the boyfriend turning into a vampire, and Gavriel, the vampire-turned-vampire-hunter. Her nurturing of friendships and communities offers new kinds of relationship beyond postfeminist rejections of feminist/lesbian feminist values and relations. Tana shows her inclusiveness, refusing to 'otherise', learning to love the vampire and to deal with her own probable change into one. Diversity and friendship are more important than the narrative of sisterhood alone, although Tana certainly is a protective sister to Pearl, who enters the coldtown to join the party. *The Coldest Girl in Coldtown* emphasises the contradictions of the two extremes of postfeminist Gothic, which are also exemplified in *Buffy the Vampire Slayer* and the *Twilight* series.

In the latter, the Cullen vampire family are fascinated with expensive clothes, cars, material wealth and family values. They avoid the unpleasant social side of being vampires, preferring vegetarianism. Edward Cullen has the glamour of the beautiful bad-boy vampire and none of the bad habits or lack of social values. It is hardly surprising that a working-class girl, Bella, with an old noisy truck, living with her divorced Dad and starting out in the constant point-scoring of a new school would find Edward attractive, a Prince Charming with wealth, beauty, longevity and perfect health. As the book/film series progresses, marriage and entry into the Cullen clan legitimates their love, and after some awkwardnesses in giving birth to a fast-growing, body-ripping vampire child, they are blessed with a happy-every-after marriage and family, even with the disruptive threat of travelling vampires. There is nothing feminist here, no radical questioning of the constraints of conservative (Mormon) values. The *Twilight* franchise is arguably a worryingly viral form of postfeminist backlash that illustrates Angela McRobbie's definition of it as a dismantling of feminism, re-selling young women a set of values focusing on body image and sexualisation which seems to free them but simply sends them back to the same old deferral to men, in a context predominantly white and heterosexual. McRobbie sees elements of postfeminist popular culture, including fashion photographs and makeover shows as constituting

> a new and expansive form of gender power which oversees and takes charge of an economically necessary movement of women, by utilizing a faux-feminist language of 'empowerment of women' so as to defuse, refute and disavow the likelihood of a new solidaristic vocabulary being invented which would challenge these emerging forms of gendered, racialized and class inequalities. (McRobbie 2009: 135)

Buffy the Vampire Slayer (1997–2003) offers an alternative postfeminist Gothic. The Buffy vs Edward fan work posted on Facebook by Jill Smo (see Pender 2016: 225) highlights a comparison of the values underlying the relationships of Edward and Bella, where Bella is dependent and emptied out by her relationship to the powerful, languid, possibly vicious Edward, while Buffy and Angel have a more equal relationship in which Buffy has the power and energy. Smo's work builds on Jonathan McIntosh's 2009 (fair use) compilation of footage from *Twilight* (Catherine Hardwicke, 2008) and *Buffy* (seasons 1–7), with a little *Harry Potter and the Goblet of Fire* (Mike Newell, 2005). In *I'm Buffy and You're History: Buffy the Vampire Slayer and Contemporary Feminism*, Patricia Pender considers Buffy as an example of third wave feminism, arguing that 'if one of the primary goals of third wave feminism is to question our inherited models of feminist agency and political efficacy, without acceding to the defeatism implicit in the notion of "post-feminism"' (2016: 76), then *Buffy* provides us with modes of oppositional praxis, of resistant femininity and, in its final season, of collective feminist activism that are unparalleled in mainstream television. Her reading enables us to see Buffy as a positive, politicised, energetic alternative to the worryingly vacuous versions of relationships and values exemplified in *Twilight* and the grim denials of hope for any kind of feminist future in, for example, Sarah Waters's *The Little Stranger* and *The Paying Guests*.

One of the points I make in this chapter is that postfeminist Gothic comes in several forms, with varied values and messages, some radical, some familiar and conformist, some rather dour. It appears as 'chick lit' anodyne returns of romantic relationships with attendant problems of a celebration of male power, both cultural and physical (*Twilight*), and as hopeless refusals of feminist agency and futures (*The Paying Guests*). These versions undermine the achievements of feminism. But postfeminist Gothic also moves beyond illusion and despair. It can be energetic and agentic ('The Loves of Lady Purple', *Buffy the Vampire Slayer*, 'The Glass Bottle Trick'). Charlaine Harris's novels in *The Southern Vampire Mysteries* (2001–13) and their TV series adaptation, *True Blood* (2008–13), *Buffy the Vampire Slayer* and YA postfeminist Gothic, such as *The Coldest Girl in Coldtown*, retain an interest in shopping, the performative self and dress codes familiar from 'chick lit', but they also focus on friendship, family, community and strong women, the latter typically a feminist concern.

Seeking romance, young women are easy targets for passive-aggressive or violent partners, whether alive or undead. Rewriting the Bluebeard tale, and 'Fitcher's bird', mixed with Caribbean myth and postfeminism's doubts about sisterhood, in her postfeminist Gothic 'The Glass Bottle Trick', Nalo Hopkinson deploys Gothic figures, the abusive controlling husband who tortures and murders his wives, ghostly figures of duppies, and the worldly-wise young woman with survival instincts and agency.

Persuaded to give up her wayward ways and her gold chain-wearing boyfriend and settle with the wealthy, ostensibly stable, boring, bookish Samuel, Beatrice seeks the security of her husband's income and romance, but pregnancy is a threat for both of them. Samuel's façade of success masks an internalised negative self-destructive version of his own blackness, offloaded onto the women in his life. He fears that producing a child would remind him of his colour, seen as ugly. Like Toni Morrison's Pecola Breedlove in *The Bluest Eye* (1969), he hates his body, himself. For his series of wives, pregnancy is death. When pregnant, they are punished as the carriers of his guilty blackness, the source of the problem. They are destroyed, kept in stasis in the back bedroom, their duppy spirits imprisoned in glass bottles. No radical feminist, Beatrice seeks a comfortable domestic life, but is jolted out of that complacency when she finds the duppy wives and realises she is next. Smashing the bottles, she smashes both the false romance and Samuel's power over them all, an act suitable for a feminist warrior reacting against a Bluebeard bully, but she has no illusions about the sisterhood of the vengeful wives. Here, some of the characteristics of feminist tales return (exposing romance and dominant partnerships, reintroducing cultural difference), while, as in *The Paying Guests*, feminist ideas of sisterhood and independence are revealed as idealised and unlikely.

There are choices for postfeminist Gothic: it can either be a form of 'chick lit' with shopping and fangs, or a critique of some of the idealistic hopes of feminist texts, and thus reassert critique, multiculturalism and agency. Postfeminist Gothic reveals the violence at the heart of romance, whether heterosexual or same sex, appearing as entrapment in deceptive, romantic, domestic histories in Sarah Waters's *The Paying Guests* and Helen Dunmore's *Birdcage Walk*. In the latter novel, feminism is erased in the same way as is the grave of Julia Fawkes, an early feminist pamphleteer – her words lost in a silent history. In doll or cyborg-focused work the stabilities of the body are queried, as are all boundaries in terms of life, death, culture, gender, self and Other. Postfeminist Gothic does not offer some new feminist utopia, although some of it attempts a tempered version of a positive future that avoids outdated, idealistic dreams of sisterhood, lesbian love and widespread equality.

Postfeminist Gothic texts leave the reader with a series of critical contradictions that reflect the contested nature of both postfeminism and the Gothic, dealing with new and old problems facing women. At their best they warn of the returned ghosts of pre-feminist inequalities and performativity constantly shadowing the present, threatening to rematerialise and undermine any progressive developments. Through their replay of ghosts, vampires and cyborg bodies, they further arguments concerning othering, bodies, history and cultures in post-industrial society. They can be edgy, unsettled, offering new truths and imaginative agentic alternatives.

Film and Television

Buffy the Vampire Slayer (The WB/UPN, 1997–2003)
True Blood (HBO, 2008–14)
Twilight (Catherine Hardwicke, USA, 2008)

References

Black, Holly (2013), *The Coldest Girl in Coldtown*, New York: Little, Brown and Company.
Brabon, Benjamin A., and Stéphanie Genz (2007), *Postfeminist Gothic: Critical Interventions in Contemporary Culture*, Basingstoke: Palgrave Macmillan.
Braidotti, Rosi (2002), *Metamorphoses: Towards a Feminist Theory of Becoming*, Cambridge: Polity Press.
Butler, Judith (1990), *Gender Trouble: Feminism and the Subversion of Identity*, New York: Routledge.

Carter, Angela (1974), 'The Loves of Lady Purple', in *Fireworks: Nine Profane Pieces*, London: Virago.
— (1987), *Nights at the Circus*, London: Chatto and Windus.
Dworkin, Andrea (1981), *Pornography, Men Possessing Women*, London: The Women's Press.
Halberstam, Judith (2007), 'Neo-splatter: Bride of Chucky and the Horror of Heteronormativity', in Benjamin A. Brabon and Stéphanie Genz (eds), *Postfeminist Gothic: Critical Interventions in Contemporary Culture*, Basingstoke: Palgrave Macmillan, pp. 30–42.
Hall, Elaine J., and Marnie Salupo Rodriguez (2003), 'The Myth of Postfeminism', *Gender & Society*, 17.6, 878–902.
Heise-von der Lippe, Anya (2017), *Posthuman Gothic*, Cardiff: University of Wales Press.
Hopkinson, Nalo (2000), 'The Glass Bottle Trick', in *Whispers From the Cotton Tree Root: Caribbean Fabulist Fiction*, Montpelier, VT: Invisible Cities Press, pp. 257–72.
Kristeva, Julia (1982), *Powers of Horror: An Essay on Abjection*, Leon Roudiez (trans.), New York: Columbia University Press.
McIntosh, Jonathan (2009), 'Buffy vs Edward: Twilight Remixed' (original version), https://www.youtube.com/watch?v=RZwM3GvaTRM&feature=youtu.be (accessed 28 July 2018).
McRobbie, Angela (2009), *The Aftermath of Feminism: Gender, Culture and Social Change*, London: Sage.
Merrick, Elizabeth (ed.) (2006), 'Introduction: Why Chick Lit Matters', in *This Is Not Chick Lit: Original Stories by America's Best Women Writers*, New York: Random House, pp. vii–xi.
Meyers, Helene (2001), *Femicidal Fears: Narratives of the Female Gothic Experience*, New York: SUNY Press.
Negra, Diane, and Yvonne Tasker (eds) (2007), *Interrogating Postfeminism*, Durham, NC: Duke University Press.
Pender, Patricia (2016), *I'm Buffy and You're History: Buffy the Vampire Slayer and Contemporary Feminism*, London: I. B. Tauris.
Punter, David (1998), *Gothic Pathologies: The Text, the Body and the Law*, Basingstoke: Palgrave Macmillan.
Rich, Adrienne (1980), 'Compulsory Heterosexuality and Lesbian Existence', *Signs: Journal of Women and Culture in Society*, 5.1, 631–60.
Weese, Katherine (2015), 'Inventing, Revising, and Reinventing Women', *Journal of the Fantastic in the Arts*, 26.2, 333–52.
Whitney, Sarah E. (ed.) (2016), *Splattered Ink: Postfeminist Gothic Fiction and Gendered Violence*, Urbana, Chicago and Springfield: University of Illinois Press.
Wisker, Gina (2007), 'Moving beyond Waste to Celebration: The Postcolonial/Postfeminist Gothic of Nalo Hopkinson's "A Habit of Waste"', in Benjamin A. Brabon and Stephanie Genz (eds), *Postfeminist Gothic: Critical Interventions in Contemporary Culture*, Basingstoke: Palgrave Macmillan, pp. 114–25.
— Wisker, Gina (2018), 'Unfinished Dark Business: Postfeminist Gothic and Sarah Waters' *The Paying Guests*', in Simon Bacon (ed.), *The Gothic Reader*, Oxford: Peter Lang, pp. 135–43.

Chapter 4

Neoliberal Gothic
Linnie Blake

Over the course of the past thirty years, a new kind of Gothic has emerged. Manifesting predominantly in novels, films, television series and graphic novels, the phenomenon I have termed 'Neoliberal Gothic' deploys the Gothic's core representational strategies and thematic concerns specifically to explore the ways in which neoliberal capitalism has wrought seismic changes both to the world we live in and the ways in which we think about ourselves as citizens, as gendered subjects, as members of particular class and ethnic groupings and as human beings (Blake 2015a, 2015b; Blake and Soltysik Monnet 2017).

Emerging in the US and the UK in the 1970s and bursting onto the global economic stage the following decade, it was neoliberalism that:

> mounted an effective propaganda campaign against 'big government;' itself seen as inimical to the liberty of the individual because it was detrimental to the necessary freedom of the market as guarantor of broader political liberties [...] The market was all and ethics were deemed an irrelevance. Hence, a doctrine of self-regulation was espoused whilst a range of programmes that mounted direct attacks on workers' rights were imposed on an international scale in return for dubious trade agreements. (Blake 2016: 231)

Of course, as spending on education, health and social welfare was slashed across the G7 nations, inequalities soared – both between countries and within them. Unemployment surged along with homelessness as manufacturing industry either collapsed or was moved to Asia and Latin America, where safeguards for workers (such as fair pay, health and safety and the right to collective bargaining) were outlawed. Meanwhile, the neoliberal self was refashioned as a self-serving individual endlessly mutating to better fit the demands of the global corporation while aspiring to the accumulation of personal wealth as the acme of human achievement. And so, as a new world came into existence, a range of Neoliberal Gothic texts emerged to chart the massive social, cultural and psychologic dislocations wrought by free market economics and to challenge the monstrosity of a system that seemed hell-bent on elevating a tiny minority while consigning billions of human beings to poverty, disease and death.

This is not, of course, to argue that Gothic texts of the post-millennial period necessarily adopt radical attitudes or that the mode itself is intrinsically critical of the time and place of its production. The Gothic has, in fact, voiced a range of highly dubious attitudes to the working class, to women and to ethnic minorities since its inception.[1] The same can be said of numerous post-millennial offerings. The gender politics of Stephenie Meyer's *Twilight* (2005–8) are so regressive as to startle. Television series such as *The Vampire Diaries* (2009–17) and *The Originals* (2013–18) proffer a highly regressive sense of bourgeois authority. Further, Isaac Marion's novel *Warm Bodies* (2010) and its filmic adaptation (Jonathan Levine, 2013) even propose heteronormative love as a means of restoring the undead to life and society to full functionality. These texts reflect their time and place, but they do not undertake the cultural work of what I have termed Neoliberal Gothic. For as the following discussion will illustrate, Neoliberal Gothic *is* socially and politically engaged. It interrogates dominant attitudes to race, class and gender and it consistently adopts the representational strategies of the Gothic to not only explore but also indict the inequalities of the contemporary world and the economic base on which they rest. Neoliberal Gothic, in other words, *repeatedly* returns us to ways in which we have been made monstrous by the workings of capital in a world that espouses free trade but in which we are far from free.

The linkage of the monster and the workings of capital is nothing new.[2] As early as 1764, Voltaire looked on the proliferating financial services sector of his own period and observed that both London and Paris were full of 'stock-jobbers, brokers, and men of business, who sucked the blood of the people in broad daylight' (Kneeland 1836: 371). Marx expanded on Voltaire's use of the metaphor to critique the exploitative and parasitical nature of contemporary industrial capitalism, affirming that 'capital comes dripping from head to toe, from every pore, with blood and dirt' (Marx 1976: 926). For Marx, of course, capital itself was a source of horror. It had given rise to the dispossession of European peasantry, slavery and the expropriation of colonial resources and, in Marx's own period, a vampiric bourgeoisie that preyed upon the industrial working class. For Marx, then, 'capital is dead labour which, vampire-like, lives only by sucking living labour, and lives the more, the more labour it sucks' (342). In the industrialising US, moreover, wealth was generated by 'the capitalized blood of children' (920), while British industry was a 'vampire-like' system that prospered 'by sucking blood and children's blood too' (Marx 1974: 79).

Neoliberal Vampires

Given such an august lineage, it is entirely unsurprising that the vampires of the neoliberal age not only embody and enact the parasitic nature of contemporary *laissez-faire* economics but enable us to observe how readily human power-brokers have abandoned their humanity in their ongoing pursuit of wealth. A superlative example of this is the Netflix Original series *Hemlock Grove* (2013–15), set in the eponymous Pennsylvania town that, for all its contemporary US setting, is essentially the fiefdom of its wealthiest family – the Godfreys. The Godfreys owe their money to steel, being owners of the Bessemer mill that 'turned pig iron into money' ('The Crucible', 1.6) by polluting the river, poisoning the air and killing innumerable workers. In the 1990s, as cheap foreign labour and entirely unregulated pay and working conditions abroad made it unprofitable to produce steel in the US, J. R. Godfrey revived the family's fortunes by closing the mill – leaving much of the town jobless. As was the case across the 'rustbelt' in this period, the loss of jobs led not only to homelessness and widespread poverty, but to the destruction of community cohesion and a widespread decline in public health and educational attainment. It is a dynamic echoed in Jim Jarmusch's Palme d'Or-nominated vampire film *Only Lovers Left Alive* (2013), in which the all-but-derelict city of Detroit illustrates how far the world has fallen not only since the sixteenth-century youth of the vampiric protagonists, but in neoliberal times. Detroit was both economically and symbolically significant in the post-war period as the home of the American automobile industry yet is now a wasteland of broken houses, ruined factories and drug-addicted people. A similar sense of despairing decay exists in Hemlock Grove, exemplified by one townsperson's critique of Roman Godfrey, the heir to the Godfrey fortune: 'there's lots of people broke because of this asshole's family' ('Children of the Night', 1.12).

But if industrial production collapsed in the US in the 1980s and 1990s, certain new industries grew exponentially, not least the biomedical sector – including corporatised pharmacology. This, as Melinda Cooper has shown in her superlative study *Life as Surplus: Biotechnology and Capitalism in the Neoliberal Era* (2008), has become so powerful over the past thirty years that it drives government policy with regards to healthcare. For example, in 2009, the World Health Organization declared swine flu – a strain of the H1N1 virus responsible for the decimation of world populations in the years following the First World War – to be a potential global pandemic. World governments responded by spending billions of dollars of public money on the antiviral drug Tamiflu, despite the fact that its manufacturers had sponsored all trials into its value and had subsequently suppressed the evidence that it was entirely ineffective in reducing the spread or severity of the illness. Fortunately, the pandemic never arrived. And while the power of the pharmaceuticals' lobby may have been exposed, Hoffmann-La Roche got to keep its profits (£500 million from the UK alone). *Hemlock Grove*'s J. R. Godfrey was, in short, extremely wise to plough his family's capital into the foundation of the Godfrey Institute. In doing so, he sought 'to buy the future' ('Catabasis', 1.8) in much the same way his grandfather had done by investing in steel production in the nineteenth-century past. In time, all profits would be reinvested into research and the development of new treatments and techniques – including the resurrection of the dead, the development of human life outside the womb and the invention of a blood stew designed to slake the thirst of Olivia Godfrey (Famke Janssen), J. R.'s vampire widow, who is now CEO of the largest privately-owned corporation in the US. Marx's condemnation of the capitalist class as bloodsucking parasites thus finds its neoliberal embodiment in Olivia Godfrey – an incestuous sociopath who has smothered innumerable of her children at birth because they failed to carry her own vampiric trait. Living high above the ruined steel town, and proclaiming 'the only thing I care about us producing is money', Olivia is a quintessential neoliberal corporatist, generating ever more capital from her innumerable global investments while producing products that add nothing to the general welfare of the world.

The self-same love of money brings about the end of the world as we know it in Justin Cronin's vampire apocalypse trilogy *The Passage* (2010), *The Twelve* (2012) and *The City of Mirrors* (2016) – the first of which charts the fall of humanity at the hands of biotechnology, corporate greed and the governmental will to US military supremacy. Opening in 2022, this is a world where 'war was everywhere, metastasizing like a million maniac cells run amok across the planet, and everyone was in it' (Cronin 2010: 108). Unsurprisingly, global ecologies struggle to survive, New Orleans having been reduced to a toxic wasteland following a storm the magnitude of Katrina – notably Katrina has been recognised as perfectly illustrative of 'the bipartisan neoliberal consensus [that] reduces government to a tool of corporations and the investor class alone' (Reed 2006). Unsurprisingly, the phenomenon of the political dynasty is alive and well: Jenna Bush (daughter of George W. and granddaughter of George) is Governor of Texas and poised for presidential office. The Middle East remains in turmoil, terrorist atrocities are commonplace within the US and, with gas prices at record levels, 'the whole economy [has] locked up like a bad transmission' (Cronin 2010: 97). And things are about to get worse. In Bolivia, an American scientific expedition funded by the US military is all but wiped out by a bat-borne virus believed to have the power to prolong life and eliminate all disease. In true neoliberal fashion, the state and the corporation come together to capitalise upon the tragedy. Project Noah is funded by the military who seek to build the self-healing soldier, for in these neoliberal times an injured combatant is nothing more than a 'broken asset' (54). So, in a bunker below the Rockies, the nation's most disposable people become test subjects: twelve death row inmates and the six-year-old daughter of a dead prostitute (a woman forced into selling her body by the dire economic state of the country) are injected with the virus. Needless to say, things end in disaster: the original Twelve mutate into super-strong, light-averse and nigh-indestructible predatory telepaths who break free of the compound and begin to feast on the populace. Of the victims, one in ten are themselves transformed into a predatory Viral/Flyer, the word 'vampire' being assiduously avoided throughout, in thrall to the psychic injunctions of whichever one of the Twelve was their progenitor. Continental North America is wiped out, not least because the government seeks to generate political capital from the crisis rather than defending those it was charged to protect. Notably, the President blames the so-called 'Colorado fever' on 'anti-American extremists, operating within our own borders but supported by extremists abroad' (286). And even as the war is lost and the military begin to shoot the infected and bomb cities and survivors alike before being wiped out themselves, all that is forthcoming from the presidency are pietistic platitudes. The nation returns to a state of (not so) splendid isolation as world nations place a 200-mile quarantine around the US. The work of weaponised science has been done and, by the second third of the first novel, the nation as we know it ceases to exist.

If Cronin's trilogy recounts the fall of human civilisation at the hands of vampires biologically engineered by the American military, then the FX television series *The Strain* (2012–17) focuses on humanity's near-destruction by the twin energies of ancient vampirism and Wall Street investment banking.[3] Here the vampires are mindless 'strigoi' who feed through a horrific ten-foot-long proboscis, which they unfurl at the behest of The Master, one of the seven ancient progenitors of the vampire race who, at the series' inception, travels to New York in a bid to take over the world through the machinations of capital. Shifting between ancient Rome, the concentration camps of wartime Poland and contemporary New York, both the novels and series draw clear parallels between vampirism and a transhistorical will to power and domination through the militarised destruction of competing belief systems and the appropriation of their holders' resources. Parallels to the War on Terror are apparent. Significant, in this context, are the paired characters Thomas Eichorst and Eldritch Palmer: the former a strigoi and one-time SS officer who acts as The Master's representative in public life, the latter one of the richest men in the world. Terrified of death, it is Palmer who facilitates The Master's entry to the US, suppresses news reports of a growing vampire plague and discredits the media and the CDC scientist who attempts to reveal it to the public. Ultimately, though, Palmer is no match for The Master, who does not deliver the immortality he promised, merely using Palmer's body as a vessel while eliminating his consciousness altogether. This is significant in the context of Neoliberal Gothic. As an investment banker, his role was to access capital markets to enable expansion of a third party. And this is exactly what Palmer does for The Master. Having acted as a conduit for capital in life he becomes conduit for the dark machinations of his vampiric creator. His is an apt, if disturbing, fate.

This sense of evil forces manipulating the destiny of the planet is echoed in the HBO television series *True Blood* (2008–14), adapted from Charlaine Harris's *Southern Vampire Mysteries* novels (2001–13). Set in the fictional Louisiana town of Bon Temps and its environs, the series traces the aftermath of the discovery of a synthetic blood product that enables the world's vampires to 'come out of the coffin' and enter civil and political life (Blake 2012). The series thus explores the ongoing conflict between the struggle for civil rights in the US and the knee-jerk thuggery, often inflected with alt-right Evangelical Christianity or neo-fascist political sympathies, that prospers in periods of economic depression. Peering beneath the surface of American social life, the series reveals not only some ugly home truths regarding racism, sexism and homophobia in the US but posits a secret vampiric society with a parallel history to our own. This is most fully realised in the fifth season, when we learn of The Authority, a quasi-religious organisation created to protect the blood of Lilith, the first vampire, and now a de facto global government. Thus, season five exposes the degree of covert control that lies beneath the ostensibly democratic surface of international political life – the Authority exerting absolute mastery over the vampire population in much the same way as the US exerts domination over us all (Pilger 2003). The Authority's use of a secret police force, assassins and mercenaries, as well as sophisticated surveillance technology, thus echoes the US following the passage of the PATRIOT Act.[4] Like successive presidents,

American Vampire League spokesperson Nan Flanagan (Jessica Tuck) is prone to assert a range of national characteristics such as 'equality – a concept all Americans will understand and be willing to fight for' ('Strange Love', 1.1). But The Authority is itself being challenged by a separatist organisation, The Sanguinistas, who espouse vampiric self-determination and in so doing challenge the might of the US state.[5] Notably, in much the same way as the neoliberal US threw its military and economic might against the Nicaraguan Sandinistas, so does *True Blood*'s administration stop at nothing to restore the balance of power by repressing vampire self-determination by whatever means are deemed necessary. *True Blood* comes, therefore, to echo the concerns that have been raised by Naomi Klein and others regarding wholesale human rights abuses committed by the US (and US proxies), from Chile and Argentina in the 1970s to Guantanamo of the present. Thus, suspected Sanguinistas are rendered to Camp Vamp, in which they are tortured, experimented upon and ultimately infected with the HepV virus – a blood-borne means of eradicating the vampire population engineered by governmental bioscientists. Thus, the series visually echoes Guantanamo Bay while conceptually evoking the past, specifically the Tuskegee syphilis experiments (1932–72), when 622 poor black sharecroppers infected with the disease were observed over a period of forty years by government scientists who failed to offer information or treatment even when antibiotics provided a cure. For as we have seen in *The Passage* and *The Strain* and, as we will see in the BBC television series *In the Flesh*, the neoliberal agenda consistently deploys not only military technology but biomedical science to ensure world domination. In so doing, therefore, Neoliberal Gothic explores the ways in which very few of us, on a global scale, are deemed deserving of life, our economic masters having become monstrous in their ongoing pursuit of profit.

Neoliberal Zombies

If vampires provide a ready means of exploring the monstrosity of our rulers, it is the zombie who most clearly articulates what the global population has become at the hands of the neoliberal elite. For as I have written elsewhere, it is the zombie who has become

> the monster of choice for a generation tired of a decade of governmental facilitation of the anti-democratic impulses of neoliberal corporatism allowing, as it does, an existentially urgent reconsideration of who we have all become under the auspices of a failed economic model that despite the cataclysmic crash of 2008, refuses to lie down and die. (Blake 2015a: 28)

From George A. Romero's pointed exploration of the inequalities engendered by neoliberalism in *Land of the Dead* (2005) onwards, zombie narratives have consistently addressed the failings of the contemporary world. These range from the governmental function of trans-global companies, to the anodyne consumerism of the American suburbs to the despoliation of the natural world.[6] What is more, economists and cultural theorists have themselves adopted the metaphor of the zombie as apposite encapsulation of the ways in which 'particular individuals and groups are considered simply redundant, disposable – nothing more than human waste left to stew in their own misfortune' in a world 'filled with destruction, decay, abandoned houses, burned-out cars, gutted landscapes, and trashed gas stations' (Giroux 2011: 2).

The zombie apocalypse narrative therefore allows consideration not only of the infection of the body politic by *laissez-faire* economics but the mutation of the neoliberal self into a corporatised brand identity struggling to find a vestigial humanity in the rubble of a broken world. And of these narratives, Max Brooks's 2006 novel *World War Z* is undoubtedly the most significant deployment of the trope of zombie apocalypse as interrogation of contemporary geopolitics. Adopting an internationally focused, multi-chapter witness-testimony format, the novel comprises perspectives and experiences drawn from every continent that allows for a comparison of the different ways in which world cultures tackle the zombie menace. Only in the US, we note, is the free market allowed to dominate government policy. The President personally pushes a bogus antiviral called Phalanyx through the FDA to calm public fears, and the Phalanx CEO Breckenridge 'Breck' Scott makes enough money to escape the cataclysm he has hastened to a fortress in Antarctica while proclaiming, in true neoliberal style, 'I never hurt anybody [. . .] and if anybody was too stupid to get themselves hurt, boo-fuckin-hoo' (Brooks 2007: 58). Brooks is, in fact, insistent in his focus on global biotechnologies as agent of neoliberalism – his depiction of the global organ trade illustrating the ways in which human lives are differentially valued in an increasingly unequal world. For it was not merely the movement of populations that enabled the Z virus to wipe out swathes of the world, it was the sale of human organs alongside '"donated" eggs from political prisoners, [. . .] sperm, the blood' (27). Thus, the zombie narrative explores how we are all made monstrous by neoliberalism, its 'comfortable, disposable consumer lifestyle' turning some into 'sedentary, over-educated, desk-bound, cubicle mice' (139) and others into nothing more than an aggregate of monetised organs. Needless to say, such concerns do not find their way into Michael Carnahan's 2013 film that bears the title *World War Z*. This abandons the book's international perspective and biopolitical concerns, focusing instead on American hero Gerry Lane (Brad Pitt), a UN investigator who embodies ideologies of home, family and military might so concertedly that, in saving the world single-handedly, he effectively retrenches US claims to both economic and moral leadership of the free world.

Dominic Mitchell's three-part television series *In the Flesh* (BBC, 2013–14) undertakes an extensive exploration of the penetration of the contemporary subject by the machinations of corporate biotechnologies while underscoring the anti-life politics of the neoliberal agenda. Its protagonist is one Kieren Walker (Luke Newberry) who, at the series' inception, returns to his isolated village in the North of England to be reintegrated into his community. For Kieren, like neoliberalism itself, arose from the dead in 2009 (reports of its demise with the economic crash of 2008 proving to be greatly exaggerated) to feast upon the living. And like neoliberalism, his rehabilitation owes a great deal to the biomedical sector. In the series, the drug Neurotriptyline, pioneered by the pharmacologists Victor Halperin and John Weston, has the capacity to restore the consciousness, speech and memory of the undead. Thus revived, zombies are 'rebranded' 'Partially Deceased Syndrome sufferers' entirely dependent on continuing supplies of the drug lest they return to their ravening zombie state. Their personhood, and hence their rights as human beings, are contingent on continued access to the products of the health industry. It is a situation remarkably reminiscent of the ways in which some 25 million people, being too poor to afford antiretroviral drugs, have been left to die of AIDS. For as *World War Z* so fulsomely illustrates, and as Ben Goldacre (2012) has argued, it is not public health but maximum profitability that drives the biomedical industry. And once personhood has been disavowed, tortuous experimentation becomes entirely permissible just as, as Klein (2007) has argued, torture proper has become a means of advancing the neoliberal agenda.

Given the nightmarish quality of the contemporary world, it is unsurprising that Donald Trump's promise to 'make America great again' through the revivification of US manufacturing industry at home and the abandonment of military intervention overseas resonated powerfully with those dispossessed by the neoliberal agenda of every president since Reagan. On the streets, the increasing visibility of neo-fascist organisations and the commensurate rise in civil rights activism, exemplified by the Black Lives Matter organisation, illustrates the brokenness of American social life – interest groups fighting for their very survival in the face of governmental indifference to the plight of an increasingly polarised citizenry. And over all of this, of course, looms the spectre of nuclear war, as the US and North Korea, and the US and Russia, square up against each other and threaten us all with global conflagration. The neoliberal US is a terrifying place, haunted by its own exceptionalist rhetoric. The situation is no less broken in the UK, where the ongoing austerity agenda of the right-wing Conservative government has massively widened the gap between rich and poor. Legions of the unemployed, the disabled and those forced to subsist on minimum wage and zero-hour contracts have become the new precariat. There too, welfare payments have been both slashed and withheld, and, in the case of people with disabilities, human rights have been so gravely flouted that the government has been publicly condemned by the United Nations. There, too, a climate of paranoid insularity predominates that has seen not only a popular vote for withdrawal from the European Union but a marked escalation in hate crime against refugees, immigrants and Muslims in recent years. Meantime, there has been no abatement in the number of novels, films and television series adopting the lexicon of the Gothic to expose and to challenge the horrors of the contemporary neoliberal world. This is the function of the Neoliberal Gothic: to proffer a challenge to dominant ideologies of identity and dominant modes of social and economic organisation through the purposeful adoption of the mode's extraordinary happenings, its heightened emotions, impossible creatures and overblown stylistics. For these are best suited to capture the peculiar terrors of the present and to show us how monstrous and how victimised we have become.

Notes

1. This dynamic is more fully explored in Bienstock Anolik and Howard (2004).
2. An excellent extended study of the topic is Nally (2011).
3. Adapted from the novels *The Strain* (2009), *The Fall* (2010) and *The Night Eternal* (2011) by Guillermo del Toro and Chuck Hogan.
4. The USA PATRIOT (Uniting and Strengthening America by Providing Appropriate Tools Required to Intercept and Obstruct Terrorism) Act of October 2001 removed many of the rights traditionally prized by Americans and was widely criticised and subsequently amended. Most controversial were measures to detain immigrants indefinitely, to enable searches of people and property without consent or court order and to undertake surveillance of those suspected of terrorist involvement.
5. The latter, of course, is a pun on the Sandinista National Liberation Front (named for Augusto César Sandino, who had led the Nicaraguan resistance against the US occupation of Nicaragua in the 1930s). It was the Sandinistas who overthrew the US-backed Somoza dynasty in 1978 and instituted a socialist regime that prioritised health and education. In response, President Reagan declared both a national emergency and a trade embargo against Nicaragua.

6. See, for example, the *Resident Evil* film franchise (2002–12), *The Santa Clarita Diet* (2017–) series and M. R. Carey's Edgar Award winning Ecogothic novel *The Girl with All the Gifts* (2014), adapted for cinema in 2016.

Film and Television

Hemlock Grove (Netflix, 2013–15)
In the Flesh (BBC, 2013–14)
Only Lovers Left Alive (Jim Jarmusch, UK/Germany, 2013)
The Originals (The CW, 2013–18)
The Vampire Diaries (The CW, 2009–17)
True Blood (HBO, 2008–14)
Warm Bodies (Jonathan Levine, USA, 2013)
White Zombie (Victor Halperin, USA, 1932)

References

Bienstock Anolik, Ruth, and Douglas L. Howard (2004), *The Gothic Other: Racial and Social Constructions in the Literary Imagination*, Jefferson, NC: McFarland.
Blake, Linnie (2012), 'Vampires, Mad Scientists and the Unquiet Dead: Gothic Ubiquity in Post-9/11 Television', in Justin D. Edwards and Agnieszka Soltysik Monnet (eds), *The Gothic in Contemporary Literature and Popular Culture: Pop Goth*, New York: Routledge, pp. 37–56.
— (2015a), '"Are We Worth Saving? You Tell Me": Neoliberalism, Zombies and the Failure of Free Trade', *Gothic Studies*, 17.2, 26–41.
— (2015b), 'All Hell Breaks Loose: *Supernatural*, Gothic Neoliberalism and the American Self', *Horror Studies*, 6.2, 225–38.
— (2016), 'Trapped in the Hysterical Sublime: *Twin Peaks*, Postmodernism and the Neoliberal Now', in Jeffrey Andrew Weinstock and Catherine Spooner (eds), *Return to Twin Peaks: Approaches to Materiality, Theory and Genre on Television*, Basingstoke: Palgrave, pp. 229–46.
Blake, Linnie, and Agnieszka Soltysik Monnet (2017), 'Introduction: Neoliberal Gothic', in Linnie Blake and Agnieszka Soltysik Monnet (eds), *Neoliberal Gothic: International Gothic in the Neoliberal Age*, Manchester: Manchester University Press, pp. 1–18.
Brooks, Max (2007), *World War Z: An Oral History of the Zombie War*, London: Duckworth Overlook.
Cooper, Melinda (2008), *Life as Surplus: Biotechnology and Capitalism in the Neoliberal Era*, Seattle, WA: University of Washington Press.
Cronin, Justin (2010), *The Passage*, New York: Ballantine Books.
Giroux, Henry A. (2011), *Zombie Politics and Culture in the Age of Casino Capitalism*, London: Peter Lang.
Goldacre, Ben (2012), *Bad Pharma: How Drug Companies Mislead Doctors and Harm Patients*, London: Fourth Estate.

Klein, Naomi (2007), *The Shock Doctrine*, London: Penguin.
Kneeland, Abner (1836), *A Philosophical Dictionary from the French of M. de Voltaire. With Additional Notes, both Critical and Argumentative*, Boston, MA: J. P. Mendum.
Marx, Karl (1974) [1864], 'Inaugural Address of the International Working Men's Association', in *The First International and After*, David Fernbach (ed.), Harmondsworth: Penguin, pp. 73–81.
— (1976) [1867], *Capital: A Critique of Political Economy, Volume 1*, Ben Fowkes (trans.), Harmondsworth: Penguin.
Nally, David (2011), *Monsters of the Market: Zombies, Vampires and Global Capitalism*, Chicago: Haymarket Books.
Pilger, John (2003), *The New Rulers of the World*, London: Verso.
Reed Jr., Adolph (2006), 'Undone by Neoliberalism', *The Nation*, 18 September, https://www.thenation.com/article/undone-neoliberalism/ (accessed 1 May 2018).

Chapter 5

Gothic Digital Technologies
Joseph Crawford

Creators of Gothic fiction have always been swift to take advantage of new media technologies: the rise of the novel led to the appearance of Gothic romances, the falling price of print in the nineteenth century led to the publication of mass-market 'penny dreadfuls', and the development of film, comics and television gave rise to new genres of horror films, horror comics and Gothic TV, respectively. The internet has proven to be no exception, and the twenty-first century has seen the rise of distinctive new forms of 'digital Gothic', which make use of the technological possibilities of online media to find new ways of constructing and distributing Gothic narratives.

Gothic fiction existed online before the rise of the World Wide Web, and amateur writers were posting horror stories onto usenet groups such as alt.horror and alt.horror.creative as early as 1990.[1] However, the online horror fiction of the 1990s was almost entirely text based, as plain text was the easiest form of data to transmit via usenet or bulletin board systems, and in most cases its only distinctively digital trait was its means of distribution. Most of its writers published their works via the internet because the barriers to entry were lower than in traditional publishing, rather than because they were interested in the formal possibilities of digital media. Many of these authors described themselves as aspiring horror writers who hoped to one day see their works in print. 'How can I get my stories accepted for publication?' was a frequently posed question in the early days of alt.horror.creative (Colin 1998; Marano 1998).

Digital Urban Legends

The early internet also played an important role in the distribution of urban legends, which often differed from horror fiction only insofar as they were presented as true stories rather than as overtly fictional narratives. Users of the alt.folklore.urban usenet group were already swapping such tales in 1990, often claiming that the events they described had really happened to them. The legend of Bloody Mary, which had already been circulating for decades, was brought to new audiences in 1994–5 thanks to its distribution via chain emails and usenet groups (Gauthaman 1995; Emery 2017), while the legend of the Black-Eyed Kids was created out of whole cloth by Brian Bethel in two short stories posted to the 'ghost-discuss' mailing list in 1998, which were subsequently reposted to the alt.folklore.ghost-stories usenet group (Bethel 1998).[2]

Much more than the usenet horror stories of the same era, these urban legends drew upon distinctive features of online communication: specifically, the ease with which stories and rumours could be quickly and cheaply distributed to large audiences via email, and the difficulties involved in knowing whether such online dissemination can be trusted. If Bethel had communicated his stories by more traditional word-of-mouth means it might have taken decades for the urban legend of the Black-Eyed Kids to become widely known. But by posting his narratives online, he was able to create a new piece of modern folklore virtually overnight. Similarly, the makers of the 'found footage' horror film *The Blair Witch Project* (Eduardo Sánchez and Daniel Myrick, 1999) pioneered the use of online misinformation as a form of viral marketing by deliberately circulating online rumours that their film was composed of genuine found footage and that all the people involved in creating it were dead or missing, thus effectively inventing new urban legends in order to raise anticipation for the film's release (Davidson 2013). The fact that they chose to circulate these rumours on the internet, rather than through traditional print media, attests to their recognition of how much harder it could be to disentangle fact and fiction online.

The flatness and anonymity of digital text-based communications played an important role in the success of these urban legends. When someone you have only interacted with online claims to have had a seemingly supernatural experience, it can be very difficult to know how seriously their claims should be taken – usually much more difficult than it would be if they told you the same story in person, with all the contextual, nonverbal clues provided by face-to-face communication as to whether they might be lying, joking, delusional or completely serious. When more stories appear in response, with dozens of other people claiming to have had similar experiences, it becomes even more difficult to sort fact from fiction. Rumours and conspiracy theories have always flourished online for precisely these reasons, and it was the acute awareness of this that led Barbara and David Mikkelson to create the snopes.com website in 1994 as a space in which such stories could be collected, compared and analysed for accuracy. David Mikkelson was himself an enthusiastic collector of urban legends – 'Snopes' was his username on the alt.folklore.urban usenet group – and since 1994 his site has moved from simply gathering such stories to systematically fact-checking them (Snopes.com n.d.; Tepper 1997: 39–51). The fact that the main business of snopes.com today is fact-checking political stories circulated via news websites and social media demonstrates the cultural continuity between the online urban legends of the 1990s and the 'fake news' and conspiracy theories of the Trump era: both thrive on the speed with which narratives can be propagated through online environments and the difficulties involved in verifying whether or not they might actually be true.

While the urban legends of the 1990s exploited the nature of online communications more creatively than most early online horror fiction, their basic format was still that of the story written in plain text. The development of distinctive forms of digital horror media began in earnest in the later 1990s, after the rise of free website building services made it easier and cheaper for individual internet users to build their own websites. Once anyone could have their own horror fiction webpage, rather than simply submitting a text file to someone else's BBS, online archive or usenet group, it became much easier for authors to incorporate elements such as animations, images or hyperlinks into their fictions, permitting the use of formal features which could not be faithfully reproduced in traditional text-based media.

One influential webpage of this kind was *Ted the Caver* (2001), a website purporting to be the online journal of a caving enthusiast, describing his experiences exploring a nearby cavern (Anonymous 2001). Created as a free website on Angelfire, its early entries were mostly indistinguishable from those on any number of other websites devoted to the hobbies of their creators, but as the entries progressed, the events described became increasingly unsettling. The final entry, posted on 19 May 2001, described the author's resolution to return to the cave one last time to find out exactly what is inside it, ending with the words '[s]ee all of you soon, with a lot of answers! Love, Ted.' This is followed by a hyperlink, marked 'Next' – but the hyperlink, if clicked, simply leads back to the same entry. It is thus implied that Ted was never able to write another entry on his website, presumably because he was killed by whatever it was that lived within the cave.

The basic narrative structure of *Ted the Caver* is familiar from any number of 'found document' or 'found footage' horror narratives, in which the unfinished nature of the text or film bears mute witness to the (presumably unrepresentably horrible) fate which has befallen its creator. The webpage itself playfully alludes to its own kinship with 'found footage' horror films: upon discovering a mysterious symbol, Ted remarks that 'The first thing I thought when I saw it was "Blair Witch Project".' But *Ted the Caver* also helped to pioneer two techniques which would become foundational to online horror fiction, the use of real-time updates and the use of hyperlinks.

In traditional 'found document' or 'found footage' horror fiction, the action is over by the time the audience arrives, the author or filmmaker is dead (or worse), and all that remains is to go through the films or papers they have left behind in order to discover what happened to them. However, over its two months of active existence *Ted the Caver* delivered its story to its readers in irregular instalments, supposedly corresponding to Ted's repeated visits to 'Mystery Cave'. Each time an update appeared, there was no way of knowing when (or if) the next instalment would be uploaded. While the site was being updated, its audience was thus involved in a story which seemed to be unfolding in real time, rather than something which had already concluded, and the final entry only became 'final' retroactively after its readers had given up hope of a new entry ever appearing. The website thus exploited the awareness of its audience that a free website, once created, can linger indefinitely in cyberspace, even if its creator has long since died, leaving the online record of their life 'frozen' at the moment of their disappearance or death, forever awaiting the next update.

Since 2001, many other creators of online horror fiction have also used this 'live update' format to build tension and anticipation among their audiences, sometimes using long periods of silence to hint that something awful may have happened to their creators. The *Marble Hornets* YouTube channel, for example, used a technique very similar to that of *Ted the Caver* in 'Entry #26' (2010), which ended with the protagonist's resolution to find his missing friend. This video was followed by a seven-month period in which no new videos were posted on the channel, implying that he, like Ted before him, had met some horrible fate (DeLage and Wagner 2009–14). Unlike Ted, he did eventually return to post 'Entry #27', but the audience had no way of knowing this during the seven months of silence which followed 'Entry #26' and could only find out by continuing to check whether any further news had been posted.

The second distinctive technique which *Ted the Caver* employed was the use of hyperlinks. When reading a book, it is obvious from the diminishing number of pages when the end is approaching, films have set run times which are advertised in advance, and even stories uploaded onto a single webpage can have their remaining length gauged using the scroll bar on the side of the screen. But the crude website form of *Ted the Caver*, in which each page ended with a link to the next, made it impossible to know in advance how many pages there were going to be. It is only when the final link turns out to go nowhere that it becomes apparent that the story had reached its end. The website's use of hyperlink structures was basic compared to some of the works which followed it, but it nonetheless gave the text a distinctive digital quality that could not have been reproduced on paper. Even more significant was its choice to illustrate its narrative with hyperlinks that led to pictures, rather than to simply embed pictures in the text. This was common practice on early websites – slow connection speeds meant that webpages would load much faster if pictures were not included – but it gained a new significance in the context of a horror narrative, as readers had to ask themselves each time whether they really wanted to see the picture that would appear on their screen when the link was clicked. None of the images in *Ted the Caver* are scary or disturbing, but the same principle of the 'horrible hyperlink', which effectively dares the reader to click on it despite their knowledge that it might lead to something awful, would go on to be used in much more aggressive ways in subsequent works of online horror fiction such as *The Grifter* (2009).

Another important early work of online horror fiction, *The Dionaea House* by Eric Heisserer, began in 2004 (Heisserer 2004–6). Much more formally ambitious than *Ted the Caver*, its narrative was spread across one LiveJournal, three blogs and a website, each of which was updated in real time as its story unfolded, leading up to a major climax on Halloween 2004. Whereas the narrative of *Ted the Caver* was confined to the personal webpage of its creator, *The Dionaea House* used fake social media accounts to create the illusion of different people independently interacting with the mysterious house at the heart of its story, each of them separately recording their experiences on the internet. At one point, even the comments section of a blog is used as a space for storytelling, with the fictional authors of different blogs communicating with one another via comments on a blog post. The fact that these were real blogs, whose time-stamped posts and comments proved that they were being updated in real time, in line with the fictional events that they described, lent *The Dionaea House* a much greater sense of authenticity and immediacy than *Ted the Caver*, and indeed the one blog on which comments were not disabled is full of reader comments anxiously enquiring whether or not the events it described had really happened (Heisserer 2004).

Similar usages of fake social media profiles to create the illusion that the fictional characters within a narrative are real people and that its events are befalling them in real time have been a feature of many subsequent works of online horror fiction. The Slenderman vlog *TribeTwelve* (2010–), for example, makes use of two YouTube accounts, livestreams, two Twitter accounts, a Vine account and an ask.fm account, requiring its audience to repeatedly shift between different websites in order to follow its narrative, as though trying to reconstruct the lives (and deaths) of real people from the multitude of digital traces they have left behind.[3] Indeed, *TribeTwelve* goes further than *The Dionaea House* by having its creators respond 'in-character' to comments posted by its audience, thus further enhancing the impression that the events of the story, far from being over and done with, are actually happening right now.

The Dionaea House is also an important example of what would become one of the trademarks of online horror fiction, the story of serial infection. The predatory house at the centre of its narrative uses each victim to lure in others. It does so primarily by physical means, such as having its minions mail tokens of previous victims to their loved ones in the hope that they will come looking for them, but by the end of the story one of its servitors also started posting taunts on the blog of its latest target, implying that the house was now also using digital means to seek out its prey (Heisserer 2004). This motif of viral infection or corruption spreading via technology was popularised by the Japanese horror films *Ringu* (*Ring*, Hideo Nakata, 1998) and *Kairo* (*Pulse*, Kiyoshi Kurosawa, 2001). The plot of *Ringu* centres on a videotape which kills anyone who watches it unless they make more copies of it, while *Kairo* depicts an epidemic of hauntings which spreads via the internet. *Kairo*, in particular, seems almost prescient in its depiction of predatory ghosts and internet addicts as virtually interchangeable parts of the same spiritual ecosystem, locked into near-identical loops of compulsive behaviour. Its scenes of alienated young people using online technology to communicate, not with each other, but with dangerous supernatural forces which use them as vectors for their own viral proliferation, prefigure the very similar set-ups used in many subsequent works of online horror fiction, including *Smile Dog* (2008), *Ben Drowned* (2010) and the extended Slenderman mythos.

The haunted internet depicted in *Kairo* infects its victims, watches them, isolates them, and drives them to madness and self-destruction. In doing so, it acts as a literalised metaphor for the anxieties which have beset the users of online communication since its popularisation in the late 1990s. As the internet has become more pervasive, worries about the ease with which it might be exploited by criminals, terrorists, ideological extremists and sexual predators have become increasingly widespread. When the protagonists of *Kairo* stumble across malevolent supernatural beings online, they are thus only experiencing a hyperbolic version of these real concerns about the extremely dark places to which our use of the internet may take us.

Internet Horror Fiction

Internet horror fiction came of age between 2007 and 2010. By this point stories of horror and the paranormal were regularly posted to internet forums such as Something Awful (founded 1999) and the /x/ board of 4chan (founded 2003). It was from these groups that specialised horror fiction websites such as 'The Holders' (founded 2007), 'The SCP Foundation' (founded 2008) and 'Creepypasta' (founded 2008) branched off, providing more permanent repositories for stories that had originated as ephemeral forum posts. Horror-themed vlogs proliferated on YouTube after the success of *Marble Hornets* and its imitators in 2009–10, while Reddit acquired a dedicated horror fiction subreddit, 'NoSleep' in 2010. Collectively, these websites now host thousands of works of user-submitted horror fiction, ranging from paragraph-length microfictions like 'The Bad Dream' (Anonymous 2008) to extended works of cross-platform multimedia fiction such as the already-mentioned *TribeTwelve* and *Marble Hornets*. Today, there is almost certainly more horror fiction being published online than via all forms of traditional media put together.

One distinctive quality of these websites is their collaborative nature. 'Creepypasta' has a team of administrators who decide which user-submitted stories merit inclusion on the site; but 'The Holders', 'The SCP Foundation' and 'NoSleep' were all groups to which anyone could contribute. This means that their fiction is of extremely variable quality, but it also means that when ideas catch on, they can be rapidly reiterated by the community. Spin-off concepts such as 'The Rake', a monster which speaks to people in their sleep; 'Candle Cove', a nightmarish children's TV show; and 'The SCP Foundation', a secret conspiracy devoted to the containment of paranormal phenomena were swiftly taken up and developed by other writers in a process which Chess has likened to a form of open-source debugging applied to fiction rather than code (Chess 2012: 375).[4] As a result, even though the original stories can be identified in each case, the narratives which have grown out of them are perhaps best understood as forms of crowdsourced modern mythology. Each story has been retold in many different ways, with those elements which are felt to be most effective retained in subsequent retellings, while less successful additions are allowed to sink into obscurity in a kind of accelerated process of Darwinian evolution.

Many of the best-known horror stories which emerged from these online communities dealt, like *Kairo* and *The Dionaea House*, with themes of viral infection via digital media. One now-classic example is *Smile Dog*, a story posted to 4chan in 2008, describing an apparently haunted image of a demonic dog. Those who see the image are supposedly afflicted with nightmares until they agree to 'spread the word' by forwarding it to others, infecting them in turn (Anonymous 2010). The narrative is thus very similar to that of *Ringu*, with one distinctive online twist. After describing how, if he was cursed by Smile Dog, he would choose to 'spread the word' rather than suffering continued nightmares, the narrator then posts the image itself, thus implying that he has already been infected – and now the reader is, too.

Like *Ted the Caver*, *Smile Dog* takes a classic horror trope – in this case, the haunted picture – and modifies it to fit a digital context. The story exploits the fact that, online, images and videos can be reproduced and shared endlessly, with a speed and efficiency that makes the copying and recopying of the cursed videotape in *Ringu* seem positively primitive. If the Smile Dog image really was haunted, the internet would allow its curse to be distributed very quickly indeed. The story thus plays upon real fears about how quickly images and videos – of child abuse or terrorist atrocities, for example – can spread across the internet, and how difficult it is to completely suppress them when they do. Many similar stories of cursed images and videos have proliferated online, giving rise to internet legends such as *The Grifter*, a video supposedly so horrific that watching it leads to insanity or death, and *Mereana Mordegard Glesgorv*, a video which supposedly drives its viewers to blind themselves. However, the layout of *Smile Dog* also takes advantage of the way in which webpages tend to be read; most internet users scroll down reflexively as they read, so that by the time they reach the text hinting at what may be coming, there is a good chance that the Smile Dog image will already be on their screens. This effect would be very different in a book, where the reader would have to deliberately turn the page to see the image. Online, such material can 'creep up on' the reader, appearing onscreen almost before they realise it is there. A more ambitious use of scrolling can be seen in the Korean webcomic *The Bongcheon-Dong Ghost* (2011), in which a comic strip that appears to be composed of still images suddenly animates, complete with sound effects, when the reader scrolls down to certain points, creating a series of images that visually and aurally assault the viewer at unpredictable intervals (HORANG 2011).

The capacity of online media to shift unexpectedly is a source of rich possibilities for creators of horror fiction. A seemingly still image can be programmed to animate unexpectedly, subliminal images can be inserted into webpages, and text can be programmed to warp and shift. Sometimes these tactics are used very aggressively, as in internet 'screamers', when a seemingly benign image or video is suddenly replaced with a loud scream and a horrific image in order to trigger instinctive fright reactions in viewers. Other works use them more subtly: the Gothic webcomics of Emily Carroll, for example, use images that flicker almost subliminally between the mundane and the horrific in order to communicate the decaying mental states of their protagonists (Carroll 2013, 2014). A similar fascination with the corruption and decay of information can be seen in many other examples of online horror fiction, which often begin with phenomena that look like ordinary computer glitches. These effects are especially associated with the internet horror meme 'Zalgo', which has been in circulation since 2004. Supposedly, Zalgo is a supernatural being whose presence is marked by the corruption of words and images, so that 'Zalgo' texts progressively disintegrate into illegible chaos. Again, the digital nature of such media is crucial here: online text, videos, images and sound files can all be programmed to glitch or corrupt in ways that often leave their audiences initially uncertain whether they are experiencing a genuine computer problem or whether this is an intended part of the fictional experience. Several internet horror stories of the 'haunted video game' subgenre, such as *Ben Drowned* (2010) and *NES Godzilla* (2011), also make use of these techniques, presenting their readers with screenshots and gameplay videos which initially seem just slightly glitched, but then escalate into increasingly bizarre and threatening forms until it becomes clear that some kind of malevolent force is at work (Cosbydaf n.d.; Hall 2017).

The Slenderman Mythos

All of these traits – the use of internet communities to collaboratively develop new urban legends, the preoccupation with themes of infection and corruption, the use of fake social media updates to create the illusion that horror narratives are unfolding in real time, the use of subliminal imagery, and the manipulation of the formal possibilities of online media to develop new ways of scaring and disturbing one's audience – can be seen in the single most iconic figure to emerge from the online horror fiction boom of 2007–10, Slenderman. Like several earlier online horror memes, Slenderman began as a throwaway forum post; Eric Knudsen simply edited a tall, faceless figure into the background of two old photographs, added an evocative snippet of text, and posted the resulting images onto the Something Awful forums in 2009. Other writers, artists and filmmakers rapidly began developing a body of legends around this enigmatic figure, leading to the development of a swiftly growing 'Slenderman Mythos' (Chess 2012: 378–81; Boyer 2013: 243).

Slenderman thrived on YouTube. The *Marble Hornets* YouTube vlog, which began in 2009, used Slenderman as the basis for a zero-budget found footage horror series in which a film student searches for clues about what has happened to his missing friend by watching the videos he has left behind. In these, Slenderman makes various, often subliminal, appearances. By watching video footage of Slenderman, the student apparently attracts the attention of the creature himself, the proximity of which causes amnesia and glitches in the video. Once he realises that he is being followed by Slenderman, he begins filming everything that happens to him so that he can check for lost time and tell-tale glitches, thus creating even more cursed Slenderman footage, which will presumably be capable of infecting others in turn (Chess and Newsom 2015: 31–3). The *Marble Hornets* series ultimately ran for five years, attracting a large audience – its YouTube channel has almost half a million subscribers – and inspiring huge numbers of imitators in the process (DeLage and Wagner 2009–14).

Why did Slenderman – or at least the *Marble Hornets* version of Slenderman – possess such appeal for creators of online horror fiction? Part of its popularity was no doubt due to how cheap and easy Slenderman was to depict on film, especially in comparison to earlier online horror monsters such as Bloody Mary or The Rake. Poor-quality hand-held camera footage was very much part of the 'slendervlog' aesthetic, so all that was needed to stand in for Slenderman itself was a faceless mannequin in a suit, or an actor with a stocking over his face; further, as the extreme proximity of Slenderman caused the film to glitch, there was a built-in excuse for never showing it in close-up. But Slenderman also neatly embodies the anxieties over online communications which I have discussed over the course of this chapter. Like so much online content, Slenderman is anonymous and faceless: 4chan's users even call themselves 'Anonymous', and wear masks when assembling in public (Chess and Newman 2015: 56). The way that Slenderman follows its victims evokes fears of cyberstalking, online harassment and internet surveillance, all of which can feel like being stalked by some faceless, omnipresent monster.[5] Like computer viruses, or online pornography and propaganda, Slenderman proliferates virally. Within the Slenderman mythology, anyone who has ever opened a Slenderman video file is a potential target. Slenderman's victims, like the figure of the internet addict in the popular imagination, tend to become unhealthy, anxious, obsessive and socially isolated, and the fact that the monster is often depicted as preying upon children reflects the anxiety that young people might be particularly vulnerable to being misled, traumatised or exploited by the individuals and content they interact with online. Like the ghosts in *Kairo*, Slenderman can thus easily be read as a representation of the fear that new communications technology, rather than bringing us together, may in fact drive us apart, infect us, corrupt us and ultimately destroy us.

Slenderman shot to international notoriety in 2014, after two twelve-year-old schoolgirls in Wisconsin stabbed one of their classmates in an attempt to impress and/or placate the fictional monster. Following this incident, something of a moral panic erupted over the supposedly malign influence of online media in general and online horror fiction such as Slenderman in particular (Chess and Newsom 2015: 2–9; Maddox 2017: 1–14). As is so often the case with such panics, the media frenzy triggered by the Wisconsin stabbing effectively mirrored the features of the very fiction it warned against, describing Slenderman as a monster dwelling in the darkest parts of the internet, waiting to corrupt any vulnerable young person who happened to chance across it, which is virtually identical to the way in which it is depicted in most actual Slenderman media (Crawford 2015: 35–47). Indeed, the ease with which Slenderman was adapted to such technophobic narratives is another strong reason for suggesting that it has effectively functioned as a metaphorical embodiment of such anxieties all along.

As figures such as Slenderman have become more widely known, the old barriers between traditional horror media (copyrighted, single-author, for-profit, overtly fictional) and online horror media (viral, anonymous, crowdsourced, non-commercial, often blurring the lines between fact and fiction) have increasingly broken down. Eric Heisserer, the creator of *The Dionaea House*, went on to become a professional screenwriter after selling an adaptation of the story to Warner Bros. *Always Watching*, a feature film adaptation of *Marble Hornets*, appeared in 2015. The online legend 'Candle Cove' was adapted for television as the first season of *Channel Zero* (2016), a television show based on internet horror fiction. Eric Knudsen, the creator of Slenderman, first asserted his copyright over the creature and then subsequently sold it to the production company Mythology Entertainment (Rogers 2016): *Slender Man*

(Sylvain White) was released in 2018. In the early 1990s, the dreams of alt.horror.creative users that they might become professional horror authors based on the stories they posted online were little more than fantasies; but, twenty-five years on, such dreams are being realised with increasing frequency.

In response to these developments, some creators of online horror fiction have become more professional, while others have retreated deeper into anonymity. An example of the former would be the paranormal-themed podcast *Welcome to Night Vale*, which since its launch in 2012 has transitioned from being a free project produced for fun into a formal production company which raises income via live shows, paid membership options and the sale of merchandise, leveraging the enormous popularity that it has acquired on the social networking site Tumblr (Weinstock 2018: 3). An example of the latter would be the 'interface series' which appeared on Reddit in 2016 in the form of snippets of interconnected horror fiction posted apparently randomly into discussion threads on unrelated topics. These snippets collectively constituted a form of anonymous guerrilla fiction, placed into deliberately incongruous contexts and posted without explanation or attribution in order to disturb and intrigue those readers who chance across it (_9MOTHER9HORSE9EYES9 2016).

This bifurcation is representative of the way in which the internet has developed in recent years. The anarchic digital landscape of the 1990s has, to a great extent, now been tamed, mapped, indexed and integrated with the global capitalist economy. Indeed, websites such as Google, Facebook and Amazon are now just as central to that economy as any old-style industry or media corporation. At the same time, however, the modern internet is difficult to police effectively because of its scale, and widespread anxieties remain about the awful things which may lurk in its hidden corners or on the 'deep web' beyond the reach of traditional search engines. Thus, while some forms of online horror fiction are being integrated into the mainstream media ecosystem, others continue to resist adaptation into traditional forms such as single-author novels or single-director feature films, clinging instead to distinctive viral and anonymous digital formats which allow them to express and exploit what is most unique, and thus potentially most terrifying, about online media. As I have discussed, Gothic is always one of the first genres to make use of new and emerging media forms because its traditional concerns with disruption and monstrosity match up so well with the anxieties that new forms of media inevitably provoke in the societies within which they appear. The time may come when the internet seems no more inherently threatening or destabilising than the novel or the newspaper; but until that day arrives, digital media is likely to continue to provide rich new materials and formal innovations for creators of Gothic fictions.

Notes

1. Usenet groups were online discussion groups, popular during the 1980s and early 1990s. Though still extant today, they are now little used, having been largely superseded by internet fora after the rise of the World Wide Web in the mid-1990s.
2. According to American urban legend, Bloody Mary is a ghost who appears to attack or terrify anyone who repeats her name in front of a darkened mirror. The Black-Eyed Kids are supposedly malevolent supernatural beings who manifest as dark-eyed children.
3. Ask.fm is a social networking site where users can send one another questions to be answered.
4. All of these originated in throwaway works of horror-themed microfiction posted to the 4chan and Something Awful message boards.
5. As Chess and Newsom note, 'The Slender Man's lurking presence has a chilling effect, just as a web-based lurker does' (Chess and Newsom 2015: 55).

Film and Television

Always Watching (James Moran, USA, 2015)
Channel Zero (Syfy, 2016)
Kairo (*Pulse*, Kiyoshi Kurosawa, Japan, 2001)
Ringu (*Ring*, Hideo Nakata, Japan, 1998)
Slender Man (Sylvain White, USA, 2018)
The Blair Witch Project (Daniel Myrick and Eduardo Sánchez, USA, 1999)

Webpages

Note: all webpages accessed 12 January 2018.
_9MOTHER9HORSE9EYES9 archive (2016), Reddit, https://www.reddit.com/user/_9MOTHER9HORSE9EYES9/comments/.
Alt.folklore.urban archive (n.d.), https://groups.google.com/forum/#!forum/alt.folklore.urban.
Alt.horror archive (n.d.), https://groups.google.com/forum/#!forum/alt.horror.
Alt.horror.creative archive (n.d.), https://groups.google.com/forum/#!forum/alt.horror.creative.
Anonymous (2001), *Ted the Caver*, http://www.angelfire.com/trek/caver/page1.html.
— (2008), 'The Bad Dream', Creepypasta, 5 April, https://www.creepypasta.com/the-bad-dream/.

— (2010), *Smile Dog*, Creepypasta, 28 April, https://www.creepypasta.com/smile-dog/.
Bethel, Brian (1998), 'They're Back', post to ghost-discuss, 14 November, http://web.archive.org/web/20050213181819/http://www.pinn.net/~royaloak/Stories/black_eyed.htm.
Carroll, Emily (2013), 'Out of Skin', http://www.emcarroll.com/comics/skin/.
— (2014), 'When the Darkness Presses', http://emcarroll.com/comics/darkness/.
Colin (1998), 'New Novel in Search of Publisher/Agent', post to alt.horror.creative, 7 September, https://groups.google.com/forum/#!topic/alt.horror.creative/cTAFKB6Y3g0.
Cosbydaf (n.d.), *NES Godzilla*, Creepypasta wiki, http://creepypasta.wikia.com/wiki/NES_Godzilla_Creepypasta.
Creepypasta (n.d.), 'Creepypasta', https://www.creepypasta.com/.
Davidson, Neil (2013), 'The Blair Witch Project: The Best Viral Marketing Campaign of All Time', 5 August, http://mwpdigitalmedia.com/blog/the-blair-witch-project-the-best-viral-marketing-campaign-of-all-time/.
DeLage, Joseph, and Troy Wagner (2009–14), *Marble Hornets*, YouTube, https://www.youtube.com/user/MarbleHornets.
Emery, David (2017), 'Explaining the Legend of Bloody Mary in the Mirror', *Thoughtco.*, 25 September, https://www.thoughtco.com/bloody-mary-in-the-mirror-3299478.
Gauthaman, Ravindran (1995), 'Bloody Mary', post to alt.folklore.urban, 17 January, https://groups.google.com/forum/#!msg/alt.folklore.urban/8VrodwBfcJQ/FSVMywo764MJ;context-place=forum/alt.folklore.urban.
Hall, Alex (2017), *Ben Drowned*, Creepypasta, 19 December, https://www.creepypasta.com/ben-drowned/.
Heisserer, Eric (2004), 'A Quiet Space', http://dionaeahouse.blogspot.co.uk/.
— (2004–6), *The Dionaea House*, http://dionaea-house.com/.
Holders (n.d.), 'The Holders', https://web.archive.org/web/20170628143253/http://theholders.org:80/.
HORANG (2011), *The Bongcheon-Dong Ghost*, 17 September, http://comic.naver.com/webtoon/detail.nhn?titleId=350217&no=31.
Marano, Michael (1998), 'How to Publish Long and Short Horror Fiction', post to alt.horror.creative, 17 November, https://groups.google.com/forum/#!topic/alt.horror.creative/K6FVHLOst1k.
Night Vale Presents (n.d.), 'Night Vale Presents', http://www.nightvalepresents.com/about.
NoSleep (n.d.), 'Reddit NoSleep', https://www.reddit.com/r/nosleep/.
Rogers, Katie (2016), '"Slender Man", a Horror Meme, Gets Ready to Step Out of the Shadows', *New York Times*, 6 May, https://www.nytimes.com/2016/05/07/movies/slender-man-a-horror-meme-gets-ready-to-step-out-of-the-shadows.html?
SCP (n.d.), 'The SCP Foundation', http://www.scp-wiki.net.
Snopes.com (n.d.), 'About Snopes.com', https://www.snopes.com/about-snopes/.
TribeTwelve wiki (n.d.), 'Home', http://tribetwelve.wikia.com/wiki/TribeTwelve_Wiki.

References

Boyer, Tina (2013), 'The Anatomy of a Monster: The Case of Slender Man', *Preternature*, 2.2, 240–61.

Chess, Shira (2012), 'Open Sourcing Horror: The Slender Man, *Marble Hornets*, and Genre Negotiations', *Information, Communication, and Society*, 15.3, 374–93.

Chess, Shira, and Eric Newsom (2015), *Folklore, Horror Stories, and the Slender Man*, New York: Palgrave.

Crawford, Joseph (2015), 'Gothic Fiction and the Evolution of Media Technology', in Justin D. Edwards (ed.), *Technologies of the Gothic in Literature and Culture*, London: Routledge, pp. 35–47, https://ore.exeter.ac.uk/repository/handle/10871/18154.

Maddox, Jessica (2017), 'Of Internet Born: Idolatry, the Slender Man Meme, and the Feminisation of Digital Spaces', *Feminist Media Studies*, 15 March, http://www.tandfonline.com/doi/abs/10.1080/14680777.2017.1300179?journalCode=rfms20 (accessed 12 January 2018).

Tepper, Michele (1997), 'Usenet Communities and the Cultural Politics of Information', in David Porter (ed.), *Internet Culture*, New York: Routledge, pp. 40–54.

Weinstock, Jeffrey Andrew (2018), 'Introduction: Between the Weather and the Void – *Welcome to Night Vale*', in Jeffrey Andrew Weinstock (ed.), *Critical Approaches to* Welcome to Night Vale: *Podcasting between the Weather and the Void*, Cham: Palgrave, pp. 1–22.

Part II

Contemporary Monsters

Chapter 6

Contemporary Zombies
Xavier Aldana Reyes

Unlike the vampire and the ghost, the zombie does not feature in any of the foundational Gothic texts of the late eighteenth and early nineteenth centuries. The lack of a 'primal narrative that established and codified its qualities and behaviors' (Bishop 2010: 13) means that the zombie as it is currently understood in popular culture is a palimpsest: it is comprised of elements taken from a huge number of texts from a similarly vast array of media spanning well over 100 years. Oral traditions from Saint-Domingue, later Haiti; Lafcadio Hearn and William Seabrook's sensational travel writing; horror films such as *Zombie Flesh Eaters* (Lucio Fulci, 1979) or *Shaun of the Dead* (Edgar Wright, 2004); video games such as *Alone in the Dark* (1992) and *The Last of Us* (2013); comics such as *The Walking Dead* (2003–); and television series such as *Z Nation* (2014–18) have all contributed to the development of the contemporary brain-eating, reanimated corpse. The varied metaphoric and ludic possibilities zombies afford have also undoubtedly aided their global expansion in the twenty-first century.[1] Although zombies, like other supernatural monsters, have been co-opted for their romantic potential, their rotting bodies, contagious nature and ontological status (neither fully living nor fully dead) have ensured they remain subjects of horror and abjection. Originally the possessed or reanimated victims of voodoo, George A. Romero's paradigm-shifting treatment in *Night of the Living Dead* (1968) crystallised the image of modern zombies as stumbling cannibals in decay.[2]

As Markman Ellis (2000: 218) suggests, the shedding of the zombie's associations with imperial resistance and colonial desire in local Haitian folklore is regrettable but was perhaps inevitable in the process of its repackaging as new creature ready for mass consumption. In fact, it is the very evolution of the zombie from an image reminiscent of American slavery into a fully-fledged 'critique of modernity itself' (218) that allowed for its success and allegorical malleability. While the sugar-mill workers exploited by 'Murder' Legendre (Bela Lugosi) in Victor Halperin's *White Zombie* (1932) read as colonial echoes of the 'dead labour' of eighteenth- and nineteenth-century sugar plantations, by the 1970s the zombies in *Dawn of the Dead* (George A. Romero, 1978) had seemingly lost all trace of their Indigenous origins. In this film in particular, the zombie stands in for the modern urban subject operating under, and subsumed by, capitalist principles. Since the zombie tends to operate on instinct and to manifest in hordes, trapped within the shiny walls of a suburban shopping mall it becomes instead a comment on the excesses of consumer culture and neoliberalism. This metaphorical layer has been further explored in a number of critical studies that have employed the zombie, especially its capacity to reanimate and function on primal drives, to denounce the ills of market liberalism (Harman 2009; Quiggin 2010) and political authoritarianism (Giroux 2010) as they have manifested in the late twentieth and early twenty-first centuries and in the legacies of Ronald Reagan's and Margaret Thatcher's economic policies. The zombie has thus become an avatar and reminder of how we have changed under free market policies, the real effects of which have been accentuated by the financial crisis of 2008. This means that zombie narratives may be simultaneously recuperated as more than gloom and doom scenarios. As Linnie Blake has suggested, they can be reinterpreted as fictional negotiations that 'enabl[e] us to attain knowledge of our condition whilst working through the existential dislocations it has engendered' (2015: 38). The championing of the zombie as metaphoric figure, portrayed as outcast and increasingly cognisant, may not be a post-millennial innovation, but it certainly gains significance when studied as part of a zeitgeist marked by a return to conservative politics in the US and Europe. It also resonates with the critical approaches that have seen a usefulness in the monster's utter alienation and uncontainable growth. The zombie is both a mirror of the present and a warning of the dangers of an uncheckered near future.

The sprawling zombie narrative is the most visible and obvious of a broader millennial obsession with the active fantasising of the imminent apocalypse (Tate 2017), the cause of which may be, as Mark Fisher proposed, that 'it is easier to imagine the end of the world than the end of capitalism' (2009: 1). Zombies do not merely continue to signify the inexorable nature of death but, increasingly, warn of the end of civilisation that may be precipitated by global crises exacerbated by national economic pressures, such as climate change, or by biological warfare. Contemporary zombie texts mark a significant move away from the moment of outbreak as the focal plot point and toward the long-lasting effects of catastrophes for which humans are directly responsible. They centre not just on moral notions of responsibility and power, but also on the specific types of social models and community structures that might prevail after a return to basic codes of survival. In contemporary texts, zombies therefore also negotiate concerns around overpopulation and the survival of the human race in a world stripped of technology and devoid of the safeguards of legal systems.

It is important to note that the zombies of the twenty-first century, in their viral and sympathetic guises, do not constitute breaks with their representational traditions, but rather continuations. Contemporary zombies have been eminently influenced and shaped by their most successful prior iterations. It is not a coincidence that Romero, and his flesh-eating slow zombies in particular, are referenced in a number of post-millennial Gothic texts. There are antecedents for the viral zombie in the twentieth-century: Richard Matheson's *I Am Legend* (1954) and its first film adaptation, *The Last Man on Earth* (Ubaldo Ragona and Sidney Salkow, 1964), are foundational in their medicalisation of the undead. Films such as the horror comedies *Day of the Dead* (George A. Romero, 1985) and *Return of the Living Dead* (Dan O'Bannon, 1985) and the melodrama *I, Zombie: The Chronicles of Pain* (Andrew Parkinson, 1998) had also already envisioned the possibility of a conscious, likable zombie in the twentieth century. However, these texts were exceptional and not symptomatic of wider shifts in zombie popular culture. The amplification and establishment of both the viral and sympathetic zombie models in the twenty-first century do not simply speak to the widespread increase and diversification of the zombie as the Gothic figure *du jour*; they also reveal concerns rooted in our scientific, pandemic-obsessed present and in the politics of exclusion that has seen a rise in jingoistic, immigration-weary governments in Britain and the US in the 2010s. The rest of this chapter charts the history and cultural implications of these two key types of contemporary zombies. It begins by considering the return of the zombie as viral monster, especially its channelling of suspicions around the capability of modern social and political forces to successfully manage imminent ecological cataclysms, and ends by suggesting that the zombie's empathetic abjection makes it particularly attractive as a monster through which to explore alterity and resistance to the status quo.

Gone Viral

The viral zombie naturally externalises social concerns about pandemics, namely their ubiquity, but also the difficulty of effective containment in a century marked by easy, cheap and fast transcontinental travel and near-immediate informational flows. *28 Days Later* and *Resident Evil* were largely responsible for reintroducing the viral zombie and established certain patterns – the virtual indistinguishability between rabid humans and zombies (zombies as infected humans or vectors of disease), and the popularisation of the zombie-human hybrid. In the sprawling viral zombie fictions that followed, especially Max Brooks's *World War Z: An Oral History of the Zombie War* (2006) and Robert Kirkman's comic series *The Walking Dead*, the complex reaction and evolution of individuals and entire nations could be explored in detail over a number of months and even years, thus privileging crisis management over zombie gore. Extending the amplified fears of global pandemics into other fictions about contagion, or what Priscilla Wald has termed the 'outbreak narrative' (2008: 2), *World War Z* portrayed the zombie apocalypse as an event with worldwide geopolitical implications. The zombie thus became less supernatural and much more microbiological. This development eventually led to the invention of new breeds of viral zombies to accompany contemporaneous medical concerns such as prion disease, in the case of Steven C. Schlozman's *The Zombie Autopsies: Secret Notes from the Apocalypse* (2011), or fungal parasites, in that of Charlie Higson's *The Enemy* book series (2009–15). If the 1990s saw the rise of emerging infectious diseases, or at least of a journalistic fascination with them, the early twenty-first century saw zombies race ahead as the favourite figures of pandemic panic: as viral metonyms they embody instant transmission and exponential growth (see Verran and Aldana Reyes 2018).

Sometimes the zombie virus does not mark the end of all things, however, but the beginning of a new stage of human evolution, especially in those narratives where zombie-human hybrids are able to retain vestigial forms of consciousness. In M. R. Carey's novel, *The Girl with All the Gifts* (2014), Melanie, a zombie child with an unusually high IQ, is ultimately revealed to have been born of 'hungries' herself, rather than transformed through contact with the zombie fungus (Ophiocordyceps unilateralis). In the second generation, the fungus has become a 'symbiote rather than a parasite' (Carey 2014: 432) – a biological interaction where the host and parasite need one another in order to survive – which means that Melanie both thinks like a human and is immune to the parasite's long-lasting damage on the brain. The novel ends with the extinction of the human race once the release of enough spores to contaminate every living human being is deliberately triggered by her. However, as Melanie explains, this moment is not so much an extinction event as the only way to ensure the survival of some form of evolved humanity:

> There's no cure for the hungry plague, but in the end the plague becomes its own cure. It's terribly, terribly sad for the people who get it first, but their children will be okay and they'll be the ones who live and grow up and have children of their own and make a new world. (456)

It is of paramount importance that all humans die in this novel because they are the only ones capable of killing second generation hungries. The dynamics of natural selection play out as Melanie's generation becomes adapted to the plague and learns to live with the fungus. This scenario reflects real microbiological behaviours: small pockets of populations affected by viruses eventually become immune to them.

A similar, if less realistic, future is proposed in *Z Nation* (2014–18), where Alvin Murphy (Keith Allan), a former convict who is vaccinated against the zombie virus, becomes the only person able to defeat it. The entire television series revolves around the premise that his blood contains antibodies that may be synthesised to cure humans, yet Alvin is also capable of creating 'blends', half-human and half-zombies, by biting humans or those who have been recently infected. He is invariably shown as a messiah or saviour of the human race, a narrative decision which stresses the idea that Darwinian imperatives prevail in contemporary zombie narratives: the future belongs to those capable of adapting quickly to the significant alterations of our ecosystem. Texts like *The Girl with All the Gifts* and *Z Nation* are therefore susceptible of reflectionist readings. Their zombies highlight how close we imagine the climactic and environmental apocalypse to be, how the twenty-first century is perceived as a tipping point for worldwide issues like climate change, population-decimating diseases and overpopulation, as well as how we almost exclusively connect these crises to failures endemic to existing systems of social, economic and political organisation.

Given that the dynamics of viral zombie narratives entail an overhaul of the status quo, the military and governmental responses to the outbreak of plagues play an important role in them. The impact of brutal law enforcement on 'tribal' communities, as well as the revival of a 'lex talionis' in the moral codes of the new societies that evolve out of the ruins of the present, suggest that the survival of civilisation must come at the expense of individual freedoms. For example, the contrast between the emotional value attributed to a person by their loved ones and the pragmatic salvation of the human race, more in keeping with the policies of organisations like NATO, constitutes the basic plot of a film like *28 Weeks Later* (Juan Carlos Fresnadillo, 2007), where a safe zone and the lives of many are compromised by two children bent on saving their infected mother. Similarly, *Fear the Walking Dead* (2015–), especially its first season, is much more interested in the process of adamant reinforcement of the containment protocols established in order to avoid the spread of the virus than in its zombies. The narrative follows a group of survivors as they are quarantined by soldiers after the release of the same zombie virus that nearly extinguishes the human race in *The Walking Dead*. The government declares a state of emergency and the National Guard is requested to quell the riots and protests that take place once rumours of the infection begin to circulate. Eventually, the military establishes neighbourhood watch programmes throughout Los Angeles which involve introducing city-wide curfews, grounding flights, putting up fences to protect safe zones and imprisoning the sick and those at risk of infection. Survivors are subjected to new rationing regulations that include limited access to electricity. These conditions do not last long, as, crucially, the protective systems in place fail. The virus steadily wins ground, triggering 'the command code' which initiates the 'humane termination' ('Cobalt', 1.5) of all civilians in the area. Human life becomes so much collateral damage for unprepared governments unable to cope with the terminal stages of the anthropocene. Viral zombies portray figures of authority (the political and military spheres in particular) as ineffective and incapable of looking after the communities they represent, thus suggesting a stark separation between citizen and state.

This suspicion translates to state-sponsored media, who are often portrayed as guilty of misinformation by omission. For example, in *Fear the Walking Dead*, this point is routinely raised by various characters. Nick (Frank Dillane) tries the radio after news footage of an attack leaks online only to conclude that 'no one's talking about this. No one's saying anything' ('Pilot', 1.1). Later, a sceptical teacher, Madison (Kim Dickens), reassures a concerned student, Tobias (Lincoln A. Castellanos), that 'the authorities would tell us' if there was anything to fear. When they meet again after Madison has seen evidence of the zombie virus, she once more attempts to comfort the boy by telling him that 'they're going to contain it'. Tobias's question, whether this 'they' is 'the same "they" that's supposed to warn [them]?', conflates the government, the military and the media. When, in the safe zones, characters complain that they have not received any news about the status of the outbreak in nine days, the implication is that total containment is dangerously close to imprisonment, and that civilians are being deliberately kept in the dark so armed forces may operate freely. As traditional means of information broadcasting (television, radio, the internet and social media) are shut down by those in power, characters are forced to rely on hearsay and their own instincts.

Misinformation, and the alignment between state and news channels, is at the heart of Mira Grant's novel *Feed* (2010), which imagines a near future where the virus infection is partially under control. In this alternative America, traditional news reporters are directly responsible for the zombie apocalypse after someone 'who cared about the scoop and being the first to report a great and imaginary injustice being perpetrated by the heartless medical community' (Grant 2010: 111–12) runs a false story that leads to the liberation of a deadly virus. As a result, traditional news channels collapse and are replaced by blogging reporters. One of them clarifies the reasons for this transition:

> The 'real' media was bound by rules and regulations, while the bloggers were bound by nothing more than the speed of their typing [. . .] People didn't trust regulated news anymore. They were confused and scared, and they turned to the bloggers, who might be unfiltered and full of shit, but were fast, prolific, and allowed you to triangulate the truth. (48, 49–50)

Aside from connecting the instant viral spread of news through the internet, blogs and social media with the equally immediate amplification of the Kellis-Amberlee zombie virus, *Feed*, like other zombie texts such as *Diary of the Dead* (George A. Romero, 2006), seems interested in criticising the ways in which traditional news channels are responsible for sensationalising and magnifying recent outbreaks of diseases such as SARS, Ebola or the Zika virus (Wald 2008: 1–11). State-sanctioned broadcasts, much like the corporations behind them and who might have vested interests in monitoring specific immunological procedures and cures, are portrayed as incompetent and greedy, and, more tellingly, as communication systems whose priorities do not map onto those of the general populace. Viral zombie narratives do more than simply metaphorise pandemic panic; they reveal a growing endemic mistrust in the heartless political and social structures that oversee and report human behaviour in purportedly 'civilised' countries.

Sympathy for the Zombie

If one set of popular texts has focused on infection and thus continued to render zombie abjection fearful, numerous others have just as affectionately strived to humanise it. The biggest barrier to sympathy for this particular type of undead has been that, unlike vampires, zombies do not traditionally display signs of cognition or feeling. Given that even monsters who are not anthropomorphic can be pitied if they show human-like feelings, the first and key step towards the socialisation of zombies, to their re-appropriation as figure of alterity and social exclusion, has been to give them an incipient consciousness. In texts that develop the figure of the sympathetic zombie, the latter tends to think and act like a human being. In fact, since sympathetic zombie stories are usually narrated from the point of view of the zombie, they become tales of transformation that decry marginalisation and celebrate tolerance and difference. S. G. Browne's *Breathers: A Zombie's Lament* (2009) is a good case in point.

Breathers follows the challenges faced by one Andy Warner upon the realisation that he has spontaneously resurrected. The signs are not merely physical – dealing for example with a 'rapidly digesting' pancreas' or 'the smell of [one's] decomposing scalp' (Browne 2009: 3, 10) – or even emotional, after his wife fails to reanimate after the car accident for which he is responsible. Rather, the qualitative changes to his life are brought about by social rejection. Systematically bullied by humans, Andy's only hope lies in group therapy, which takes the shape of a community centre, Undead Anonymous. As the name and its slogan 'YOU ARE NOT ALONE' (6) suggests, the novel establishes a clear link between the othering of zombies, who are not violent from the outset, and the social processes of outcasting whereby certain groups of people and communities are rendered pariahs. These segregationist connections are made explicit, and racialised, when Andy reveals that the existence of zombies in America can be traced back to the Civil War. He sarcastically explains that, although zombies are now apparently widely '*accepted*', they are still 'being denied basic human rights' (39, italics in original) and 'have no legal representation' (82).[3] Andy's resistance, which initially takes the form of protests and pledges for constitutional amendments, in turn becomes a celebration of difference and uniqueness. *Breathers* does not seem interested in a conciliatory ending (the zombies turn to guerrilla warfare), but rather in pointing out that what we call civilisation is, at heart, a hierarchical form of human supervision. Comparing zombies with pre-vote women, 1940s Japanese Americans and post-9/11 Muslims, the novel clarifies that '[z]ombies are just the latest in a long line of those who've been oppressed by the ruling elite' (263).

In adapting the zombie from Gothic monster to tragic hero/ine, contemporary texts simultaneously reposition the source of conflict or evil, so that zombies are no longer those who inflict violence, but those who become subjugated by the regulatory processes which promote socialisation. Nowhere is this more evident than in *In the Flesh* (2013–14), a television series that centres on the difficult life of Kieren (Luke Newberry), a formerly rabid and rehabilitated zombie (or PDS, Partially Diseased Syndrome, sufferer) as he struggles to return to his rural community. Apart from facing prejudice from those who will not accept that zombies and humans can happily cohabit, Kieren's new life depends on the pharmacological industry that manufactures the medication necessary to suppress his zombie drives. Strongly reminiscent of the market monopolies of big pharmaceutical companies, the medical management of zombies in *In the Flesh* lays bare, as Barry Murnane argues, the ways in which humans themselves are currently suffering from 'the infiltration of political regimes of health by damaging practices of neoliberal privatization and profiteering' (2016: 229). As in the vampire show *True Blood* (2008–14), the only way to survive the system is to accept its demands, however punitive and unethical these may seem. As often happens in the sympathetic zombie narrative, Kieren's rejection by the local community, one based on the fear of the Other and the desire to preserve the status quo, allows the text to critique the normative discourses that legitimise homophobia and disablism, among other discriminatory views.

In a similar vein, other contemporary texts have used zombies to decry social injustices and champion civil rights by introducing romantic attachments between humans and zombies. These texts are sometimes referred to as 'rom zom coms', although this term may also be applied to less socially-invested zombie erotica. Novels such as Daniel Waters's *Generation Dead* (2008) or Isaac Marion's *Warm Bodies* (2010), as well as the latter's 2013 film adaptation, trace the vagaries of human-zombie emotional attachments, as well as the inevitable examples of discrimination and prejudice which protagonists must endure. The way in which attraction works in these texts is important, especially because the zombie body is in a constant process of decay and is thus more rightfully a source of disgust than of sexual appeal (Botting 2012: 19–20). *Generation Dead* resolves this issue by making its teenage zombies incapable of rotting or giving off bad smells, although the physiological reasons for this state of affairs are never offered – '[m]aybe odor-causing bacteria couldn't live off their skin, or something' (Waters 2008: 263). Protagonist Phoebe's apparent attraction to dead boy Tommy Williams is both a result of her goth-driven taste for the morbid (his skin resembles that of sculptures and his touch is cold) and of his personality, particularly after Tommy proves himself to be a staunch lobbyist for the rights of the 'differently biotic' (101). In the novel *Warm Bodies*, R is also a zombie in the early stages of decay. His intimate connection to Julie, achieved after the act of eating her boyfriend's brains earns him exclusive access to their couple's shared memories, inevitably blossoms into a full-blown romance. This love has transformative qualities: it can 'cure' the dead by replenishing their humanity. In these texts, the zombie does not work as explicit metaphor for race, gender or sexuality, but as a more general marker of alterity. The marginalisation and bullying of zombies, alongside denouements that highlight the possibility of co-existence and regeneration, underscore the importance of tolerance and the need to end discrimination of all sorts.

R narrates the novel *Warm Bodies*, which means that the story invites readers to enter the mind of the zombie. Scenes that, if experienced through the point of view of humans, might elicit disgust or fear are complicated and presented as either funny or tragic, drawing attention to the value of problematising quick value judgements that may lead to hatred or fear. The film *Wasting Away* (Matthew Kohnen, 2007) literalises these ambiguities in its aim to show how zombies' perceptions of themselves do not match those of humans. Different footage – colour for the zombies' perspective and, tellingly, black and white for the humans' – is used to distinguish between points of view. The film thus deconstructs the main staples of the zombie genre while still exploiting them for their affective value, successfully complicating the 'good versus evil', 'human versus monster' dyads. Stacey Abbott (2016: 163) has termed this developing mode of narration the 'I-zombie', and pointed out that, in an extreme example like the film *Colin* (Marc Price, 2008), told exclusively through a zombie first-person point of view, perspectival reversions also carry a social message: humans are portrayed 'as unknowable and therefore defined by violence and self-serving need; that is, the positions are reversed between human and zombie' (167).

Yet, a different approach to the sympathetic zombie has involved the further erasure of the differentiating markers between the bodies of the undead and those of their previous selves. In *Hanteringen av odöda* (*Handling the Undead*, 2005), the reanimated return to their homes in a seemingly catatonic state, displaying little more than 'a certain rudimentary brain function' (Ajvide Lindqvist 2009: 148). As characters come to terms with events and grieve for the second loss of their loved ones, the novel recasts the zombie narrative as tragedy and zombies as a metaphor for the difficulties of accepting human loss or the ravages of life-altering medical conditions. In the television series *Les Revenants* (*The Returned*, 2012–15) and its American remake, *The Returned* (2015), those who come back are not even psychologically very different from who they once were. This means that their difficulty in readjusting to society comes from the passing of time – the dead have been mourned and people's lives have moved on – and from the natural laws-defying impossibility of their presence. It also makes them difficult to classify as supernatural phenomena, with the characters in the series referring to themselves as both 'zombies' and 'ghosts'. These cognisant and sensitive zombies could not be further away from the abject, hive-minded, instinctual creatures of splatter films; they are pathetic rather than abject.

Naturally, the cognitive and empathetic turn of the contemporary zombie has also entailed a problematic blurring of ontological boundaries – just where do zombies begin and humans end? If zombies can think and temporarily suppress their raw urges, what separates them from the living? In the television series *iZombie* (2015–) the borderline between the zombie and the human is particularly permeable, with characters like Major (Robert Buckley) and Blaine (David Anders) toggling between human and zombie as temporary cures are found and infections re-occur. Since heroine Olivia (Rose McIver) can think as she used to, practically inhabits the human memories stored in the brains she consumes, and, through make-up and hair dye, passes for human, the series continues to mark the zombie as an outcast who has to choose between the limitations of assimilation or a more 'natural', but radically oppositional, acceptance of alterity. This scenario is played out in particular detail in season three. Here, some zombies attempt to keep their existence a secret via their self-segregation to a hypothetical zombie island while others decide that mass infection with the zombie virus is the only way forward. Since both humans and zombies show themselves to be capable of destruction, the lines between them disappear. In *Santa Clarita Diet* (2017–), the variations in Sheila's (Drew Barrymore) behaviour after her transformation are so subtle at first that the television series can be read as consciously positioning the endless craving of the zombie as a grotesque mirror for its protagonists, Californian real estate agents.

Similarly, Darren Shan's *Zom-B* book series (2012–16) uses ontological ambiguity to ask questions about the expendability of zombie bodies and about the moral dimensions of monstrosity. The first instalment, *Zom-B* (2012), presents a conflicted protagonist, B, who gradually comes to question her family's many prejudices. The daughter of a rampant racist, her attack by zombies and subsequent transformation into one of the cognisant undead (the '*revitalizeds*', as opposed to the mindless zombies, or '*reviveds*' (Shan 2014: 205)), serves various narrative purposes, especially given that her physical changes follow B's discovery of the Nazi's torture, experimentation and execution of Jews in concentration camps during the Second World War. On the one hand, zombies as dehumanised and feared subjects stand in for the racial or religious Other, the Muslims and blacks actively despised by B's father. As B awakens after an attack in her school to discover she is now a heartless monster (a literalised metaphor, since she is zombified when a student she once bullied tears her heart out), she learns to empathise with zombies by proxy, and becomes incapable of torturing or killing them for the purposes of scientific advancement. Although conscious, B is discriminated against by the scientists who tell her that, as she is technically dead, she no longer has any rights. The series deliberately conflates conscience and consciousness, for B's refusal to become a 'killer' (296) means she is starved of human brains by her captors, and brain deficiency leads to the eventual regression to a revived state – to a sense of moral unconsciousness. On the other hand, the line dividing the revitalised from the revived is, as in *Warm Bodies* or *Generation Dead*, very thin and concerned primarily with the zombies' capacity to think, feel and react morally to situations. As B complains, she 'can't see the revieds as monsters. They're still people in [her] eyes' (302), but her dad, formerly a figure of adoration, can safely be recast as 'a bigger monster than any bloody zombie' (177).

Zombies, if less common until the twentieth century, are crucial Gothic monsters, for they are as embedded in the cultural and folkloric past as they are in prophetic visions of the dystopian future. Contemporary zombie fiction spins both cautionary tales of who we might become and of who we already are, prompting us to question what it is exactly that we, as a species, may want to preserve for any possible descendants. Zombie narratives, in their channelling of environmental fears, in their questioning of the effectiveness of extant social structures and in their foregrounding of the value of tolerance and difference, continue to offer rich ground for literal and metaphorical explorations of what it means to be both human and humane in the twenty-first century.

Notes

1. As Roger Luckhurst (2015: 167–96) has argued, the zombie has also been used to self-reflexively explore the very global nature of the markets that have enabled its spread through popular culture.
2. It is worth noting that Romero did not originally refer to his creatures as 'zombies', but as 'ghouls'.
3. The novel subsequently compares Andy's triumphant glee upon boarding a bus to Rosa Parks's activism (151).

Film and Television

28 Days Later (Danny Boyle, UK, 2002)
28 Weeks Later (Juan Carlos Fresnadillo, UK, 2007)
Colin (Marc Price, UK, 2008)
Diary of the Dead (George A. Romero, USA, 2006)

Fear the Walking Dead (AMC, 2015–)
iZombie (The CW, 2015–)
Resident Evil (Paul W. S. Anderson, UK/Germany/France/USA, 2002)
Santa Clarita Diet (Netflix, 2017–)
The Walking Dead (AMC, 2014–)
Wasting Away, aka *Aaah! Zombies!!* (Matthew Kohnen, USA, 2007)
Z Nation (Syfy, 2014–18)

References

Abbott, Stacey (2016), *Undead Apocalypse: Vampires and Zombies in the 21st Century*, Edinburgh: Edinburgh University Press.
Ajvide Lindqvist, John (2009), *Handling the Undead*, London: Quercus.
Bishop, Kyle William (2010), *American Zombie Gothic: The Rise and Fall (and Rise) of the Walking Dead in Popular Culture*, Jefferson, NC: McFarland.
Blake, Linnie (2015), '"Are We Worth Saving? You Tell Me": Neoliberalism, Zombies and the Failure of Free Trade', *Gothic Studies*, 15.2, 26–41.
Botting, Fred (2012), 'Love Your Zombie: Horror, Ethics, Excess', in Justin D. Edwards and Agnieszka Soltysik Monnet (eds), *The Gothic in Contemporary Literature and Popular Culture: Pop Goth*, Abingdon and New York: Routledge, pp. 19–36.
Browne, S. G. (2009), *Breathers: A Zombie's Lament*, London: Piatkus.
Carey, M. R. (2014), *The Girl with All the Gifts*, London: Orbit.
Ellis, Markman (2000), *The History of Gothic Fiction*, Edinburgh: Edinburgh University Press.
Fisher, Mark (2009), *Capitalist Realism: Is There No Alternative?*, London: Zero Books.
Giroux, Henry A. (2010), *Zombie Politics and Culture in the Age of Casino Capitalism*, Oxford: Peter Lang.
Grant, Mira (2010), *Feed*, London: Orbit.
Harman, Chris (2009), *Zombie Capitalism: Global Crisis and the Relevance of Marx*, Chicago: Bookmarks.
Luckhurst, Roger (2015), *Zombies: A Cultural History*, London: Reaktion.
Murnane, Barry (2016), '*In the Flesh* and the Gothic Pharmacology of Everyday Life; or Into and Out of the Gothic', *Text Matters*, 6.6, 228–44.
Quiggin, John (2010), *Zombie Economics: How Dead Ideas Still Walk among Us*, Princeton and Oxford: Princeton University Press.
Shan, Darren (2014), *The Zombie Chronicles: Zom-B, Zom-B Underground, Zom-B City*, New York and Boston, MA: Little, Brown.
Tate, Andrew (2017), *Apocalyptic Fiction*, London: Bloomsbury.
Verran, Jo, and Xavier Aldana Reyes (2018), 'Emerging Infectious Literatures and the Zombie Condition', *Emerging Infectious Diseases*, 24.9, 1774–8.
Wald, Priscilla (2008), *Contagious: Cultures, Carriers, and the Outbreak Narrative*, London and Durham, NC: Duke University Press.
Waters, Daniel (2008), *Generation Dead*, London: Simon & Schuster.

Chapter 7

Contemporary Vampires
Sorcha Ní Fhlainn

The figure of the vampire has a long and deep significance within the Gothic tradition, vacillating across the past three centuries from villainy to anti-heroism, from distant invasions to contemporary domesticity. Vampires have walked among us for some time; like other undead monsters, vampires are crucial figures because they allow for investigations of political, social and cultural unrest. As amorphous beings, vampires rise up at the margins and work their way inward, from the strange stirrings of Coleridge's 'Christabel' (1816), and the infiltration of high society by Polidori's Lord Ruthven in 'The Vampyre' (1819) in the first wave of Gothic literature, to the vast adventure of James Malcolm Rymer's penny dreadful *Varney the Vampyre* (1847) and J. Sheridan Le Fanu's alluring 'Carmilla' (1872), to arguably the most influential offering in vampire literature, Bram Stoker's *Dracula* (1897), in which the Count invades the capital of the British Empire: vampires occupy and contest centres of power and influence in the home, the family and the nation. Vampires thrive in their adaptability – they characteristically shift as each cultural era demands while remaining physically immutable in the face of time. The twentieth century, in particular, rewarded the vampire's ability to change and morph; since the birth of cinema, vampires had featured in some silent short films (McNally and Florescu 1994: 257–9; Rhodes 2017), albeit largely as parasitic vamps, and would soon appear in later influential feature length productions. In 1922, F. W. Murnau's German expressionist masterpiece *Nosferatu*, an unofficial screen adaptation of Stoker's *Dracula*, became a huge visual influence on the vampire. Despite its significant violation of Mrs Stoker's rights (Skal 2004: 139–62), Murnau's film endures for its profound cultural and artistic importance: Max Schreck's iconic portrayal of the horrific Count Orlok terrifies with his supernatural reach, manifested through the deep chiaroscuro shadows he casts and his piercing mesmeric gaze. *Nosferatu* contributed to the ever-evolving nature of vampirism onscreen; it furthered the rules by introducing the fatal consequences of scorching sunlight, a feature which has remained a staple of vampire destruction (particularly on screen) ever since.

As Nina Auerbach observes, 'vampires go where power is: when, in the nineteenth century, England dominated the West, British vampires ruled the popular imagination, but, with the birth of film, they migrated to America in time for the American century' (Auerbach 1995: 6). Vampires had found a new and popular medium in which to thrive. Universal Studios' *Dracula* (Tod Browning, 1931) launched the screen career of Bela Lugosi and immortalised the (now clichéd) screen look for Dracula, comprised of formal evening wear complete with a cape, borrowed from the successful Hamilton Deane (1924) and John Balderston (1927) theatre productions. These authorised and successful stage versions of *Dracula* also formed the basis of Browning's 1931 film, including the casting of Bela Lugosi as the Count following his successful turn as this character on Broadway in 1927. On screen, Browning focused on Lugosi's mesmeric stare and slow and heavily-accented delivery to hint at the Count's sexual prowess and distinct otherness. As Stacey Abbott notes, *Dracula* 'not only established the formula of gothic horror for other key universal films of the classic period [. . .] but was also followed by a series of sequels including *Dracula's Daughter* (1936), *Son of Dracula* (1943), and *House of Dracula* (1945)' (2007: 63). Universal's Gothic and horror titles gained significant momentum and subsequently spawned sequels and cross-over titles which quickly faded into parody and self-citation. Lugosi would continue to try to recapture the screen power bestowed unto him through his influential portrayal of *Dracula* but would never regain roles of similar screen status again. Following the Second World War, vampires and other undead creatures declined in their seriousness, as there were greater known fears and horrors at work than the Gothic shadows cast by Lugosi, Karloff and their ilk. Nevertheless, the vampire had become a staple of American cinema, a true source of cultural symbolism, by way of Universal's monster movies. Furthermore, the lasting influence of Lugosi's portrayal of the Count would also heavily inform future Dracula productions, emphasising the count's erotic allure and sensuality.

Vampires and the reanimated undead would later be revived and remoulded in Richard Matheson's superb vampire novel *I Am Legend* (1954), which recasts the vampire from its familiar guise as a foreign and invading Gothic spectre to a bacterial plague which has overtaken the earth. The last man on Earth, Robert Neville, places the vampire under the microscope to discover the horrors of vampirism at a cellular level, further diminishing the supernatural hold vampirism previously had through its nineteenth-century antecedents. Nonetheless, Matheson's pathogenic vampirism permits the unimpeded proliferation of undeath on a catastrophic global scale, to which only Neville is immune. The horror of Matheson's vision is that vampirism is no longer an exceptional state but rather an inevitability that obliterates humanity. Stacey Abbott identifies this viral development as an important nexus point between the vampire and the zombie in her book *Undead Apocalypse*, arguing that twenty-first-century scientific discourse surrounding the vampire can be traced back to Matheson's brilliant realignment of infectious vampire pathogens. Vampirism would be unleashed from its Gothic dusty past in the late 1960s as a pandemic by transgressing national borders triggered by satire and the near exhaustion of Hammer Horror's vampire scares (1958–74). Roman Polanski's Hammer satire *The Fearless Vampire Killers* (aka *Dance of the Vampires*, 1967) plays with and inverts the expected beats of Hammer cinema through its sexual politics (gay vampires frolic at its margins in musty eighteenth-century court costumes) and violates expectations by indirectly enabling vampirism's further proliferation. In its final moments, we are informed by the unseen narrator that the undead have run amok following Professor Abronsius (Jack MacGowran) and his servant Alfred's (Roman Polanski) fateful intervention to save the captured maiden (and soon-to-be vampirised) Sarah (Sharon Tate) from a vampire enclave; the vampire hunters' successful quest turns disastrous as they unwittingly bring vampirism to new civilisations, proving that the undead, however isolated, find a way back into our modern world, and soon spread their undead influence across new borders and on to new populations. This image neatly encapsulates the vampire's infectious growth in the late twentieth and early twenty-first centuries, bringing elements of sympathy to vampire subjectivity and confessions of their proximity to human existence. As we near the close of the twentieth century, vampire profusion becomes increasingly evident and celebrated.

Key Changes in the Late Twentieth Century

Opening up new physical and psychological spaces for the undead to transgress, not least on television with the popularity of supernatural spectres in Dan Curtis's Gothic soap opera *Dark Shadows* (1966–71) (see Wheatley 2006; Jowett and Abbott 2013), vampires now live in American suburbs and small towns, and while still regarded as altogether strange or comedically jarring, their slow encroachment into such familial and everyday spaces furthers vampiric fascination with our domestic spaces, and normalises their belonging within them. By the 1970s, influential authors and filmmakers utterly revised and transformed revenants from their earlier moulds by bringing the undead into modern suburbia in Romero's stunning vampire film *Martin* (1977). Martin (John Amplas) embodies the angst of immortality which rails against the expected backdrop of ancient European vampirism and faded Gothic aesthetics of plush grandeur and costumed menace; for Martin, his penchant for drugging and sexually assaulting his victims, while drinking their blood using a razor blade, neatly demarcates his vampirism as a modern update on a well-worn Gothic trope. He repeatedly warns us that 'there is no magic!' about his form of vampirism – he is merely a more modern expression of vampirism's violence, experienced through his mental illness (or perhaps, it is hinted, past life regression) and crushing isolation. The 1970s witnessed a revolutionary plethora of important vampire fiction and film, recasting vampires as unlikely anti-heroes – in Fred Saberhagen's *The Dracula Tape* (1975); Anne Rice's *Interview with the Vampire* (1976), the first of her ongoing *Vampire Chronicles*; Chelsea Quinn Yarbro's *Hôtel Transylvania* (1978), which introduced her immortal hero Saint Germain; and Dan Curtis's TV Film *Dracula* (1974), which reunited long-lost lovers across time – thus providing contesting accounts of undeath which realigned vampirism with the figures of the outsider and the adventurer. Reclaimed as a subjective experience, vampirism became a revelatory platform for the undead to narrate their own fantastical tales; many confess to a personal tragic loss with narrative confessions steeped in sympathetic turns. Ranging from the enormous successes of stage and screen Draculas to new articulate fledglings keen to share their insights, 1970s and 1980s vampirism diversified the undead and imbued them with a tantalising erotic allure and a lingering sympathetic sadness. The most significant of these were John Badham's *Dracula* (1979), starring the doe-eyed Frank Langella in a mesmeric performance, and, in the same year, Werner Herzog's refracted Count Orlok through Klaus Kinski's tragic emptiness in *Nosferatu: Phantom der Nacht* (*Nosferatu The Vampyre*, 1979). Herzog's film is a meditation on collective guilt and national German horror which unleashes a pandemic of undeath. The numerous revisions of *Dracula* during the 1970s alone gathered momentum and overtly influenced Gary Oldman's sympathetic and romantic warrior Dracula in Francis Ford Coppola's lavish 1992 adaptation *Bram Stoker's Dracula*, bookending this version with the influential romance and gallantry borne of late 1970s vampire literature and cinema.

Alongside intimacy, the increased visibility of vampires culminated in their evident proximity to our everyday existence. Teenage vampires and vampire killers ran amok in American suburbia (Tom Holland's *Fright Night*, 1985), infiltrated families (Joel Schumacher's *The Lost Boys*, 1987), or roamed the American heartland (Kathryn Bigelow's *Near Dark*, 1987) in search of new pleasures and places to conquer. Anne Rice's brat prince, the vampire Lestat, became a rock icon on MTV in the 1980s, awakening a whole new host of vampire brethren in the novels *The Vampire Lestat* (1985) and *Queen of the Damned* (1988), while new diseases (allegories for sickness, addiction and later in the decade, HIV+ infection) emerged in Whitley Strieber's *The Hunger* (1981) and its 1983 film adaptation to warn of vampirism's hedonism and thinly-veiled codification of queer desire. While vampirism proved fatal for many of the emergent youthful undead in the 1980s, when 'many crawled out of their stories to die' (Auerbach 1995: 192), the queer tinge suggested by half-vampirism, a feature of *The Lost Boys* in particular, permitted undeath to become a reversible state; a forbidden or queer encounter which can, under conservative politics, be undone with appropriate, if not outwardly fatal, action (Benshoff 1997: 254). 'Kill your brother, you'll feel better', the vampire hunter brothers Edgar (Corey Feldman) and Allen Frog (Jamison Newlander) advise Sam (Corey Haim), whose brother Michael (Jason Patric) is exhibiting some strange new symptoms of undeath. Tapping into vampirism's coded transgressions of quasi-queered teenage desire as a source of suggested shame and potential terror by restoring the masquerade of normalcy through the successful reversal of half-vampirism, the film parodies the suppression of one's own queer desires and temptations, which must remain in check in conservative 1980s America. Sexuality, repressed or otherwise, would continue to be a prevalent aspect of the vampire throughout the 1990s and into the twenty-first century.

Gothic television of the 1990s reinforces the proximity and sympathy of the undead in our own world once their distinctive otherness melts away. Shows such as *Forever Knight* (1992–6) and *Buffy the Vampire Slayer* (1997–2003) featured strong vampire protagonists and love interests alongside fanged villains. *Buffy* mediated complex relationships between vampires, humans, demons and slayers, their fantastic world allegorically standing in for the hellish perils of high school and its various cliques. In non-vampire Gothic series such as *The X-Files* (1993–2002, 2016–), various types of Gothic creatures manifested in their 'monster of the week' episodes, including variations on revenants as sanguinarian cults ('3', 2.7) or performative vampire rednecks with plastic fangs ('Bad Blood', 5.2) to articulate the decade's paranoid cultural mood in general (Ní Fhlainn 2017), and marked the vampire's necessary inclusion in Gothic-inflected popular texts. Neil Jordan's screen adaptation of Rice's *Interview with the Vampire* (1994) revels in the duality of the vampire condition (as does *Buffy the Vampire Slayer* and, later, *True Blood* (2008–14)), wherein its leading vampires are torn between the damnation of the soul and a strange desire to recapture what has been lost in their previous mortal life. This also informs Anne Rice's 1990s instalments of the *Vampire Chronicles* in which Lestat performs a body swap to re-experience the human condition, in *The Tale of the Body Thief* (1992), and in which vampire spirituality and theodicy are explored, in *Memnoch the Devil* (1995). As vampires move ever closer to the human world, they increasingly replicate (or perhaps develop) human emotions and familial bonds, and seek out human culture and human familiars. As Susan Chaplin notes on Rice's impact on the genre, Louis and Lestat's vampiric 'nature, against which they so often struggle, appears to signify not a condition of monstrous otherness so much as a dislocated alienation that represents a postmodern human existential despair' (2017: 37). The filmic adaptation of Rice's fiction is particularly significant in foregrounding the popularity of vampires in 1990s popular culture, with A-list star Tom Cruise openly campaigning for the role as part of a renewed interest in Gothic and horror films in the early 1990s at the highest echelons of the film industry. At the close of the twentieth century, the undead were everywhere: from popular TV series *Buffy* and *Angel* (1999–2004), cult TV series such as *Ultraviolet* (1998), popular Hollywood films such as *Interview with the Vampire*, *From Dusk Till Dawn* (Robert Rodriguez, 1996), John Carpenter's *Vampires* (1998) and *Blade* (Stephen Norrington, 1998); and independent and international films, including *Cronos* (Guillermo del Toro, 1993), *Nadja* (Michael Almereyda, 1994), *Habit* (Larry Fassenden, 1995), *The Addiction* (Abel Ferrara, 1995) and *Irma Vep* (Olivier Assayas, 1996). Vampires also thrived in other media: in novels such as Poppy Z. Brite's *Lost Souls* (1992), Laurell K. Hamilton's *Anita Blake: Vampire Hunter* series (1993–) and Anne Rice's ongoing *Vampire Chronicles* (1976–), and even video games (for example, *Vampire: The Masquerade* (1991) and *Vampire Hunter D* (1999)). The fin-de-millennium was a welcome and fertile breeding ground for the undead.

Vampiric Intimacy in the Twenty-First Century

The late twentieth and early twenty-first centuries saw the Gothic bring the undead from the margins to the centre of the postmodern world. As J. M. Tyree notes, the post-millennial vampire enjoys increased intimate contact with humans in the everyday world, forming unlikely partnerships and providing fruitful ground for further vampire proliferation:

> The way a victim gets 'unclean' from a vampire bite involves illicit intimacy, and these pictures run the gamut of marginalised sex acts contained in the political unconscious: premarital hook-ups, gay and bisexual relationships, adultery, cheating, polygamy, S&M, the sexuality of children, and the hovering specter of quasi-willing sexual violence. (Tyree 2009: 31)

While romantic and sexual relations with vampires are more pronounced in vampire literature since the 1970s, and are no longer symbolically codified through penetrative fangs alone, early twenty-first counterparts flourished in the vacuum left at the conclusion of both *Buffy* and *Angel* on network television (by 2004), with competing TV series and films quick to contend for audience share. In *True Blood*, the intimacy of the undead boyfriend matched the generic signatures of paranormal romance in general, but also actively sought to carve out its own distinctive adult sexual and violent content aided by HBO's status as a network cable channel. In combining Southern Gothic-tinged dark fantasy and explicit sexuality with vampires, faeries, demons and other fantastical hybrids, *True Blood* extended much of the underpinning narrative of *Buffy* (the weird supernaturally-doomed town, the beautiful suitors, dark humour and the maturation of its central and gifted female protagonist) and rendered visible that which could only be suggested before. Ball's series delights in exploring the polyamorous nature of contemporary vampirism, addiction, queer politics and graphic violence which *Buffy*, due to its target demographic and airing on network TV, could not. The freedom to pursue a more adult tone is playfully and excessively realised onscreen: Sookie's (Anna Paquin) vampire suitors Bill (Stephen Moyer) and Eric (Alexander Skarsgård) are framed as beautiful hyper-sexual undead bodies, 'shifting their generic co-ordinates away from mystery and romance (as found in Charlaine Harris's source novels, *The Southern Vampire Mysteries*) and towards horror and softcore pornography instead' (Crawford 2014: 250). Sookie, notably flat and distant in her own narrative in the novels, is also transformed along with the population of Bon Temps into a hyper-emotional character caught up in perennial and often playfully absurd Gothic crises (Crawford 2014: 250–1) in which she frequently oscillates between two brooding and emotionally negligent lovers. These two beautiful vampires also match on to previous undead suitor dyads – Bill, like Buffy's Angel and Rice's Louis, is emotionally haunted by his human history and wishes to abstain from blood drinking, while Eric, as a pin-up amalgam of Spike and Lestat, engenders a rebellious streak which both fascinates and frustrates Sookie. Vampires are surprisingly fragile and emotionally fraught throughout the series too: they weep tears of blood and make declarations of love in their complex relationships with other vampires and humans alike; they are often manipulated (by demons or necromancers) or targeted by church groups (The Fellowship of the Sun) and human cabals for nefarious ends; their blood has the power to heal the dying and to intoxicate (with effects similar to those of LSD); and their bodies – beautiful and sleek and sexually powerful – abjectly explode into a glut of sticky sinew and gunge once staked or beheaded. Contemporary vampirism is mediated in the series as a repository for Gothic excess by explicitly intermixing and problematising representations of romance, sex and violence – elements typically kept separate in other vampire texts.

Other vampire intimacies focus on the pain of isolation quelled and soothed by the arrival of an unexpected vampire. In John Ajvide Lindqvist's 2004 novel, *Let the Right One In* (English translation 2007), twelve-year-old Oskar, a bullied and marginalised boy, becomes fascinated with his new neighbour Eli, a seemingly similarly-aged vampire whose isolation is equally and painfully evident. Eli fosters a genuine friendship with Oskar to find an emotional connection beyond sexual exploitation; her existing relationship with her paedophile guardian Håkan, who sources fresh blood in exchange for sexual favours, casts vampirism as a form of unsavoury dark circulation, a mirroring of unpalatable appetites tinged with exploitation and violence for the sake of mutual survival. Vampirism remains separate and substantially less horrific on the surface from other domestic concerns evident in the novel and its faithful Swedish film adaptation (Tomas Alfredson, 2008), wherein the suburb Blackeburg is unveiled as a hotbed of violence and addiction, broken homes and lost dreams. Eli heals Oskar's crushing isolation by encouraging him to fight back against his school bullies and by trusting him with secrets – Eli, once a mortal boy, now dresses as a girl and bears a slit where s/he was ceremonially cut to remove his male genitalia when made immortal – and sharing traumatic memories of his vampiric transformation. The intimacy of their relationship is tender and warm, in stark contrast with more traditional sources of solace (families and human peers) that are presented in this text as distant or damaged beyond repair. As in *True Blood*, such intimate relationships often enable disclosures of vampiric vulnerabilities; the rule of needing to invite a vampire into a home comes into focus in both *True Blood* and *Let the Right One In* to emphasise the importance of home ownership, intrusion and consent: Bill and Eric are physically ejected from Sookie's home once their invitation is revoked, while Eli's unstable porous skin begins to spectacularly bleed inside Oskar's home when he withholds his verbal invitation. At its conclusion, after murdering Oskar's school bullies, Eli and Oskar run away together to begin a new life; the tragedy of their intimacy is that Oskar desires to grow up with Eli, and yet his devotion ultimately seals his fate – he is doomed to become the new Håkan, Eli's deceased former guardian. As *Let the Right One In* (and its American remake *Let Me In* (Matt Reeves, 2010)) concludes, intimacy with undead neighbours frequently invites tragedy and emotionally drains and damages the vampire's beloved (as is also evidenced across the seven seasons of *True Blood*). Neil Jordan's *Byzantium* (2012) ruminates on isolation and male chauvinism in the creation of vampirism and vampires' intrinsic need to share the emotional burden of their tale. Thought to be in the remit of men only, vampiric creation is extended in this text as a form of elemental promethean fire, stolen knowledge of a secret place which confers immortality and known only to patriarchal vampire elders. Sharing a political response to misogyny and timely retribution in a similar vein to *A Girl Walks Home Alone at Night* (Ana Lily Amirpour, 2015), vampirism can clearly become a vehicle for feminist liberation from violent patriarchal oppression. Eleanor (Saoirse Ronan) and Clara (Gemma Arterton) exist in secrecy and desolation due to their forbidden immortal existence, hesitant to form bonds for fear of inevitable tragedy at the hands of a puritanical and patriarchal vampire hierarchy which secretes immortality for itself. Despite these dangers, Eleanor, in an echo of Anne Rice's tragic protagonist Louis of *Interview with the Vampire* (and in the Jordan film), finds solace in sharing her secret existence (in whispers with lovers and in diaries and short stories) and in aiding only those worthy of vampirism to benefit from its restorative powers and the unique closeness it affords. What becomes increasingly prevalent in these contemporary vampire narratives is the desire to form emotional ties and quasi-familial bonds to overcome the unbearable isolation of immortality.

In 2005, Stephenie Meyer's novel *Twilight* became a publishing sensation, capturing young readers with its central love story between the 'vegetarian' vampire Edward Cullen and Meyer's ordinary teenage protagonist Bella Swan. Bella and Edward's romance surveys typical vampire fare: it features a burgeoning romance stifled by temptation, ancient rules which govern vampire-kind and romantic propriety at the cusp of adulthood, and is replete with concerns about sexual chastity, virtue and love in the face of steady emotional development (in contrast with the vampire's tragic gift of timelessness). The novel consolidated many overt romantic themes in vampire fiction as far back as the 1970s, and repackaged and marketed them explicitly for a teenage audience. Most crucial of all in this vampiric evolution was not Edward's stern abstinence from human blood drinking (a growing phenomenon in postmodern vampires as they attempt to curb their bloodlust) but rather his strangely scintillating skin. Meyer's vampire set possess marble white skin which sparkles in the sunlight, utterly transforming the undead body from an abject corpse to gemstone perfection. The initial popularity of the series (and its film adaptations) with younger readers in particular spoke to an audience which had not been explicitly catered for in vampire fiction. As Hannah Priest cogently observes on the perceived 'delegitimised' nature of Meyer's sparkly vampires, particularly in Gothic studies, 'the reason so many of us hate sparkly vampires is because, simply put, they are not written for us [. . .] [W]e are railing against another generation's gothic' (Priest 2011). As Priest argues, Meyer's timely material spoke to a generation explicitly invested in undead romance written for a teenage audience, with few evident drawbacks to this version of undeath: the prolonged and shared adoring gazes they exchange, the 'special' nature of a seemingly ordinary schoolgirl chosen by a 'godlike' creature and the delayed gratification (be it coitus or matrimony) of their maturing and meaningful relationship, all successfully transform this vampire into 'the symbol onto which the woman maps her desires' (Wasson and Artt 2013: 188). Inviting strong feminist and political criticism and commentary during the height of its cultural saturation, the series sits apart from its recent teenage-focused predecessors (such as *Buffy*) and guards its vision (however conservative its outlook) of near-aspirational undeath as rooted in coded discipline, propriety and the preservation of the American family.

Vampiric Assimilation, Contagion and Synthesis

While the vampires of Charlaine Harris's *Southern Vampire Mysteries* and Alan Ball's loose TV adaptation, *True Blood*, feature vampires vying for equal rights (as a metaphor for marginalised LGBTQ+ groups) within mainstream culture, their assimilation is hard fought and regularly confronts horrific prejudice. The VRA (Vampire Rights Amendment) is described as the 'Great Revelation' when, akin to 'coming out of the closet' and gay rights movements and protests since Stonewall, vampires stage a necessary intervention in the series as a collage of representative minorities and marginalised queer groups in mainstream American society. That these vampires describe their undead status openly as 'mainstreaming' solidifies its significance. *Twilight*'s Cullen family do fraternise with humans at a safe distance (and abstain from blood drinking), attempting to mesh in with American culture by, for example, playing baseball for recreation to broadly affirm their cultural assimilation. Yet, they live alongside, rather than within, human culture, opting in and out of it as they please. In *Only Lovers Left Alive* (Jim Jarmusch, 2013), Adam (Tom Hiddleston) and Eve (Tilda Swinton), led by their creative and emotional impulses, are sensuous, beautiful vampires who also exist in parallel with human history instead of mainstreaming. Attempting to live 'ethically' (sourcing nourishment from blood banks and doctors), they exist at the margins, knowing that, should blood supply run dry or become contaminated, they will have to hunt humans again. Visually coded as yin and yang via their costuming, Adam and Eve's duality and shared sense of immortal exhaustion, depression and purposelessness seems rooted in their seemingly harmonious coexistence with humans. Vampires that exist alongside humanity may temporarily quell their appetites and desires, but a prolonged denial of purpose, in the end, dulls the senses. Adam's emotional isolation is mirrored in the decay of his surroundings in contemporary suburban Detroit, articulating his acute need to be revived as a depressed representation of the modern American vampire. By its conclusion, Adam is restored with purpose through his relocation to Eve's home in Tangiers, Morocco. This gateway city to older worlds and the continents of Africa and Europe enables this duo to remember and rediscover their historical past and purpose as reawakened by place. Adam's and Eve's domesticated appetites were only temporarily lulled, and their Gothic selves are liberated by necessity in Jarmusch's final frames. Rice's Lestat returns in the twenty-first century, enthralled by, if not slightly out of step with, digital technology but as isolated and detached in a digital world as any human. Rather, Lestat's new adventure in *Prince Lestat* (2014) after Rice's hiatus from the *Chronicles* over a decade earlier pits this vampire against the eternal mystery of religion, faith and belief, and the spiritual purpose of undeath with which her vampire clan continue to struggle.

Vampire contagions and horrific hybridities, however, also remain serious obstacles and sources of concern in the twenty-first century. As examined in detail in Abbott's study (2016), vampirism becomes a harbinger of contamination and apocalyptic annihilation in more recent fiction and film, from scientific experiments gone awry (Justin Cronin's *The Passage* trilogy, 2010–16) to hyper-vampire consuming Reapers, the 'eating machines' whose morphology is described as 'cancer with a purpose' in *Blade II* (Guillermo del Toro, 2002). *I Am Legend* (Francis Lawrence, 2007), another screen adaptation of Richard Matheson's classic vampire novel, transforms virus-afflicted hordes into quasi-zombies, victims infected with a 'vaccine-cure' for cancer. A timely if worrying expression of vaccine hesitancy and post 9/11 conservative backlash, apocalyptic vampire narratives tend not to offer much hope for the survival of society, save for isolated pockets of survivors. Icy isolation does not protect against vampire infiltration in *30 Days of Night* (David Slade, 2007) and *Frostbiten* (*Frostbite*, Anders Banke, 2006) either. Both texts depict vampire infiltration and destruction at the very margins of the Arctic Circle, where isolation aids the vampire to wipe out whole communities. In more temperate climes, apocalyptic destruction bears a striking resemblance to the popular representation of the twenty-first-century zombie-styled apocalypse in films such as *Stake Land* (Jim Mickle, 2011) and *Priest* (Scott Stewart, 2011), with nations being reduced to horrific states of nature. The ravaging appetites of vampires as contaminators and hyper-consumers manifest as expressions of rage, unable (or indeed unwilling) to slake the thirst which reduces contemporary society to ruin. *Daybreakers* (Peter and Michael Spierig, 2009) also imagines a world in which scarce resources run dry (exchanging the contemporary finite resource of crude oil for blood), resulting in a societal breakdown which presages the horrors of late capitalism in the hoarding of blood resources by the economic 1 per cent at the expense of the vampiric masses. In the wake of the 2008 financial crisis, it is felicitous to read the film's vampiric and economic circulations as fuelling centralised greed while populations and economies are hollowed out to near ruin. Driving the metaphor further, it is only through the discovery of reversing vampirism itself (reclaiming the body from the vampiric economic system) that permits renewable alternatives to quash the stranglehold of vampiric hyper-capitalism.

The desire to break free of blood drinking has frequently resurfaced since Rice's *Interview with the Vampire*. While Louis survives on a diet of rats and sustains his hunger (as a form of penance for the sin of immortality), twenty-first-century vampires look to advance their survival beyond the necessity of killing humans. Some use blood banks, others ration their access to blood to curb their thirst, but it is the use of synthetic blood, complementing their increasingly synthetic screen bodies, that liberates and engenders their full assimilation. Tru Blood, the artificial blood substitute in *True Blood*, enables the status of cultural visibility and equality under the law as vampires are no longer bound to their historical role as human predator. Ironically, this commodity creates a new means of economic currency, as vampire blood becomes a black-market resource for its healing and hallucinatory properties. In *Dracula 2000* (Patrick Lussier, 2000), Dracula's (Gerald Butler) own blood is extracted and used by Van Helsing (Christopher

Plummer) to artificially extend his mortal life as custodian of Dracula's gravesite, vainly attempting to prevent Dracula from rising again. While the twenty-first century remains quietly bereft of Hollywood Draculas, vampire bodies have become territorialised by narratives which redeploy their folkloric influence through religion (as Butler's Dracula is revealed to be Judas Iscariot in *Dracula 2000* in a millennial return to Christologically-informed immortality), or are supplanted onscreen by the increased prominence of computer generated special effects, as in *Dracula Untold* (Gary Shore, 2014), which transforms its Count into a reluctant superhero. Thirst again plays a significant role in this Dracula's transformation. Dracula (Luke Evans) is warned by a secret master vampire (Charles Dance) that he may borrow his supernatural powers – 'to have dominion over the night and all its creatures' – to defeat the invading Turkish army but must not succumb to his newfound thirst for blood for three days; the price for even a taste is eternal vampiric damnation. *Dracula Untold* extends the opening of Coppola's iconic *Bram Stoker's Dracula* into a feature-length exploration of Dracula's emotional and Faustian transformation, but unlike Coppola's film, which is rooted in early twentieth-century cinematic trickery and illusion, Evans's vampiric body frequently morphs into pixelated impossibilities, a synthesis echoing contemporary Hollywood-styled spectacle and computer-game stylisation over (physical) substance.

Most revealing of all, in its hilarious and playful exploration of contemporary vampirism as confessional captured in mockumentary format, *What We Do in the Shadows* (Jemaine Clement and Taika Waititi, 2014) documents the (often banal) trials and tribulations facing vampires in the contemporary world. Such modern frustrations include hatred of werewolves, the claustrophobic nature of flat-sharing and how to deal with new recruits desperate to become part of the undead scene. Articulating vampire evolution and cliché through five popular archetypes across twentieth-century culture in its iconic visual citations of *Dracula* (Schreck's Graf Orlok, Bela Lugosi and Gary Oldman's epochal Draculas) and recent popular undead variations of Rice's Lestat and Meyer's Edward, the documentary discloses that daily life, human assimilation and maintaining intimate friendships – as well as accidental contamination and being up to date with modern technology – is trying for vampires too. In the end, *What We Do in the Shadows* encapsulates the progress of twentieth-century and contemporary vampires since the advent of popular vampire literature and cinema: these vampires underscore the blurring of the monstrous with the human, transforming vampires into proxies of human experience while satirising the proximity vampires share with human culture. The undead are certain to continue to be revelatory and subjective storytellers willing to reveal their histories, and in turn mirror our own deepest (and most human) fears and desires.

Film and Television

Bram Stoker's Dracula (Francis Ford Coppola, USA, 1992)
Byzantium (Neil Jordan, UK/Ireland, 2012)
Dark Shadows (ABC, USA, 1966–71)
Dracula 2000 (Patrick Lussier, USA, 2000)
Dracula Untold (Gary Shore, USA, 2014)
Frostbiten (*Frostbite*, Anders Banke, Sweden, 2006)
Låt den rätte komma in (*Let the Right One In*, Tomas Alfredson, Sweden, 2008)
Only Lovers Left Alive (Jim Jarmusch, UK, 2013)
30 Days of Night (David Slade, USA, 2007)
True Blood (HBO, 2008–14)
What We Do in the Shadows (Jemaine Clement and Taika Waititi, New Zealand, 2014)

References

Abbott, Stacey (2007), *Celluloid Vampires*, Austin: University of Texas Press.
— (2016), *Undead Apocalypse: Vampires and Zombies in the 21st Century*, Edinburgh: Edinburgh University Press.
Auerbach, Nina (1995), *Our Vampires, Ourselves*, Chicago: University of Chicago Press.
Benshoff, Harry M. (1997), *Monsters in the Closet: Homosexuality and the Horror Movie*, Manchester: Manchester University Press.
Chaplin, Susan (2017), *The Postmillennial Vampire*, Basingstoke: Palgrave.
Crawford, Joseph (2014), *The Twilight of the Gothic?: Vampire Fiction and the Rise of the Paranormal Romance*, Cardiff: University of Wales Press.
Jowett, Lorna, and Stacey Abbott (2013), *TV Horror: Investigating the Dark Side of the Small Screen*, London: I. B. Tauris.
McNally, Raymond T., and Radu Florescu (1994), *In Search of Dracula: The History of Dracula and Vampires*, Boston, MA: Houghton Mifflin.
Ní Fhlainn, Sorcha (2017), 'A Very Special Vampire Episode: Vampires, Archetypes, and Postmodern Turns in Late 1980s and '90s Cult TV Shows', *Horror Studies*, 8.2, 255–74.
Priest, Hannah (2011), 'What's Wrong with Sparkly Vampires?', *The Gothic Imagination*, 20 July, http://www.gothic.stir.ac.uk/guestblog/whats-wrong-with-sparkly-vampires/ (accessed 6 June 2018).
Rhodes, Gary (2017), 'The First Vampire Films in America', *Palgrave Communications*, 3, https://www.nature.com/articles/s41599-017-0043-y#Abs1 (accessed 19 July 2018).
Skal, David J. (2004), *Hollywood Gothic: The Tangled Web of Dracula from Novel to Stage to Screen*, rev. edn, New York: Faber & Faber.

Tyree, J. M. (2009), 'Warm Blooded: *True Blood* and *Let the Right One In*', *Film Quarterly*, 63.2, 31–7.
Wasson, Sara, and Sarah Artt (2013), 'The Twilight Saga and the Pleasures of Spectatorship: The Broken Body and the Shining Body', in Sam George and Bill Hughes (eds), *Open Graves, Open Minds: Representations of Vampires and the Undead from the Enlightenment to the Present Day*, Manchester: Manchester University Press, pp. 181–91.
Wheatley, Helen (2006), *Gothic Television*, Manchester: Manchester University Press.

Chapter 8

Contemporary Serial Killers
Bernice M. Murphy

The emergence of the serial killer as one of the post-millennial Gothic's most pervasive obsessions began in the late 1950s, when Robert Bloch, inspired by the case of Wisconsin murderer and necrophiliac Ed Gein, wrote his seminal potboiler *Psycho* (1959). Because Gein could only be conclusively tied to two deaths, he cannot accurately be categorised as a serial killer. Nevertheless, Bloch's novel, in which the supernatural was decisively superseded by human horrors, was immensely influential, primarily thanks to the impact of Alfred Hitchcock's 1960 film adaptation. Gein's crimes also inspired *The Texas Chain Saw Massacre* (1974) and Thomas Harris's novel *The Silence of the Lambs* (1988).

Hannibal Lecter, who remains the most iconic (fictional) serial killer of our times, made his first appearance in Harris's second novel, *Red Dragon* (1981), which featured two plot elements which still recur in many contemporary serial killer narratives, including *The Silence of the Lambs*. The first is the trope of the empathic profiler. The second is the prominence the novel gives to procedural 'insider information' Harris gleaned from his research at the FBI's real-life Behavioural Science Unit (BSU). As Philip L. Simpson has argued, Harris's 'contributions to the serial killer sub-genre are even more self-destabilizing than most, because the Gothic conventions he adopts are in opposition to the rationalist assumptions of the detective genre in which he also works' (2000: 73). So, although his novels may on one level present us with the seemingly reassuring presence of highly-trained, insightful law enforcement investigators who can apply all manner of scientific, medical and technical insight to the horrific acts perpetrated by the killer(s) in question, 'at the same time, they quickly realise the limitations of narrowly defined academic knowledge when faced with "the real thing" – the evil and unknowable serial killer' (72). Even when the prowess of the FBI is supplemented by the quasi-supernatural insight of gifted criminal profilers such as *Red Dragon*'s Will Graham, the real victor is always

Lecter. He has always had much more in common with the eighteenth- and nineteenth-century classical Gothic villain – and as Simpson has highlighted, with the vampire in particular – than any 'real life' serial killer.

Recent years have seen the consolidation of Lecter's iconic status. In the TV show *Hannibal* (2013–15), Danish actor Mads Mikkelsen portrays pre-incarceration Lecter as a modern-day Lucifer who delights in getting away with murder under the noses of his friends in the FBI. In addition, Lecter's conflation here with the folkloric figure of the Wendigo lends the character a specifically *American* mythic significance, and further underlines the ease with which the serial killer can be conflated with Gothic supernaturalism. As Simpson notes, the fact that 'the contemporary serial killer inhabits Gothic territory so easily is no accident' (2000: 14). He continues:

> The serial killer as labelled by the FBI during the American 1980s and passed in to mass-media instruments of popular culture, ever quick to cater to the prevailing ideological winds, is a fantastic confabulation of Gothic/romantic villain, literary vampire and werewolf, detective and 'pulp' fiction conceits, film noir outsider, folkloric threatening figure, and nineteenth-century pseudo-sociological conceptions of criminal types given contemporary plausibility. (15)

The Gothic has always privileged 'excess and exaggeration' and embraced emotion over Enlightenment rationality (Punter 1996: 5). As such, it is hardly surprising that a criminal threat which embodies disorder, irrationality and chaos should ally itself so readily to many of the mode's most resonant themes and conventions. Furthermore, although fictional depictions of female serial killers have become more common than they used to be, these stories still overwhelmingly revolve around 'rogue males' who target women and children and cannot (or choose not to) restrain their most savage impulses.

This notion of society being under threat from dangerously unregulated men is one that again overlaps with a long-standing Gothic tradition, and in particular, with the 'male Gothic':

> The plot of the male Gothic, typified by novels such as M.G. Lewis's *The Monk* (qq.v.), primarily focuses on questions of identity, and on the male protagonist's transgression of social taboos. It involves the confrontation of some isolated overreacher with various social institutions, including the law, the church, and the family. *In such texts women characters tend to be objectified victims, their bodies, like the Gothic structures, representations of the barriers between inside and outside that are to be broached by the transgressive male.* (Byron and Punter 2010: 278, my italics)

In addition to the focus on lurid sexual violence Byron and Punter also identify as being key facets of the 'male Gothic' (278), this emphasis upon the objectification and victimisation of women at the hands of transgressive men further allies the contemporary serial killer narrative with the Gothic mode. As Philip Jenkins observes of evolving American attitudes towards criminality from the mid-1970s onwards, '[t]he worst criminals were seen as irrational monsters driven by uncontrollable violence and lust. Far from being the products of an unjust society, such criminals (usually deranged men) were nothing short of demonic' (2006: 12). It was during the 1980s that the modern-day conception of the serial killer as a distinct category of pop-culture villain and real-life threat emerged. Jenkins notes of the US during this time that although the notion of 'serial murder' had only recently entered the cultural lexicon, 'the serial killer came to epitomise violent crime in the popular imagination' (2006: 69). In the UK the serial killer had also 'quickly become an eminently marketable form of contemporary folk legend', in large part thanks to killers such as Ian Brady and Myra Hindley, Peter Sutcliffe and Dennis Nielsen (Simpson 2000: 2). It is in relation to the many small-screen serial killer procedurals which emerged in the wake of *The Silence of the Lambs* that we start to see the tropes of the contemporary serial killer narrative gain truly mainstream prominence. In their consistent conflation of the detective/crime story with familiar Gothic themes and tropes, these shows underline the Gothic underpinnings of the twenty-first-century serial killer narrative.

Crime Procedurals

The prime-time television landscape, since the late 1990s, has been populated by a succession of shows featuring FBI agents/profilers/cops whose investigations of the darkest facets of human nature are interspersed with scenes in which the brutal mechanics of violent death take centre stage. One of the first, *Profiler* (1996–2000) featured a talented female forensic psychologist who, like Harris's FBI consultant Will Graham, can 'see' into the mind of the killer. As would become standard, 'serial killer of the week' storylines were interspersed with the ongoing struggle to take down a maniacal Lecter-style 'super' serial killer. It is a basic plot arc exploited most prolifically by *Criminal Minds* (2005–), which also focuses on cases tackled by a team from the FBI's BSU.

Harris's emphasis on forensics, dead bodies and crime scenes ('an aesthetics of the aftermath', as Mark Seltzer (2007: 37) describes it) would be taken to their most extreme extent in movies, novels and TV shows which focused on physical evidence rather than psychological profiling. The most obvious examples are *CSI: Crime Scene Investigation – Las Vegas* (2000–15) and its numerous spin-offs and *Bones* (2005–17), *very* loosely based on the novels by Kathy Reichs, herself a real-life forensic anthropologist. The intense focus on the forensic examination of the corpse found in both shows also owed much to Patricia Cornwell's best-selling series of Kay Scarpetta novels, which began with *Postmortem* (1990).

More recently, the law enforcement versus serial killer premise has been employed in *The Following* (2013–15), which concentrates on a serial killer – and, interestingly, Poe scholar – who has amassed a Manson-like cult of brainwashed groupies. By far the most self-consciously Gothic recent show of this type is the acclaimed first series of *True Detective* (2014–15). It combined what were by now wearily familiar elements – the ritualised murder of young women, mismatched but dogged investigators – with a refreshing degree of formal and stylistic originality. Creator Nic Pizolatto also incorporated thematic elements drawn from late nineteenth-century pulp horror (Robert W. Chambers's 1895 collection *The King in Yellow*), H. P. Lovecraft, Thomas Ligotti and the Southern Gothic tradition.

In 2017, the serial killer procedural cycle came full circle with the Netflix series *Mindhunter*, which dramatised the work of the individuals whose work had inspired the subgenre to begin with. Based upon the memoirs of former FBI profiler John Douglas, *Mindhunter* is shot in the same desaturated visual style as executive producer David Fincher's acclaimed 2007 film *Zodiac*. Climactic set pieces revolve around formal interviews with convicted serial killers and suspects rather than on shoot-outs and autopsies, and the period-specific 'newness' of the very concept of the serial killer is given considerable emphasis.

The UK has also had some notable serial killer procedurals, including *Wire in the Blood* (2001–8), based upon the novels by Scottish crime writer Val McDermid. *Luther* (2010–), starring Idris Elba, was notable both for its violent set pieces, as well as the fact that Luther's sardonic nemesis, Dr Alice Morgan (Ruth Wilson) is, essentially, a female Lecter, and, unusually for a fictionalised female serial killer, does *not* have a tragic backstory. Another BBC hit, Belfast-set show *The Fall* (2013–16), divided the narrative focus between Detective Inspector Stella Gibson (Gillian Anderson), brought over from England to help catch a serial murderer of young women, and the killer, Paul Spector (Jamie Dornan). As the show, and Stella's frequent pronouncements on this matter, frequently remind us, Spector's crimes are only a particularly overt manifestation of the dehumanisation, misogyny and objectification women already face in everyday life. Combined with its consistent focus upon sexual violence and its traumatic aftermath, this tendency means that *The Fall* represents a particularly resonant example of the continuation of classic 'male Gothic' themes of male transgression and female victimisation.

Although the recent arrival of 'Domestic Noir' as a major publishing category has tended to move the contemporary thriller towards crimes of a more intimate nature, there remains no shortage of serial killer procedurals, many of which are part of an ongoing series. Notable UK and US authors working in this vein include Lisa Gardner, Richard Montinari, P. J. Tracey, Chelsea Cain, Chris Carter, Peter James and Val McDermid. South African writer Lauren Beukes's *The Shining Girls* (2013) provided a genuinely original and genre-blending take on familiar tropes, while another outstanding recent effort is French crime writer Pierre Lemaitre's *Alex* (2011). As is the case with several of the other female serial killers discussed in this chapter (real world and fictional), Lemaitre's murderer is both victim *and* villain, driven to violence by her desire to avenge a brutal act of sexual torture she endured as a youngster.

What these procedural narratives tend to have in common is the implication that the danger posed by the serial killer is one that not only threatens the individual (and in particular, young women and children), but 'civilised' society as a whole. Furthermore, the moral and psychological integrity of the professional investigators featured here is invariably compromised the closer they get to understanding/capturing their quarry. The chaos created by the killer, particularly in those narratives which focus upon a single long-running investigation, is almost always seen as a contagion which undermines the stability of everyone who is pulled into his/her orbit. As in *Red Dragon*, the worst-case scenario is inevitably the possibility that the 'good guys' may end up as morally bankrupt as their prey.

Victim-Focused Narratives

Although procedurals remain the most common variety of fictional serial killer narrative, another notable sub-category revolves around prospective victims and other innocent parties who are pulled into the serial killer's chaotic wake. *Wolf Creek* (Greg McLean, 2005), *Death Proof* (Quentin Tarantino, 2007), *Funny Games* (Michael Haneke, 2007, a remake of his 1997 film), *Vacancy* (Nimród Antal, 2007), *The Bunny Game* (Adam Rehmeier, 2011) and *Road Games* (Abner Pastoll, 2015) all focus on characters who battle to survive – not always successfully –

their ordeal at the hands of a killer. More unusually, a *deceased* victim is the focus of Alice Sebold's novel *The Lovely Bones* (2002), which begins with the memorable lines, '[m]y name was Salmon, like the fish; first name, Susie. I was fourteen when I was murdered on December 6th, 1973' (2002: 5). As befits the novel's suburban Gothic atmosphere, the fact that Susie's murderer is the seemingly harmless middle-aged man next door is revealed in the opening pages.

Although these victim-centred narratives tend to take place over a very short period of time, things usually spool out in a more leisurely fashion in those stories in which a loved one discovers by chance that someone very close to them is a serial killer. A prime example can be found in *A Good Marriage* (Peter Askin, 2014), based on a Stephen King story and loosely inspired by the case of Dennis Rader, the Midwestern 'family man' who had secretly been butchering people for decades as the notorious 'BTK'. Events here are related from the perspective of the killer's shell-shocked wife. As in William March's *The Bad Seed* (1954), her dilemma ultimately revolves around whether to bring the police into matters or 'keep things in the family' by dispensing rough justice in her own fashion.

A similar plot features in Guillermo del Toro's *Crimson Peak* (2015), which eventually turns out to be a cross between *The Honeymoon Killers* (Leonard Kastle, 1970) and the *Bluebeard* fairy tale. Here, a naive young American heiress eventually figures out that her aristocratic but impoverished English husband has long been working with his deranged sister to bump off his besotted new brides. The most disturbing recent take on the 'my loved one is a monster' trope is explored in the 2012 film *Found* (Scott Schirmer, based on the 2004 novel by Todd Rigney). *Found* opens as a lonely young boy discovers a rotting human head in his older brother's room – and then decides to keep this information to himself, with horrific consequences.

In contrast to the police procedural narratives, in which serial murder is depicted as a deeply aberrant act that is still, nonetheless, encountered as part of the protagonist's job, family-and-victim centred serial killer narratives focus much more intently upon the horror of everyday life horrifically disrupted by the violent Other. In victim-centred narratives, the frantic struggle to survive into which the protagonist is suddenly propelled emphasises the devastating physical and psychological consequences of the killer's violence. In narratives where the serial killer is a loved one whose 'dark side' is suddenly exposed, there is always a moment when the protagonist struggles to reconcile this shocking revelation with their previous, seemingly 'normal' relationship with the killer. Even husbands, brothers and sons cannot be trusted here, and in a trope that again intersects considerably with long-standing Gothic themes (in particular, subgenres such as the 'Family Gothic' and the 'Suburban Gothic') the most unthinkable criminal urges are concealed beneath a façade of middle-class familial 'normality'.[1]

Biopics and True Crime

In the twenty-first century, serial killer biopics and true crime accounts now span an even wider network of publication and media formats than ever before. Of course, this seemingly insatiable appetite for true crime narratives is nothing new. It was anticipated by the long-standing popularity of the Newgate Calendar, 'a number of eighteenth and nineteenth-century texts that comprised collections of criminal biographies' taken from prisoners in London's Newgate prison (Worthington 2010: 14), and the avid Victorian readership for gothicised true crime-inspired 'Penny Bloods', plays and broadsides (Flanders 2011). As Harold Schecter notes, it was little different in the so-called 'New World', which was, 'from the beginning, fertile ground for true narratives of crime' (Schecter 2008: xii).

The late twentieth-century market for 'true crime' paperbacks, which owed much to the success of Anne Rule's Ted Bundy memoir *A Stranger Beside Me* (1980), still exists, with titles revolving around prominent new cases appearing as soon as the killer in question hits the headlines. The serial killer also remains a staple ingredient of magazines such as *True Detective* (1924–95), *Master Detective* (1929–95) and *Real Crime* (2015–). Digital publishing has also provided a forum for publications such as the downloadable e-magazine *Serial Killer Quarterly* (2014–), which features 'real cases of serial killing from around the globe' and regularly publishes articles by established authors such as Katherine Ramsland, Harold Schechter, Lee Mellor (one of the magazine's founders) and Carol Anne Davis. Themed issues have so far included '21st Century Psychos', 'Cruel Britannia' and 'Partners in Pain'; their tone tends to be unsentimental and sensationalist.

Broadly speaking, it is still the case that, as David Schmid noted in 2005, 'serial killers are generally depicted in true crime as individualised monstrous psychopaths whose crimes tell us noting about the societies in which they live' (176). This was certainly true of most of the low-budget, straight-to-DVD serial killer biopics which were released in the early 2000s, among them *Ed Gein* (Chuck Parello, 2000), *Dahmer* (David Jacobson, 2002), *Ted Bundy* (Matthew Bright, 2002) and *Gacy* (Clive Saunders, 2003), although *Dahmer* did have a degree of nuance absent from the other efforts of this sort. However, societal and familial factors were implicated in Patty Jenkins's *Monster* (2003), which fictionalised the life and crimes of Florida serial killer Aileen Wournos. Featuring an Oscar-winning performance from Charlize Theron, the film depicted Wournos as an abused and vulnerable individual whose mental illness and dire circumstances were inherently linked with her acts of murder. As with the success of *The Silence of the Lambs*, the respectful critical reception afforded the film marked another key point at which the serial killer narrative entered the mainstream pop-culture consciousness. Although the film tends to lean more towards tragic melodrama than horror, as Caroline Joan (Kay) S. Picart notes, Wournos is still framed in distinctly Gothic terms. However, in stark contrast to the suave, 'vampire'-like Lecter, she is instead associated with one of the mode's most iconic misfits: 'the Frankensteinian monster – a lumbering, lonely misfit desperately in search of love, a neglected child in a body too large for it to control' (2006: 12).

By far the most significant post-millennial fictionalisation of a real-life case is found in David Fincher's film *Zodiac* (2007), which focused on the killer whose crimes terrorised San Francisco during the 1970s. Fincher's staging of one of the killer's crimes in particular – a savage knife attack that takes place on a bright summer's day – is a directorial *tour de force* which emphasises the profoundly destabilising potential of the serial killer. As audience members, we watch knowing that in real life, the Zodiac has yet to be identified. If Wournos's story in *Monster* is all the more upsetting because we feel that we know exactly why she commits her crimes, the unavoidable mystery that surrounds the Zodiac's true identity and motivations circumvents what Schmid describes as 'the danger that the monster could collapse back into the ordinary man' (2005: 183) found in other true crime narratives. As such, the film's ambiguous narrative resolution means that the Zodiac remains the epitome of the 'evil and unknowable' serial killer identified by Simpson (2000: 72).

Fictionalisations of American cases tend to be the most common – both because the US has a thriving film industry and, like the UK, a well-publicised history of serial murder – but serial killer films based on true events are, like such crimes themselves, a worldwide phenomenon. Two of modern Australia's most notorious cases inspired *Snowtown* (Justin Kurzel, 2011) and *The Hounds of Love* (Ben Young, 2016), respectively. In *Snowtown* a run-down, working-class Adelaide suburb becomes the home of a self-styled vigilante named John Bunting (Daniel Henshall) who, almost openly, brutally murders those he deems to be 'paedos'. Jamie, a vulnerable teenager already desensitised by sexual abuse, poverty and neglect, gradually succumbs to the toxic influence of Bunting, a charismatic father figure. Here the serial killer is not only a corruptive force who makes monsters out of the young, but also an embodiment of the endemic social ills and prejudices of a chronically deprived and dysfunctional social underclass.

In an act that seemed to represent only the most recent attempt to grapple with the collective trauma wrought by the most infamous British serial murder case of the 1960s, in 2006 UK television screened two dramas inspired by the notorious 'Moors Murders', the year that marked the fortieth anniversary of the crimes: *Longford* and *See No Evil: The Moors Murders*. In both dramas, Ian Brady is depicted as an entirely 'evil', corruptive presence, while there is a great deal of speculation about both the motives and post-trial inner life of Myra Hindley. As in *See No Evil*, the narrative focus was split between serial killer and an innocent party in the 2011 drama *Appropriate Adult*, which was about the police investigation into the crimes of Fred and Rose West. What these dramas have in common is a decidedly 'respectful' and realist approach which seeks to downplay the more sensationalised aspects of the cases concerned. Nevertheless, all three still frame their killers as ultimately unfathomable figures whose moments of apparent humanity make their actions even more difficult to understand, or forgive.

Following the ground-breaking success of the first season of *Serial* (2014–), true crime podcasts have proliferated, many revolving around (or frequently featuring) serial murder cases. One of the most prominent is the US podcast *Sword and Scale*, which debuted in 2013. As its website tells us, *Sword and Scale* 'covers the underworld of criminal activity and the demented minds that perform the most despicable and unthinkable actions', and holds fast to the conviction that 'the worst monsters are real' (indeed, one can even buy a T-shirt in their online store featuring this slogan).[2] Much the same can be said of the grim 'horror amidst the everyday' worldview perpetuated in other podcasts of this kind, such as *Casefile: True Crime Podcast* (2016–), *True Crime Garage* (2015–), *Crime Feed* (2015–) and the much more tongue-in-cheek effort *My Favourite Murder* (2016–). Podcasts devoted to serial killers exclusively at the time of writing include *The Serial Killer Podcast* (2016–) and *Serial Killers* (2017–). Anecdotally at least, it appears that, as with true crime books, the audience for these podcasts is predominately female.[3] Although formats tend to vary, shows such as *Sword and Scale* and *Casefile* provide the listener with straightforward narrative accounts of the 'case of the week'. Others, such as *My Favourite Murder*, have a much more informal, 'chatty' and unstructured approach. Nevertheless, in both formats 'keeping up' with both the latest cases and notable historical crimes is presented as a vaguely disreputable but understandable 'guilty pleasure' for the listener. As in true crime and fictional serial killer narratives more generally, many of the most 'popular' individual shows focus upon lurid cases involving children and younger women. There is a consistent emphasis on the everyday nature of the setting of the crime and the 'niceness' and 'ordinariness' of the victims. The success of the shows themselves further underlines the veracity of David Schmid's important work on the serial killer and celebrity and his observation that, '[a]s the variety and scale of media technologies evolved, the opportunities for publicising criminals expanded enormously' (2005: 13). Although the medium is obviously very different, the fixation upon violent death, transgressive males and 'innocent' (and usually female) victimhood displayed in the contemporary true crime podcast has a great deal in common with eighteenth- and nineteenth-century popular reading material such as the Newgate Calendar.

Through the Eyes of the Killer

Perhaps the most notable trend within fictional twenty-first-century serial killer narrative has been the increasing tendency to relate events from the perspective of the killer. The first major serial killer movie of the new millennium was *American Psycho* (2000), directed by Mary Harron from Bret Easton Ellis's notorious 1991 novel. *American Psycho* focused on the darkly satirical elements of the source text, jettisoned many of its infamously gory set pieces and emphasised Ellis's scathing critique of consumer capitalism. The film effectively immerses us in Bateman's unreliable worldview and underlines the relationship between late capitalism and toxic masculinity.

In contrast, Jeff Lindsay's *Dexter* novels (2004–15) represent the apotheosis of the 'serial killer as vigilante' idea first explored by Harris. Lindsay's sarcastic anti-hero refers to his murderous urges as 'the dark passenger', and covers for his nefarious urges by working as a police blood spatter analyst. In the novels, as in the hit TV show (2006–13) that followed, we are arguably 'disposed to accept, if not actually approve, Dexter's murderous activities because his victims are themselves reprehensible criminals who have, for the most part, molested and killed children and other innocents' (Buchbinder and McGuire 2013: 228). As was the case with the activities of Hannibal Lecter, whose killings were on occasion motivated by a desire to avenge 'discourtesy', many of the murders committed by Dexter place the audience in the position of empathising with the vigilante actions of the killer. It is an uncomfortable moral position underlined by the fact that, as in *Hannibal*, these carefully curated – even 'artistic' – acts of murder continually serve as pivotal visual and narrative set pieces. Whereas *Henry: Portrait of a Serial Killer* (1986) aroused profound moral queasiness by obliging the audience to unknowingly identify with the killers during the notorious home-invasion sequence, in *Dexter* a tacit yet 'guilty' identification with the killer is encouraged but seldom problematised in the same manner. After all, at least to begin with, Dexter is mainly ridding the world of deeply unpleasant characters we do not approve of ourselves. On this show, serial murder, rather like meth dealing or being a New Jersey mob boss, is depicted as another activity undertaken by middle-class white male anti-heroes who refuse to 'play by the rules' and, for the most part, get away with it.

Interest in the origins of the fictional serial killer has inspired numerous contemporary stories in which his/her formative years are documented. The most notable example is the TV show *Bates Motel* (2013–17), which focuses on the teenage years of Norman Bates. The show was grounded by sympathetic performances from Freddie Highmore as Norman and Vera Farmiga as his well-meaning but troubled mother. Over five seasons, it conveyed an effective and ultimately tragic portrait of familial dysfunction, toxic co-dependence and mental illness, and transformed the previously one-dimensional 'Norma Bates' into a complex and sympathetic figure. In this iteration, Bates murders ten people over the course of the series, and so at last finally qualifies as *definite* serial murderer. Unlike *Dexter*, our understanding of Norman in no way lessens the moral impact of his inevitable crimes, but instead deepens both the horror and the tragedy.

The shadow of Ed Gein also lies heavily upon Nicolas Pesce's debut film *The Eyes of My Mother* (2016). This black-and-white effort revolves around Francisca (Kika Magalhaes), a dangerously isolated young woman of Portuguese descent living in the rural US. Having witnessed the horrific shocking murder of her mother, Francisca becomes a remorseless killer whose crimes are informed by her profound longing for intimacy. Francisca's inability to separate reality from psychotic fantasy resembles that of Jerry, the protagonist of Marjane Satrapi's horror comedy *The Voices* (2014). In a standout scene, the viewer suddenly realises that the relentlessly upbeat and pastel-hewed vision of the world we had previously been subjected to was relayed entirely from Jerry's dangerously deluded perspective.

The trope of the psychotic serial murderer is also treated with thematic innovation in British writer/director Alice Lowe's 2016 film *Prevenge*. The film is about a heavily pregnant widow (played by Lowe, pregnant herself at the time of filming) who stalks and kills those she deems responsible for her husband's death, urged on by her unborn child. Like *The Voices*, it starts off as black comedy but morphs into a tragic portrait of delusional obsession. We also have here a protagonist who exploits – to both witty and disturbing effect – society's tendency to infantilise pregnant women. Within recent popular fiction, female serial killers who also manipulate expectations regarding 'appropriate' behaviour can also be found in C. J. Skuse's *Sweetpea* (2017), Ali Land's *Good Me, Bad Me* (2017) and Peter Swanson's *The Kind Worth Killing* (2015), although again, childhood abuse – and sexual abuse in particular – is provided as part of the killer's backstory. Although still greatly outnumbered by their male counterparts (as in real life), the increasing regularity with which female serial killers feature in film, TV and popular fiction provides yet another indication of the by now entirely mainstream nature of this character type.

Indeed, as the range of texts and mediums discussed here has suggested, the serial killer remains one of the twenty-first-century Gothic's most resonant (and fecund) imaginative preoccupations. Although, as Richard Dyer observes, '[a]ctual serial killing is a phenomenon so rare as to be worth remarking only for its curiosity value' (2015: 3), the *idea* of serial murder is one that has, for a wide range of reasons, decisively taken hold in the popular imagination, not least because in an increasingly secular age, the horrors perpetrated by other humans strike us as much more appalling – and fascinating – than those of the classic, 'old-school' supernatural Gothic monsters. Yet, at the same time, the entirely disproportionate prominence afforded these crimes in both popular media and popular culture is due in no small part to the fact that our reactions have been shaped by long-standing cultural templates and, as both Philip L. Simpson and David Schmid have persuasively argued, by the conventions and language of the Gothic in particular. For all of these reasons, then, although serial murder narratives may initially appear to be a subject more fittingly associated with the crime and suspense genres, their substantial debt to the Gothic mode cannot be denied. Whether we consume these stories in the form of news media, true crime paperbacks, Hollywood movies, serialised TV shows, podcasts or best-selling thrillers, the serial killer's standing as one of the twenty-first-century Gothic's most disturbing, yet perversely appealing, 'monsters' appears unassailable.

Notes

1. For more on these topics and the subject of serial murder, see Murphy (2009: 136–65) and Schlegel (2013).
2. The podcast *Sword and Scale* is available at http://swordandscale.com/ (accessed 9 November 2017).
3. As outlined by Browder (2006). Anecdotal references to the predominately female true crime podcast audience are made in Hall (2017) and Fitzpatrick (2017).

Film and Television

A Good Marriage (Peter Askin, USA, 2014)
American Psycho (Mary Harron, USA, 2000)
Bates Motel (A&E, 2013–17)
Bones (Fox, 2005–17)
CSI: Crime Scene Investigation (CBS, 2000–15)
Criminal Minds (CBS, 2005–)
Crimson Peak (Guillermo del Toro, USA/Canada, 2015)
Dexter (Showtime, 2006–13)
Found (Scott Schirmer, USA, 2012)
Hannibal (Ridley Scott, USA, 2001)
Hannibal (NBC, 2013–15)
Mindhunter (Netflix, 2017–)
Monster (Patty Jenkins, USA, 2003)
Prevenge (Alice Lowe, UK, 2016)
Snowtown (Justin Kurzel, Australia, 2011)
The Eyes of My Mother (Nicolas Pesce, USA, 2016)
The Fall (BBC Northern Ireland, 2013–16)
The Hounds of Love (Ben Young, Australia, 2016)
The Silence of the Lambs (Jonathan Demme, USA, 1991)
The Voices (Marjane Satrapi, USA/Germany, 2014)
True Detective, season 1 (HBO, 2014)
Zodiac (David Fincher, USA, 2007)

References

Browder, Kaura (2006), 'Dystopian Romance: True Crime and the Female Reader', *The Journal of Popular Culture*, 39, 928–53.
Buchbinder, David, and Ann Eizabeth McGuire (2013), 'Homme Fatal: Illegitimate Pleasures in *Darkly Dreaming Dexter*', in Alzena Macdonald (ed.), *Murder and Acquisitions: Representations of the Serial Killer in Popular Culture*, London: Bloomsbury, pp. 227–42.
Byron, Glennis, and David Punter (2010), *The Gothic*, Oxford: Blackwell.

Dyer, Richard (2015), *Lethal Repetition: Serial Killing in European Cinema*, London: Palgrave Macmillan.
Fitzpatrick, Molly (2017), 'How Two Hilarious Women Turned a Murder Podcast into a Phenomenon', *Rolling Stone*, 30 May, http://www.rollingstone.com/culture/features/how-two-women-turned-a-murder-podcast-into-a-phenomenon-w483989 (accessed 9 November 2017).
Flanders, Judith (2011), *The Invention of Murder: How the Victorians Revelled in Death and Detection and Created Modern True Crime*, London: HarperCollins.
Hall, Katy (2017), 'The True Crime Podcast Everyone's Talking About', *The Daily Telegraph*, 12 October, http://www.dailytelegraph.com.au/rendezview/the-true-crime-podcast-everyones-talking-about/news-story/f4e1c8bab286fd4547b4051625c59ee1 (accessed 9 November 2017).
Jenkins, Philip (2006), *A Decade of Nightmares: The End of the Sixties and the Making of Eighties America*, Oxford: Oxford University Press.
Murphy, Bernice M. (2009), *The Suburban Gothic in American Popular Culture*, Basingstoke: Palgrave.
Picart, Caroline Joan (Kay) S. (2006), 'Crime and the Gothic: Sexualizing Serial Killers', *Journal of Criminal Justice and Popular Culture*, 13.1, 1–18.
Punter, David (1996) *The Literature of Terror: A History of Gothic Fiction from 1765 to the Edwardian Age, Vol. 1*, London: Routledge.
Schechter, Harold (2008), *True Crime: An American Anthology*, New York: The Library of America.
Schlegel, Johannes (2013), '"They Fuck You Up": Revaluations of the Family in Contemporary British Horror Film', in Agnes Andeweg and Sue Zlosnik (eds), *Gothic Kinship*, Basingstoke: Palgrave, pp. 211–30.
Schmid, David (2005), *Natural Born Celebrities: Serial Killers in American Culture*, Chicago: University of Chicago Press.
Sebold, Alice (2002), *The Lovely Bones*, London: Picador.
Seltzer, Mark (2007), *True Crime: Observations on Violence and Modernity*, New York: Routledge.
Simpson, Philip (2000), *Psycho Paths: Tracking the Serial Killer through Contemporary American Film and Fiction*, Carbondale: Southern Illinois University Press.
Worthington, Heather (2010), 'From the Newgate Calendar to Sherlock Holmes', in Charles J. Rzepka and Lee Horsley (eds), *A Companion to Crime Fiction*, Oxford: Wiley-Blackwell.

Chapter 9

Contemporary Ghosts
Murray Leeder

At the end of the second millennium, one academic book about ghosts opined that '[c]hances are, ghosts will make another comeback' (Buse and Stott 1999: 1). Eleven years later, another confirmed the prophecy had come true: '[i]t seems that ghosts are everywhere these days' (Blanco and Peeren 2010: ix). The twenty-first century has given rise to countless ghosts, old and new – and often a combination of the two. Academia's 'spectral turn' (Luckhurst 2002), nominally stemming from the publication of Jacques Derrida's *Specters of Marx* (1993, in English in 1994) and only growing in intensity in the decades since, has mirrored a broader interest in the ghost in popular culture. Introducing another academic collection, Jeffrey Andrew Weinstock writes:

> It is also no coincidence that the contemporary American fascination with ghosts seems to have reached a high-water mark at the turn of the millennium and has yet to abate. Ghosts [. . .] reflect the ethos and anxieties of the eras of their production [. . .] Millennial spectres ask us to what extent we can move forward into a new millennium when we are still shackled to a past that haunts us and that we have yet to face and mourn fully. (2004: 6)

Thus, in contemporary texts, ghosts are tethered to ancient traditions and yet are also fundamentally new, adaptable and malleable.

There is some temptation to think of ghosts and other things supernatural as fundamentally out of place in our world, linked to premodern superstition and an enchanted world dispelled by rationalisation, bureaucratisation and science/technology. In such a paradigm, belief in, or even cultural resonance of, the supernatural needs to be regarded as an atavistic trace of the previous order. But many scholars have come to think differently: that the interest the supernatural generates in the most rational and technologised of societies is natural, perhaps even inevitable. And ghosts are indeed popular in our century: bookstores are lined with specialised books about haunting places in most any city or region; reality television has plundered the haunted house trope; alleged ghost sightings populate YouTube; they straddle low and high art and all points in between.[1] They can still be found in cemeteries and Gothic mansions, but they now also populate many aspects of everyday life as well.

'Ghost stories' and 'the Gothic' are by no means perfect synonyms, but there is a significant overlap between the two, especially in iconographies like gloomy cemeteries and dark houses and themes like inheritance and the relationship of past and present, modernity and the archaic premodern. The figure of the ghost, a spectral testimonial to the past's survival, becomes a central figure in Gothic literature. In Horace Walpole's *The Castle of Otranto* (1764), generally considered the first Gothic novel in the English language, the giant ghost of Alfonso appears looming over the ruins, declaring that the peasant Theodore is his true heir and that Manfred is an interloper, dramatically ascending to heaven only once the crisis of his succession is resolved. Few of the literary ghosts to follow would be as large, but many would share the need to complete unfinished business before achieving rest. Other strands of the Gothic have favoured what Tzvetan Todorov would call 'fantastic-uncanny' (1975: 44) narratives, in which apparent ghosts prove to have naturalistic explanations, mostly deceptions driven by greed; this is overwhelmingly the case in the fiction of Ann Radcliffe. Yet even 'fake' ghosts are significant, pointing as they do to the increasing association between the supernatural and the inner spaces of the mind, 'haunted' by our thoughts and delusions (Castle 1995). In Edward Bulwer-Lytton's 'The Haunted and the Haunters' (1859), a London house proves to be haunted not by the spirits of the dead but by the psychic residuals of a previous evil occupant. It thus emblematises the 'scientificised' Gothic that came to prevail in the last half of the nineteenth century as things supernatural were subjected to scientific scrutiny in the nascent field of psychical research. During the Victorian Gothic revival, the ghost story served as a prism for thinking about empire, modernity, gender and a plethora of other topics, and it would remain so into the twentieth century and beyond. In recent decades, the neo-Victorian and related literary movements treat the past itself as a kind of haunting force for which the ghost is a powerful figure.

One difficulty in speaking of the ghost is that the very term 'ghost' has been extremely elastic over time. It has meanings now that it did not have a scant few years ago. Some senses of the word 'ghosting' have largely vanished, but there is a new usage tailored to the stratified human interactions of the digital age: securing distance by deliberately becoming a ghost. The ghost seems to be powerfully part of how we live today, a force that works to gothicise our world.

The Media Ghosts of the Twenty-First Century

The most influential, or at least representative, ghost of the twenty-first century was actually invented in the twentieth. Sadako Yamamura was created by Japanese author Koji Suzuki in his novel *Ringu* (*Ring*, 1991), which was subsequently filmed by Hideo Nakata in 1998. She has taken on a life (or unlife) not only in the literary and cinematic sequels but in a range of cultural translations. In the Korean version, *The Ring Virus* (Kim Dong-bin, 1999), she becomes Park Eun-Suh; in the American *The Ring* (Gore Verbinski, 2002) and its sequels, she is Samara Morgan. In her ascension into the hierarchy of iconic horror movie monsters, she has become a fluid, protean, transmedia and transcultural property. On one hand, she is an *onryō*, one of the traditional vengeful female ghosts of Japanese folklore, and shares their traditional look: white burial garb, white bloodless skin and long black hair. But on the other, she is a figure of electronic media, her soul trapped on a cursed videotape, who contacts her victims by phone and ultimately emerges from television screens to claim them. She is at once a traditional and specifically Japanese figure: her backstory draws on the experiments Dr Tomokichi Fukurai conducted on female clairvoyants in the 1910s, and the film reflects on Japan's status during the 'Lost Decade'. At the same time, Sadako is a Gothic monster for the age of global media; her haunting updates the technological media horrors of *Poltergeist* (Tobe Hooper, 1982) and *A Nightmare on Elm Street* (Wes Craven, 1984). The key image associated with all iterations of Sadako is her terrifying emergence from a television screen, a powerful visualisation of the blurring of media landscapes and the perceptible world in our contemporary media age.

Sadako and related figures like Kayako in the *Ju-on* (2000–) franchise, Mitsuko in *Honogurai Mizu no soko Kara* (*Dark Water*, 2002) and Mimiko in *Chakushin Ari* (*One Missed Call*, 2003) have been dubbed 'technoghosts': 'spirits that display the physical properties of electronic or technical media [. . .] their physical appearance involve[s] static, appearing blurring, featuring interference, as if they [a]re being broadcast'; their 'manifestation is both made possible by technology and mediated through it' (Wetmore 2008: 73). While the linkage of ghosts and technology is not new (Sconce 2000), what has changed is how openly ghosts are presented as mediated phenomena. This is evidence of Sadako's long shadow.

In the Japanese horror cycle associated with directors like Hideo Nakata, Takashi Shimizu and Kiyoshi Kurosawa and labelled 'J-Horror' in the English-language world, Sadako's successors proliferated.[2] In fact, the representative figure of J-Horror became the 'dead wet girl' (McRoy 2008: 82). One of the most impressive of the J-Horror films is Kurosawa's *Kairo* (*Pulse*, 2001). In *Kairo*, an overfull afterlife results in the bleeding of spirits back into the world through the internet, resulting in an apocalyptic struggle between material and immaterial regimes. Affected humans even crumble into ash. A philosophical meditation on alienation and technology in the digital era through the prism of the ghost story, *Kairo* may be at its most overt when a character points to images of alienated, secluded youths (referencing the Japanese phenomenon of the *hikikomori*, youths who seclude themselves for months or longer), lit vaguely before their webcams. One wonders if they are different from living ghosts themselves.

Like so many J-Horror and other Asian horror films of its period, *Kairo* was remade in Hollywood as *Pulse* in 2005. The haunted technology of J-Horror seemed to infect Hollywood in other ways. *FeardotCom* (William Malone, 2002), which plays like an unofficial J-Horror remake, was an early iteration of a haunted internet, an idea realised more successfully in *Unfriended* (Leo Gabriadze, 2014). *Unfriended* plays out in real time entirely on a computer screen, with most of the events unfolding through social media platforms like Facebook, Chatroulette and Skype. Its villain, who first appears to be someone using the handle 'billie227', is actually the ghost of Laura Barns, a teenage victim of cyberbullying now getting revenge on those who actively or passively contributed to her death by virally distributing a humiliating image of her. After dispatching her former friends one by one in their digital shared environment, 'billie227' seems to achieve her own Sadako-like breaching out of the digital world. A timely film, *Unfriended* speaks to contemporary concerns about revenge porn and the uncontrollable 'spreadability' of social media through its variation on the ghost story.

Unfriended is rife with visual and auditory mistakes, and 'billie227' is likened in dialogue to a 'glitch': '[t]he glitch just typed!', cries one of her victims. Indeed, the breakdown of digital media has provided its own distinctive aesthetic of haunting in the twenty-first century, a stock form in found footage horror. Marc Olivier writes that in 'Glitch Gothic' the 'jarring spectacle of data ruins is becoming to the twenty-first century what the crumbling mansion was to Gothic literature of the nineteenth century: the privileged space for confrontations with incompatible systems, nostalgic remnants, and restless revenants' (2015: 253). The glitch ghost is a logical digital-age continuation of that centuries-old association of the supernatural and technological.

A related breed of millennial horror reflects on 'obsolete' technologies and their ghostly status in the digital age. One example is *White Noise* (Geoffrey Sax, 2005), in which widowed architect Jonathan Rivers (Michael Keaton) becomes obsessed with contacting his wife through electronic voice phenomena (EVP), a method for communicating with the dead through radio waves pioneered in the early twentieth century. *White Noise*'s focus on analogue media, radio waves and static seemed peculiarly antiquated when it was released, but it is part of a pattern of tales that deal with the ghostly return of 'obsolete' media. It even offers a contrast between the kind of 'legitimate' contact with the dead practised by a female medium and the more dangerous technological version embraced by Rivers; he turns out to be manipulated by evil spectres. In *Sinister* (Scott Derrickson, 2012), *The Canal* (Ivan Kavanagh, 2014) and *The Quiet Ones* (John Pogue, 2014), ghosts manifest through film – more precisely, through older formats like 8mm and 16mm. Other narratives place emphasis on how media ghosts survive platform migration, including *Playback* (Michael A. Nickles, 2012) and the unsuccessful sequel *Rings* (F. Javier Gutiérrez, 2017).

There has also been a striking boost in Gothic texts reflecting on spiritualism, psychical research and related practices. One example is the UK film *The Awakening* (Nick Murphy, 2011), written by ghost specialist Stephen Volk, which explores competing spiritualist and rationalist discourses in the aftermath of the First World War. *The Haunting in Connecticut* (Peter Cornwell, 2009) roots its supernatural goings-on in the history of dark psychical research. Multiple fiction television shows have been built around characters who can communicate with ghosts, such as *Ghost Whisperer* (2005–10), *Afterlife* (2005–6) and *Medium* (2005–11).

Recent decades have not only invented new media ghosts but also have shown a willingness to reflect on how media have always had their ghosts. There has been special interest paid to spirit photography in the last fifteen years. Spirit photography and the 1869 fraud trial of its American populariser William Mumler has received attention in academic writing (Jolly 2006; Harvey 2007; Kaplan 2008; Natale 2016), in the spaces of high art (exhibits like *The Disembodied Spirit*, at the Bowdoin College Museum of Art in 2003, and *The Perfect Medium: Photography and the Occult*, at the Metropolitan Museum of Art in 2005), in fiction (Van Young 2016) and in popular nonfiction (Manseau 2017). Spirit photography shows us that the history of photography, so often looked upon as a medium that conveys referentiality, authenticity and reality, is inescapably entangled with both fakery and fantasies about other worlds. The original aesthetic of the spirit photograph, where superimpositions layer different portraits together like a ghostly palimpsest, visualised the spiritualist understanding of multiple worlds co-existing largely unaware of each other. Its mode of visualising the overlap between our world and the next is a gentler variation on the Sadako-style violent irruption of one world into the other.

Nor is the fantasy of documenting ghosts through photographic means a thing of the past. The proliferation of ghost-hunting reality television shows like *Most Haunted* (2002–10), *Ghost Hunters* (2002–16) and *A Haunting* (2005–7, 2012–) attest to its continued vitality. As Alison Williams notes, the paranormal reality show has become 'a reliable standard for many cable networks, including the Travel Channel, Discovery Kids, SciFi Channel and A&E, each tailoring the subject matter to their own branded network identity' (2010: 151). These programmes are generally filmed at old hospitals, cemeteries, castles and other familiar Gothic locales yet favour a scientific, empiricist and generally masculine outlook towards the supernatural. In exploiting documentary aesthetics and the relative crudity of the digital image (with night vision as a stock aesthetic) to make ghosts and other paranormal imagery plausible and convincing, these programmes share many principles with so-called 'found footage horror', including the *Paranormal Activity* franchise (2007–15). Some, such as the *Grave Encounters* films (2011–12) and *Hell House LLC* (Stephen Cognetti, 2016), even depict the production of ghost-hunting documentaries. A close parallel can be found in the uploading of videos to YouTube and other hosting sites that purport to depict supernatural events, where again crudity and simplicity are linked to authenticity. Rather in parallel to the intimate relationship between spiritualist performances and anti-spiritualist exposés in the nineteenth century, ghost videos and footage hoping to debunk them feed off each other in a symbiotic circle.

Ghosts of Times Present and Past

Relatively low-brow phenomena like reality television and found footage horror are but one face of the contemporary ghost. The ghost story has been more available to categories of taste and class than other kinds of Gothic and horror narratives. For example, the fondness for ghost narratives on British television, as with the beloved BBC annual series *A Ghost Story for Christmas* (1971–8), has much to do with the ghost story's potential gentility, and films like *The Haunting* (Robert Wise, 1963) and *The Innocents* (Jack Clayton, 1961) are celebrated for their qualities of restraint and suggestion. The cultural cachet of the tasteful and restrained mode of the ghost story has if anything increased in the twenty-first century, as evidenced by revived attention to the foundational authors of the literary ghost story, with reprints of authors like M. R. James, Elizabeth Gaskell, Algernon Blackwood and Lord Dunsany, as well as collections of the ghost stories of such authors as Charles Dickens, Henry James and Arthur Conan Doyle.

In addition to the appreciation of older works, there has been a proliferation of historical fiction exploring 'classic' ghosts and their role in the shaping of the modern world. Hilary Mantel's *Beyond Black* (2006), Tananarive Due's *Joplin's Ghost* (2006) and Kim Newman's *An English Ghost Story* (2014) are all examples, but the most acclaimed prose ghost story of the twenty-first century (at least in English) is probably Sarah Waters's *The Little Stranger* (2009). Waters authored an early academic article about the supernatural and the internet (1997), so it is no surprise to find that *The Little Stranger* is an exceptionally thoughtful engagement with the history and idea of the ghost and of Gothic fiction. *The Little Stranger* takes place in the late 1940s in Warwickshire and is narrated by a country doctor of humble background. Its 'haunted house' is Hundreds Hall, a once-great Victorian manor house now given over to neglect, literally crumbling as its owners maintain an impoverished parody of the aristocratic 'gentle life' in a vastly changed post-war society. Waters places considerable emphasis on the nascent welfare state and the foundation of the National Health Service. Stripped of the labour force that once maintained it, its contents become rebellious against its owners, slowly driving them to insanity and suicide. Its haunting force, neither named nor anthropomorphised, is at once supernatural, psychological and linked to class anxieties.

The Little Stranger has also been adapted into a 2018 film directed by Lenny Abrahamson, a natural fit with 'quality' ghost cinema in the last two decades. The surprise success of M. Night Shyamalan's *The Sixth Sense* (1999) motivated the production of a series of well-budgeted ghost films, often with movie stars, in subsequent years. *The Others* (2001) was among the first of these, a decidedly 'old-fashioned' period piece set in a nearly vacant mansion on the island of Jersey, directed with a Gothic flair by Spain's Alejandro Amenábar. The same year, Mexican director Guillermo del Toro made *El espinazo del diablo* (*The Devil's Backbone*, 2001). It takes place in an orphanage during the Spanish Civil War, where a newcomer finds himself approached by the ghost of a murdered boy who needs help; the narrative of the dead returning seeking justice and vengeance plays out against a backdrop of war and tragedy. It asks suggestively:

> [w]hat is a ghost? An emotion, a terrible moment condemned to repeat itself over? An instant of pain, perhaps? Something dead which still seems to be

alive. An emotion suspended in time. Like a blurred photograph. Like an insect trapped in amber.

Like *The Little Stranger*, *The Devil's Backbone* offers a critical commentary on the ghost story itself alongside its own engaging narrative.

In its use of the ghost as a figure through which to channel notions of national trauma and cultural memory, *The Devil's Backbone* displays another key feature of the ghost in general and of the twenty-first-century ghost in particular. Such narratives have appeared in many parts of the world: for example, the South Korean film *Gidam* (*Epitaph*, Jung Sik and Jung Bum-shik, 2007) takes place in 1942 and deals with the traumatic legacy of the Japanese occupation. *The Devil's Backbone* also debuted del Toro's aesthetic of haunting, a mix of practical and digital elements that suggest both embodied physicality and intangibility. Del Toro's other ghost film, *Crimson Peak* (2015), is an overt homage to the nineteenth-century Gothic novel, using cutting-edge special effects to tell a decidedly old-fashioned story. His status as an auteur of the ghost story and of the Gothic goes beyond his films (and those he has produced, such as *El orfanato* (*The Orphanage*, J. A. Bayona, 2007) and *Mama* (Andrés Muschietti, 2013)). For example, he curated and introduced a series of Penguin Classics collections by Gothic masters of the ghost story such as M. R. James, Arthur Machen and Algernon Blackwood.

A new and very commercially successful breed of ghost cinema came to thrive late in the first decade of the twenty-first century. The proliferation of haunted house films about suburbia and domestic spaces in the wake of the 2008 crisis (especially in films by Blumhouse Pictures such as the *Insidious* (2010–), *Sinister* (2012–) and *The Conjuring* (2013–) franchises) reflects an upswing in economic uncertainty (Murphy 2015). These films evince the long-standing artistic convention of utilising Gothic tropes to process modern financial insecurities, real estate anxieties and class precarity. More recently, the Netflix series *The Haunting of Hill House* (2018), produced, written and directed by Blumhouse regular Mike Flanagan, borrows the cultural prestige of Shirley Jackson's classic novel but uses little more than its name. The fact that it has proved to be Netflix's first successful horror series speaks to the continued viability the ghost story to middle-brow consumption, especially on television.

Ghosts have their place in world art cinema as well, somewhat in parallel to the international perambulations of popular ghost films such as the J-Horror cycle. French art-house director Olivier Assayas's *Personal Shopper* (2016) features Kristen Stewart as an American medium residing in Paris and attempting to contact her deceased twin brother. *Personal Shopper* melds familiar haunted house film scenarios and social media hauntings with art film aesthetics; possibly its most memorable image is a glass levitating, in soft focus and unobserved by any character, at the extreme back of the frame. American director David Lowery's *A Ghost Story* (2016) also uses Hollywood stars (Casey Affleck, Rooney Mara) in a slow, quiet, yet sweeping narrative that dares its audience to take seriously the kitschy 'sheet ghost'.

Yet it is, again, in Asian cinema that the ghost film and the art film crossed over most visibly. Apichatpong Weerasethakul's *Lung Bunmi Raluek Chat* (*Uncle Boonmee Who Can Recall His Past Lives*, 2010) became not only the first Thai film to win the Palme d'Or at Cannes, but the first ghost film to do so too. Meditating on memory, Thai history and the relationship between nature and civilisation, and featuring beautiful and startling images, *Uncle Boonmee* is an example of the art film's 'slow cinema'. Another haunting piece of slow cinema was *Bú sàn* (*Goodbye, Dragon Inn*, 2003) by Taiwanese director Tsai Ming-liang. Taking place and shot in a closing movie theatre in Taipei, inhabited by the ghosts of films and audiences past, *Goodbye, Dragon Inn* holds a static camera on empty spaces to mediate the experience of loss. Near its end, it holds what appears to be a point-of-view shot from the perspective of the screen itself out onto the empty chairs for more than five minutes. Slow cinema, with its emphasis on the experience of time unfolding, seems a perfect match for the ghost story.

Also obsessed with how loss and absence haunt the history of cinema, the acclaimed Canadian director Guy Maddin has been tangling with ghosts since his debut short *The Dead Father* (1985). His twenty-first-century features *Cowards Bend the Knee* (2003), *Brand upon the Brain!* (2006), *My Winnipeg* (2007) and *Keyhole* (2011) are particularly populated with eccentric ghosts and spectral landscapes. In 2010 he began an art installation project called *Hauntings* that involved the remaking, or in some cases making, of lost and unrealised films. *Hauntings* evolved into the online project *Seances*, which debuted on the National Film Board of Canada's website in 2016. Found at seances.nfb.ca, *Seances* promises a unique film experience for every viewer. Built around the video rendering platform Imposium, *Seances* algorithmically generates a unique set of segments built out of dozens of short films shot by Maddin in 2012 and 2013 that use digital techniques to approximate the gauzy ephemerality of the decaying photochemical image. The viewer gets a unique title and the following experience is unpausable, unrewindable and unsavable. Furthermore, it uses audio-visual effects like data-moshing, sound interruption, sound flowing, rotoscoping and motion tracking to make every 'conjuration' unique. Congruent with the 'Glitch Gothic' Olivier identifies in found footage horror, competing images flow in and out seemingly at random, and visual and audio digital noise shatters the integrity of the image. The film is then lost, never to be viewed again. Maddin has spoken about a desire to haunt the internet, which reminds him

> a lot of some sort of afterlife: a space that doesn't really seem to exist in three dimensions [...] a place where it's promised data will live forever [...] the promise that the Internet has of storing things forever that almost promises the kind of immortality that an afterlife does, or that's impossible. And so introducing intentional data destruction online intrigues me. (Leeder 2015: n.p.)

Embodying the strange millennial interplay of analogue and digital media, past and present, transience and permanence and absence and presence, as well as reflecting the ghost's simultaneous allegiance with high and low culture, *Seances* may be the definitive ghost artwork for our time.

Our Ghosts, Ourselves

Interviewed for Ken McMullen's 1983 film *Ghost Dance*, Jacques Derrida himself opined that, 'ghosts are part of the future, and that the modern technology of images like cinematography and telecommunication enhances the power of ghosts and their ability to haunt us'. We look to the solidity of the past and find that, like Hundreds Hall in Waters's *The Little Stranger*, it is crumbling. And to withdraw from the world of social interactions into the unprecedented electronic solitude available to people now is to 'ghost'. It is striking how many twenty-first-century narratives end with characters either realising that they were always ghosts, as in *The Others* and *Static* (Todd Levin, 2012); becoming ghosts, as in *The Orphanage* and *The Innkeepers* (Ti West, 2011); learning that a putative ghost is really a living human, as in *Volver* (Pedro Almodóvar, 2006); penetrating a ghost world, as in *Mirrors* (Alexandre Aja, 2008), 'the Further' in the *Insidious* films and the 'ghost dimension' in the *Paranormal Activity* films; or more generally thriving on uncertainty about who is alive and who is not, as in *American Horror Story: Murder House* (2011). Our Gothic media seems to be telling us that the line between our ghosts and ourselves is increasingly untenable.

Ghosts are versatile, adaptable metaphors. The new century reveals them as simultaneously domestic and global, with national particularities but subject to the international flows of media. They are rooted in the past – an old-fashioned figure linked to an old-fashioned kind of storytelling – but they are endlessly adaptable to new contexts and, especially, new technologies, often revealing the dark, Gothic aspects that trouble narratives of progress, connectivity and convenience. Whether the future, as Derrida said in *Ghost Dance*, belongs to ghosts or not, it is definitely hard to imagine a future without them.

Notes

1. Recently, examples of popular nonfiction about ghosts include Roach (2006), Dickey (2016) and Owens (2017).
2. The international attention paid to the J-Horror cycle unfolded against a proliferation of ghost and otherwise supernatural narratives produced in other Asian cinemas, including Hong Kong (*Gin gwai* (*The Eye*, Oxide Pang Chun and Danny Pang Phat, 2002)), the Philippines (*Sigaw* (*The Echo*, Yam Laranas, 2004)), South Korea (*Janghwa, Hongryeon* (*A Tale of Two Sisters*, Kim Jee-won, 2003)), Thailand (*Shutter* (Banjong Pisanthanakun and Parkpoom Wongpoom, 2004)) and India (*Bhoot* (*Ghost*, Ram Gopal Varma, 2003)).

Film and Television

Bú sàn (*Goodbye, Dragon Inn*, Tsai Ming-Liang, Taiwan, 2003)
El espinazo del diablo (*The Devil's Backbone*, Guillermo del Toro, Spain/Mexico, 2001)
Ghost Dance (Ken McMullen, France/UK, 1983)
Gidam (*Epitaph*, Jung Sik and Jung Bum-shik, South Korea, 2007)
Kairo (*Pulse*, Kiyoshi Kurosawa, Japan, 2001)
Lung Bunmi Raluek Chat (*Uncle Boonmee Who Can Recall His Past Lives*, Apichatpong Weerasethakul, Thailand, 2010)
Ringu (*Ring*, Hideo Nakata, Japan, 1998)
Unfriended (Leo Gabriadze, USA, 2014)
White Noise (Geoffrey Sax, Canada/UK/USA, 2005)

Webpages

Seances (2016), interactive website, created by Guy Maddin, Evan Johnson and Galen Johnson, National Film Board of Canada, http://seances.nfb.ca/ (accessed 4 June 2018).

References

Blanco, María del Pilar, and Esther Peeren (eds) (2010), *Popular Ghosts: The Haunted Spaces of Everyday Culture*, New York: Continuum.
Buse, Peter, and Andrew Stott (eds) (1999), *Ghosts: Deconstruction, Psychoanalysis, History*, New York: St. Martin's Press.
Castle, Terry (1995), *The Female Thermometer: Eighteenth-Century Culture and the Invention of the Uncanny*, New York: Oxford University Press.
Derrida, Jacques (1994), *Specters of Marx: The State of the Debt, the Work of Mourning and the New International*, London: Routledge.
Dickey, Colin (2016), *Ghostland: An American History in Haunted Places*, New York: Viking.
Harvey, John (2007), *Photography and Spirit*, London: Reaktion Books.
Jolly, Martin (2006), *Faces of the Living Dead: The Belief in Spirit Photography*, London: British Library.
Kaplan, Louis (2008), *The Strange Case of William Mumler, Spirit Photographer*, Minneapolis: University of Minnesota Press.
Leeder, Murray (2015), 'Ektoplasm-o-vision! with Guy Maddin', *Luma – Film & Media Art Quarterly*, 1.1, n.p.
Luckhurst, Roger (2002), 'The Contemporary London Gothic and the Limits of the "Spectral Turn"', *Textual Practice*, 13.3, 527–46.
McRoy, Jay (2008), *Nightmare Japan: Contemporary Japanese Horror Cinema*, Amsterdam: Rodopi.
Manseau, Peter (2017), *The Apparitionists: A Tale of Phantoms, Fraud, Photography, and the Man Who Captured Lincoln's Ghost*, Boston, MA: Houghton Mifflin Harcourt.
Murphy, Bernice (2015), '"It's Not the House That's Haunted": Demons, Debt, and the Family in Peril in Recent Horror Films', in Murray Leeder (ed.), *Cinematic Ghosts: Haunting and Spectrality from Silent Cinema to the Digital Era*, New York: Bloomsbury, pp. 235–52.
Natale, Simone (2016), *Supernatural Entertainments: Victorian Spiritualism and the Rise of Modern Media Culture*, University Park: Pennsylvania State University Press.
Olivier, Marc (2015), 'Glitch Gothic', in Murray Leeder (ed.), *Cinematic Ghosts: Haunting and Spectrality from Silent Cinema to the Digital Era*, New York: Bloomsbury, pp. 253–70.
Owens, Susan (2017), *The Ghost: A Cultural History*, London: Tate Publishing.
Roach, Mary (2006), *Spook: Science Tackles the Afterlife*, New York: W. W. Norton.
Sconce, Jeffrey (2000), *Haunted Media: Electronic Presence from Telegraphy to Television*, Durham, NC: Duke University Press.
Todorov, Tzvetan (1975), *The Fantastic: A Structural Approach to a Literary Genre*, Richard Howard (trans.), Ithaca: Cornell University Press.
Van Young, Adrian (2016), *Shadows in Summerland*, Toronto: ChiZine Publications.
Waters, Sarah (1997), 'Ghosting the Interface: Cyberspace and Spiritualism', *Science as Culture*, 6.3, 414–43.
— (2009), *The Little Stranger*, Toronto: Emblem.

Weinstock, Jeffrey Andrew (2004), 'Introduction: The Spectral Turn', in Jeffrey Andrew Weinstock (ed.), *Spectral America: Phantoms and the National Imagination*, Madison: The University of Wisconsin Press, pp. 3–17.

Wetmore, Kevin J. (2008), 'Technoghosts and Culture Shocks: Sociocultural Shifts in American Remakes of J-Horror', *Post Script: Essays in Film and the Humanities*, 28.2, 72–81.

Williams, Karen (2010), 'The Liveness of Ghosts: Haunting and Reality TV', in María del Pilar Blanco and Esther Peeren (eds), *Popular Ghosts: The Haunted Spaces of Everyday Culture*, New York: Continuum, pp. 149–61.

Chapter 10

Contemporary Werewolves
Kaja Franck and Sam George

The twenty-first-century werewolf is at its most distinctive in that generic conjunction of horror with romantic fiction that forms paranormal romance. Werewolves (following vampires) have become humanised, even romanticised, alongside the assimilation of the Other as identity politics which became mainstream around the 1980s (Hughes 2013: 246–7). Thus werewolves, formerly existing as monsters at the edges of Gothic narratives, have been brought to the centre and made sympathetic. Young Adult Gothic fiction, which gathered momentum as a genre from the late twentieth century onwards, is often where the most radical transformations of the werewolf theme occur, inspired by concerns over agency and subjectivity. Ecology, too, has shaped our understanding of creatures which oscillate between nature and culture, and there is a new focus on the wolf behind the werewolf myth in response to narratives around extinction and to the growth of Animal Studies (McKay and Miller 2017: 2–5). The twenty-first century has seen new werewolf hauntings and sightings, and a revival of folkloric elements from urban myth which posit the twenty-first-century werewolf as the spectre wolf, in place of the absent flesh and blood animal. Thus, while the monstrous werewolf in the tradition of Gothic horror persists in the twenty-first century, a new avatar has become firmly established alongside it. This version is characterised by a new-found sympathy towards the creature, often through representing its subjectivity and autonomy; by an attention to femininity, with female werewolves appearing as protagonists; and by concerns with the environment, often coupled with an increased awareness of the actual wolf as animal.

Gothic texts deal with a variety of themes as pertinent to contemporary culture as they were to the eighteenth and nineteenth centuries, when Gothic novels first achieved popularity. The werewolf is easily situated within themes of monstrosity, liminality and the divided self, showing it to be a decidedly Gothic creature. The Gothic is a genre profoundly concerned with its own past, self-referentially dependent on traces of other stories, familiar images, narrative structures and intertextual allusions (Spooner 2006: 10). To understand the twenty-first-century werewolf as a Gothic figure, it is necessary to first revisit its incarnations in the past.

In literature, accounts of man-into-wolf transformations can be found in the epic of *Gilgamesh* (approximately 2000 BC); the werewolf tale in Petronius's *Satyricon* (c. AD 1–3) and Ovid's rendition of the Greek myth of Lycaon in *Metamorphoses* (c. AD 8). The werewolf came to life outside of literature due to the existence of werewolf trials. Witchcraft trials are common knowledge, but many readers are unaware that people were tried and executed as werewolves. The werewolf became a frightening reality for this reason during the sixteenth and seventeenth centuries. The year 1589, which saw the rise of werewolf trials in France, appears to have been the werewolf's *annus mirabilis* (Douglas 1992: 127–50, 266; Sconduto 2008). Jean Grenier, the 'Werewolf of Chalons', and the Gandillon family, all of whom were executed as werewolves at this time, were murderers who had a taste for human flesh. The werewolf trials confirmed the identity of the werewolf as a monster. It was cannibalistic, anti-Christian and murderous. Of particular importance to the history of the werewolf, however, is the transition of the werewolf from a courtly figure, exemplified in early French poetry, to the cannibalistic peasant of the werewolf trials (Sconduto 2008: 180–200).

The werewolf's association with sorcery, seen in the trials, was challenged by its depiction in the Gothic novel in the early nineteenth century. It appeared to understand lycanthropy as a mental disorder rather than a magical, supernatural transformation. *The Albigenses* (1824), by Charles Maturin, references John Webster's *Duchess of Malfi* (1614) in depicting the werewolf as a product of lunacy and superstition. Such narratives end with a logical explanation (in the manner of Ann Radcliffe's novels) for why credulous peasants have mistakenly identified someone as a werewolf (Bourgault du Coudray 2006: 33). By the middle of the nineteenth century, the depiction of the werewolf was becoming more sensational through texts such as G. W. M. Reynold's *Wagner, the Wehr-Wolf* (1846–7), a serialised penny dreadful. The publication of Sabine Baring-Gould's *The Book of Werewolves* (1865) and Kirby Flower Smith's *An Historical Study of the Werewolf in Literature* (1894) suggests a renewed interest in both the history of the werewolf and its importance as a cultural figure at this time. Surprisingly, Baring-Gould's work is an important source for Bram Stoker's *Dracula* (1897), yet the werewolfish qualities of the Count are often overlooked in histories of Gothic fiction, which only focus on his identity as a vampire.

Clemence Housman's *The Were-Wolf* (1890) is notable for being female, anticipating the twenty-first-century manifestations below.

Although nineteenth-century werewolf narratives tended to locate the werewolf in the medieval past, the publication of Charles Darwin's *On the Origin of Species* (1859) suggests a Victorian origin for the fear of the werewolf. The werewolf marks a threshold, neither animal nor human. Kelly Hurley describes hybrid creatures such as the werewolf as a site where the notion of the human and animal collapse (2007: 139). Thus, like Darwin's theory of evolution, the werewolf dissolves clear notions of human superiority. Stephen Asma further confirms this potential of the werewolf to uncover the precarity of human understanding of the natural world, defying taxonomic categorisation (2009: 26). Important here, too, is the Gothic version of liminality. Werewolves cannot be categorised as either human or wolf; they remain monsters on the boundaries of humanity. This is troubling, suggesting that the human subject is not inviolable. The typical nineteenth-century werewolf embodies the Gothic fear that civilisation is a veneer and that our animal origins may burst from within at any moment. The rise of psychoanalysis consolidated this anxiety in the early twentieth century, where werewolves can be seen as depicting humanity's latent animalistic violence. Thus, lycanthropy came to represent the 'beast within' or everything animal that we have repressed in terms of our human nature. The twenty-first century has seen a shift from understanding werewolves through Freud's 1914 case study of the individual male psyche ('Wolf-Man') to an interest in the links between the lunar cycle, werewolfism and menstruation.

Wolf children or stories of children raised by wolves have also been influential in shaping contemporary manifestations of the werewolf myth, together with late twentieth-century accounts of the last wolf – fictional, mythical and factual (Morpurgo 2002; Crumley 2010; Weymouth 2014). There are contemporary writers who are reinventing wolf children myths, such as Jill Paton Walsh in her *Knowledge of Angels* (1994). These are often written for young adults, as with Marcus Sedgwick's *The Dark Horse* (2002), Jennifer Lynn Barnes's *Raised by Wolves* (2010) and Manoru Hosadu's anime film, *Wolf Children* (2012). The story of wolf children has endured alongside the fairy tale narratives of Red Riding Hood and the Big Bad Wolf. Throughout all these manifestations, sometimes contradictory and ambivalent, two key archetypes have endured: the monstrous and the sympathetic.

Monstrous Werewolves

The new millennium opened with the original and inventive werewolf film *Ginger Snaps* (John Fawcett, 2000). Apparently reacting to the lack of female werewolves, the central monster in the narrative is Ginger (Katharine Isabelle), a teenage girl. Ginger and her sister abhor the vapid world of their adolescent peers, planning to commit suicide before they enter adulthood. Attracted to the scent of blood, Ginger is attacked during her first period, an event that plays on the association between menstruation, werewolves and the lunar cycle. Her transformation into a werewolf coincides with her experience of puberty. In keeping with the traditional monster narrative, the film ends with the death of Ginger. Rather than rejecting her status as a werewolf, she revels in the pleasure of violence, along with the concomitant overtones of sexuality. Despite this, femininity and monstrosity are not aligned. Ginger is not monstrous because she is female; she is monstrous because she is a werewolf. While this narrative reacts to the woman as Other in Gothic texts, it still situates the werewolf in a place of monstrosity. The cult success of the original spawned both a sequel and a prequel, *Ginger Snaps 2: Unleashed* (Brett Sullivan, 2004) and *Ginger Snaps Back: The Beginning* (Grant Harvey, 2004), although neither was as effective as the original in interrogating female lycanthropy.

The *Ginger Snaps* trilogy typifies the varied quality of early twenty-first-century filmic werewolves. The 1980s is often seen as the golden age of the werewolf film, with key examples such as *An American Werewolf in London* (John Landis, 1981), *The Howling* (Joe Dante, 1981), *The Company of Wolves* (Neil Jordan, 1984) and *Teen Wolf* (Rod Daniel, 1985) premiering in close proximity. Increasingly sophisticated special effects meant that the werewolf's transformation could appear on the cinema screen in gory detail. More recent incarnations of the werewolf film have failed to retain surprise and horror, in part because the death of the werewolf has become less desirable. The repetitive quality of werewolf narratives is characterised by the remakes and reboots of twenty-first-century werewolf cinema. *The Wolf Man* (George Waggner, 1941), starring Lon Chaney Jr, with its iteration of the curse of lycanthropy, is one of the archetypal werewolf narratives, notable too for its faux folklore around wolfbane. It was remade as *The Wolfman* by Joe Johnston in 2010. Despite the appeal of serious actors such as Anthony Hopkins and Benicio del Toro, the film did little to reinvigorate its source material. The 1980s *Howling* film series was rebooted in 2011 with *The Howling: Reborn* (Joe Nimziki). The narrative arc of identifying and hunting down the werewolf has become a staple of the genre (Bourgault du Coudray 2006: 42–3) and one to which many werewolf films still adhere. However, the new sympathetic werewolf has rendered this both unsophisticated and unoriginal. Unproblematic depictions of monstrosity where the monster is killed create a one-dimensional and conservative version of the Gothic.

The death of the monstrous werewolf is central to another key twenty-first-century film, *Dog Soldiers* (Neil Marshall, 2002). It is set in the highlands of Scotland, where a group of soldiers have been sent on a training exercise. Ultimately, the mission is a cover for attempting to capture a werewolf in order to use it to engineer the ultimate soldier. The trope of animal testing and scientific discourse situates the text within the wider genre of medical Gothic and of twenty-first-century werewolf narratives more broadly. This resonates with the Ecogothic perspective, which often depicts human protagonists and werewolves as equally monstrous. The Scottish setting itself speaks to this, as Scotland was the final place in the British Isles to have wolves. In this narrative, Scotland is depicted as a wilderness inhabited by preternaturally rapacious creatures. *Dog Soldiers* problematises this by suggesting that the English soldiers are invaders, displacing the werewolves and manipulating the (super)natural world for their own pernicious aims.

Perhaps the most successful werewolf franchise is the *Underworld* series. The first film, *Underworld* (Len Wiseman, 2003), features an ancient battle between vampires and Lycans (werewolves). Starring Kate Beckinsdale as the werewolf-hunting vampire, Selene, the films depict the vampires as undead aristocrats and the Lycans as a violent underclass. Visually, the series appeals to Goth(ic) sensibilities. As in other contemporary werewolf narratives, the idea of a genetic trait causing lycanthropy is central, although the bite is still able to transform humans into either creature. The film was followed by a number of sequels, but the prequel, *Underworld: Rise of the Lycans* (Patrick Tatopoulos, 2009), is more noteworthy for its charting of the history of the Lycans' escape from slavery under their vampire overlords. The series' longer narrative arc allows the Lycans to be rescued in terms of their monstrosity. Selene is misled in her view of werewolves and she comes to understand, along with the viewer, that monsters are not born – they are created.

The monstrous Other is depicted in Benjamin Percy's novel *Red Moon* (2013), which imagines an alternate reality in which 'lycans', victims of a blood-borne prion, are a minority group within human society. The Lupine Republic is established, where many lycans, treated with fear and hatred, choose to live, while others take silver-based medication to prevent aggressive outbursts. Set mainly in the US, the narrative follows various terrorist skirmishes which lead to an all-out war. Percy's novel is a post-9/11 political dystopia. Ostensibly, then, the lycans, as in *Underworld*, are introduced as monstrous, but the narrative problematises the reader's understanding of monstrosity. In both narratives, werewolves are violent and aggressive, but this is a reaction to their treatment by humans.

The hunting and destruction of werewolves is central to the plot of both Toby Barlow's *Sharp Teeth* (2008) and Glen Duncan's *The Last Werewolf* series (2011–14). The former, written in free verse, is about packs of werewolves living in Los Angeles. The storyline depicts infighting between packs and the cruel fate of stray dogs, some of whom are werewolves. Through the plight of the homeless, it engages with the flaws of the human world. Isolated from other humans, and constantly threatened with extermination, the werewolves find comfort in creating packs, despite the machinations involved in maintaining a stable hierarchy. Human society is depicted as cruel and violent, no better than the pack dynamics of the werewolves. The treatment of the werewolves at the hands of various hunters and scientists working for the World Organisation for the Control of Occult Phenomena (WOCOP) highlights issues regarding both animal and human rights. It also exemplifies the new focus on the wolf behind the werewolf in response to prevalent debates around the extinction and re-wilding of wolves.

Central to the effectiveness of Duncan's novel is the first-person narrative. The novels are told from the point of view of the monstrous werewolf. It is a tale told by a werewolf, rather than a tale told about a werewolf, an important shift. The reader experiences both Duncan and Talulla's (his lover) delight in killing humans and the extremity of their pain at the hands of sadistic scientists. By allowing the reader to inhabit the position of the monstrous Other, at once human and animal, the werewolf moves from liminality to hybridity. The werewolf is no longer at the boundary of subjectivity but the subject of the narrative. The most brutal scene of violence against Talulla can be read as an allegory for animal testing and human torture without diminishing either. Rather, it shows that the hierarchal structures of power used against both human and animal 'others' parallel one another.

Similarly, the Gothic horror series *Penny Dreadful* (2014–16) draws on human/wolf relations and racialised violence in Western society. Set mainly in Victorian London, the werewolf Ethan Chandler/Ethan Lawrence Talbot (Josh Hartnett) is an American, hiding from his bloody past. His transformations at the full moon lead to many deaths. However, the narrative is sympathetic to Chandler, portraying him as a hunted animal. The series engages intertextually with previous depictions of the werewolf, as evidenced by Chandler's true name, which pays homage to Larry Talbot, the werewolf in *The Wolf Man*. In doing so, it highlights historical representations of the werewolf as a creature which must be killed. But despite his violent nature, the audience is encouraged to react sympathetically to the werewolf. Chandler is haunted by his own persecution of Native Americans; even before he was a werewolf, he already was a killer. Humanity, it appears, is as monstrous as the monsters it fears.

The monstrous werewolf has not entirely disappeared from twenty-first-century Gothic narratives. Rather, the understanding of what is monstrous and what makes an individual monstrous has changed. Contemporary werewolves can threaten humanity, feeding on us, transforming us, invading our cities and towns, yet this does not mean that their death is necessarily desired. Instead, the presumed monstrosity of the werewolf is problematised through narratives that make explicit the role of humanity in the creation of monsters, holding a mirror up to ourselves.

Sympathetic Werewolves

The landscape of twenty-first-century lycanthropic literature and the rise of the sympathetic werewolf have, in large part, been shaped by the success of Young Adult (YA) fiction and paranormal romance. As with the sympathetic vampire, this werewolf is less a fighter than a lover, or at least shows significant remorse about its more violent actions (Crawford 2014: 46–57). This shift began towards the end of the twentieth-century (Frost 2003: 215–17), becoming the defining trend of the early twenty-first century. To facilitate this transformation, many authors allow werewolves to retain their humanity and sense of self; they are increasingly able to transform at will. In an interview about her werewolf series, *The Wolf Gift Chronicles* (2012–13), Anne Rice declared, 'I could make the werewolf theme acceptable [. . .] by dealing with a conscious "man wolf," a man that doesn't lose his self-awareness when he becomes a werewolf' (Riddle 2013). The monstrous loss of identity is replaced with a hybrid experience of being the animal Other in which human and wolf are balanced.

Stephenie Meyer's YA paranormal romance *Twilight* series (2005–8) has played a major part in the redemption of the werewolf. Despite the central male protagonist, Edward Cullen, being a vampire, readers became immersed in the love triangle between Edward, Bella Swan and Jacob Black, a werewolf. Commentators were quick to note that due to issues of race and class – Jacob is a blue-collar Native American in comparison to the starkly white doctor's son Edward – Bella Swan, the female protagonist, was almost predestined to choose Edward (Leggatt and Burnett 2010: 26–46). Jacob's physical transformation from adolescence into adulthood coincides with his burgeoning lycanthropy. This parallel between adolescence and the werewolf state is a common theme; shapeshifters are peculiarly suited to dramatise the transition to adulthood because of their own indeterminate status.

The Gothic has always had a strong link to adolescence. The heroines of early Gothic novels were invariably young girls on the verge of adulthood. Contemporary YA Gothic continues this relationship. For example, Annette Curtis Klause's *Blood & Chocolate* (1997) features a love affair between a werewolf and a teenage human girl (see Franck 2018). Following the release of Meyer's *Twilight* in 2005 and its commercial success, there was an explosion in the publication of YA Gothic (Crawford 2014: 229). Within this field, romances between teenage humans and werewolves are common. In using lycanthropy as a way of exploring the experience of adolescence, these novels foreground the teenager as a liminal entity and always 'other' to the mature phase of adulthood. The adolescent's disgust with changes in his or her own emerging body, from acne to menstruation, is easily mapped onto the shapeshifting werewolf.

Martin Millar's *Kalix MacRinnalch* (2007–13) and Maggie Stiefvater's *Wolves of Mercy Falls* (2009–14) series offer more multifaceted narratives of the teenage werewolf. Millar's novels follow the experience of Kalix, an adopted female werewolf who suffers from anxiety, depression, anorexia and an addiction to laudanum. She moves to London where she is 'adopted' by two humans. Her lycanthropy is not depicted as a simple allegory of puberty; rather, it is used to draw attention to the difficulties and pressures that shape individual identity in general. In comparison, Stiefvater's *Wolves of Mercy Falls* uses a more conventional trajectory of paranormal romance in order to explore the notion of choice in adolescent identity. Grace Brisbane is a human who falls in love with Sam Roth, a werewolf. Together, they find a way for Sam to remain human, allowing them to be together. As Bill Hughes suggests, it is possible to read these novels as a celebration of 'the distinctively human powers of language, of individual identity, and goal-oriented agency as her [Stiefvater's] characters find their voice and define their projects' (2017: 244–5).

As with Stiefvater, many contemporary YA werewolf novels fall within the genre of paranormal romance. Paranormal romances typically have female protagonists, and these may be werewolves, countering the traditional depiction of werewolves as masculine monsters (Priest 2015: 1–23). The newly sympathetic monster also means that female werewolves continue the shift away from the threatening incarnations of female sexuality that Bourgault du Coudray charts (2006: 112–29). Leigh McLennon's analysis of urban fantasy argues that paranormal romances 'challenge the boundaries between self and the monstrous Other when a romantic attraction causes two potential lovers to re-evaluate their identities and philosophies' (2014). Similarly, Roz Kaveney describes this genre as 'to some degree revisionist fantasy' (2012: 220), humanising the monstrous Other.

However, despite the way many of these YA novels attempt to redeem the monstrous Other, criticism has been levelled at their normative aspects. They typically centre on white, middle-class, cisgendered, ablebodied, heterosexual characters. Moreover, the romance elements of paranormal romance have been critiqued for their biological essentialism and sexist ideologies of gender difference. The symbolism of 'Little Red Riding Hood' and its latent sexuality recur in many YA werewolf narratives, potentially reaffirming an idea of masculinity as rapacious and lustful in contrast to the perceived passivity of femininity. Thus, in Jackson Pearce's *Sisters Red* (2010), Scarlett, wearing a red cloak, hunts the Fenris, aggressive werewolves who prey on young women and are always male.

Following the success of the *Twilight* franchise, *Blood & Chocolate* (Katja von Garnier, 2007), an adaptation of Curtis Klause's 1997 novel of the same name, and *Red Riding Hood* (Catherine Hardwicke, 2011) were aimed at a teenage audience and depicted the werewolf as a romantic interest. *Blood & Chocolate* made the male protagonist human and the female protagonist a werewolf. The film moves away from the original narrative, in which the female werewolf is rejected by her human lover, by ending with the promise of a successful relationship. This change acknowledges the influence of twenty-first-century YA and paranormal romance werewolf narratives. A retelling of 'Little Red Riding Hood', Hardwicke's film ends with a male werewolf and female human falling in love. Aesthetically, the film draws on Gothic conventions: it is set in medieval France, in the manner of early nineteenth-century narratives, taking place in a community surrounded by forests. The werewolf emerges from the wooded wilderness but is also one of the human inhabitants, and thus threatens from both the outside (as a wild animal) and the inside (as a member of society). The romance elements of the film compromise the horror, and the love between human and werewolf overcomes species difference.

In the twenty-first century, the televisual werewolf offers empathetic explorations of lycanthropy. Reimagining the werewolf as the protagonist rather than the antagonist reiterates the power of fictional narratives to give subjectivity to the Other. As an embodiment of the animal Other, the repositioning of werewolf characters in twenty-first-century Gothic draws attention to the voiceless animal.

The literary werewolves of YA and paranormal romance have their televisual equivalents; the most successful teenage werewolf show has been *Teen Wolf* (2011–17). Adapting the premise of the film (Rod Daniel, 1985), the TV series follows Scott McCall (Tyler Posey), a teenager who is bitten by a werewolf in the first episode and must come to terms with his new identity with the help of his non-werewolf best friend, Stiles Stilinski (Dylan O'Brien). Scott navigates pack issues, other supernatural characters, werewolf hunters and various romantic entanglements. Central to Scott's characterisation is his lack of violence. He is referred to as a 'true Alpha', an Alpha wolf who is able to become the leader of his pack without shedding blood. Moreover, werewolves are able to learn how to control their transformations so that they are not a threat to humans. Anastassiya Andrianova suggests that the series is more celebratory of the wolf and 'human animality' than previous werewolf narratives (2016: 65–84); it also responds well to the homophobic elements of the original film (Koetsier and Forceville 2014: 50–1).

Paranormal romances for older readers also make much of the sympathetic werewolf. These are often superimposed onto a *noir* detective plotline. In texts such as Kelley Armstrong's *Bitten* (2001) and Patricia Briggs's *Mercy Thompson* series (2006–), the werewolf or shapeshifter narrates in the first person, further enhancing the sympathy with the monster. However, the inclusion of the werewolf in paranormal romances can be read as biologically essentialist. Paranormal romance featuring werewolves typically concentrates on the importance of pack politics and the primal nature of werewolf sexuality (Hughes 2017: 229–30). Werewolf packs in these novels tend to adhere to strict hierarchies in which the male Alpha is the leader and his mate is second in command, and fights for dominance between male and female werewolves are a recurring theme. Thus, the depiction of gender politics in many of these novels often observes both heteronormative and patriarchal models, explaining these behaviours as 'natural' to the werewolf and reinforcing the idea that gender difference is biologically determined.

The changing role of the werewolf has dictated that the term 'shapeshifter' is now more frequently used. This can also connote the transformation into animals other than the wolf. Patricia Briggs's Mercy Thompson is a 'skinwalker' who transforms into a coyote. She has inherited this trait from her Native American ancestors. During the series she becomes involved with her local werewolf pack, and the differences between the two kinds are demarcated accordingly. This differentiation is also used by Charlaine Harris in her *The Southern Vampire Mysteries* book series (2001–13), where 'shapeshifters' can transform into any animal of their choosing, but 'weres' are only able to become one specific animal. Similarly, in the *Twilight* novels, Stephenie Meyer differentiates between shapeshifters and werewolves. In the final novel, *Breaking Dawn* (2008), Aro, the vampire leader of the Volturi, explains that Jacob cannot be a werewolf because he is able to transform at will. This differentiates him from the 'Children of the Moon', and it is implied that Jacob's Quileute Pack are less monstrous. In Leitich Smith's YA novels, there are different types of were-animals which have traits that reflect their real-world animal counterparts. In *Feral Nights* (2013), Clyde the werepossum becomes a werelion under extreme stress. This allows him to step more easily into the role of protagonist, in part due to the more active connotations of lion over possum.

This lexical distinction between werewolves and shapeshifters enables a number of effects. Firstly, renaming the werewolf replaces previous negative depictions of the creature with something more affirmative. Secondly, the influx of other were-animals allows further exploration of ideas of biological essentialism and hierarchy which appear in werewolf fiction. The change in terminology suggests that the rules of lycanthropy have been reimagined, including how one becomes a werewolf. It was not until the twentieth century that the bite became the catalyst. But now, in a number of texts, werewolves can be born as well as created by infection. This change, drawing on evolutionary biology, emphasises the materialist element of contemporary werewolf narratives. It allows werewolves to be natural creatures, knowable by science, rather than mysterious supernatural monsters. It demystifies the werewolf, eliminating, to a certain extent, the unknowable quality of the Other. Similar shifts can be found in the portrayal of werewolves in other media, to which we now turn.

The role of science in demystifying, and sometimes controlling, the werewolf is important in the BBC's *Being Human* (2008–13). The series follows the lives of a vampire, a ghost and a werewolf sharing a flat in Bristol. George Sands (Russell Tovey) must transform into a monstrous werewolf every full moon. George does not adhere to the typical hypermasculine traits of this monster (Bourgault du Coudray 2006: 71–2), however, as he is intelligent, thoughtful and, when in human form, gentle. He attempts to manage his transformation so that he can neither attack nor infect other people. In the first series, his character is contrasted with Tully (Dean Lennox Kelly), a werewolf who delights in his animal nature and portrays himself as an alpha male. The contrast between George and Tully suggests that werewolves' identities are not fixed; they have free choice over their behaviour. Medical intervention is central to the narrative arc. Werewolves are subjected to torturous tests at the hands of scientists as they attempt to control the moon's influence over their transformations. Despite the threatening nature of the werewolf, the viewer is invited to feel sympathy and empathy with their pain as the series is focalised through the monstrous Other.

The CBBC series *Wolfblood* (2012–17) added another dimension to the werewolf. Aimed at a younger audience than *Teen Wolf*, the narrative follows a family of 'wolfbloods', a species who can transform into wolves at will, although they must transform at full moon. The episodes concentrate on the youngest members of the pack as they learn how to secrete themselves and control their behaviour. The wolfbloods are no more dangerous or violent than their human counterparts. Accompanied by online and spin-off information that focuses on the wolf itself, *Wolfblood* reimagines the figure of the werewolf through an Ecogothic lens. The inclusion of such positive traits of the wolf as loyalty and altruism revises pre-twenty-first-century depictions of the werewolf as monster.

The diversity of forms the werewolf adopts speaks to its continued relevance in the twenty-first century. A creature defined by its ability to transform, the newly-humanised werewolf has adapted by presenting new challenges to the threshold between human and animal. This is shown in Ecogothic concerns and in the reappraisal of our relationship with the animal Other. The werewolf is still a Gothic creature but romance has cleaned up its darker counterpart, transforming or ennobling its violent Gothic energies. In its quest for love, the werewolf has found itself increasingly humanised.

Present-day werewolfism is also inextricably bound up with humankind's treatment of wolves. The contemporary myth of Old Stinker, the Werewolf of Hull, illustrates our complex relationship to werewolves in the present, originating as it does, in the Yorkshire Wolds, a landscape which saw some of the last wolves in England (George 2019). It coincides with a phase of severe environmental damage. This has not taken the form of sudden catastrophe, but rather of a slow grinding away of species, particularly the native wolf. The result is a landscape constituted more actively by what is missing than by what is present. This is the climate in which the spectre of the twenty-first-century werewolf has re-emerged (rising from the grave of the flesh and blood wolf).

Wolves have long been represented as the archetypal enemy of human company, preying on the unguarded boundaries of civilisation, threatening the pastoral of ideal sociality and figuring as sexual predators. Yet, in their way, with their complex pack interactions, they have also served as a model for society. Lately, this ancient enemy has been rehabilitated and reappraised, and re-wilding projects have attempted to admit wolves more closely into our lives. Their reintroduction has been seen as a symbolic process of atonement for the sins of the destruction of wild environments and the eradication of species due to human wrongdoing. In the twenty-first century, an era of late capitalism, new werewolf myths have emerged from our cultural memory around humans and wolves. Thus, to cite Kathryn Hughes, 'in our dog-eat-dog world, it's time for werewolves' (2015).

Film and Television

Being Human (BBC Three/BBC HD, 2008–13)
Blood & Chocolate (Katja von Garnier, USA/Germany/Romania/UK, 2007)
Dog Soldiers (Neil Marshall, UK/USA/Luxembourg, 2002)
Ginger Snaps (John Fawcett, Canada, 2000)
Penny Dreadful (Showtime/Sky, 2014–16)
Red Riding Hood (Catherine Hardwicke, Canada, 2011)
Underworld (Len Wiseman, UK/Germany/Hungary, USA, 2003)
Underworld: Rise of the Lycans (Patrick Tatopoulos, USA, 2009)
Wolfblood (CBBC, 2012–17)

References

Andrianova, Anastassiya (2016), 'Teen Drama with a Bite: Human Animality in Teen Wolf', *Supernatural Studies*, 3.1, 65–84.
Asma, Stephen T. (2009), *On Monsters: An Unnatural History of Our Worst Fears*, Oxford: Oxford University Press.
Baring-Gould, Sabine (2007) [1865], *The Book of Werewolves*, Dublin and Chelford: Nonsuch.
Bourgault du Coudray, Chantal (2006), *The Curse of the Werewolf: Fantasy, Horror and the Beast Within*, London: I. B. Tauris.
Crawford, Joseph (2014), *The Twilight of the Gothic: Vampire Fiction and the Rise of the Paranormal Romance*, Cardiff: University of Wales Press.
Crumley, Jim (2010), *The Last Wolf*, Edinburgh: Birlinn.
Douglas, Adam (1992), *The Beast Within: A History of the Werewolf*, London: Chapmans.
Franck, Kaja (2018), 'Growing Pains of the Teenage Werewolf: YA Literature and the Metaphorical Wolf', in Sam George and Bill Hughes (eds), *In the Company of Wolves: Sociality, Animality, and Subjectivity in Narratives of Werewolves, Shapeshifters, and Feral Humans*, Manchester: Manchester University Press (forthcoming 2019).

Frost, Brian (2003), *The Essential Guide to Werewolf Literature*, Wisconsin: The University of Wisconsin Press.

George, Sam (2019), 'Wolves in the Wolds: Late Capitalism, the English Eerie, and the Weird Case of "Old Stinker" the Hull Werewolf', *Gothic Studies*, 21.1 (forthcoming).

Hughes, Bill (2013), '"Legally Recognised Undead": Essence, Difference and Assimilation in Daniel Waters's *Generation Dead*', in Sam George and Bill Hughes (eds), *Open Graves, Open Minds: Representations of Vampires and the Undead from the Enlightenment to the Present Day*, Manchester: Manchester University Press, pp. 245–63.

— (2017), '"But by Blood No Wolf Am I": Language and Agency, Instinct and Essence: Transcending Antinomies in Maggie Stiefvater's *Shiver* Trilogy', in Robert McKay and John Miller (eds), *Werewolves, Wolves and the Gothic*, Cardiff: University of Wales Press, pp. 239–63.

Hughes, Kathryn (2015), 'In our Dog-Eat-Dog World, It's Time for Werewolves', *The Guardian*, 30 August, https://www.theguardian.com/commentisfree/2015/aug/30/werewolves-scarcity-fear-vampires-sexual-anxiety (accessed 17 February 2018).

Hurley, Kelly (2007), 'Abject and Grotesque', in Catherine Spooner and Emma McEvoy (eds), *The Routledge Companion to Gothic*, Abingdon and New York: Routledge, pp. 137–46.

Kaveney, Roz (2012), 'Dark Fantasy and Paranormal Romance', in Edward James and Farah Mendlesohn (eds), *The Cambridge Companion to Fantasy Literature*, Cambridge: Cambridge University Press, pp. 214–24.

Koetsier, Julius, and Charles Forceville (2014), 'Embodied Identity in Werewolf Films of the 1980s', *Image & Narrative*, 15.1, 44–55.

Leggatt, Judith, and Kristin Burnett (2010), 'Biting Bella: Treaty Negotiation, Quileute History, and Why "Team Jacob" Is Doomed to Lose', in Nancy C. Reagin (ed.), *Twilight & History*, Hoboken, NJ: John Wiley & Sons, pp. 26–46.

McKay, Robert, and John Miller (eds) (2017), *Werewolves, Wolves and the Gothic*, Cardiff: University of Wales Press.

McLennon, Leigh (2014), 'Defining Urban Fantasy and Paranormal Romance: Crossing Boundaries of Genre, Media, Self and Other in New Supernatural Worlds', *Refractory: A Journal of Entertainment Media*, 23, http://refractory.unimelb.edu.au/2014/06/26/volume-23/ (accessed 14 January 2018).

Morpurgo, Michael (2002), *The Last Wolf*, London: Doubleday.

Priest, Hannah (ed.) (2015), *She-Wolf: A Cultural History of Female Werewolves*, Manchester: Manchester University Press.

Riddle, Tina (2013), 'Anne Rice Started Her Werewolf Series on a Whim', *Phoenix New Times*, 13 November, http://www.phoenixnewtimes.com/arts/anne-rice-started-her-werewolf-series-on-a-whim-6577867 (accessed 2 January 2018).

Sconduto, Leslie A. (2008), *Metamorphosis of the Werewolf: A Literary Study from Antiquity through the Renaissance*, Jefferson, NC: McFarland.

Spooner, Catherine (2006), *Contemporary Gothic*, London: Reaktion.

Weymouth, Adam (2014), 'Was This the Last Wild Wolf in Britain?', *The Guardian*, 21 July, http://www.theguardian.com/science/animal-magic/2014/jul/21/last-wolf (accessed 3 October 2015).

Part III

Contemporary Subgenres

Chapter 11

The New Weird
Carl H. Sederholm

Narrating a history of the New Weird would be easy were it not for the nagging problem of pinning it down. What started as a means of labelling, let alone understanding, a number of novels and short stories that began to appear in the early years of the twenty-first century quickly shifted into a debate concerning the nature of a new subgenre within speculative literature. From the start, the authors associated with the New Weird emphasised originality through an 'uninhibited commingling of fictional genres' that mostly included elements of fantasy, science fiction, Gothic and horror, but might also freely draw on Westerns, New Wave science fiction, slipstream or steampunk (Harvey 2012: 87). Despite all this variety, the New Weird was never simply about combining genres, but was more interested in transforming them in ways that created something new while also preserving certain key questions fundamental to the weird itself. Xavier Aldana Reyes underscores this idea when he explains that the New Weird is 'a re-imagining of [the weird's] motifs and characters, via transplantation into a more obviously fictitious, more recognizably science fiction or fantastic environment' (2016: 206). One of the clearest signs of this deep change came from the way the New Weird transformed the practice of some weird writers to imitate Lovecraft too closely or to borrow too much from his plots. Instead, the New Weird embraced weird fiction's general tendency to interrogate the human experience of the world and the cosmos and added to them an interest in exploring how human beings perceive the world. In the New Weird, everything – including the experience of reading and understanding – is potentially strange and unknowable.

The New Weird's initial phase is most commonly associated with a handful of texts from the early 2000s, particularly China Miéville's *Perdido Street Station* (2000), Jeff VanderMeer's *City of Saints and Madmen* (2001), K. J. Bishop's *The Etched City* (2003) and Steph Swainston's *The Year of Our War* (2004). Aside from these novels, Ann and Jeff VanderMeer's anthology of short stories and commentary, *The New Weird* (2008), provided an important bookend to this first wave not only by attempting to define the New Weird, but also by expanding its range significantly. In that sense, *The New Weird* performed three major critical functions. Firstly, it introduced readers to even more authors, stories, themes and influences within the New Weird. Secondly, it reflected critically on the New Weird by including essays by scholars and practitioners debating the nature of the New Weird, its name, scope and aims. Thirdly, *The New Weird* stressed the larger philosophical questions central to weird tales of any sort. In that light, Jeff VanderMeer's closing statement in his introduction to the anthology – 'New Weird is dead. Long live the Next Weird' (2008: xviii) – should be read not as the death knell for the movement but as a reminder that, when it comes to the weird, labels matter less than atmosphere and purpose.

New Weird, Weird, Gothic

Much of the initial excitement over New Weird texts comes from their breathtaking range, including the ways they blend various strands of horror, science fiction and fantasy into a hybrid whole. Because of that, there is some risk of misunderstanding any experimental text or any blending of genre as examples of the New Weird. The essential difference between the New Weird and other kinds of genre mixing lies in the way the weird itself is deployed. As Roger Luckhurst describes it, the weird is 'less a genre than a *mode*, far more expansive and supremely difficult to demarcate' (2015: 203). In that light, even if the New Weird is broadly associated with science fiction, horror and fantasy, it maintains its weirdness by staying philosophically connected to questions concerning the nature of the world and the cosmos and whether they are truly knowable. Because the weird does not naturally fit into stable notions of genre, including their familiar tropes and expectations, it can easily serve as a broad means of interrogating those very tropes and expectations. Put another way, the weird makes everything potentially uncanny and mystifying.

Jeff VanderMeer captures this essential difference when he argues that the New Weird takes 'its visionary power' from a knowing 'surrender to the weird', one that expands all imaginative possibilities rather than limiting them to an old house in New England or 'a cave in Antarctica' (VanderMeer 2008: xvi). This development also makes explicit what was long implicit in Lovecraft's work – that the weird questions the ways human beings experience the world to the point of epistemological and ontological rupture. Mark Fisher likewise emphasises this point when he explains that the weird 'involves a sensation of *wrongness*' (2016: 15, italics in the original), a feeling that we need to reconceive our notions of the world and the objects within it.

Although the impulse toward the weird has a long history, one could find an incipient weird tradition in the early to mid-nineteenth century, perhaps most notably in stories by Edgar Allan Poe, Mary Shelley, Washington Irving and others. Later writers commonly connected to the early weird include Ambrose Bierce, Arthur Machen, Lord Dunsany, M. R. James and many others. In its most recognisable form, the weird took shape mostly in the early decades of the twentieth century in the pages of pulp magazines like *Weird Tales* (founded in 1923). These magazines published a wide range of stories from writers interested in exploring new possibilities within the larger speculative tradition. Much of Lovecraft's fiction, including 'The Call of Cthulhu' (1928), originally appeared in *Weird Tales*. Some of the other significant writers associated with the weird in that period include Robert E. Howard, E. Hoffmann Price, Robert Bloch, Robert W. Chambers, C. L. Moore, Seabury Quinn and Clark Ashton Smith.

Theorising about the weird largely began with Lovecraft's *Supernatural Horror in Literature* (1927), a long essay that attempted to establish the weird tale as a distinctive 'literature of cosmic fear' rather than just a loose style that borrowed from the Gothic (1945: 15). For Lovecraft, the weird differed from other genres by going further in the ways it attempted to shake the foundations of experience. In his words,

> [t]he true weird tale must have something more than secret murder, bloody bones, or a sheeted form clanking chains according to rule. A certain atmosphere of breathless and unexplainable dread of outer, unknown forces must be present; and there must be a hint, expressed with a seriousness and portentousness becoming its subject, of that most terrible conception of the human brain – a malign and particular suspension or defeat of those fixed laws of Nature which are our only safeguard against the assaults of chaos and the daemons of unplumbed space. (1945: 15)

For Lovecraft, the emphasis was always on that 'something more', the unstated quality that shifts weird narratives into texts more engaged with questions than answers. At their best, weird tales do not merely frighten readers; they transform feelings of fear and dread into actual concern for one's safety and sanity. An effective weird tale may even leave readers feeling stunned and helpless, unable to process what they know to be real. The point is to turn the world upside down, transforming the ordinary into the inexplicable, leading to an 'undermining of the quotidian' (Miéville 2011: 510) that is as destructive as it is philosophical. Ultimately, weird tales point readers toward fundamental problems of representation and reality. As Graham Harman argues, 'reality itself is weird because reality itself is incommensurable with any attempt to represent or measure it' (2011: 51). This push from fictional worlds to the real world lies at the heart of the weird.

As noted above, Lovecraft believed that the traditional Gothic novel did not have enough power to frighten readers deeply enough to provoke cosmic fear. For example, he described *The Castle of Otranto* (1764) as 'flat, stilted, and altogether devoid of the true cosmic horror which makes real literature' (1945: 25). He was similarly dismissive of texts such as *The Mysteries of Udolpho* (1794), *The Monk* (1796) and *Melmoth the Wanderer* (1820), even though he acknowledged that each of them expanded the possibilities of both the Gothic and the weird. Although few critics would deny the connections between these two styles, they tend to emphasise the distinctions between them. As Ann and Jeff VanderMeer suggest, the weird tale 'is a story that has a supernatural element but does not fall into the category of traditional ghost story or Gothic tale' (2011: xv). That is largely true, but in Lovecraft's mind, the main difference was that the Gothic lacked the power to sustain the right levels of dread to generate true cosmic horror. For him, it simply lacked those additional narrative qualities or speculative elements that brought readers to the point of doubting their place in the universe (1945: 15). In this light, the Gothic could only send shivers down the spine but the weird could burrow directly – and permanently – into the mind.

Despite Lovecraft's interest in distinguishing the weird from the Gothic, he also clearly understood how much the two had in common. He dedicated three chapters of *Supernatural Horror in Literature* to the rise, fall and aftermath of the Gothic novel and he acknowledged that 'the typical weird tale of standard literature is a child of the eighteenth century' precisely because of those Gothic influences (1945: 21). In the broadest sense, both styles share an interest in overwhelming audiences with situations culled from the religious to the psychological to the frenzied. They also both represent an ongoing effort to understand the ways past actions challenge present hopes, the impact of hidden secrets and the possibility of facing supernatural or monstrous foes.

Rather than simply list what the Gothic and the weird have in common, it is more useful to see them broadly as variations on common themes rather than as sharp points of contrast. Jeffrey Andrew Weinstock articulates this idea best when he writes, '[t]he weird tale for Lovecraft is a late nineteenth-century development coming out of the earlier Gothic novel; but in place of the familiar trappings of the Gothic' the weird provides its own conventions instead (2016: 182). Similarly, both the Gothic and the weird thrive on themes of excess and transgression. Following Fred Botting's description of the Gothic, both styles could be described as a 'writing of excess', the sort that 'signified an overabundance of imaginative frenzy, untamed by reason and unrestrained by conventional eighteenth-century demands for simplicity, realism or probability' (Botting 1996: 1, 3). The Gothic and the weird interrogate the world in ways that powerfully demonstrate human limitations both in terms of understanding our place in the world and also how we perceive reality in the first place. Even though the New Weird is commonly associated with science fiction, fantasy and horror, the broad ties between the Gothic and the weird remain significant.

At the turn of the twenty-first century, the New Weird made its initial appearance. The most representative works of that period include China Miéville's *Perdido Street Station* (2000), Caitlín Kiernan's *Threshold* (2001), Jeff VanderMeer's *City of Saints and Madmen* (2002) and K. J. Bishop's *The Etched City* (2003). Together, these novels demonstrated how the New Weird could build dense and epic worlds, suggest new thematic possibilities and creatively partner with other genres. They also demonstrated the ways the New Weird could interrogate literary conventions by showing just how strange and unknowable everything really is. Whether or not the 'New Weird' label ultimately proves helpful, it nevertheless signifies a moment when multiple authors independently reinvigorated speculative fiction by exploring just how much it could shed light on the problems associated with things as fundamental as reading, writing, perception, time and setting. Collectively, these novels also demonstrate Michael Cisco's point that the New Weird never operates from a fixed set of instructions, but that it represents 'a great proliferation of correspondences on a more intimate level, like a sprawling coincidence of idiosyncratic choices' (2008: 335). In what follows, I discuss in more detail these four texts in order to highlight the reasons why they serve as essential starting points for approaching the New Weird.

New Weird Fiction

China Miéville's *Perdido Street Station* is widely considered to be the standard-bearer for the New Weird, partly because of Miéville's impressively epic scale and partly because it was so commercially successful. *Perdido Street Station* did not create the New Weird – no single work did that – but it certainly marked an important 'flash point' in its development by joining explicitly progressive politics with a wide range of novelistic techniques based on writers as diverse as Charles Dickens, Clive Barker, M. John Harrison, Mervyn Peake and others (VanderMeer 2008: xi). Miéville's own ambitious storytelling and rich prose style likewise demonstrated a considerable talent for building worlds and creating characters that are simultaneously alien and yet remarkably familiar. Similarly, New Crobuzon, the sprawling city at the heart of the novel, blends the seedier side of Victorian-era London with contemporary world conditions in ways that give the novel's politics an extra sense of urgency and intrigue. *Perdido Street Station* is not a perfect novel – it sometimes struggles to bring its various strands together – but it nevertheless expanded the possibilities of New Weird expression to give readers something concrete to associate with this new genre. Scholarly commentary on *Perdido Street Station* likewise focuses on its connections to the New Weird, but it also examines the author's socialist politics, his hybrid approaches to genre and his impact on weird fiction generally.

As a representative New Weird text, *Perdido Street Station* should be read as a brash exploration of the aesthetic possibilities connected to hybridity, transition and the grotesque. Such interests are essential to the New Weird because they underscore the central premise that language cannot represent reality adequately; at its best, language may allude to, but never capture, reality (Harman 2011: 51). Miéville develops this theme primarily by taking readers directly into the strange and uncanny streets of New Crobuzon, a city so alive and so heterogeneous that it has no sense of stasis or stability. If some cities never sleep, New Crobuzon cannot even rest for all its shifting and pulsing energies. Miéville captures this side of it in a long sentence filled with multiple prepositional phrases that reflect the city's restlessness:

> New Crobuzon's architecture moves from the industrial to the residential to the opulent to the slum to the underground to the airborne to the modern to the ancient to the colourful to the drab to the fecund to the barren. (Miéville 2000: 41)

The point is not simply that the city has endless variety, but that it moves from one thing to another with the kind of breathlessness and range suggested by Miéville's language. Because New Crobuzon cannot be contained or described adequately, it mirrors weird fiction.

If New Crobuzon should be read as a life force, one that is best described as a 'constantly shifting, highly adaptive, heterogeneous topos' (Gordon 2003: 46), its inhabitants are no less unusual and overwhelming. The novel introduces several key characters, including Isaac Dan der Grimnebulin, a human scientist obsessed with 'crisis energy'; Lin, a Khepri woman (the Khepri have human bodies and scarab beetle heads) who is also a rebellious sculptor and Isaac's lover; and the Remade, once recognisable beings who were forcibly modified into grotesque shapes or forms in consequence of breaking the law or otherwise challenging authority (Miéville 2000: 9, 170). The Remade, grotesque and terrible, underscore this novel's consistent interest in hybridity and change, not to mention the ways human beings regularly exploit and abuse one another. And then there is Mr Motley, the heavily Remade gangster who embodies so many different shapes, sizes, forms and qualities at once that he cannot be described with any accuracy. His body, like New Crobuzon itself, is never stable; instead, it constantly transitions from the hybrid to the uncanny. As Motley explains, such points of transition are essential to understanding the world from his perspective: '[t]ransition. The point where one thing becomes another. It is what makes you, the city, the world, what they are' (41). This interest in constant change and fluctuation – Miéville calls it the 'hybrid zone' (41) – suggests *Perdido Street Station*'s larger creative attempt to imagine something truly impossible to describe or understand but that is nevertheless real.

Attempts to represent Motley's form artistically actually play a significant role in the novel because Motley commissions Lin to make a sculpture of his 'lunatic anatomy' (77). Lin initially feels overwhelmed by the prospect of having to capture Motley's body in a relatively static sculpture. How would she 'impose order on his chaos' (109)? She begins by focusing on one detail at a time, telling herself that

> it felt absurdly prosaic to *count* the razor-sharp shards of chitin that jutted from a scrap of pachyderm skin, just to make sure she had not missed one in her sculpture. It felt almost vulgar, as if his anarchic form should defy accounting. And yet, as soon as she looked at him with such an eye, the work of sculpture took shape. (109, italics in the original)

Like any other artist of the weird, Lin understands that she cannot capture the real completely. Instead, she decides to mark each point of transition, places where the impossible skin meets unlikely muscle. In doing so, she can gesture toward the real by suggesting how things join together and to what extent they demonstrate a larger reality.

Jeff VanderMeer's *City of Saints and Madmen: The Book of Ambergris* introduces readers to Ambergris, another expansive and filthy New Weird topos that helps to underscore the generally unknowable conditions of our world. *City of Saints and Madmen* is less a novel than a collection of related stories, all of which demonstrate the inherent tensions and complexities within that strange city, its history and inhabitants. To make it even stranger, VanderMeer regularly focuses on kinds of life other than human, including the noticed, but often ignored, 'lichen, creepers, and mushroom dwellers' that are also a major part of the city (2002: 27).

Because *City of Saints and Madmen* brings multiple components together, literally and thematically, it may be described as a weird archive, one that constantly brings to mind the tensions that occur when narratives clash and when past and present meet and vie for primacy. Since VanderMeer's text also draws on multiple genres and discourses – including elements of history, fantasy, scientific writing, psychological interviews, personal letters, illustrations and folklore – it also suggests just how complex even the most seemingly simple stories truly are. In *City of Saints and Madmen,* stories of every kind are more likely based on faulty perceptions and on human ego than on anything resembling real truth. This is one of the reasons why VanderMeer pays so much attention to those mysterious mushroom dwellers within Ambergris. Their presence serves as an ongoing reminder that even the most thriving civilisations are founded on attempts to repress other cultures.

City of Saints and Madmen questions fundamental notions of perception and writing. It explores the ways human beings understand reality and how words never quite overcome human subjectivity. For example, the title character in 'Dradin, In Love' discovers that a woman he has observed (and loved) only from a distance is actually a mannequin. And yet, he refuses to give up his feelings by reasoning that 'it did not matter that she was in pieces, that she was not real, for he could see now that she was his salvation' (VanderMeer 2002: 97). Fantasy may overwhelm reality, thereby allowing a mannequin to appear as an ideal partner. In fact, Dradin prefers his imaginative powers because 'he had invented an entire history for this woman and now his expectations of her would never change and she would never age, never criticise him, never tell him he was too fat or too sloppy or too neat' (97). Accepting this fantasy, Dradin takes the mannequin's head and tries to steal away from the world, all the while knowing that even if he gets as 'as far as he might wish', it will always be 'perhaps not far enough' (99).

Likewise, in 'The Strange Case of X' – and one of its companion pieces, 'A Note from Dr. V to Dr. Simpkin' – VanderMeer explores the problem of words and reality through the story of a writer (known only as 'X') who begins to find himself lost in Ambergris, a city he believes only exists in his imagination. Has he lost his mind or is there something unusual happening to him? 'X' faces an ongoing dilemma: how does a writer live with 'two separate versions of reality', one of which is constantly in his head while the other is (presumably) all around him (297)? VanderMeer captures this problem nicely when he wonders how a writer may successfully 'question the validity of his world' when he only has 'his senses to describe it' (297)? Human perception clouds proper understanding and makes it impossible to know what lies beyond the self. In 'A Note from Dr. V to Dr. Simpkin', VanderMeer addresses the problem further by revealing that 'X' actually wrote in numbers and that his work has to be decrypted by Dr V. This process, however, raises new challenges as V finds himself terrified by the possibility that 'the book had changed and was now writing me' (n.p.). Contrary to V's denial that 'words on a page can affect reality', he must now face the possibility that he is wrong and that his so-called 'affliction' is actually a case of an active imagination (n.p.). By leaving the problems of 'X' and 'V' unresolved, *City of Saints and Madmen* broadly suggests that we cannot experience reality directly. The only way to navigate our way through present complexities is to surrender to the weird.

On the surface, K. J. Bishop's *The Etched City* might seem like an outlier in this discussion because some may see it as a Western rather than a New Weird text. However, readers quickly discover that, despite the novel's initial interest in the bleak desert – and the outlaws connected to it – there is something more complex at stake. Jonathan Harvey describes the novel in terms of the ways it transforms the Western into something very unusual. In his words, *The Etched City* 'make[s] the Western *weird*, not comfortable, by transplanting it from its original region and adding elements of the supernatural and alien' (2012: 93, italics in the original). Like other New Weird texts, *The Etched City* shifts the novel away from convention and into spaces where those very conventions may be interrogated deeply.

Like *Perdido Street Station* and *City of Saints and Madmen*, *The Etched City* introduces readers to a fascinating new city – Ashamoil – that is as complex, vibrant and dirty as New Crobuzon or Ambergris. The novel likewise weaves together multiple genres and styles – including Westerns, urban fantasy and medieval romance – into a tale that comments on the nature of art and storytelling, life and death, faith and doubt. As Harvey also points out, the novel is ultimately an extended meditation on the ways its two different settings, 'the Western desert and the New Weird city', impact on the main characters in ways that transform them forever (94).

At the centre of *The Etched City* are two intersecting characters. One of them is Raule, a physician fascinated by the ephemeral line between life and death and by her expansive collection of biological prodigies, creatures with mismatched bodies and heads that throw all known systems of understanding into question. The other character is Raule's sometime companion, Gwynn, a gangster, gunslinger and – ultimately – an 'eccentric' or 'calamitous' person who 'tears the curtain between life and death' (Bishop 2003: 367). Central to Gwynn's progress is Beth Constanzin, his lover who is also an artist of the unnatural and the prodigious. When Gwynn sees her work for the first time, he immediately recognises it as something well beyond convention: '[a]ll the actors in these baroque fairylands were prodigies: not legendary creatures, these ones, but beings straight – or crookedly – out of private hallucination' (156). For Beth, art makes real certain forms of power and perception thought to be lost. As she puts it, 'art is the conscious making of numinous phenomena' (297), objects teeming with such life and possibility that they infuse the world with power. Because most human beings overlook this power, there is an ongoing 'quelling of the numinous, an ashening of the fire of life' (297) that transforms art either into empty gestures or simple tributes to ancient possibilities. If people are to understand art's true purpose, they must rediscover the numinous. Beth's solution is both to create extraordinary works of art and to discover ways she can become 'strange' (298). As she explains to Gwynn, 'Only by being strange can we move forward, for strange acts cause us to be rejected by whatever normality we have offended, and to be propelled towards a normality that can never accommodate us' (298). By pressing beyond normality, artists ultimately transcend human limitation. In Gwynn's own climactic journey from the mortal to the strange to the 'calamitous' (367), he recalls Beth's paean to strangeness and transforms into something more than human. Gwynn sees the world without constraint, even to the point of wondering 'where, when, how, and who was he' (367).

The Etched City is also an extended reflection on the withering power of time, particularly the way it reduces cities to ruins and human beings to corpses. From the beginning, time is a constant source of 'decrepitude' that works against everything: art, medicine, religion and gun slinging (Harvey 2003: 3). But if time leads everything towards death and decay, it also transforms human events into stories and stories into legends – or even into outright lies. Gwynn's exploits multiply so much they are described as 'a monkey with many tails' (Bishop 2003: 380), stories that can no longer be verified, tracked or classified. *The Etched City* offers little consolation against this power and yet it also suggests that one may learn how to read time in puzzling ways through its twists, turns and deceptions.

Learning how to read time is also a major theme in Caitlín Kiernan's *Threshold: A Novel of Deep Time*. Kiernan, a long-term admirer of H. P. Lovecraft, is particularly influenced by his interest in deep time, suggesting that it is 'critical to [Lovecraft's] cosmicism, the existential shock a reader brings away from his stories. Our smallness and insignificance in the universe at large. In all *possible* universes. Within the concept of infinity' (VanderMeer 2012: n. p.). Kiernan also shares Lovecraft's interest in human insignificance, something that comes through in *Threshold*'s fascination with 'time, and what people find when they start looking in time' (Kiernan 2001: 232).

In *Threshold*, time shifts and bends, suggesting that human notions of linear time are not only wrong, but naive. The novel also points to the ways in which events in one reality impact events in others. In particular, Kiernan draws on Algernon Blackwood's 'The Willows' (1907), particularly its suggestion of a strange mental or physical connection between human beings and some uncanny entities to suggest a similar kinship between her characters and the creatures lurking just below the surface in *Threshold*. Kiernan is especially fond of Blackwood's line 'our thoughts make spirals in their world' (Blackwood 2002: 53) because of its suggestion of an unexpected impact between worlds and beings. Actions create equal and opposite reactions, but in weird fiction these reactions often take place in different times, places and circumstances. *Threshold*'s plot similarly twists and turns as the main characters struggle to understand a scientifically impossible fossilised trilobite and how it challenges conventional notions of prehistory and time. Chance Matthews, the novel's protagonist, compares her paleontological studies to 'learning to *read* [. . .] and not just the handful of things men have been around long enough to write down. The history of the whole damned *planet* is written in rocks, just lying there waiting for us to learn how to read the words' (Kiernan 2001: 147, italics in original). In his own study of fossils, W. J. T. Mitchell suggests that 'when new objects [like fossils] appear in the world, they also bring with them new orders of temporality, new dialectical images that interfere with and complicate each other' (2001: 183). For Chance, reading fossils brings to light a similar set of new problems, none of which requires mastering the difference between signifier and signified. Unlike written language, fossils represent non-human records, traces of a past that do not speak for themselves. Learning to read a fossil requires learning 'how to read *time*' (147, italics in original). This process is not only difficult, it also risks undermining scientific understanding in general. In *Threshold*, this means crossing seemingly impossible barriers and 'reaching back across epochs' (247).

Chance eventually learns that the trilobite signifies realities beyond human knowledge. As Chance draws closer to her own limits, she discovers that there is no accurate human language for representing her current experience: '[a] thousand metaphors and she'd never come any closer, a seeping place where two worlds meet, where all worlds and all times meet, black hole, white hole, a *crossroads* and that's as good a way as any other of looking at it' (246, italics in the original). Entering this liminal space, Chance experiences time from every perspective at the same time: 'she stands someplace, sometime, everywhere and nowhere' (250). In that state, she encounters a mysterious 'tall man' who tells her, '[t]ime is your cathedral. You *know* the present is only a pretty illusion in the minds of men. And I think you know that nothing has ever passed away, not entirely' (251, italics in original). In this moment, Chance learns to read time in ways that make it bend, twist or change (250). But she is no fantasy hero; instead of saving the world she only gets a glimpse into how her own reality may be altered. In the end, she must learn to act in a world where everything has changed but very few people seem to have actually noticed. In weird fiction, strange new insights always come to those who are most open to them. The rest of the world simply continues going about its business.

Each of the four texts covered above helps illustrate the ways in which the New Weird takes up the problems of artistically representing the world and expands them into new settings and circumstances. It should be clear from this what the New Weirdists have borrowed from the Gothic, but also where they have gone beyond it. Even if the New Weirdists leave aside the specific style, settings and creatures directly associated with Lovecraft's fiction, they nevertheless hold fast to his fundamentally strange and overwhelming questions. Whether the works of the New Weird represent just another phase in weird expression, or something essential in their own right, they nevertheless represent a key literary post-millennial moment in which several like-minded writers experimented with fictional possibilities that reinvigorated the weird and its power to suggest just how strange and unknowable the world that surrounds us is. At its best, the New Weird is also a reminder that the weird's reach must always exceed its grasp; otherwise it could not attempt to expand our knowledge of the cosmos or challenge our perception and portrayal of the real.

References

Aldana Reyes, Xavier (2016), 'Post-Millennial Horror, 2000–16', in Xavier Aldana Reyes (ed.), *Horror: A Literary History*, London: British Library, pp. 189–214.
Bishop, K. J. (2003), *The Etched City*, New York: Bantam.

Blackwood, Algernon (2002), 'The Willows', in S. T. Joshi (ed.), *Ancient Sorceries and Other Strange Tales*, New York: Penguin, pp. 17–62.
Botting, Fred (1996), *Gothic*, New York: Routledge.
Cisco, Michael (2008), '"New Weird": I Think We're the Scene', in Ann VanderMeer and Jeff VanderMeer (eds), *The New Weird*, San Francisco: Tachyon, pp. 333–6.
Fisher, Mark (2016), *The Weird and the Eerie*, London: Repeater.
Gordon, Joan (2003) 'Hybridity, Heterotopia, and Mateship in China Miéville's *Perdido Street Station*', *Science Fiction Studies*, 30.3, 456–76.
Harman, Graham (2011), *Weird Realism: Lovecraft and Philosophy*, Alresford: Zero Books.
Harvey, Jonathan (2012), 'The Wild West and the New Weird in K. J. Bishop's *The Etched City* and China Miéville's *Iron Council*', *Contemporary Literature*, 53.1, 87–113.
Kiernan, Caitlín (2001), *Threshold: A Novel of Deep Time*, New York: ROC.
Lovecraft, H. P. (1945), *Supernatural Horror in Literature*, New York: Ben Abramson.
Luckhurst, Roger (2015), 'American Weird', in Eric Carl Link and Gerry Canavan (eds), *The Cambridge Companion to American Science Fiction*, New York: Cambridge University Press, pp. 194–205.
Miéville, China (2000), *Perdido Street Station*, New York: Ballantine.
— (2011), 'Weird Fiction', in Mark Bould, Andrew M. Butler, Adam Roberts and Sherryl Vint (eds), *The Routledge Companion to Science Fiction*, New York: Routledge, pp. 510–15.
Mitchell, W. J. T. (2001), 'Romanticism and the Life of Things: Fossils, Totems, and Images', *Critical Inquiry*, 28.1, 167–84.
VanderMeer, Ann, and Jeff VanderMeer (2011), 'Introduction', in Ann VanderMeer and Jeff VanderMeer (eds), *The Weird: A Compendium of Strange and Dark Stories*, New York: Tor, pp. xv–xx.
VanderMeer, Jeff (2002), *City of Saints and Madmen*, New York: Bantam.
— (2008), 'The New Weird: "It's Alive?"', in Ann VanderMeer and Jeff VanderMeer (eds), *The New Weird*, San Francisco: Tachyon, pp. ix–xviii.
— (2012), 'Interview: Caitlín Kiernan on Weird Fiction', *Weird Fiction Review*, 12 March, http://weirdfictionreview.com/2012/03/interview-caitlin-r-kiernan-on-weird-fiction/ (accessed 17 November 2017).
Weinstock, Jeffrey Andrew (2016), 'The New Weird', in Ken Gelder (ed.), *New Directions in Popular Fiction: Genre, Distribution, Reproduction*, New York: Palgrave, pp. 177–99.

Chapter 12

Ecogothic
Sharae Deckard

New approaches to the 'greening' of Gothic explore how Ecogothic represents cultural anxieties about the human relationship to the non-human world through uncanny apparitions of monstrous nature. Literary Ecogothic constitutes nature as 'a space of crisis which conceptually creates a point of contact with the ecological', thus mediating fears surrounding climate crisis and environmental damage (Smith and Hughes 2013: 3). If Gothic often turns around a 'return of the repressed' that reveals buried social truths, Ecogothic turns around the uncanny manifestation of the 'environmental unconscious', particularly those forms of environmental violence that have been occulted. Whether this revelation is a cause for fear or for triumph is a question of the politics of the text.

Ecogothic aesthetics can express *ecophobia*, Simon Estok's term for the 'contempt and fear we feel for the agency of the natural environment' (2009: 207). Ecophobic narratives are suffused with loathing, fear, disgust and horror, often attributing a capacity for retribution to a vengeful Nature, personified as malevolent antagonist. These tales turn on a 'nearly ubiquitous cultural fascination with the hostile and deadly aspects of the otherwise nurturing image of "Mother Nature"', commingled with resentment at this perceived betrayal of the maternal (Hillard 2009: 688). If Gothic is characterised by excess, in Ecogothic environments are themselves excessive, sites of monstrous fecundity that threaten human civilisation, where vines and vegetation run rampant, or where plagues and vermin spread deliriums. In many narratives, the natural immanence of death and decay is a source of terror – corporeality or mortality as embedded in the external environment or in the human body itself – in others, nature itself becomes a character, often incarnated in spirit form.

However, Ecogothic can also be critical or subversive, expressing critique of the domination of nature in late capitalism, criticising dualist myths that separate notions of the human from nature rather than embracing humanity-in-nature, or summoning spectres of past ecological disasters in order to explore the complex causality of compound catastrophes. Ecogothic revenants offer a powerful method of conjoining short and long *durées*, in which environmental histories and geophysical forces outside the capacity for memory of individual human protagonists manifest as apparitions that disturb the present (Deckard 2015: 288). In so doing, Ecogothic narratives often rely on 'a momentary derangement of the perceptual apparatus' during which 'characters struggle to adjust their perceptions of sensory experience against the rational structures that sustain their world view' (Sage 2003: 176). Such perceptual shifts enable *telesthesia* – the extension of perception beyond the normal range of the empirical senses to apprehend other situations in time and space. Telesthesia can telescope multiple temporalities, capturing the way in which different moments of socio-ecological crisis over long historical periods are over-layered on fractured environments. The spatial dispersion of the senses can also figure the radical alterity of non-human nature, as in Swamp Thing's rhizomatic perception of all the forms of life across the Louisiana wetlands in Alan Moore's landmark of Ecogothic graphic narrative, *Saga of the Swamp Thing* (issues #20–6, 1984), when his human consciousness 'leak[s] away down the shoots and streams, dissipating, trickling out into the swamps' (Moore 2012: 72).[1]

The social relations Ecogothic embeds in its form must be understood as 'socio-ecological': representing the organisation of the whole range of human and non-human relations within any given environment. As Kerstin Oloff has argued, Ecogothic from postcolonial societies 'has long pointed towards the need to re-conceptualise the relation between humans and their environment as central to the project of decolonization', foregrounding the 'dialectical relation of racial/human and natural alterity' in Ecogothic, where ecocritical concerns are not merely 'added on' to the 'Gothic mode's well-documented entanglement in discourses on race, class and gender, but [are rather . . .] mutually constitutive' (Oloff 2012: 21–32). Reading ambivalent depictions of nature in 'global Ecogothic' from cultural traditions outside of Euro-America can help reveal how socio-ecological relations are inextricably bound up with hierarchies of race, class, gender and ideas of natural alterity, but also how the cultural experiences of environmental catastrophe in other nations intersect with wider geopolitical contexts such as imperialism (Deckard 2013: 177). This chapter will compare contemporary examples of 'resource gothic' fictions that figure the socio-ecological violence of extractivism, plantation and ecological imperialism in postcolonial nations, including the sugar Gothic of Roger McTair's 'Just a Lark (or the Crypt of Matthew Ashdown)' (2000), set in Jamaica, the oil Gothic of Helon Habila's *Oil on Water* (2010), set in Nigeria, and the toxic nuclear Gothic of Robert Barclay's *Meḽaḽ* (2003), set in the Marshall Islands. It will also address the prominence of Ecogothic aesthetics in contemporary television and video games by exploring the oil and sugar imaginary of the first season of HBO television series *True Detective* (2014) and the nuclear magnetism of Bethesda Game Studios' *Fallout 4: Far Harbor DLC* (2016).

Plantation Gothic

Caribbean Ecogothic teems with monsters, spirits and creatures such as the *duppy* (ghost), the *zombi*, the *lagahoo* (shapeshifter) and the *soucouyant* (fire-hag: a vampiric woman who transforms into a flying ball of fire and sucks blood). These figures emerge from syncretic folklore and African-derived belief systems such as Haitian *vodou*, Jamaican *obeah* and Cuban *Santeria*, and are explicitly linked to the slave trade and to postcolonial identities fraught with doubled consciousness, as Alison Rudd has argued in her account of 'postcolonial Gothic' (2010). However, they are also ecological figures that express multivalent understandings of Caribbean nature. When ecophobic, they often figure the imperialist imaginary of the environment's supposed malevolence as a threat to colonial order and the regimented organisation of the plantation system. When subversive, they imagine non-human nature as an ally to the insurgency of the oppressed, and express animist beliefs of the environment as charged with the consciousness of spirits and ancestors. These latter tales often write back to earlier significations of Gothic nature, reversing the valence of green monsters in order to embrace their capacity for transgression, or to attribute terror to the unjust operations of power.

Roger McTair's short story 'Just a Lark' is a powerful example of the contemporary use of Ecogothic to criticise ecological imperialism – the domination of both humans and non-human nature within Caribbean plantation society – and to represent the capacity for political insurrection. McTair's story is couched within a frame narrative, presented by a nameless historian as a found manuscript from twentieth-century Jamaica. In a knowing nod to nineteenth-century Gothic imaginaries of the racialised political unconscious of plantation societies, the frame narrator addresses a third expert known for his 'more than a serious interest in the sources of men like Poe, Lovecraft, and Stoker', asking if the enclosed manuscript registers 'one of those junctures where history meets with the monstrous' (McTair 2000: 53).

The use of the monstrous to figure repressed histories can be read in all three authors. Poe's macabre writings have been interpreted as registering racialised fears of slave insurrection and the threat to the plantation economy of the nineteenth-century American South, but they are also markedly ecophobic; Tom Hillard, for instance, reads Poe's 'The Raven' as an example of an unsettling encounter with the alterity of non-human animal intelligence that sets the human narrator 'deep into that darkness peering' (2009: 685). Similarly, Stoker's vampires mediate fears around female sexuality, class degeneracy and external racial threats to British imperial supremacy, particularly anxieties about the power of the Anglo-Irish ascendancy in Ireland's plantation economy, but they also evoke Ecogothic fears of a predatory nature opposed to bourgeois social order through the Count's monstrous transformations into wolves and bats. The Afro-Caribbean writer Eric Walrond's 'The Vampire Bat' (1926) recalibrates Stoker's racialised figure of the vampire to embrace a black baby that shapeshifts into a vampire bat as an exultant symbol of revenge against the colonial *buckra* (white master), who is drained dry. In Walrond's story, Ecogothic nature crystallises around the chronotope of the sugar cane field as a landscape fraught with terror and haunted by spirits. After the cane is set on fire by protesting field hands, it is overshot with a series of hallucinatory visions focalised through the perception of the white protagonist. 'Barbaric *obeah* images' fill 'his buckra consciousness' (Walrond 2013: 156, italics in original) of 'sugar canes burning – men in the canes – fire hags – nigger corpses –' (156) and 'a river red as burning copper' (156). The infernal glow of the burning cane signifies the white master's fears of the colonised labourers and their increasing demands for independence, but also subversively imagines the land as animated by the blood and spirits of slaves and insurgents past.

Similarly, in McTair's brilliantly parodic story, the ecophobic aesthetics of Lovecraft's tales are subversively reconfigured to represent plantations in the West Indies and their relation to the wider Atlantic economy. Caribbean ecologies were subjected to ecocide in the course of converting them into plantations – deforesting entire islands and eradicating native flora and fauna in order to specialise in cash crop monocultures, exhausting soil fertility and draining watersheds to produce input-intensive crops such as sugar and deploying forms of unfree labour such as slavery and indenture. As such, plantations were violent in both environmental and human terms, culminating in mass extinctions of species and centuries of social oppression. Due to this particular intensity of violence, Michael Niblett argues that literary texts which represent sugar plantation are more likely to deploy an Ecogothic aesthetics which he calls 'saccharine-irrealism' (2015: 268). As a subgenre of plantation Gothic, sugar Gothic frequently personifies 'King Sugar' as an autonomous agent and represents plantation ecologies as sensuously tangible yet seemingly unreal, saturated both with the commodity-fetishism of an export monoculture and with the supernatural residues of past brutality.

McTair's sugar Gothic, like Walrond's, turns around plantation violence. At the story's climax, a group of young white men in post-Second World War Jamaica, the rich descendants of British sugar planters, recite aloud a necromantic acronym from the *Necronomicon* – an occult text recurrent in the plots of H. P. Lovecraft's stories – in an attempt to resurrect the corrupt body of despotic plantocrat Matthew Ashdown, exclaiming '[t]he form would evoke any number of unreal or not-real situations' (McTair 2000: 70). Roger Luckhurst has argued that Lovecraft's peculiar style is intended to evoke the seemingly unreal reality of what Lovecraft called '"*supplements* rather than *contradictions* of the visible and mensurable universe." Horror erupts from the edges of the known frontier or else slithers from the recesses of the body' (Luckhurst 2013: xiv–xv, italics in original). The formal correlation between weird style and the horrific revelation of a repressed or hitherto unimaginable reality – whether historical past or cosmic totality – is a crucial element for Lovecraft's more progressive successors like McTair, who deploys Ecogothic aesthetics to rectify historical amnesias around the frontier violence of colonialism in plantation isles.

While the frame narrative is set in the present, the story's body is retrospective, looking back on the post-war period in Jamaica from the perspective of a narrator who left the island in 1962. This is described as a period of political quiescence following labour unrest. The island's elites cling to Churchill's promises to not 'preside over the dissolution of the British Empire', waiting for the island to return to the 'placidity of the early thirties' (McTair 2000: 55). Part of a coterie of decadent youth who live off the profits of their families' estates, the depoliticised narrator is drawn into a 'cryptic picnic' organised by Eddie Shears, an amateur practitioner of the occult, who is nostalgic for the plantocracy.

Travelling out of Kingston to a peasant village to consult with an *obeah* man about the dangers of performing the resurrection spell, the narrator receives an uncanny lesson from Teacha Paul in the island's environmental history:

> The sea not touch a shore on which there is no dead. The sun shine on no tree on which rope or gibbet not hang. No field, no gully without a bed of bones. Evil and vile; evil Eyre, evil Ashdown; evil Milner, evil Niembhard, evil Jonas,

evil Edward, evil Riland [. . .] To my horror I recognized many of the names of prominent families on the island. (McTair 2000: 66)

The landscape of Morant Bay subsequently assumes an ecophobic aspect that voices the narrator's repressed knowledge of the horrific reign of King Sugar that has saturated the earth with the blood of slaves, lynched planters and executed revolutionaries. A 'clammy unhealthy' heat and 'viscous humidity' oppresses his party, the 'vegetation seems stricken', mosquitoes 'eat' them, the country roads are 'dense, bleak and rare of humanity', trees slash their faces and draw blood, and the cottonwood tree – in whose roots duppys reside – gives off 'agonizing wrenching' sounds (60). Parodying common tropes of imperial Tropical Gothic, this wounded and wounding landscape bears witness to the ecological exhaustion of the land and the parasitic exploitation of human labour concomitant with plantation.

When Ashdown's undead corpse is summoned up out of the 'necrophagous abyss' (78), the passage explicitly reconfigures Lovecraft's 'The Call of Cthulhu' (1928), in which a monstrous horror escapes its 'aeon-long imprisonment' on 'flapping membranous wings' (Lovecraft 2013: 49):

> Cries and shrieks reverberated in the air. Somewhere in the treetops I could hear frantic fluttering, as if some large winged thing's passage had been disturbed. The vile effluent of the tomb rolled up and out in the graveyard. It hung over the silk cotton tree and climbed and caressed its trunk. I swear I heard that tree grunt and groan in venereal response. (McTair 2000: 77)

The tomb emits an 'oozing ichor' (72), an image that evokes the sickly treacle by-products of the sugar refining process. The horror here is not of natural immanence, nor even of some supernatural ancient creature, but rather of the planter himself, whose monstrous brutality infects all he touches. The terror is not cosmic in origin, but rather historical. When 'the entire landscape heave[s] with unspeakable terror' (77), it is as if nature were crying out in protest at the forces of colonial domination that Ashdown encapsulates. The plot's resurrection recuperates Lovecraftian aesthetics to narrate the 'evaded history' (81) of the 1865 Morant Bay Rebellion – in which Ashdown and all his estate were burnt alive – and the subsequent bloody execution of Boyle's rebels by Governor Edward Eyre. This history seems 'unreal' because the ruling classes have written it out of official narratives in order to forestall anti-colonial and class insurrection, preferring to believe that 'the peasants were happy' (67). The racialised connotations of Lovecraft's stylised representation of dark nature are reconfigured to reflect the political unconscious of the white elites and their repressed fears of the peasants and proletarians whom they once used as chattel and now maintain in conditions of poverty, while Lovecraft's obsession with the occult is refashioned to express planter fears of *obeah* as capable of instigating political insurrection.

When the undead Ashcroft sears the young men's bodies with the family seal with which he used to brand African slaves, the narrator is forced to recognise the 'charnel pit of yesteryear' (75) – the violence of nineteenth-century resource imperialism that continues to haunt the present. This revelation exemplifies how Ecogothic narratives transform memory into imagination and articulate what often cannot be expressed in other forms under conditions of cultural erasure. Significantly, it is Teacha Paul's amulet that the narrator uses to exorcise Ashdown's shuffling corpse and revitalise the haunted land, in a counter-spell that weaponises *obeah* knowledge against the colonial episteme. The story summons the prospect of a counter-hegemonic knowledge-system, rooted in a relation to nature that emphasises interdependent reciprocity rather than domination.

McTair's story also exemplifies the formal capacity of Ecogothic to evoke situated periodicity – 'any number of unreal or not-real situations' – through the device of telesthesia – the shift in temporal perception that telescopes multiple periods of crisis into one moment of revelation. The narrative telescopes multiple temporal moments of labour unrest and ecological crisis related to boom-bust cycles – the 1930s labour strikes, the 1865 Morant Bay Rebellion and the 1830s Baptist war – thus evoking synchronic contexts across a diachronic *durée* of what Jason W. Moore calls 'the intertwining of resistances from labouring classes, landscape changes and market flux – all specific bundles of relations between humans and the rest of nature' (Moore 2011: 46). Periodicity denotes a logic of recurrence rather than linear progression and explains the tendency of Gothic narrative devices to reappear in clusters in ways that 'are both historically specific to the time of their production and representative of the general logic of capitalist time-space contortions' (Shapiro 2009: 24). McTair's use of earlier Gothic intertexts illustrates a propensity within Ecogothic narratives to mine or recalibrate literary resources produced in response to prior contexts of environmental crisis. Reconfiguring the Gothic-effects of folklore and culture from earlier historical periods enhances their ability to represent nested temporalities, imagining past catastrophes as cumulative processes undergirding compound crises in the present.

Oil on Sugar

This capacity for periodic representation is deeply associated with Ecogothic narratives representing resource violence. The chronotopes of the Big House and cane field haunt contemporary narratives, appearing not only in literature but in other media, often using explicitly intermedial references. One powerful example can be found in the first season of the anthology television series *True Detective*, a murder mystery whose noir aesthetics swerve into the supernatural through the uncanny perceptions of detective Rust Cohle, a mystical nihilist given to reading weird fiction and philosophical horror, including Ambrose Bierce's 'An Inhabitant of Carcosa' (1918), Robert W. Chambers's *The King in Yellow* (1895) and Thomas Ligotti's *The Conspiracy Against the Human Race* (2010).

The season begins with the dead body of Dora Lange, sprawled in a cane field of the Oak Alley estate, and in the climactic scene of the season finale, Cohle tracks a serial killer to his lair in 'Carcosa', set in the eerie, root-pierced ruins of Fort Macomb. Here again are central *topoi* associated with the resource Gothic of the sugar plantation – the bloodied cane field, the Confederate fortress 'where black stars rise' – that continue to haunt the present, revenants of the past which is not past. These are reinforced by Antibody and Elastic's title sequence, which opens with 'Sugar Cane and Refinery', a photograph by Robert Misrach from *Petrochemical America* (Misrach and Orff 2012) of a cane field bisected by a dirt road over which looms an oil refinery clouded in smog. The image offers a visual analogue to Cohle's later evocation of Bierce's description of the ruined lands of Carcosa:

> Over all the dismal landscape a canopy of low, lead-colored clouds hung like a visible curse. In all this there were a menace and a portent – a hint of evil, an intimation of doom. Bird, beast, or insect there was none. The wind sighed in the bare branches of the dead trees and the gray grass bent to whisper its dread secret to the earth; but no other sound nor motion broke the awful repose of that dismal place. (Bierce 2012: 203)

However, rather than signifying mystical evil, as in Bierce, the leaden clouds in *True Detective* are portents of the real effects of ecocide and petroleum extraction across the American Gulf states. Oil and sugar frontiers are superimposed in the credits – fading in and out like 'ghosts' – and throughout the season's cinematography, which features long shots of the detectives driving along roads flanked by rigs, refineries and post-industrial ruins. The petroleum uncanny is thus conjoined to the sugar uncanny in the depiction of Louisiana's wetlands as simultaneously real and unreal, where new petrochemical regimes of extraction are nested onto earlier agricultural regimes of sugar production – what Michael Niblett calls 'oil on sugar' (2015: 269).

The Gothic nature of *True Detective* does not represent ecophobic fears of natural immanence or excessive fecundity, but rather states of permanent disaster characterised by the 'slow violence' of toxic contamination. As defined by Rob Nixon, this is environmental 'violence of delayed destruction that is dispersed across time and space', which is often incremental or imperceptible, but which accumulates over time, as in processes of biomagnification resulting from radiation or pollution (Nixon 2011: 2). The narrative's nested temporalities – cycling between the 1990s and the diegetic present of 2012, and reaching back to the nineteenth century through its reimagination of Civil War geographies through Cohle's visions of 'Carcosa' – evoke the periodicity of the compound catastrophes that structure contemporary life in Louisiana, from the 'natural' disasters of Hurricanes Andrew (1992) and Katrina (2005) to the 'industrial' disaster of the Deepwater Horizon oil spill (2010), to the social violence lingering in the aftermath of the privatisation of education, the corruption of government institutions, and socio-economic and racial inequalities persisting long after the failures of post-bellum Reconstruction and the incomplete processes of desegregation. In contrast to the plot's sensational focus on the satanic killing sprees orchestrated by a cabal of politicians, NGO heads, businessman, police and drug dealers, the 'true reveal' of the show's cartographic aesthetics is not who committed the murders, but rather the uncanny revelation of the structural violence emerging from the 'nexus of corporate-produced inequality, fragile bodies, toxic waste, indigence, political bullying, and an unruly ecosystem' in the Southern Louisiana wetlands (Lirette 2014).

Oil on Water

We can see a similar use of what Lawrence Buell calls 'toxic gothic' to depict the 'gothicized environmental squalor' (Buell 2001: 42–3) of the oil-contaminated wetlands of the Niger Delta in Helon Habila's *Oil on Water* (2010). Akin to *True Detective*'s conjoining of realist and non-realist genre conventions, Habila's novel is initially narrated in a more naturalistic style by its first-person narrator, a journalist, but Rufus's attempt at documentary realism is constantly subverted by spectral irruptions of Ecogothic imagery as he struggles to represent the extraordinary violence attendant on oil extraction in Nigeria. The plot follows his investigation of the alleged kidnapping of an oil-man's wife by militants opposed to the extraction of petroleum in the Niger Delta by transnational corporations and the subsequent poisoning of ecosystems and dispossession of local populations.

As Rufus wanders from island to island, the novel's topochronic poetics – similar to the telesthesic geographies in *True Detective* – move associationally between spaces, rather than sequentially in linear time, so that each locality stimulates a different fragment of event, often in the forms of dreams or hallucinations. Rufus persistently deploys ghostly terms to describe the polluted landscapes he traverses, as in the following passage:

> The next village was almost a replica of the last: the same empty squat dwellings, the same ripe and flagrant stench, the barrenness, the oil slick, and the same indefinable sadness in the air, as if a community of ghosts were suspended above the punctured zinc roofs, unwilling to depart, yet powerless to return. In the village centre we found the communal well. Eager for a drink, I [. . .] peered into the well's blackness, but a rank smell wafted from its hot depths [. . .] Something organic, perhaps human, lay dead and decomposing down there, its stench mixed with that unmistakable smell of oil. (Habila 2010: 9)

Organic matter is putrescent or reduced to 'dead matter': rivers and wells are clogged by decaying flesh, whether of 'white-bellied' fish or of the human corpses of villagers and militants executed by state security forces; poisoned birds and bats plummet from a sky turned orange by flaring gas and 'lie draped over tree branches, their outstretched wings black and slick with oil' (9). Rather than ecophobic fears of the natural immanence of decay, this is the death-of-nature, the deathworld produced by the toxification and pollution of the environment by the oil industry. The vibrant ecology of the wetlands is reduced to a 'dead place, a place for dying' (90) by the 'necrotic' logic of capital accumulation, which 'devours all life' and leaves in its wake 'the disappearance of species, languages, cultures, and peoples' (McBrien 2016: 116). The rift in the social metabolism of nature perpetrated by the extractivist economy, in which oil is drained from under the earth and exported for consumption in capitalist cores, is embodied in the physical dispositions of the protagonists, repeatedly described as feeling emptied out or enervated: '[w]e felt drained just standing there [. . .] By now Zaq seemed to have lost even the energy – and the will – to lift the bottle to his mouth' (Habila 2010: 9–10).

In contrast, oil, that bloodstream of capitalist economy, seems to assume an uncanny life of its own, so that pipelines 'sprout' from the 'evil-smelling, oil-fecund earth' and 'the land gr[ows] only gas flares'

(39). Popular understandings of petroleum are frequently framed in Ecogothic tropes of oil as 'the devil's excrement', 'socially polluting, magical and powerful' (Watts 2001: 212). The fevers suffered by Zaq indicate a literal embodiment of the diseases arising in degraded ecologies where epidemiological vectors tend to multiply – but also a symbolic figuration of the infernal reality of petrolic extraction, the orange fire of the gas flares of the delta that roar as they combust, burning twenty-four hours a day. Similarly, the mists that perpetually blind Rufus as he attempts to navigate a delta that is 'vaporous and shape-shifting, appearing and disappearing' (4), the fog that 'rises and covers the faces and places' (3) as he struggles to reconstruct his memory of the journey, are the optics corresponding to oil, which is paradoxically invisible – subterranean, flowing through pipelines – but omnipresent.

The strange fetishism of the water-spirit religion that Rufus encounters at the shrine of Irikefe seems at first to evoke the petro-fetishism corresponding to the phantasmagoria of oil commodification in the popular imagination. However, in the cult's emphasis on the cyclic redemption associated with living water, and their refusal to comply with state forces protecting the oil company interests, there is an intimation of people's agency; it suggests local resistance motivated by desire for resource sovereignty rather than mere conservation, and contests the environmental destruction that threatens their way of life. When the state security forces mutilate their holy statues, the cult builds them again, literally piecing together their severed parts, so that the new forms bear the fissures of history but suggest the possibility of recuperation.

Nuclear Hauntings

I want to conclude with two contrasting visions of nuclear irradiation that deploy Ecogothic tropes to very different ends. The first is *Far Harbor*, a downloadable content extension to the *Fallout 4* video game, set in a post-apocalyptic wasteland in the twenty-second century, after the world has been destroyed by nuclear war. In *Far Harbor*, the player's avatar takes a case from Valentine's Detective Agency that leads her on a search for a missing young girl to a mysterious island off the coast of Maine, where 'higher levels of radiation have created a more feral world', as Bethesda's promotional blurb describes it. Taking its inspiration from H. P. Lovecraft's short story 'The Shadow over Innsmouth' (1936), the DLC populates the island with radioactive ghouls, crazed cultists that worship nuclear radiation, human Trappers turned cannibals, and Anglers and Gulpers, eldritch abominations from the deep.

Ecogothic   185

In contrast to the sun-bleached aesthetics of the main game, *Far Harbor* is decidedly more Gothic, shrouded in perpetual mist and darkness, and the player must battle through thick waves of toxic, radioactive fog from which monsters loom unexpectedly.

As in the rest of the *Fallout* series, the storyline is deeply contradictory in its exploration of contemporary anxieties around nuclear technology, gesturing to the supposed horror of nuclear fallout and environmental destruction but granting the Vault Dweller (the player character) near-invincibility in their radiation-proof, atomic-powered suit. While the plot turns around the revelation of dark secrets concealed by the island's inhabitants, the DLC's imagination of the post-nuclear environment is ultimately less horrifying than it is magnetising, depicting nature as a waste to be conquered and domesticated through the creation of frontier homesteads where settlers drive back the fog and dark. Post-nuclear nature is essentially conceived as a playground where the player can revel in fantasies of nuclear empowerment and annihilate swarms of mutants without remorse – this is ecophobia become ludic, rendered a source of sheer pleasure.

In contrast to this nuclear playground for players, Robert Barclay's novel *Meḷaḷ* offers a searing vision of the Marshall Islands as a 'playground for demons, not habitable for people' in the wake of Pacific nuclearisation and militarisation (Barclay 2003: i). The novel's revelation of the history of nuclear crisis centres around the Pacific island of Ebeye, to which almost 10,000 Marshallese have been exiled after the nuclear contamination of their home islands by US missile testing. As toxic casualties of the US nuclear military-industrial war machine, the islanders suffer not only the trauma of alienation from their homelands, condemnation to structural poverty and unemployment and the political domination of US imperialism, but also the adverse health effects of radiation exposure, which lead to birth defects and cancers. Drawing on Marshallese folklore, the novel depicts the invisible residues of nuclear contamination – the half-lives unfolding over lifetimes – as a host of demons infesting the island:

> Soul stealers, decay makers, child eaters, sickness spreaders, brain suckers, the foulest of all conjurable demons clinging to people and things like sea slugs sucking the reef, feverishly intent in the service of their masters on wringing death from life, on replacing everything pure and natural and pleasurable with stinking rot and ruin, a living death, life inside-out. (Barclay 2003: 14)

As Huggan and Tiffin observe, 'these malevolent spirits of nuclear fallout are the spectral emanations of a continuing toxic nightmare' (2010: 59). As in *Oil on Water*, the slow violence of toxic contamination renders their ecology a deathworld. In the nuclear Gothic of this text, it is again not natural immanence that is terrifying, but rather degradation and extinction – the unravelling of the whole web of life as a result of nuclear colonialism. The novel's demons not only embody the historicity of colonial ecological violence, but also raise questions about the possibility of futurity in an environment 'as poisoned and disabling as the irradiated atolls of the Marshall Islands' (Straß 2016: 238). Yet, at the same time, the narrative emphasises the capacity for survival of its lead characters, Rujen Keju, a waste worker, and his sons Jebro and Nuke, who struggle against cultural erasure and poverty, and strive to preserve their Indigenous oceanic vision of the environmental cycles of the Pacific archipelago. Thus, in its reconfiguration of folkloric materials, the novel seeks not only to represent the trauma of post-nuclear life and dispossession, but to reactivate earlier cultural materials in order to embody collective memory from below, in opposition to imperial cultures of governance. This is one of the most powerful aesthetic effects of Ecogothic: to offer a portal into the contemporary imagination of compound ecological crises with complex temporal antecedents, to materialise with an uncanny immediacy those revenants of 'undead' processes in the past that continue to shape contemporary environments.

Note

1. The Alan Moore-scripted issues were not collected together and published as a single graphic novel book under the title *Saga of the Swamp Thing* until 2012.

Film and Television

True Detective, season one (HBO, 2014)

Videography

Fallout 4: Far Harbor DLC (Bethesda Game Studios, USA, 2016)

References

Barclay, Robert (2003), *Meḷaḷ: A Novel of the Pacific*, Honolulu: University of Hawai'i Press.
Bierce, Ambrose (2012), 'An Inhabitant of Carcosa', in *Can Such Things Be?*, Portland: The Floating Press.
Buell, Lawrence (2001), *Writing for an Endangered World: Literature, Culture, and Environment in the U.S. and Beyond*, Cambridge, MA: Harvard University Press.
Deckard, Sharae (2013), 'Uncanny States: Global EcoGothic and the World-Ecology in Rana Dasgupta's *Tokyo Cancelled*', in Andrew Smith and William Hughes (eds), *Ecogothic*, Edinburgh: Edinburgh University Press, pp. 177–94.
— (2015), 'Ghost Mountains and Stone Maidens: Ecological Imperialism, Compound Catastrophe, and the Post-Soviet Ecogothic', in Elizabeth DeLoughrey, Jill Didur and Anthony Carrigan (eds), *Global Ecologies and the Environmental Humanities: Postcolonial Approaches*, London: Routledge, pp. 286–306.
Estok, Simon (2009), 'Theorizing in a Space of Ambivalent Openness: Ecocriticism and Ecophobia', *ISLE*, 16.2, 203–25.
Habila, Helon (2010), *Oil on Water*, London: Hamish Hamilton.
Hillard, Tom (2009), '"Deep Into That Darkness Peering": An Essay on Gothic Nature', *ISLE*, 16.4, 685–95.
Huggan, Graham, and Helen Tiffin (2010), *Postcolonial Ecocriticism*, London: Routledge.
Lirette, Christopher (2014), 'Something True about Louisiana: HBO's *True Detective* and the *Petrochemical America* Aesthetic', *Southern Spaces*, 13 August, https://southernspaces.org/2014/something-true-about-louisiana-hbos-true-detective-and-petrochemical-america-aesthetic (accessed 8 June 2018).
Lovecraft, H. P. (2013), *H. P. Lovecraft: The Classic Horror Stories*, Oxford: Oxford University Press.
Luckhurst, Roger (2013), 'Introduction', in *H. P. Lovecraft: The Classic Horror Stories*, Oxford: Oxford University Press, pp. vii–xxviii.
McBrien, Justin (2016), 'Accumulating Extinction: Planetary Catastrophism in the Necrocene', in Jason W. Moore (ed.), *Anthropocene or Capitalocene? Nature, History, and the Crisis of Capitalism*, Oakland: PM Press, pp. 116–37.
McTair, Roger (2000), 'Just a Lark (or the Crypt of Matthew Ashdown)', in *Whispers from the Cotton Tree Root: Caribbean Fabulist Fiction*, Montpelier, VT: Invisible Cities Press, pp. 53–83.
Misrach, Richard, and Kate Orff (2012), *Petrochemical America*, New York: Aperture Foundation.
Moore, Alan (2012), *Saga of the Swamp Thing: Book One*, art by Stephen Bissette, John Totleben, Dan Day and Rick Veitch, coloured by Tatjana Wood, lettered by John Constanza and Todd Klein, Burbank: DC Comics.
Moore, Jason W. (2011), 'Wall Street Is a Way of Organizing Nature', *Upping the Anti: A Journal of Theory and Action*, 12, 39–53.
Niblett, Michael (2015), 'Oil on Sugar: Commodity Frontiers and Peripheral

Aesthetics', in Elizabeth DeLoughrey, Jill Didur and Anthony Carrigan (eds), *Global Ecologies and the Environmental Humanities: Postcolonial Approaches*, London: Routledge, pp. 268–85.

Nixon, Rob (2011), *Slow Violence and the Environmentalism of the Poor*, Cambridge, MA: Harvard University Press.

Oloff, Kerstin (2012), '"Greening" The Zombie: Caribbean Gothic, World-Ecology, and Socio-Ecological Degradation', *Green Letters*, 16, 31–45.

Rudd, Alison (2010), *Postcolonial Gothic Fictions from the Caribbean, Canada, Australia and New Zealand*, Cardiff: University of Wales Press.

Sage, Victor (2003), 'The Ghastly and the Ghostly: The Gothic Farce of JG Farrell's Empire Trilogy', in Andrew Smith and William Hughes (eds), *Empire and the Gothic: The Politics of Genre?*, London: Palgrave Macmillan, pp. 172–91.

Shapiro, Stephen (2009), 'Transvaal, Transylvania: Dracula's World-System and Gothic Periodicity', *Gothic Studies*, 10.1, 24–47.

Smith, Andrew, and William Hughes (2013), *Ecogothic*, Edinburgh: Edinburgh University Press.

Straß, Hannah (2016), '"A Living Death, Life Inside-Out": The Postcolonial Toxic Gothic in Robert Barclay's *Meļaļ: A Novel of the Pacific*', in Jernej Habjan and Fabienne Imlinger (eds), *Globalizing Literary Genres: Literature, History, Modernity*, New York: Routledge, pp. 228–53.

Walrond, Eric (2013) [1926], *Tropic Death*, New York: Liveright Publishing Corporation.

Watts, Michael (2001), 'Petro-Violence: Community, Extraction, and Political Ecology of a Mythic Commodity', in Nancy Lee Peluso and Michael Watts (eds), *Violent Environments*, New York: Cornell University Press, pp. 189–212.

Chapter 13

Gothic Comedy
Catherine Spooner

In July 2018, the auditions round of popular television show *America's Got Talent* featured a stand-up comedian called Oliver Graves. Graves appeared on stage with black bird's nest hair, black panda eyes and black lipstick, wearing an artfully ragged red sweater. The audience and judges were initially bemused: the cameras cut to sceptical audience reaction shots and the judges joked among themselves about Graves's implied lack of desirability as a romantic partner. His set traded on his outsider status with self-deprecating one-liners delivered in a melancholic monotone: 'I'm trying to find the woman of my dreams, but it's a struggle, because I'm an insomniac.' The result was a standing ovation and unanimous approval from the judges, reducing him to tears on stage.

Graves's impact on *America's Got Talent* was short-lived, as he was eliminated in the second round of the competition. Nevertheless, the way that his audition was presented by the mainstream talent show is highly revealing about the status of Gothic comedy in twenty-first-century popular perception. There were traditionally Gothic elements to Graves's set – his jokes characteristically set up a cheerfully normative scenario only to flip it into something gloomier, thus enacting the Gothic tendency to provide a dark underside to an Enlightenment narrative of progress. His physical presentation, however, played into popular notions of the goth outsider, resembling subcultural icons such as The Cure frontman Robert Smith, and this is how the show incorporated him into its own narrative. From the outset, the show set up Graves as an underdog, enabling the sentimental manipulation of the audience. Famously acerbic judge Simon Cowell showed a rare moment of softness when he said, 'I think you didn't get the reaction you expected. So, you're not used to this, are you?' The judges' comments then went on to cement Graves's role as someone who by his very outsider nature had something unique to bring. Judge Mel B struck the keynote when she declared, 'You're so different!' Graves himself, in his post-performance interview with host Tyra Banks, perpetuated the theme by agreeing, 'I'm not the norm.' Banks replied, 'That's what makes you special.'

Graves's shtick is a variation on the familiar trope of the sad clown. *America's Got Talent*, however, makes a series of revealing presuppositions in its framing of Graves's act. Firstly, it elides Gothic with goth, condensing the Gothic literary and cultural tradition into mainly visual and behavioural signifiers of subcultural difference (a difference that is therefore recognisable and commodifiable). Secondly, it betrays the expectation that someone with a Gothic appearance should *not* be funny, or rather more precisely that they should be the butt of the joke rather than the source of humour. Finally, it proposes a sentimental narrative borrowed from Tim Burton's 1990 film *Edward Scissorhands* (the eponymous character of which Graves nominally resembles) that redeems the outsider as loveable and misunderstood.

It is in this notion of difference that twenty-first-century Gothic comedy finds its most potent, and most recurrent, material. Comedy has always been intrinsic to the functioning of Gothic, as Avril Horner and Sue Zlosnik show in their foundational book *Gothic and the Comic Turn* (2004). As they point out, Horace Walpole deliberately modelled *The Castle of Otranto* (1764) on Shakespearean tragedy with its graveyard humour and 'low' comic scenes. Thus 'the comic turn in Gothic is not an aberration or corruption of a "serious" genre but rather a key aspect of Gothic's essential hybridity' (12). They suggest that comic Gothic exists on a spectrum, with hysterical laughter at one end and self-conscious deployment of parody and wit at the other. Although their book focuses on the British literary tradition, exploring examples ranging from Jane Austen's early nineteenth-century parody, *Northanger Abbey* (1818), to later twentieth-century fiction such as Fay Weldon's *The Life and Loves of a She-Devil* (1983), other commentators have recognised the significance of Gothic comedy in American film. Kamilla Elliott (2008) establishes a long tradition of Gothic parody beginning with early Hollywood films such as *Abbott and Costello Meet Frankenstein* (Charles Barton, 1948), arguing that these parodies tend to interrogate the presumptions of Gothic criticism as well as the form itself. William Paul identifies a surge of horror comedy in the 1980s encompassing popular classics such as *The Evil Dead* (Sam Raimi, 1981) and *Ghostbusters* (Ivan Reitman, 1984), a trend that he finds offers 'a radical challenge to taste and value, but not in the programmatic way of self-consciously avant-garde art that could still make these works acceptable to arbiters of taste and value' (1994: 20).

If Gothic has always had a comic aspect, however, in the twenty-first century the *kinds* of comedy found in Gothic texts have diversified: from the witty repartée of *Buffy the Vampire Slayer* (1997–2003) to the parodically earnest 'mockumentary' *Trolljegeren* (*Trollhunter*, André Øvredal, 2010); the mordant irony of *Lemony Snicket's A Series of Unfortunate Events* (1999–2006) to the whimsical satire of Chris Riddell's *Goth Girl* series (2013–); the celebratory camp of drag queen Sharon Needles to the carnivalesque romp of Tim Burton's *Corpse Bride* (2005). Moreover, comic Gothic has increasingly spread beyond its 'traditional' media of novel and film to advertising, television sitcom, music video, stand-up, comics and graphic novels, animation and, of course, internet memes.

Gothic comedy takes multiple forms, some of which I will explore in this chapter – it is not reducible to a single theme or effect. However, in the twenty-first century it has increasingly taken on a new inflection in the light of the growth of identity politics and renewed attention to ideologies of the family. In many of these comic texts, the *tone* of Gothic comedy has changed. As Graves's performance shows, in Gothic comedy outsiderdom has become something to be cherished and redeemed. Graves's shtick may have allowed the audience to feel superior to his haplessness, but it also enabled them to feel sympathetic towards him – and his tears following his positive reception were in this respect a crucial part of the performance. Twenty-first-century Gothic comedy often exploits the idea of the sympathetic monster, a concept that was popularised in Gothic cultural products from the 1960s onwards, particularly Anne Rice's *Interview with the Vampire* (1976), but which reached a tipping point in the 1990s with Francis Ford Coppola's *Bram Stoker's Dracula* (1992). In this film the archetypal vampire was recast as a romantic hero with a tragic backstory, thus inaugurating a series of novels, films and television programmes in which first vampires and then other monsters were pitched as viable romantic partners or, indeed, protagonists. The sympathetic monster characteristically has a voice and is able to express their point of view. This fundamentally changes the comedic narrative as it means that the audience laughs with the monster rather than laughs at them. Cultural difference has become something to be celebrated rather than feared, and Gothic comedy has accordingly become more generous and inclusive.

Comic Monsters

In twenty-first-century Gothic, difference is frequently embodied in the figure of the monster, who enacts or stands in for a variety of different kinds of marginalised social groups, including (but not limited to) subcultural, queer, disabled and racial or ethnic identities. As Jeffrey Jerome Cohen states, '[a]ny kind of alterity can be inscribed across (constructed through) the monstrous body, but for the most part monstrous difference tends to be cultural, political, racial, economic, sexual' (1996: 7). Comic monsters, however, undergo a particular kind of transformation. According to Noël Carroll, for monsters to become funny the threat they pose 'must be sublated or hidden from our attention' (1999: 158). Removing monsters' frightfulness makes them objects of humour rather than horror: '[o]nce their fearsomeness is factored out, what remains is their status as category errors, which, of course, makes them apt targets or objects of incongruity humor' (156). Carroll uses the example of *Abbott and Costello Meets Frankenstein*, in which the only thing that changes about the Universal horror monsters Dracula and Frankenstein (played by regular actors Bela Lugosi and Glenn Strange) is the context. However, this effect can be seen more widely in the way that the figures of Dracula and Frankenstein are appropriated in texts aimed at children, in popular merchandise and in advertising. For Fred Botting, the process of factoring out fear has resulted in a domestication of the monster: in twenty-first-century culture, monsters have become thoroughly incorporated into the discourse whose limits they once troubled and have lost their power to disturb. Drawing on Derrida, he claims that '[a]s monsters are sought out, radical difference is diminished: they become familiar, recognized, expected, "normal" rather than "monstrous" monstrosities, domesticated to the point of being pets' (2014: 500). It would seem, therefore, that contemporary monsters are primed for comic treatment.

Carroll's and Botting's arguments are persuasive but do not fully account for the forms of black humour found in a television series like *The League of Gentlemen* (1999–2017). Here, comedy operates simultaneously with horror; the fact that the audience laughs does not mean that they are not frightened. When Papa Lazarou (Reece Shearsmith), a circus ringmaster in blackface, appears at the door of a suburban housewife (Steve Pemberton), he plays the archetypal villain of female Gothic in hyperbolised form: he insists on calling her Dave; coerces her into speaking gibberish and finally abducts her with the gleeful declaration, '[y]ou're *my* wife now!' His wilful refusal to recognise the woman's identity or participate in a rational conversation is a transgression of norms of communication and as such is *both* nightmarish *and* funny. The scene's humour, however, is dependent on rendering the female victim grotesque through costume, make-up and performance and thus reducing audience empathy. Told from the perspective of a sympathetic heroine, this story would not be funny at all. As Horner and Zlosnik argue, '[c]omic Gothic moments [. . .] invite a conscious, self-reflexive engagement with the Gothic mode that sets up a different kind of contract between the reader and the text, offering a measure of detachment from scenes of pain and suffering that would be disturbing in a different Gothic context' (2012: 125). Scenes of pain and suffering in *The League of Gentlemen* do not stop being disturbing but are so in a different way: they partly disturb *because* they elicit laughter, revealing the audience's own cruelty.

The Papa Lazarou scenes in *The League of Gentlemen* are further complicated by the character's appearance in blackface, which combined with his reliance on Traveller stereotypes (Roma and Irish Travellers sold wooden pegs from door to door, read palms and were believed to abduct young women) flirts uncomfortably with racism. Papa Lazarou combines a number of signifiers of ethnic difference, which while clearly self-consciously *performed*, and thus not intended to represent actual ethnic groups, are nevertheless discomforting – and this discomfort is part of the character's power. If Papa Lazarou provides an example of a comic monster whose threat is not defused, he also suggests a form of humour that is increasingly unpalatable to twenty-first-century audiences. The series' return for a Christmas special in 2017 provoked much media commentary about how it would revisit characters that might now be regarded as racist or transphobic in the light of shifting cultural politics, and its success or otherwise in doing so (see, for example, Bassett 2017). This highlights the fact that the reason many twenty-first-century monsters have lost their power to shock is because the forms of difference they once represented are increasingly tolerated and often celebrated by contemporary culture. It is no longer acceptable to laugh at cultural others. Rather than comic targets or objects, therefore, contemporary Gothic monsters are increasingly presented as comic subjects: we laugh with them and not at them.

The monster as comic subject often possesses a distinctive voice, in which the ironic detachment Horner and Zlosnik associate with Gothic comedy is expressed through wit. This is often a variation on the subject position of the dandy in the Byronic or Wildean mode, whose sardonic witticisms skewer the follies of the society to which they belong. The combination of monstrosity and dandyism might seem surprising, but dandies were regularly figured as monstrous in nineteenth-century writing and monstrous dandies feature recurrently in Gothic novels, where they trope on the idea of the demonic outsider or glamorous exile, most prominently in Oscar Wilde's *The Picture of Dorian Gray* (1890–1). Wit, as Andrew Stott argues, enables the construction of a 'comic identity [. . .] conceived as a means of refusing incorporation into a communal identity defined by the sobriety of the establishment' (2005: 59). This is perhaps most eloquently embodied in Jake Marlowe, the suavely literate and irreverent hero of Glen Duncan's *The Last Werewolf* (2011), prone to pronouncements such as, 'Reader, I ate him' (131). However, it also appears in Young Adult novels such as Catherine Jinks's *The Reformed Vampire Support Group* (2009), in which the permanently fifteen-year-old Nina projects a jaded world-weariness that is equal parts dry Australian and eternal teenager: 'being a vampire [. . .] is like being stuck indoors with the flu watching daytime television, for ever and ever' (5). Similarly, deadpan zombie Andy in S. G. Browne's adult novel *Breathers: A Zombie's Lament* (2009) finds his newly undead perspective offers comic insight into the nuclear family, self-help culture and consumer capitalism. His catchphrase, '[i]f you've never... you probably wouldn't understand', highlights the ludicrous disparities between zombie and human experience and the consequent difficulty of reconciling cultural difference. In *Breathers*, the zombies' campaign for their civil rights is doomed to failure: '[i]f you've never been dismembered or crushed or allowed to slowly disintegrate until you turn into chicken soup, then you probably wouldn't understand' (2009: 310).

Monster Heterotopias

The monster as comic subject in twenty-first-century Gothic texts often meets and multiplies in what might be described as monster heterotopias. The heterotopia, according to Michel Foucault (1986), is a space that gathers together simultaneously a number of different possible orders or worlds. Examples include graveyards, prisons and brothels. The monster heterotopia takes these spaces and fills them with monsters: different orders of being which would seldom meet in the folkloric and literary texts they derive from, but which become incongruous twenty-first-century companions. While it is possible to replay these monster mash-ups in a serious mode, as in the television series *Penny Dreadful* (2014–16), the clashes that derive from bringing different narrative conventions together are a rich resource for comedy.

Monster heterotopias have important precedents in the twentieth century, in particular the cult animation *Mad Monster Party?* (Jules Bass, 1967), in which the Baron Boris von Frankenstein (voiced by Boris Karloff) summons all the members of the Worldwide Organization of Monsters to stay at his castle on the Isle of Evil in order to announce his retirement and, in a nod to the atomic age, reveal his secret weapon of total destruction. Although most of the monsters are destroyed at the climax of the film, the ending, which parodies the final line of *Some Like It Hot* (Billy Wilder, 1959), 'nobody's perfect', proposes a romantic embrace of monstrosity and difference. This celebratory and inclusive finale resonates with subsequent monster heterotopias, which are often pitched at a family audience. Recalling Northrop Frye's influential theory of comedy (2006), the comic monster heterotopia moves towards social integration and renewal.

This inclusive narrative becomes still more overt in the animated *Hotel Transylvania* franchise (2012–). Hotel Transylvania is an exemplary monster heterotopia, a refuge for monsters who are tired of persecution by humans, set up by Count Dracula (voiced by Adam Sandler). The first film in the series inverts the usual marginalisation of the monster by having a human backpacker, Jonathan (Andy Samberg), trespass into monster territory and have to 'pass' as a monster in order to integrate into their community. Both sides must overcome their dislike and distrust of one another in order to resolve the romantic plot, in which Jonathan falls for Dracula's goth daughter, Mavis (Selena Gomez). In a particularly self-reflexive sequence, the monsters find themselves in a town celebrating a Monster Festival, filled with admiring humans dressed up as themselves. As if in response to Fred Botting's claim that in the contemporary age Gothic has become exhausted, the monsters are forced to confront their own redundancy within postmodern culture. Frankenstein (here referring to the creature, and voiced by Kevin James) exclaims, '[w]e haven't scared people in centuries! I don't think I've got it in me anymore!' As he rampages through the town, he is met not with terror but with appreciative cheers. In a crucial moment that turns the vindictive mob of James Whale's *Frankenstein* (1931) on its head, an attractive girl asks, 'Can you sign my torch?' The monsters are no longer feared by humans but have become celebrities. Although they do, ultimately, assert their difference from their crowd by means of their monstrous abilities, this difference is constructed as positive and is embraced, rather than rejected. Gothic is not exhausted, the film seems to be saying, so much as shifting into a new mode in which the outsider is enabled to preserve and celebrate their difference within an inclusive community.

The Whimsical Macabre

Mad Monster Party? and *Hotel Transylvania* draw attention to the fact that comedy is particularly prevalent in Gothic cultural products aimed at child and teen audiences. Again, this is not new: Heinrich Hoffmann's *Struwwelpeter* (1845, English translation 1848) blended horror and humour in its series of extravagant cautionary tales, and Edward Gorey dispatched with children in inventive alphabetised ways in *The Gashlycrumb Tinies* (1963), while Count von Count has been a fixture of the American pre-school show *Sesame Street* (1969–) since 1972. All of these texts draw on an aesthetic that I have elsewhere termed the 'whimsical macabre' that has become particularly widespread in the twenty-first century (Spooner 2017: 99–119).

The whimsical macabre combines whimsy, defined by the *Oxford English Dictionary* as '[a] sudden fancy; a caprice' and 'something odd or quaint', with the grim and gruesome. It deliberately blends the cute, fanciful and quirky with the gloomy, grisly and morbid. On one level the whimsical macabre simply operates according to the incongruity theory of comedy, established in the eighteenth century. As James Beattie, who was influential in formulating this theory, wrote in 1776, '[l]aughter arises from the view of two or more inconsistent, unsuitable, or incongruous parts or circumstances, considered as united in one complex object or assemblage, or as acquiring a sort of mutual relation from the peculiar manner in which the mind takes notice of them' (1779: 320). However, the whimsical macabre also provides a tool with which to challenge the sanctimonious idealisation of the child in Western culture. As such it is an appropriate aesthetic for a cultural climate in which childhood is undergoing a category crisis, continually construed as under threat even as it is idealised and fetishised. Lucie Armitt, commenting on the prevalence of haunted and haunting children in contemporary texts, writes 'Gothic takes on a kind of pathological direction, tracing an obsession in society which cannot make up its mind whether it is appalled or enthralled by children and the dangers by which, in their name, *we* are haunted' (2011: 46–7). The whimsical macabre takes a different direction, acknowledging childhood as an artificial construct, revealing the predatory drives of adults as well as children's agency, and opening up a space in which more playful and sometimes revisionary versions of childhood can emerge.

Rather like comic Gothic itself, the whimsical macabre exists on a spectrum. At one end, there are texts like the Canadian animated television show (and sometime clothing brand) *Ruby Gloom* (2006–8), in which a perky goth dubbed 'the happiest girl in the world' has low-stakes adventures with a variety of cute spooky creatures. At the other, is a text like Roman Dirge's comic *Lenore: The Cute Little Dead Girl* (1998–) in which cute graphics are despoiled with high levels of gore and deliberate bad taste. At either end of the spectrum, however, these texts work to expand and disrupt conventional ideas of childhood and, more specifically, girlhood. Pre-adolescent or teenaged girls are the typical focus of the whimsical macabre. Texts in this mode tend to reject narrow definitions of contemporary Western femininity and offer a range of alternative possibilities for identity construction: black replaces, or augments, the ubiquitous pink associated with girls' culture. This is accentuated in products influenced by Japanese culture, in which, as Sharon Kinsella (1995) establishes, cuteness is already constructed as a mode of resistance to a dominant patriarchal culture and a narrow range of adult feminine roles.

Accordingly, many whimsical macabre texts play with romance frameworks. Tim Burton's stop-motion animated film *Corpse Bride* has Emily, the undead bride of the title (voiced by Helena Bonham Carter), disrupt the logical progress of dynastic romance in a festive interlude from the gloomy conventions of the everyday world that reveals the whimsical macabre's origins in the medieval *danse macabre* and the carnivalesque. She transports the protagonist, Victor (Johnny Depp), to the underworld where he is greeted with an upbeat, jazzy song and dance routine by the skeleton Bonejangles (Danny Elfman) and his deceased companions. The lyrics trope on the medieval theme of *memento mori*, or 'remember you must die':

> Die, die we all pass away
> But don't wear a frown cause it's really okay
> And you might try and hide
> And you might try and pray
> But we all end up the remains of the day.

Meanwhile, the skeletons caper in a modern version of the dance of death, playing each other's bodies like instruments and swapping heads in a Busby Berkeley-style routine. The depiction of the underworld thus draws on the topsy-turvy space of Mikhail Bakhtin's carnival (1984), a space in festive opposition to the routine, everyday world. It is filled with grotesque, capricious bodies that contrast with the ordered, buttoned-up world of the living: one character is a severed head; another is a grave worm living behind Emily's eyeball; someone's nose falls off into the wedding cake mix. Nevertheless, nothing is really disgusting in Burton's film, as befitting its PG certificate: decay is heavily stylised and the corpse bodies are comical, whimsical, even cute, as in the case of the skeleton dog Scraps. Similarly, whereas in the Middle Ages the *danse macabre* had a moral and didactic purpose, encouraging sinners to repent while there is still time, in *Corpse Bride* this is secularised into a message of romantic love and self-sacrifice, focused on the dyad of the heterosexual couple. The patriarchal villain, Barkis (Richard E. Grant) may be vanquished, but familial wealth and power is consolidated through Victor and Victoria's marriage and, despite (or because of) the anarchic intervention of the dead, the social order is reconfirmed. Curiously, the end of the film, in which Emily dissolves into a cloud of moths, contrasts the temporary nature of carnival with the permanence of death, re-separating the two.

In its most arch and self-conscious form, the whimsical macabre shades into camp. In Paul Magrs's Brenda and Effie novels, beginning with *Never the Bride* (2006) and *Something Borrowed* (2007), many of the motifs of twenty-first-century Gothic comedy collide: the series is wittily narrated by a sympathetic monster (in this case, Brenda, the Bride of Frankenstein), is set in a monster heterotopia (a Whitby populated by diverse monsters), and displays a whimsical approach to plot (characterised by, for example, a bamboo wickerwork god that possesses a hotel's garden furniture). Magrs, an openly gay writer, invests these motifs with a camp sensibility in which, as Susan Sontag writes, '[o]ne can be serious about the frivolous, frivolous about the serious' (1994: 288). Sontag's notoriously apolitical description of camp identifies eighteenth-century Gothic novels as among the origins of camp taste, but twenty-first-century Gothic comedy often self-consciously politicises this aesthetic. In Magrs's novels, for example, the frivolous tone contains a serious message: in his fictional Whitby, monsters, Goths, gays and other outsiders are brought together in a mutually supportive community, one in which difference is welcomed and eccentricities embraced. The paranormal romance narrative, moreover, is parodied and disrupted: Brenda is *never* the bride while supporting characters have unlikely and often hyperbolically queer relationships, for example between a gay human and a lizard-boy from the land before time (*The Bride That Time Forgot*, 2010).

Happy Families

Paul Magrs's Brenda, as the Bride of Frankenstein, is not born into a family and has no natural kin; as the novels progress she gathers a surrogate queer family around her composed of companions she has chosen for herself. The monsters of twenty-first-century Gothic comedy challenge normative family values: from Papa Lazarou's collection of wives to Andy of *Breathers* storing his parents' bodies in the fridge to the vampire-human miscegenation of *Hotel Transylvania*, the middle-class, nuclear family unit is repeatedly questioned and frequently travestied.

This has its roots in the Gothic family sitcoms of the 1960s, *The Addams Family* (1964–6) and *The Munsters* (1964–6), which Helen Wheatley argues 'simultaneously satirised and venerated the all-American family' (2006: 145). A similar ambivalence characterises *Desperate Housewives* (2004–12), in which a suburban housewife's murder brings the dark secrets of her neighbours to light, and *Santa Clarita Diet* (2017–), in which a Californian property realtor contracts a particularly violent sickness bug and finds herself transformed into a zombie, thus miraculously revitalising her middle-class lifestyle. In their focus on the domestic, these texts are centrally located within a Gothic tradition bound up with the exploration of the homely and unhomely, and with women's domestic entrapment.

These themes are brought together in the vampire 'mockumentary' *What We Do in the Shadows* (Jemaine Clement and Taika Waititi, 2014), which presents an unexpected take on the domestic Gothic by addressing it through male relationships. The film depicts another version of the monster heterotopia, in that it brings together five vampires from different kinds of vampire narratives in an urban flat-share. Each vampire inhabits a different order of being and set of narrative conventions, and the clash between these is translated into character clash. The mockumentary format is the logical end point of giving monsters a voice, as each character contributes a candid account of their own backstory as well as frank commentary on their companions.

Significantly, *What We Do in the Shadows* was made in New Zealand, and its directors are of mixed Maori heritage. They previously worked together on hit television comedy series *The Flight of the Conchords* (2007–9), and this show resonates through the film, not least in the casting of Rhys Darby as werewolf pack leader Anton. *The Flight of the Conchords* depicts the eponymous band (Jemaine Clement and Bret McKenzie) as they try to build a music career in New York. Darby plays their inept manager, Murray Hewitt. Hewitt is moonlighting from his job at the New Zealand Consulate, where he inhabits a shabby, run-down cubicle, decorated with posters with reticent slogans such as 'New Zealand. Better than Old Zealand' and 'New Zealand. It's not part of Australia'. These posters encapsulate the series' comic construction of New Zealand as marginal and insular: Flight of the Conchords are always too provincial and obscure to succeed in the big city. This dynamic resonates through *What We Do in the Shadows*. Shot on location in Wellington, the film places the glamour of the vampire myth in tension with a marginal, provincial New Zealand identity. The culture's supposed ordinariness and lack of ambition is transferred to the vampires, who bicker pettily in their domestic setting.

The domestic setting is crucial to the film's message. Ultimately, *What We Do in the Shadows* is as much a film about masculinity as it is about vampires, and especially about the homosocial bonds men develop when living without women. The most celebrated scene in the film depicts a stand-off between the vampires and a group of local werewolves when they are both out on the town. When a pack member angrily uses an expletive, Darby's mild-mannered alpha reprimands him, '[w]hat are we? Werewolves, not swearwolves.' The werewolves are otherwise meek men who struggle to control their animal urges (including the impulse to chase after sticks) while the vampires jockey for position within their internal hierarchy, their struggles for status expressed through fights over the washing-up rota.

Within this seething morass of conflicted masculinity, there is one important female character: junior vampire Deacon's 'servant', Jackie (Jackie van der Beek), who carries out his most arduous domestic chores in return for the long-deferred promise of immortality. After a night spent cleaning a particularly grim bathroom, Jackie escapes Deacon's thrall, gets his rival Nick to turn her into a vampire, and makes her husband into her own slave. Jackie's liberation from domestic servitude is significant because it is a reminder that the refusal of domesticity is always at the expense of someone else, and traditionally it is women who been unrewarded for their domestic labour. The domestication of the monster, therefore, is an inevitable and, in many respects, welcome reconfiguration of conventional power hierarchies. We do not need to lament the loss of '"monstrous" monstrosities', for those 'familiar, recognized, expected, "normal"' monsters herald the emergence of a more progressive society.

Conclusion

In twenty-first-century Gothic comedy, the monstrous outsider stands redeemed: given a voice and allowed to become a comic subject rather than the butt of the joke. Thus, far from being frivolous or disposable, contemporary Gothic comedy forms a politically significant function I have elsewhere described as 'happy Gothic' (Spooner 2017) in its tendency to promote a celebratory politics of difference and inclusion. Contemporary Gothic comedy champions the outsider and their resistance to mainstream taste even as it creates a space where they can be safely heard. It often functions to travesty culturally significant concepts of family, domesticity and childhood in the light of a liberal identity politics. Nevertheless, the comedy of difference is double-edged, as in its emphasis on the rights of the individual to self-expression it buys into neoliberal ideologies of self-care and freedom of choice. 'It's not just a diet, it's a whole new lifestyle', Drew Barrymore announces in one of the teaser trailers for *Santa Clarita Diet*. In this ambivalence, twenty-first-century Gothic comedy retains its power to provoke, critique and disturb.

Film and Television

Abbott and Costello Meet Frankenstein (Charles Barton, USA, 1948)
America's Got Talent, season 13 (NBC, 2018)
Bram Stoker's Dracula (Francis Ford Coppola, USA, 1992)
Buffy the Vampire Slayer (The WB/UPN, 1997–2003)
Corpse Bride (Tim Burton, UK/USA, 2005)
Desperate Housewives (ABC, 2004–12)
Edward Scissorhands (Tim Burton, USA, 1990)
Ghostbusters (Ivan Reitman, USA, 1984)
Hotel Transylvania (Genndy Tartakovsky, USA, 2012)
Mad Monster Party? (Jules Bass, USA, 1967)
Penny Dreadful (Showtime/Sky, 2014–16)
Ruby Gloom (YTV, 2006–8)
Santa Clarita Diet (Netflix, 2017–)
Sesame Street (NET, PBS, HBO, 1969–)
Some Like It Hot (Billy Wilder, USA, 1959)
The Addams Family (ABC, 1964–6)
The Evil Dead (Sam Raimi, USA, 1981)
The Flight of the Conchords (HBO, 2007–9)
The League of Gentlemen (BBC 2, 1999–2017)
The Munsters (CBS, 1964–6)
Trolljegeren (*Trollhunter*, André Øvredal, Norway, 2010)
What We Do in the Shadows (Jemaine Clement and Taika Waititi, New Zealand/USA, 2014)

References

Armitt, Lucy (2011), *Twentieth-Century Gothic*, Cardiff: University of Wales Press.
Bakhtin, Mikhail (1984), *Rabelais and His World*, Hélène Iswolsky (trans.), Bloomington and Indianapolis: Indiana University Press.
Bassett, Jordan (2017), 'We Need to Talk about Barbara: Why *The League of Gentlemen* Feels out of Time', *NME*, 20 December, https://www.nme.com/blogs/nme-blogs/we-need-to-talk-about-barbara-why-the-league-of-gentlemen-feels-out-of-time-2178013 (accessed 30 August 2018).
Beattie, James (1779) [1776], 'On Laughter and Ludicrous Composition', in *Essays*, E. and C. Dilly and W. Creech: Edinburgh, pp. 297–450.

Botting, Fred (2014), 'Post-Millennial Monsters: Monstrosity-No-More', in Glennis Byron and Dale Townshend (eds), *The Gothic World*, London: Routledge, pp. 498–509.
Browne, S. G. (2009), *Breathers: A Zombie's Lament*, New York: Broadway Books.
Carroll, Noël (1999), 'Horror and Humor', *The Journal of Aesthetics and Art Criticism*, 57.2, 145–60.
Cohen, Jeffrey Jerome (1996), 'Monster Culture (Seven Theses)', in *Monster Theory*, Minneapolis: University of Minnesota Press, pp. 3–25.
Duncan, Glen (2011), *The Last Werewolf*, Edinburgh: Canongate.
Elliott, Kamilla (2008), 'Gothic – Film – Parody', *Adaptation*, 1.1, 24–43.
Foucault, Michel (1986), 'Of Other Spaces', Jay Miskowiec (trans.), *Diacritics*, 16.1, 22–7.
Frye, Northrop (2006) [1957], *The Anatomy of Criticism: Four Essays*, Toronto: University of Toronto Press.
Horner, Avril, and Sue Zlosnik (2004), *Gothic and the Comic Turn*, Basingstoke: Palgrave.
— (2012), 'Comic Gothic', in David Punter (ed.), *A New Companion to the Gothic*, Oxford: Wiley-Blackwell, pp. 321–34.
Jinks, Catherine (2009), *The Reformed Vampire Support Group*, London: Quercus.
Kinsella, Sharon (1995), 'Cuties in Japan', in Lise Skov and Brian Moeran (eds), *Women, Media and Consumption in Japan*, London/Honolulu: Curzon/University of Hawai'i Press, pp. 220–54.
Paul, William (1994), *Laughing Screaming: Modern Hollywood Horror and Comedy*, New York: University of Columbia Press.
Sontag, Susan (1994), *Against Interpretation*, London: Vintage.
Spooner, Catherine (2017), *Post-Millennial Gothic: Comedy, Romance and the Rise of Happy Gothic*, London: Bloomsbury.
Stott, Andrew (2005), *Comedy*, New York and London: Routledge.
Wheatley, Helen (2006), *Gothic Television*, Manchester: Manchester University Press.

Chapter 14

Steampunk
Claire Nally

In 2007, James Richardson-Brown (aka Captain Sydeian) organised the first UK steampunk get-together at Whitby Gothic Weekend (WGW). Since then, steampunks have congregated alongside the traditional goth community in a series of fringe events hosted at Whitby's The Rifle Club. Whitby was already an important location for alternative culture: in 1994, Jo Hampshire assembled around forty goth penpals at The Elsinore pub, in the small North Yorkshire seaside town. Goth (as distinct from Gothic) emerged in the late 1970s and is often associated with the popularity of the band The Sisters of Mercy (although the lead singer, Andrew Eldritch, rejects any association), as well as The Damned, Bauhaus, Siouxsie and the Banshees and Joy Division. The music has a wide range of themes and sounds but is often composed of a heavy drum beat (on a drum machine), rock guitars, low-register male vocals and, as a counterpoint, a high-register female voice. But it is not simply a music culture. For many, goth is a lifestyle choice, imbued with a dark aesthetic that overlaps with steampunk in a surprising number of ways. One of the most pre-eminent steampunk bands, Abney Park, have headlined at the WGW event several times, having moved from an industrial to a steampunk sound. This suggests a diversification of the goth subculture and a fluidity between the genres. This chapter offers a definition of steampunk and its relationship to the goth subculture in terms of revisiting and adapting historical aesthetics, while paying close attention to the inherent differences between these two practices. The central argument employs the post-subculture model (Muggleton and Weinzierl 2003), which sees subcultures as elective and postmodern in terms of identity politics. Using WGW as a starting point for this analysis, the chapter then undertakes a survey of themes in steampunk music, fashion and literature, including its increased popularisation and visibility, while also theorising the subculture in terms of a range of issues, including activism, the politics of neo-Victorianism and, relatedly, postcolonialism.

Defining Steampunk

Unlike many other subcultures (including goth), steampunk first emerged as a literary, rather than a music, phenomenon. The author K. W. Jeter is usually credited with coining the term, which he later identified as 'a taste for brass and copper and the ticking, hissing mesh-&-grind of Victorian technology' (Jeter 2011: 6). Indeed, he characterises steampunk as an aesthetic resistance to the smooth surfaces of contemporary mass production, explaining that 'there is something nauseatingly pre-digested about the look of late 20th and early 21st century industrial design, all those Steve Jobs-approved rounded edges like cough lozenges sucked on for a minute or so before being spat out into your hand' (8). This aesthetic resistance has been incorporated into the wider subcultural practice of steampunk: many participants embrace this aspect of retro-technology in their attire, so cogs and clockwork, mechanical prostheses, brass and wood, as well as militaria, often make their way into the design of clothing, accessories and millinery. Interestingly, there are aspects of both goth and steampunk that hark back to the Victorian era – for steampunk, this is technological as well as sartorial, whereas in goth the imagery is often far more melancholy, morbid and related to 'the perverse sexuality of fetish wear and the graveyard exoticism of nineteenth century mourning costume to create a macabre aesthetic' (Spooner 2004: 162). Both subcultures, however, share the notion of spectacle, for, as Dick Hebdige explains in his seminal work on subculture,

> spectacular subcultures [. . .] are *obviously* fabricated [. . .] They *display* their own codes (e.g. the punk's ripped T-shirt) or at least demonstrate that the codes are there to be used and abused (e.g. they have been thought about rather than thrown together). In this they go against the grain of a mainstream culture. (Hebdige 1979: 101–2)

While later critics (such as Muggleton 2000), have complicated the model of subcultural affiliation and resistance, noting that subcultures are nonetheless subject to commercial imperatives (Spooner 2004: 165), the idea of the spectacular subculture is still persuasive insofar as both goth and steampunk are self-conscious, visual articulations of dissimilarity from everyday style.

Steampunk is synonymous with sepia tones (unlike the black garb traditionally invoked in relation to goth), alongside a nostalgic but often critical approach to the Victorian period, as well as the present. It encompasses technology, DIY arts and crafts practice, but is not necessarily about replicating the past as much as it is invested in interrogating and complicating it by invoking the perspective and sensibilities of the present. Therefore, Jeff VanderMeer identifies steampunk as follows: '[f]irst, it's simultaneously retro and forward-looking in nature. Second, it evokes a sense of adventure and discovery. Third, it embraces divergent and extinct technologies as a way of talking about the future' (VanderMeer 2011: 9). Unsurprisingly, given this focus on the future, steampunk also embraces anachronism and science fiction, with key literary reference points including figures such as H. G. Wells, Mary Shelley and Jules Verne. This idea of repurposing historical material extends across literature, film, art, music and craft, with sources being adapted and reconfigured to comment upon both the present and the past. From a literary perspective, there has been an explosion of novels broadly embracing the steampunk aesthetic: K. W. Jeter's *Infernal Devices* (1987), William Gibson and Bruce Sterling's *The Difference Engine* (1990), James P. Blaylock's *Langdon St. Ives* book series (1986–2015), Tim Powers's *The Anubis Gates* (1983), as well as the works of Cherie Priest, China Miéville, Gail Carriger, Paolo Bacigalupi, G. W. Dahlquist, Neal Stephenson, Robert Rankin, Margaret Killjoy and Scott Westerfeld.

Steampunk at its best is avowedly political. For instance, *The Steampunk Magazine* represents a repository of radical politics, including debates around gender, activism and anti-capitalism. But there are also elements of the subculture which might be seen to invoke nostalgia for a bygone imperial age, rather than a challenge to it. Here, it is useful to address the ways in which steampunk participates in some of the issues also plaguing neo-Victorianism more broadly. Elizabeth Ho comments that

> the visual vocabulary of imperialism that dominates steampunk texts and culture (modified pith helmets, military uniforms and weaponry, maps, the gear and trappings of space and terrestrial exploration, Asian(-inspired) materials and costuming) and a certain position toward the Victorian that leaves in place orientalist structures and understandings of 'the East' has prompted a re-examination of the steampunk archive. (2012: 148)

Thus, the subculture might be seen to be multifaceted in its approach, being simultaneously radical and conservative in its practice. A clear example of this double-bind might be demonstrated in the ubiquity of the corset in steampunk's (and goth's) sartorial repertoire. Steampunk Couture, a clothing line developed by Kato (erotic model, fashion designer and presenter of the GSN short-lived *Steampunk'd* reality TV series from 2015), showcases in its fashion collections the instability of the corset as signifier. Steampunk Couture's (n.d.) photoshoot for the 'Ryonen' corset (from the Spring 2011 collection) seems to combine utility and traditional femininity. The corset itself might be interpreted as armour: the Red Riding Hood trope is discernible in the forest setting and the red cape sported by the model, so here the corset is protection, implying the self-sufficiency and survival instincts present in the heroine from different versions of the fairy tale tradition. However, like many interpretations of the Red Riding Hood story (see Zipes 1993), there is also the trace of patriarchal injunctions relating to womanhood (the model is young, stereotypically attractive, slender, a touch provocative). The corset seems very serviceable and practical (beige in colour, it has buckle features and is accessorised with a coin purse, dispensing with the need for a handbag), but at the same time the accentuation of breasts and feminine curves insinuate the importance of feminine convention and sexual allure. Thus, in this instance at least, steampunk style is ambivalently positioned as conservative and revolutionary. Indeed, this also reflects subcultural co-option of Victorian clothing more generally. Valerie Steele has noted that the corset is not related to simple binary oppositions 'in terms of oppression versus liberation, and fashion versus comfort and health. Corsetry was not one monolithic, unchanging experience that all unfortunate women experienced before being liberated by feminism. It was a situated practice that meant different things to different people at different times' (Steele 2001: 1).

While we have already noted that steampunk interconnects with goth in some ways (most notably at music festivals), it is also important to register how far this intersection has prompted tension between the two communities, resulting in a gatekeeper stance from some of the key voices in the two scenes. Following the Manchester bombing in May 2017 which killed 23 people at an Ariana Grande concert, WGW headquarters reissued a statement about the prohibition of replica weaponry at all its events and identified elements of the steampunk community as being especially divisive on this issue. Certainly the use of military paraphernalia is an element of some steampunk practice, and this has prompted criticism from a number of circles, especially when it is aligned with politically- and racially-charged colonial signifiers such as pith helmets. Whereas the official festival statement indicates a section of the goth community want to distance themselves from carrying imitation weaponry (and this is not generally associated with goth sartorial choice), elements of the steampunk arts and crafts community happily customise replica weaponry. However, it is also worth noting that The Asylum Steampunk Festival in Lincoln has issued a Dress and Etiquette Code, which included a highly nuanced provision for weaponry and safety (Rostov 2015). The issue of replica weaponry is not the only example of tension between goths and steampunks at the festival, as an article from 2016 in *The Steampunk Journal* makes clear (Moriarty Viccar 2016). Indeed, Whitby Steampunk Weekend, first held in the town in 2017, seems to codify a distinction between the two communities, beyond the stereotype of a brown versus black colour palette.

More generally, Robert Brown ('Captain Robert'), lead singer with steampunk icons Abney Park, has engaged in an effort to demarcate the steampunk community from perceived commodification:

> I'm fairly annoyed by people dressing Steampunk, then making music with zero vintage in the sound, and calling themselves Steampunk music makers [. . .] There are also a ton more clones these days. Cosplayers playacting they are Steampunks in a hotel lobby. People, instead of being their own original interpretation on Steampunk, show up looking almost identical to everyone else. (Quoted in VanderMeer and Boskovich 2014: 202)

In the light of these comments, it is useful to reflect upon Sarah Thornton's conceptualisation of subcultural capital as 'confer[ring] status on its owner in the eyes of the relevant beholder [. . .] subcultural capital is objectified in the form of fashionable haircuts and well-assembled record collections' (Thornton 1995: 11). So while Captain Robert rails against the commodification of the steampunk subculture, and suggests individuality is key to the practice, it is also clear that certain steampunk performances are (to him) inadmissible as authentic markers of subcultural identity. This is perhaps where the DIY ethos of steampunk is crucial – as a maker culture, it celebrates the unique, the handmade, the one-of-a-kind object. To buy one's steampunk outfit from a mass market retailer suggests inauthenticity, a lack of commitment to the ethics behind the varying and disparate articulations of the scene.

The popularity of steampunk has certainly meant not only increased visibility in the mainstream, but also its co-option in terms of its very specific iconography. Justin Bieber's flirtation with steampunk in the music video 'Santa Claus is Coming to Town' in 2011 provoked incredulity and anger from many aficionados of the subculture (Stubby the Rocket 2011). In each instance, this gestures towards how subcultures are subject to internal policing and how authenticity is a major issue for participants. In defining subcultures as they are articulated in the late twentieth and early twenty-first centuries, David Muggleton has argued that they are not 'internally homogenous and externally demarcated' (2000: 21). Rather, he has suggested, in common with others (Bennett and Harris 2004: 31), that a monolithic approach to subcultures, with ideas of static membership and fixed identities, does a disservice to the plethora of practice within any one subculture (Muggleton 2000: 23). Moreover, with the advent of postmodern articulations of fluid identities and aesthetic play, it may be the case that participants can deploy signifiers from more than one subculture. As Paul Hodkinson has argued in his discussion of goth, 'participants engaging in their subcultural stylistic pick 'n' mix tended to select one or two items of clothing or accessories associated with related scenes or subcultures' (2002: 56). In this sense, the broader idea of 'alternative' culture is perhaps a more useful way of thinking about the cross-references between goth and steampunk.

Cultural Contributions

In terms of steampunk outputs we might address several key areas where the subculture has contributed to arts and culture: literature, music, film, art and fashion. Addressing these in turn is crucial in order to offer a broader picture of the movement. In terms of literature, *The Steampunk Magazine*, which was first published in 2007, is one of the best examples of the politically radical thread which informs some aspects of steampunk practice, and emphasises the anarchist influences on steampunk. If steampunk offers a vision of an alternative future from the perspective of the nineteenth-century past (or a future that never was), then it also aligns itself with utopian politics: '[p]roblems can be discussed by way of dramatizations, and the appeal of an alternative society can be evoked for people to contemplate, to wish for, to work for' (Robinson 2009: 3). This utopianism is foregrounded in the first issue of *The Steampunk Magazine*, in an article by The Catastrophone Orchestra and Arts Collective. Keen to distance themselves from a nostalgia which replicates the Victorian age without censure, the Collective suggests that

> [s]teampunk rejects the myopic, nostalgia-drenched politics so common among 'alternative' cultures. Ours is not the culture of Neo-Victorianism and stupefying etiquette, not remotely an escape to gentlemen's clubs and classist rhetoric [. . .] Too much of what passes as steampunk denies the punk, in all its guises. (The Catastrophone Orchestra and Arts Collective 2012: 11)

As a manifesto for the radical strand of the movement, this also summarises the ethos of the magazine very effectively. Running to nine issues, *The Steampunk Magazine* presented interviews with writers, such as

Michael Moorcock and Alan Moore, as well as musicians and bands like Ghostfire, The Men That Will Not Be Blamed For Nothing, Dr Steel and Unwoman (some of whom will be discussed below). The magazine also featured fiction and poetry on steampunk themes, but a large part of the publication was nonfiction articles, including definitions of the subculture and lifestyle advice for makers and DIY practitioners ('It Can't All Be Brass, Dear: Paper Maché in the Modern Home', 'Sew an Aviator's Cap', 'Sew Yourself a Lady's Artisan Apron'). At the centre of many articles is a clear political agenda ('The Courage to Kill a King: Anarchists in a Time of Regicide', 'Nevermind the Morlocks: Here's Occupy Wall Street', 'On Race and Steampunk: A Quick Primer', 'Riot Grrls, 19th Century Style'). Notably, many articles suggest a feminist imperative which is entirely resistant to the mainstream model of gender and sexuality. In 'The Steampunk's Guide to Body Hair', the reader is enjoined that 'in regards of the growing or shaving of body hair, people of all genders ought to feel free to do either' (Anonymous 2012: 102), while one article by Miriam Roček (aka Steampunk Emma Goldman) contests 'the fascism in fashion' (Roček n.d.: 96–101).

Related to the political inflection of steampunk, the UK-based artist Geof Banyard (Doctor Geof) has featured in *Steampunk Magazine* as well as enjoying visibility on the goth subculture scene. Doctor Geof produces line drawing artwork which also combines historical anachronism, whimsy, discussions of subculture, fetish and gentle satire. In terms of his steampunk work, we might point to The Great Tea Referendum at The Asylum Steampunk Festival in Lincoln, UK, in August 2016, which spoofs the EU Referendum in the UK (June 2016) by refiguring the EU-Brexit debate as a comedic reflection on preference regarding 'Milk First' or 'Milk Last' in a cup of tea. The hyperbole of the divisive political propaganda in circulation at the time is lambasted through Doctor Geof's artwork accompanying the Lincoln event, where the Milk First contingent reflect upon the broken promises of earlier generations: '[o]n 24th August 1863 "MILK LAST" cracked this cup of tea and in doing so BROKE THEIR PROMISE TO US ALL. Don't Let Them Win. Vote Milk First' (The Island of Doctor Geof 2016a). This is pitted against Milk Last's denunciation of the opposition: 'MILK FIRST is responsible for all cases of Untraceable Orphan Gruel-Fatigue Syndrome. And you're a good person, aren't you? You wouldn't do THAT to ORPHANS would you? Surely not. Not like THEM' (The Island of Doctor Geof 2016b).

In terms of novels, possibly the most prolific of steampunk literary outputs, there is a wealth of material to identify and explore. This chapter has already noted how works such as K. W. Jeter's *Infernal Devices* and William Gibson and Bruce Sterling's *The Difference*

Engine are cornerstones of steampunk fiction. *The Difference Engine* is a complex reflection on the development of Industrial Age London in 1855, where Charles Babbage's success in developing a calculating machine has propelled society onto a different path. Lord Byron, Ada Lovelace (Byron's daughter who worked with Charles Babbage on his calculating machines) and various other historical figures such as Isambard Kingdom Brunel and Charles Darwin feature alongside fictional characters such as the heroine from Disraeli's *Sybil* (1845). In some ways, this curious fusion of (alternative) historical fact with fiction is a feature of many steampunk fictions. Alan Moore's graphic novel series *The League of Extraordinary Gentlemen* (1999–) rewrites history and literature in a similar fashion, while K. W. Jeter's *Morlock Night* (1979) transports the pitiless Morlocks of H. G. Wells's *The Time Machine* (1895) to Victorian London, where they present an increasing threat to the population, who in turn are rescued by a reincarnation of King Arthur. Notably, the poverty of nineteenth-century London is reflected through Henry Mayhew's research, published in *London Labour and the London Poor* (1851), and indeed Mayhew briefly features in an anecdote retold by one of the 'toshers' (sewer scavengers), who works in the sewers under the city. Each of these examples suggests that steampunk literature has an anachronistic and irreverent approach to its historical predecessors, yet also reimagines or fabricates an alternative history (uchronia).

Gail Carriger's work in the Parasol Protectorate book series (2009–12) is useful insofar as it showcases the intersection of popular romance fiction and steampunk tropes. Mike Perschon has argued that Carriger's heroine, Alexia, is a 'romanticized New Woman of steampunk [who] can have career and family' (2013: 34). However, rather than a New Woman, Alexia's status is much more that of the postfeminist romantic heroine (think Helen Fielding's Bridget Jones), a woman who represents society's enjoinder to 'have it all', despite the gross inequalities still discernible in the culture as a whole. Alexia inhabits a steampunk world where vampires and werewolves live openly in society, and in the first novel, *Soulless* (2009), is happy with her spinster status. However, by the end of the first novel, she marries a werewolf, Lord Maccon, and is thus brought into normative femininity (she subsequently has a daughter, Prudence). As Diane Negra notes with reference to postfeminist tropes, 'it is taken to be self-evident that single and non-parenting women's lives are empty, deficient, or not yet fully underway' (2009: 61).

At this stage, it will be apparent that not all steampunk fiction is radical or paradigm-shifting – quite the opposite. What all steampunk fiction shares, however, is an alternative worldview, usually in an urban environment where scientific development has altered the trajectory of history (and this is where steampunk's science fiction credentials become apparent). For instance, dirigibles become a normal part of everyday transportation, clockwork automatons or time travel become possible. This is also the case with many popular steampunk films: *Wild Wild West* (Barry Sonnenfeld, 1999), *The League of Extraordinary Gentlemen* (Stephen Norrington, 2003) and *Sherlock Holmes* (Guy Ritchie, 2009), as each reference steampunk in their representation of steampunk accoutrements, technology and retro-engineered weaponry. The use of such paraphernalia is also where the arts and crafts aspect of steampunk overlaps with popular culture: Ian Finch-Field (of SkinzNhydez) makes leather goods, film props and steampunk gear, which underscores the ethos of arts and craft – the original, authentic and individualised art object, rather than the mass-produced and sleek lines of twenty-first-century commodity. As Bruce Sterling summarises,

> the Industrial Revolution has grown old. So machines that Romantics considered satanic now look Romantic [. . .] the heaviest guys in the Steampunk scene are not really into 'steam.' Instead, they are into punk. Specifically, punk's do-it-yourself aspects and its determination to take the means of production away from big, mind-deadening companies who want to package and sell shrink-wrapped cultural product. (Quoted in VanderMeer 2011: 12)

These resistant gestures are also perceptible in the work of Richard Nagy ('Datamancer'), whose work underscores the functionality of these aesthetically pleasing objects. His steampunk computers, while being fully operational, reference the intersection of modern technology and retro design: typewriter keyboards, telegraph computer mice, display monitors, each register through the use of wood, metal and brass the affective physicality of historical materials (see Donovan 2011: 105–9). As Datamancer's website articulates, '[t]he mechanical keys give the keyboards a tactile "click" or "snap" to them, which lends itself nicely to the "typewriter" theme of the keys and provides a nice sense of touch-feedback' (Datamancer n.d). Joey Marsocci (Dr Grymm) similarly combines functionality and design in his objects: the 'Victrola Eye-Pod' (Donovan 2011: 88) is a modded iPod Nano, featuring a large mechanical eye, while other outputs, such as his 'Vampire Blood Lust Goggles' (84), emphasise the intersection between Gothic and steampunk.

The adventure narrative is also crucial to steampunk films such as *Les Aventures extraordinaires d'Adèle Blanc-Sec* (*The Extraordinary Adventures of Adèle Blanc-Sec*, Luc Besson, 2010), where the stereotypical 'boy's own adventure story' is reconfigured with a female lead. *The City of Lost Children* (Jean-Pierre Jeunet and Marc Caro, 1995), *Suchîmubôi*

(*Steamboy*, Katsuhiro Otomo, 2004) and *Hugo* (Martin Scorsese, 2011) each demonstrate the international appeal and global reach of steampunk – it has incarnations across Europe, in the US, but also in East Asia, where it garners other influences from traditions such as Japanese anime. The Australian short film *The Mysterious Explorations of Jasper Morello* (Anthony Lucas, 2005) combines gothic and steampunk aesthetics (dark, oppressive silhouettes combine with black and sepia colour through the use of shadow puppetry and origami) with a post-apocalyptic narrative of plague in the city of Gothia, from where Jasper Morello embarks on a fantastical dirigible journey in search of a cure. The tropes of the solitary, tormented and enigmatic Gothic hero converge here with ecological and humanitarian anxieties about where our world might be headed.

While literature, film and visual culture provide a formidable contribution to steampunk, other cultural activities, such as music, have equally important roles in the subculture. However, perhaps unlike steampunk's visual and literary culture, music has less of a unitary style or perceptible features which can pinpoint it as a steampunk sound. Steampunk music draws on metal, rock, goth, classical, hip-hop and jazz, among others, meaning its chief hallmark is aural eclecticism. In this respect, thematic correspondences suggest steampunk is far more than a sound or music style as such:

> The actual sound of steampunk is all over the map, so in that regard I would leave it up to the individual's music taste. I would hope they would dress the part and that the lyrics conjured up some nice, fantastical imagery. I would definitely have a violin, cello, banjo, accordion, or some instrument that would give it an 'old-timey' feel. And for extra credit, I would add in a bit of machinery to the mix by way of electronic instruments or percussive elements to represent the fantastic machines, crazy intentions, or the Industrial Revolution in general. (Captain Robert, quoted in VanderMeer and Boskovich 2014: 187)

In light of this comment it is clear that historical instruments, juxtaposed with a more contemporary or electronic component, highlight the steampunk ethos. The importance of a musician's or band's spectacle, 'dress[ing] the part' in order to visualise this alternate world, also identifies how the music genre intersects with subculture more generally. Appearance as well as sound is a hallmark of steampunk in music.

A musician such as Unwoman, whose stage name is tellingly derived from Margaret Atwood's dystopian novel, *The Handmaid's Tale* (1985), engages with many of these issues in her 2012 album *The Fires I Started*. Her music is a fusion of her classical cello playing and electronica beats. Thematically, she addresses feminist politics, revolution and social class, and employs literary models such as George Orwell ('The Future, The Boot'), William Blake ('A Poison Tree') and the anarcho-feminist writer Voltairine de Cleyre ('Written in Red'). As with steampunk literature, and the arts and crafts element of the movement, the music scene is highly intertextual as well as political, borrowing and adapting prior models and sources (Unwoman has also released covers of classic goth singles like The Sisters of Mercy's 'Temple of Love' (1983/1992) and 'More' (1990), Joy Division's 'Love Will Tear Us Apart' (1979) and The Velvet Underground's 'Venus in Furs' (1967), the latter also covered by Christian Death). Although a much more thrash, metal, punk and heavy outfit than Unwoman, like her, the political alignment of The Men That Will Not Be Blamed For Nothing (name derived from supposed evidence in the Jack the Ripper case) emphasise the '-punk' aspect of the genre, castigating the inequalities of the Victorian age in songs like 'Third Class Coffin' and 'Miner'. Andy Heintz of TMTWNBBFN explains they 'decided to take the "punk" part of Steampunk literally and imagine what a punk band would be singing about if they were from 1880 instead of 1980' (quoted in VanderMeer and Boskovich 2014: 188). Andrew O'Neill's vocals and guitar accompany Heintz's vocals (and musical saw!), and both these band members in particular present a striking subcultural spectacle onstage: O'Neill's cross-dressing and Heintz's garishly dyed beard imply a sartorial punk style to accompany their sound. They have also playfully released songs on limited edition wax cylinders. The song 'Sewer' was released in 2010, limited to forty copies, with the proviso that '[a]nyone buying one of the 40 copies of the track on wax will also get instructions for building a phonograph to play the cylinder' (Anonymous 2010). The DIY maker culture of steampunk is codified here with the technologies of the past, the political radicalism of punk and the aesthetic pleasure garnered from antiquated machinery. Thomas Truax similarly explores the affective physicality of steampunk in his custom-made instruments: the Hornicator (a 'pimped up gramophone') and the Mother Superior ('delivering a dizzying array of grooves, clacks, snaps and thumps'), among others, testify to the hands-on, individualised maker culture of steampunk (Truax n.d.)

Comparatively, the band Abney Park (named after the graveyard in London) showcase a stage presence, lyrical content and image which melds steampunk with industrial and goth. As a testimony to the way in which steampunk has achieved greater visibility in recent years, as well as its links with goth, it is useful to note that the Abney Park song 'Sleep Isabella' (from the album *Lost Horizons*, 2008) featured in HBO's *True Blood* series (2008–14). In fact, the whole album *Lost Horizons* locates the themes associated with steampunk very effectively. 'Airship Pirate' contributes to the pseudo-biography of the band, with band members having alternative identities as airship pirates in an imagined steampunk world. The intertextuality of the steampunk narrative on the album is obvious from the song titles: 'Herr Drosselmyer's Doll' (from *The Nutcracker*), 'I Am Stretched On Your Grave' (a seventeenth-century Irish poem, 'A Taim Sinte air do Thuamba'), and 'The Secret Life of Dr Calgori' (presumably riffing on the 1920 German Expressionist horror film, *The Cabinet of Dr Caligari*, as well as the theme of the mad inventor scientist so prominent in steampunk).

The construction of a steampunk persona (or *steamsona*) is especially noteworthy in the context of Professor Elemental, who has summarised steampunk music as being defined by '[p]oliteness, camaraderie, invention [. . .] exploration and adventure' (quoted in VanderMeer and Boskovich 2014: 187). This definition presents something of a contrast to the raw, aggressive punk of bands like TMTWNBBFN, and, conversely, shows more allegiance to the 'chap-hop' movement in music. This is a variant of hip-hop (shared by his arch-nemesis Mr. B The Gentleman Rhymer), but it is one which celebrates English values and satirises stereotypes such as tea-drinking, gin, cricket and gentlemanly codes of politeness. His homage to tea, 'A Cup of Brown Joy' (from the 2010 album *The Indifference Engine*) combines an expansionist travel narrative citing tea from around the world and a wry commentary on tea drinking as drug addiction.

In issue 4 of *Steampunk Magazine*, Libby Bulloff commented that 'many people who self-identify as or are actively involved in the goth/industrial/punk scenes are currently taking an intense interest in steampunk' (Bulloff 2012: 210). As this chapter has sought to demonstrate, the relationship between goth and steampunk is marked, but it is also fraught with contestations and difficulties. There are numerous, inherent differences between these two practices. Science fiction and invention are perhaps more overt in steampunk, and the music of the subculture is perhaps more disparate in terms of its influences. While Whitby is a place of pilgrimage for many goths due to the seaside town featuring in Bram Stoker's *Dracula* (1897), goth is first and foremost a music scene, which derives inspiration from Gothic literature and horror, among other sources. Steampunk, by comparison, originated as a literary subculture, and has spiralled into a plethora of cultural practices, including music, art, film and DIY practice. Both subcultures, however, share a common ethos in terms of attempting to interrogate the wider culture's aesthetic values, through performative dress and spectacle, often referencing the nineteenth century. As a close relation of twenty-first-century Gothic, it is worthwhile noting how far the darker elements of steampunk overlap in sartorial style, especially with the influence of Victoriana. Steamgoth, which Richardson-Brown and others have characterised as steampunk infused with horror, is a testament to how far the distinct subcultures have also found common ground: 'Steamgoth is a far darker view of the steampunk world. Whereas steampunk can often be said to be science fiction set in an alternative Victorian-era world, Steamgoth would be horror set in that same world' (Alfaya n.d.). Similarly, as we have seen, both goth and steampunk have wrestled with the issue of increased commodification and what this means for the subculture. Ultimately, the complexities associated with the radicalism or conservatism of steampunk practice ensure it will remain a dynamic and contested field of enquiry for scholars and wider culture.

Film and Television

Hugo (Martin Scorsese, France/UK/USA, 2011)
Les Aventures extraordinaires d'Adèle Blanc-Sec (*The Extraordinary Adventures of Adèle Blanc-Sec*, Luc Besson, France, 2010)
Sherlock Holmes (Guy Ritchie, UK/USA, 2009)
Steamboy (Katsuhiro Otomo, Japan, 2004)
The City of Lost Children (Jean-Pierre Jeunet and Marc Caro, France/Germany/Spain, 1995)
The League of Extraordinary Gentlemen (Stephen Norrington, UK/Germany, Czech Republic/USA, 2003)
The Mysterious Explorations of Jasper Morello (Anthony Lucas, Australia, 2005)
Wild Wild West (Barry Sonnenfeld, USA, 1999)

Webpages

Alfaya, J. F. (n.d.), 'Steamgoth in a Nutshell', http://www.decimononic.com/blog/steamgoth-in-a-nutshell-1-of-6-intro (accessed 18 January 2018).
Anonymous (2010), 'Tech Know: A Journey into Sound', http://www.bbc.co.uk/news/10171206, (accessed 15 January 2018).
Datamancer (n.d.), https://datamancer.com/faq/ (accessed 15 December 2017).
Moriarty Viccar (2016), 'The Future of Steampunks at Whitby Goth Weekend: Could it be Time to Throw in the Towel?', https://www.steampunkjournal.org/2016/11/14/future-steampunks-whitby-goth-weekend/ (accessed 3 February 2018).
Rostov (2015), 'What to Do about Steampunk Weapons', 25 August, https://www.asylumsteampunk.co.uk/steampunk-weapons/ (accessed 3 February 2018).
SkinzNhydez (n.d.), https://www.etsy.com/uk/shop/SkinzNhydez?ref=condensed_trust_header_title_items (accessed 19 January 2018).

Steampunk Couture (n.d.), https://www.steampunkcouture.com/forsale/c/spring-2011/the-ryonen-corset-97/ (accessed 17 January 2018).

Stubby the Rocket (2011), 'Justin Bieber Has Gone Steampunk', https://www.tor.com/2011/12/06/justin-bieber-has-gone-steampunk/ (accessed 18 January 2018).

The Island of Doctor Geof (2016a), 'Milk First: The Broken Cup', http://shop2.islandofdoctorgeof.co.uk/index.php?route=product/product&product_id=241&tag=tea+referendum (accessed 23 January 2018).

The Island of Doctor Geof (2016b), 'Milk Last: Blame Them', http://shop2.islandofdoctorgeof.co.uk/index.php?route=product/product&product_id=235&tag=tea+referendum (accessed 23 January 2018).

Truax, Thomas (n.d.), 'Instruments', https://www.thomastruax.com/instruments/ (accessed: 2 February 2018).

References

Anonymous (2012) [n.d.], 'The Steampunk's Guide to Body Hair', *The Steampunk Magazine*, issue 2, from *The Steampunk Magazine, The First Years: Issues #1–7*, Combustion Books, 102–3.

Bennett, Andy, and Keith Kahn-Harris (2004), *After Subculture: Critical Studies in Contemporary Youth Culture*, Basingstoke: Palgrave Macmillan.

Bulloff, Libby (2012) [n.d.], 'Paint It Brass: The Intersection of Goth and Steam', *The Steampunk Magazine*, issue 4, from *The Steampunk Magazine, The First Years: Issues #1–7*, Combustion Books, 210–11.

Donovan, Art (2011), *The Art of Steampunk*, East Petersburg, PA: Fox Chapel Publishing.

Hebdige, Dick (1979), *Subculture: The Meaning of Style*, Abingdon: Routledge.

Ho, Elizabeth (2012), *Neo-Victorianism and the Memory of Empire*, London: Bloomsbury.

Hodkinson, Paul (2002), *Goth: Identity, Style and Subculture*, Oxford: Berg.

Jeter, K. W. (2011), *Infernal Devices*, Oxford: Angry Robot.

Muggleton, David (2000), *Inside Subculture: The Postmodern Meaning of Style*, Oxford: Berg.

Muggleton, David, and Rupert Weinzierl (eds) (2003), *The Post-Subcultures Reader*, Oxford: Berg.

Negra, Diane (2009), *What a Girl Wants? Fantasizing the Reclamation of Self in Postfeminism*, Abingdon: Routledge.

Perschon, Mike (2013), 'Useful Troublemakers: Social Retrofuturism in the Steampunk Novels of Gail Carriger and Cherie Priest', in Julie Anne Tadeo and Cynthia J. Miller (eds), *Steaming into a Victorian Future: A Steampunk Anthology*, Lanham, MD, and Plymouth: Scarecrow Press, pp. 21–42.

Robinson, Kim Stanley (2009), 'Introduction', in Margaret Killjoy (ed.), *Mythmakers and Lawbreakers: Anarchist Writers on Fiction*, Edinburgh: AK Press, pp. 1–5.

Roček, Miriam (n.d.), 'A Healthy Alternative to Fascism in Fashion', *The Steampunk Magazine*, issue 9, 96–101.

Spooner, Catherine (2004), *Fashioning Gothic Bodies*, Manchester: Manchester University Press.
Steele, Valerie (2001), *The Corset: A Cultural History*, London and New Haven, CT: Yale University Press.
The Catastrophone Orchestra and Arts Collective (2012) [n.d.], 'What Then, Is Steampunk? Colonizing the Past So We Can Dream the Future', *The Steampunk Magazine*, issue 1, from *The Steampunk Magazine, The First Years: Issues #1–7*, Combustion Books, 10–11.
Thornton, Sarah (1995), *Club Cultures: Music, Media and Subcultural Capital*, Oxford: Blackwell.
VanderMeer, Jeff (2011), *The Steampunk Bible*, New York: Abrams.
VanderMeer, Jeff, and Desirina Boskovich (2014), *The Steampunk User's Manual*, New York: Abrams.
Zipes, Jack (1993), *The Trials and Tribulations of Little Red Riding Hood: Versions of the Tale in Sociocultural Context*, Abingdon: Routledge.

Chapter 15

Posthuman Gothic
Anya Heise-von der Lippe

The posthuman Gothic is concerned with humanity's widespread sense of unease regarding our biomedical and technological involvements and their capacity to change our perceptions of what it means to be human. It revolves around our fear of becoming Other, of losing ourselves in a multitude of corporeal as well as discursive possibilities. While attempts at systematically defining the posthuman Gothic are relatively recent (Bolton 2014; Heise-von der Lippe 2017), the narrative exploration of related phenomena – Gothic technologies and machineries of textual production for instance – can be traced back to earlier Gothic texts and predecessors in adjacent genres like cyberpunk (William Gibson's *Neuromancer* (1984), or Philip K. Dick's *Do Androids Dream of Electric Sheep?* (1968)) or hypertext (Shelley Jackson's *Patchwork Girl* (1995), for instance). Mary Shelley's *Frankenstein* (1818) is an important predecessor of these discussions as it had a lasting impact on later posthuman narratives as well as posthuman Gothic criticism. Humanity's relationship with uncanny machineries and man-made monstrous others is a key element of the Gothic mode, which has long been fascinated with the more liminal states and involvements of the human. Posthuman Gothic texts shift these concerns (and fears) towards questions of (human) identity constructions. By aestheticising the uncanniness of the automaton – the almost-but-not-quite human cyborg or the abject, biotech human-animal hybrid – posthuman Gothic texts not only draw attention to the many ways in which these processes can and will go wrong, they also highlight the instability and ultimate unsustainability of our most basic ontological category – the human – along with the essential ethical and epistemological paradigms we derive from it.

The near-future television series *Black Mirror* (2011–) plays on common fears of a dark future in which technology is so ingrained within human bodies and lives that it has an immediate impact on our existence, life and death. Season three's penultimate episode 'Men

Against Fire' (2016) poses a prime example of how the posthuman Gothic challenges culturally ingrained dichotomies of humans and non-humans and shifts the boundaries between 'us' and 'them' through the use of dehumanising technologies. The narrative follows a group of high-tech-equipped North American soldiers on a mission to hunt 'roaches', who are introduced as sub-human or even monstrous, based on how the soldiers perceive them through their high-tech 'MASS' implants. 'You can't still see them as human', the commanding officer admonishes a roach-sympathiser, pointing out how killing the roaches will stop their 'sickness' from being passed on to future generations, and army psychologist Arquette explains the underlying eugenic ideology: '[d]o you have any idea of the amount of shit that is in their DNA? Higher rates of cancer, muscular dystrophy, MS, SLS, sub-standard IQ, criminal tendencies, sexual deviances – it's all there. The screening shows it.' The episode's narrative angle shifts when the protagonist Stripe Koinange's 'MASS' implant is damaged and he is able to see the 'roaches' in a new light – as normal human beings. Stripe's (and the viewer's) unease is corroborated by the apparent extent of the kill list, which would mark a large percentage of the world's population as 'roaches' (vermin) and 'it' (objects), rather than human beings. The repeated use of the term 'screening' in this context establishes a connection to the current highly contested issue of pre-natal diagnostics (see Shakespeare 2018: 164–7). The episode's posthuman horror relies on the shift in perspective, which draws attention to the construction of otherness through the use of specific technologies and discourses of power. This scenario is not an infrequent one, as it is, for instance, echoed in other recent films – *Ex Machina* (Alex Garland, 2014), *Ghost in the Shell* (Rupert Sanders, 2017) – as well as television series – *Westworld* (2016) and various other episodes of *Black Mirror*. Interestingly, these texts also often foreground the reinforcement of gender stereotypes under late techno-capitalism by introducing hyper-sexualised female cyborg bodies (Gillis 2007: 9–10) which draw attention to processes of technological as well as gendered dehumanisation and objectification. 'Men Against Fire' addresses this issue by introducing the sexualised dream imagery of the 'MASS' implants, which manipulate the soldiers in an uncanny approximation to the usually uncontrolled, unconscious process of sleep, further inviting viewers to question the soldiers' humanity.

(Re)Presenting the Posthuman

Posthuman Gothic fears reflect this destabilisation of the human and, consequently, 'indicate a shift in concern from external to internal threats to subjectivity and human agency' (Bolton 2014: 2). Micheal Sean Bolton argues that

> [w]hereas subgenres coupling the Gothic and the postmodern often derive horror and/or terror from fear of the eradication of humanity at the hands of monstrous technologies, the posthuman Gothic finds instances of terror and horror arising from the interfaces and integrations of humans and technologies; specifically, in the inevitability and exigency of these unions as a matter of the continued existence of the human subject reconstituted as posthuman. (2)

As he points out, the 'source of dread in the posthuman Gothic lies not in the fear of our demise but in the uncertainty of what we will become and what will be left of us after the change' (3). Bolton's definition draws on both Gothic criticism and critical posthumanist theory – for instance Cary Wolfe's definition of the posthuman as 'a historical moment in which the decentering of the human by its imbrication in technical, medical, informatic, and economic networks is increasingly impossible to ignore' (Wolfe 2010: xv). Confrontations with humanity's involvements and integrations with (bio-)technologies undermine our sense of what it means to be human, necessitating, as Wolfe argues, 'new theoretical paradigms [. . .] a new mode of thought that comes after the cultural repressions and fantasies, the philosophical protocols and evasions, of humanism as a historically specific phenomenon' (xvi). Critical posthumanism is, consequently, less concerned with what might come after the human, but rather with how 'the human' as a category, which traditionally excludes both machine and animal as radically Other, can no longer be upheld; what might come after it; and what this means for derivative concepts like human rights or the humanities.

Transhumanists may essentially celebrate technology-driven evolution processes as well as integrations of the human body with various technologies, but there is something distinctly disturbing about the necessary shifts in perspective away from the human which accompany these developments, the necessity to 'read as if one were not human, or at least from a position of analytical detachment' (Herbrechter and Callus 2008: 95). Posthuman Gothic texts like the *Black Mirror* episode 'Men Against Fire' foreground humanity's fears of what we might be becoming by drawing attention to the discourses of difference we use to establish categories like 'human' and 'non-human', thus presenting a particularly useful textual basis for a posthumanist reading.

Technologies of representation and the representation of technology play an important role in this context as posthuman Gothic texts often question the principles of perception – and reflect these processes in their own narrative means. 'Men Against Fire' provides an example of this kind of visualisation of posthuman Gothic narrative means as camera perspectives shift between Stripe's point of view – influenced by his glitching 'MASS' implant – and an outside perspective, which ostensibly shows the 'real' world – although 'reality' and 'existence' are concepts undermined early on in the episode. In this context the name of 'Heidekker' (the 'roach'-friendly farmer) evokes Heideggerian existentialist philosophy as well as the German philosopher's problematic ties to national socialist ideology (see Sheehan 1988). The final scene, which shows Stripe returning home with full military honours to a warmly lit house and the seductively smiling woman of his earlier dreams, is quickly revealed as an illusion created by the implant; a countershot shows that he is, in fact, returning to an empty, dilapidated house. The prevalent cultural discourse, this ending suggests, can only be upheld through continued technological control of the human.

Westworld and *Ex Machina* use filmic means and meta-narrative elements like surveillance camera feeds to create similar effects and to tap into an older Gothic narrative tradition of metatextual reflection of the often-monstrous content on a structural, aesthetic or textual level. As Fred Botting argues, this is indeed an ingrained feature of 'Gothic fiction [which] begins in an age of mechanism and deploys an array of machines' (2005: 1). Gothic machineries are inextricably 'tied to the mechanisms of narrative' (6) and modes of textual production. While hypertext novels like Mark Z. Danielewski's *House of Leaves* (2000), whose layouts already draw attention to their various textual levels, present the most tangible example of posthuman Gothic textuality, the last decades have seen the publication of a number of other examples in both text and film. The most obvious filmic example would be the various incarnations of *Ringu* (*Ring*, Hideo Nakata, 1998)/*The Ring* (Gore Verbinski, 2002), in which the monster manages to traverse medial levels – not only through the monstrous girl's iconic ability to climb out of television sets, but also in the simple but deadly necessity to replicate the monster tale by copying the videotape which guarantees its continued existence. Horror is created by immersing the viewer in the experience of watching the deadly video along with the doomed protagonists and, thus, replicating at least part of the materiality of their medial experience. Marisha Pessl's novel *Night Film* (2013) attempts a similar effect by providing its readers with interspersed media snippets (images, websites) related to the main narrative about a reclusive film director and his mysterious, ostensibly horrific films. These narrative breadcrumbs can be traced beyond the novel itself with the help of a '*Night Film* Decoder app' (Pessl 2013), but the immersive experience of the added media remains limited. As Steven Poole summarises, 'the internet is here framed as a guarantor of reality for fiction: Pessl has also posted some short videos and other paraphernalia related to the novel online, in a hopeful stab at transmedia virality' (Poole 2013). The integration of printed text and digital elements is, however, disruptive to the reading flow and the creation of suspense in the narrative arc itself. Hypertext, more than other forms of narrative, relies on reader immersion, as the reader plays an active role in the creation of the narrative experience (Heise-von der Lippe 2015). Jarring the immersive experience not only limits the enjoyment of the text but also undermines its overall aesthetic, which, as N. Katherine Hayles has argued, relies on the reader's ability to develop 'cyborg reading practices' (2000: 13) to engage with the multiple threads of the text in a 'posthuman conjunction[:] bodies of texts and bodies of subjects evolve together in complex configurations that carry along the past even as they arc toward an open and unknown future' (51). While a truly posthuman reading would involve more than the use of a different medium, namely a shift in perspective away from the human (Herbrechter and Callus 2008), the formal peculiarities of hypertext networks force the reader to engage with and become aware of the technological elements of textual production and, thus, serve to undermine their sense of a fixed human(ist) subject position. This is, as Christopher Keep argues, a central element of the Gothic, which manifests itself not so much as a literary genre, but as

> a recurring moment within the history of modernity, that point in which the material substrate of signification, whether it takes the shape of the book or a computer-mediated network, is momentarily visible, when it has not yet become so much a natural fact of our reading practices as to disappear from view. (Keep 2006: 12)

Posthuman Gothic texts engage with other, often technologically more demanding media, and thus not only draw attention to their own textual construction but also make a point about our posthuman technological involvements.

Similar to *Night Film*, although with no extra-textual immersive technologies, Gemma Files's *Experimental Film* (2015) evokes the posthuman possibilities of the medium of film. Files's text – purportedly a film researcher's autobiographical narrative about the discovery of an early

Canadian filmmaker – creates a number of textual levels: a documentary film, a set of notes concerned with the production of the film, as well as the filmmaker's personal experiences of engaging directly with the medium. Reader immersion is created by a sense of documentary rather than fictional writing, created by the narrator's meta-commentary. As John Langan observes, 'Lois is a self-conscious narrator, always aware of how she's framing the story she's recounting, and including the reader in her strategizing' (Langan 2016). The text creates the impression of a posthuman Gothic traversal of medial levels through uncanny doublings between the protagonist's discoveries and her own life, as well as a sense of intrusion of the monstrous into the immediate health and safety of her family. The latter becomes uncannily clear when the protagonist's autistic son throws up 'dirt, and [. . .] some sort of bulb – a flower, probably' (Files 2015: 229) after a ghostly image of the monstrous 'Lady Midday' seems to bend over him in a recording on his iPad, which nobody seems to have filmed (see Files 2015: 229). Several types of film create an embodiment of a monster, whose effect is blinding and whose attempt at claiming new victims is connected to the filmic medium in a manner similar to *The Ring*'s ghostly antagonist. Lady Midday manages to traverse textual levels through the use of media (film) as well as the powers of a medium (a person) who possesses the ability to transfer mental images to film. The destructive materiality of the ancient, highly combustible silver nitrate film the early filmmaker worked with underlines these effects, suggesting posthuman integrations between media technology, its creators and audiences.

Various episodes of *Black Mirror* ('The Entire History of You' (2011), 'Be Right Back' (2013), 'Nosedive' (2016), 'Shut up and Dance' (2016), to name only a few examples) also focus on the horrors of medial intrusions into people's personal lives – albeit on more recent technological levels than silver nitrate film. Season three's final episode 'Hated in the Nation' (2016) manages to visualise the immense scale of these integrations with the help of an extended swarm metaphor involving both autonomous swarms of drone insects and the seemingly uncontrolled spreading of viral hate through social networks. The narrative, which is presented in retrospect at a court hearing, focuses on a deadly mass-attack of hacked drone insects (originally created to replace the extinct bee population) on social media users who spread and shared the hate campaign 'death to...'. As the investigators struggle to protect individual targets of the 'death to'-hashtag from drone insect attacks, the uncontrollability of social media campaigns becomes painfully clear. In a recent article in *Washington Monthly*, Roger McNamee (2018) explains how the use of data algorithms to determine what social media users see and bots, which can start and spread news stories, have a major political and cultural impact – and we are beginning to see the extent of this in the Facebook data-mining scandal (IAME 2018). 'Hated in the Nation' visualises these connections by introducing a direct threat to social media users in the figure of a vengeful hacker, intent on punishing anyone who would support a hate campaign. The episode portrays how people sharing a popular hashtag ignore the fact that their simple act of clicking might actively harm someone, nor do they take any responsibility, as they are not its original creators. As one of the women involved (a pre-school teacher who also sent one of the victims a cake with a threatening message) argues, '[i]t was funny, okay? And I can see if I'd done it myself then that would be a bit weird, but I'm not mental [. . .] It's not [. . .] real. It's a joke thing.' The reversal of perpetrators and victims challenges the illusion of detachment created by the filter of social media. By introducing the possibility of murder (and mass murder) by hijacked, remote-controlled drone insects, the episode further highlights how the use of social media would make the choice of victims both self-perpetuating and, ultimately, inescapable, as internet users vote first for the victims by spreading the 'death to'-hashtag and in the process nominate themselves as later victims. The episode highlights the horror of large quantities of data, which dominate or even manipulate human lives as they evolve beyond our control as well as the essentially non-human quality of viral patterns.

Apart from human-machine and, at least to an extent, human-animal integrations and blurrings, the posthuman Gothic is also interested in the viral as a form of posthuman distribution of biological or computational data. The graphic novel series *The Beauty* (2016–), for instance, is concerned with the spread of a sexually transmitted disease, which people are actually eager to catch because it enhances the carriers' physical appearance. As the side effects seem minimal at first, the series describes the rapid spread of the virus in a world obsessed with impossible (Western) beauty standards. The narrative takes a further posthuman angle when, at the end of the first volume, the cure against 'the beauty' has a disturbing effect on the test subject's appearance, drawing attention to the monstrous becomings of the posthuman. The different volumes of the graphic novel series also reflect the concept of viral patterns on a narrative level, as they present a far-reaching network of narratives of infection. Shifting between different protagonists and time frames they also focus on questions of otherness, exploitation and objectification.

(De)Constructing the Human(ist) Subject (Position)

The issues explored above are rooted in critical posthumanist thought, which draws attention to the constructedness of the human as a discursive category and argues that it is no longer tenable – it may even never have been tenable in the first place. As Rosi Braidotti points out,

> [n]ot all of us can say, with any degree of certainty, that we have always been human, or that we are only that. Some of us are not even considered fully human now, let alone at previous moments of Western social, political and scientific history. (2013: 1)

In this context, critical posthumanism specifically focuses on the exploitation of those who are not considered fully human by contemporary techno-capitalist consumer cultures. As Braidotti argues 'the bodies of the empirical subjects who signify difference (woman/native/earth or natural others) have become the disposable bodies of the global economy' (111). The exploitation of these bodies is, as Braidotti points out using Achille Mbembe's terminology, becoming increasingly necropolitical, that is, focused on the administration of death on a large, often international scale (Braidotti 2013: 122; Mbembe 2003). Few films visualise this concept in as literally a manner as the military science fiction film *Spectral* (Nic Mathieu, 2016) in its weaponisation of the dead, but the fatal exploitation of bodies has, nevertheless, become a recurring motif in posthuman Gothic texts. *Westworld*, for instance, also foregrounds the exploitation of artificial bodies in a hyper-realistic theme park modelled on an imaginary 'Wild West'. The non-human status of the robotic 'hosts' is visualised when they are routinely stripped naked for maintenance. Their vulnerable bodies are presented in stark contrast with the high-tech environment of the theme park's control centre (and the fully dressed human employees). The visitor's attitude towards the theme park androids/gynoids as disposable gadgets foregrounds the inhumanity of the humans, while the focus on the main gynoid characters, Dolores (Evan Rachael Wood) and Maeve (Thandie Newton), highlights their essential humanity as they begin to question the circumstances of their existence. The first episode's opening scene already combines key components of posthuman Gothic aesthetics (a perfectly still female body in a clean, subtly lit, high-tech space) with a nod to the 'Spaghetti Western' tradition (the opening scene of Sergio Leone's 1968 genre classic *Once Upon a Time in the West*). The unlikely uniting factor between the two is a fly, which first lands on the woman's face, then begins to crawl over the glassy, unblinking surface of her eye.

It is this tiny detail, brought into stark focus by a close-up of her face, which tips the scale towards the posthuman Gothic, as her immobility underlines both her vulnerability and her non-human object status.

Advanced neoliberal techno-capitalism has led to an automatisation and systematisation of the biopolitical exploitation of human bodies (as well as other species and the planet as a whole), and 'the concept of the human has exploded under the double pressure of contemporary scientific advances and global economic concerns' (Braidotti 2013: 1). This specific type of capital- and technology-driven progress has a tendency to further marginalise specific minorities, as Donna Haraway suggests in her 1984 'A Cyborg Manifesto' (a text which has since become a classic of cyber-theory). Haraway proposes an ironic post-gender myth focused on 'women in the integrated circuit' (2000: 291) – the female workers of various global tech industries. The text foregrounds the potential of otherness and the challenging of binaries through technological developments, arguing that '[w]riting is pre-eminently the technology of cyborgs' (312), and draws attention to the disruptive potential of posthuman narratives in the process.

Westworld, *Ex Machina* and *Ghost in the Shell* pursue similar concerns revolving around the authority over and control of the (female) body, but they do so by foregrounding the technological otherness of their protagonists, who are not only likened to cyborgs via their integration into networks of technology production, but possess artificial bodies and, at least in *Ex Machina* and *Westworld*, artificial intelligence. While *Westworld* hinges on the uncanny discovery that a convincingly replicated human would, at some point, cease to be an automaton and develop a consciousness, *Ex Machina* describes an elaborate Turing Test scenario (see Turing 1950) in which an artificial intelligence developed from a powerful search engine manages to convince a programmer that it is sentient and worth saving from destruction. While the AI's curiosity and ultimate cruelty may seem to stem from its origin in technology, both features can be traced back to its origins in a search engine – and, thus, some of humanity's basest technology interactions. The film was proven correct in this observation when interaction with Twitter users turned Tay (a chatbot originally designed by Microsoft to improve the conversational understanding skills of AI projects) into a 'racist asshole' in under twenty-four hours (Vincent 2016).

Ex Machina plays with the idea of surfaces and what may lie beneath them by undermining the main protagonist's sense of a human subject position. Disturbed by the work of search engine magnate and AI developer Nathan Bateman (Oscar Isaac) and his sentient gynoid Ava (Alicia Vikander), the protagonist, Caleb Smith (Domhnall Gleeson), cuts the skin on his arms in a moment of nocturnal panic to see if there is, indeed, flesh and blood underneath. While Caleb bleeds profusely, smearing the blood from his cuts on the deceptive surface of the mirror (which hides a camera), the scene is echoed by a number of shots throughout the film in which various gynoids appear completely or at least partially without skin. The most horrifying of these shows Nathan's mute servant, Kyoko (Sonoya Mizuno), who has been stripped of her facial skin in a fight, revealing the technology that lies underneath and undermining the previously created impression of humanity in the process. The film presents the gynoid bodies as not only interchangeable but also composed of exchangeable parts, their seeming 'humanity' clashing oddly with their artificiality. In an almost cannibalistic act the escaping Ava can simply borrow the skin of one of her decommissioned predecessors, which Nathan keeps in a row of cabinets in his bedroom. The discovery of Nathan's gynoid 'skeletons in the closet' serves as a reminder of Ava's own transience and dependence on her creator's whim (as he might decide to 'turn her off' (Garland, 2014) and reuse her body parts to create the next, improved model). Ava's discovery of the inanimate gynoid bodies is reminiscent of another cinematic collection of failed experiments: the lab of the USM Auriga in *Alien: Resurrection* (Jean-Pierre Jeunet, 1997), in which the last and only successful human-alien clone, Ripley 8 (Sigourney Weaver), discovers a row of monstrous predecessors, displayed in ominously green-lit tanks. *Alien: Resurrection* marks a shift in the source of horror from the external alien creatures, which invade the human body in the previous instalments of the franchise, to the 'monster's mother' fusing Ripley's DNA with that of the alien queen. In these parallel scenes Ava and Ripley are confronted with the artificiality and seriality of their existence and the biopolitical exploitation of their bodies, but while Ripley kills the last living clone and destroys the laboratory, Ava uses her predecessors' skin to escape from Nathan's underground high-tech facility and move undetected among humans. Her escape possesses the potential to turn the human world on its head (as the last shot of the film suggests), harking back to the film's earlier framing of Nathan's work as 'Promethean' (Garland, 2014). The film's ultimate source of horror is the fear of artificial intelligence becoming smarter than, and thus unpredictable for, humanity in 'the singularity' (see Eden et al. 2012) – a posthuman development foreshadowed by a number of references to the creation of the atomic bomb: Nathan recites J. Robert Oppenheimer's use of a verse from the *Bhagavad Gita* 'I am become Death, the destroyer of worlds' (Oppenheimer 2015) and the film's soundtrack switches to OMD's ominous 'Enola Gay' shortly after Caleb's arrival at the facility, suggesting a sense of nostalgia for the treacherous illusion of an unblemished human past.

Like Haraway's cyborg manifesto, *Westworld*, *Ex Machina* and *Ghost in the Shell* also focus on the objectification and biopolitical exploitation of female bodies through the posthuman integration of the body and technology as 'the line between human and machine [. . .] disappear[s]' (Sanders 2017), along with any sense of a stable human subject position. The gynoids' (*Westworld*, *Ex Machina*) and cyborgs' (*Ghost in the Shell*) rebellion against their own creators harks back to Frankenstein's doubts about his female creature, who

> might become ten thousand times more malignant than her mate, and delight, for its own sake, in murder and wretchedness [. . .] she, who in all probability was to become a thinking and reasoning animal, might refuse to comply with a compact made before her creation. (Shelley 2012: 114–15)

In *Ghost in the Shell*, the failed Project 2571's pleas for Major (Scarlett Johansson) to join him and 'evolve [. . .] beyond' (Sanders, 2017) their creators present a contemporary play on this constellation of monster and mate. Similar to *Ex Machina*'s Promethean hubris of creating an evolving AI, the various attempts at destroying the cyborgs in *Ghost in the Shell* also invoke Shelley's timeless warning of the dangers of playing god and making monsters. As Herbrechter points out, '[t]he posthuman must [. . .] be entirely other and new' (2013: 87) in the sense of Derrida's 'monstrous monstrosities' which can only be recognised retrospectively, when the monstrosity 'has become normal' (Derrida 1990: 79), categorised and domesticated. The posthuman Gothic texts discussed in this chapter ultimately revolve around humanity's fears of the unfathomable monstrous becomings of these technology-driven evolutionary processes, which societies in the late-capitalist Global North are clearly ignoring at our own peril as the anthropocene progresses.

Film and Television

Alien: Resurrection (Jean-Pierre Jeunet, USA, 1997)
Black Mirror (Channel 4/Netflix, 2011–)
Ex Machina (Alex Garland, UK/USA, 2014)
Ghost in the Shell (Rupert Sanders, USA, 2017)
Ringu (*Ring*, Hideo Nakata, Japan, 1998)
Spectral (Nic Mathieu, USA, 2016)
The Ring (Gore Verbinski, USA, 2002)
Westworld (HBO, 2016–)

References

Bolton, Micheal Sean (2014), 'Monstrous Machinery: Defining Posthuman Gothic', *Aeternum: The Journal of Contemporary Gothic Studies*, 1.1, 1–15.
Botting, Fred (2005), 'Gothic Technologies: Virtualities in the Romantic Era – Reading Machines', *Romantic Circles*, http://www.rc.umd.edu/praxis/gothic/botting/botting (accessed 8 January 2018).
Braidotti, Rosi (2013), *The Posthuman*, London: Polity.
Derrida, Jacques (1990), 'Some Statements and Truisms about Neologisms, Newisms, Postisms, Parasitisms, and Other Small Seismisms', in David Carroll (ed.), *The States of 'Theory*, Stanford: Stanford University Press, pp. 63–94.
Eden, Amnon H., et al. (eds) (2012), *Singularity Hypotheses*, Berlin: Springer.
Files, Gemma (2015), *Experimental Film*, Peterborough: ChiZine Publications.
Gillis, Stacy (2007), 'The (Post)Feminist Politics of Cyberpunk', *Gothic Studies*, 9.2, 7–19.
Haraway, Donna (2000), 'A Cyborg Manifesto', in David Bell and Barbara M. Kennedy (eds), *The Cybercultures Reader*, London: Routledge, pp. 291–324.
Hayles, N. Katherine (2000), 'Flickering Connectivities in Shelley Jackson's *Patchwork Girl*: The Importance of Media-Specific Analysis', *Postmodern Culture*, 10.2, https://muse.jhu.edu/article/27720 (accessed 21 August 2014).
Heise-von der Lippe, Anya (2015), 'Hypertext and the Creation of Choice: Making Monsters in the Age of Digital Textual (Re)Production', in Lorna Piatta-Farnell and Donna Lee Brien (eds), *New Directions in 21st Century Gothic: The Gothic Compass*, London: Routledge, pp. 117–31.
Heise-von der Lippe, Anya (2017), 'Introduction: Post/Human/Gothic', in Anya Heise-von der Lippe (ed.), *Posthuman Gothic*, Cardiff: University of Wales Press, pp. 1–16.
Herbrechter, Stephan (2013), *Posthumanism*, London: Bloomsbury.
Herbrechter, Stephan, and Ivan Callus (2008), 'What Is a Posthumanist Reading?', *Angelaki*, 13.1, 95–111.
IAME (2018), 'The Facebook Data-Mining Scandal – What Happened', *Medium*, 29 March, https://medium.com/@IAMEIdentity/the-facebook-data-mining-scandal-what-happened-82154855aeca (accessed 6 April 2017).
Keep, Christopher (2006), 'Growing Intimate with Monsters: Shelley Jackson's *Patchwork Girl* and the Gothic Nature of Hypertext', *Érudit*, 41–2, http://id.erudit.org/iderudit/013156ar (accessed 8 January 2018).
Langan, John (2016), 'John Langan Reviews Gemma Files', *Locus*, 13 July, http://locusmag.com/2016/07/john-langan-reviews-gemma-files/ (accessed 8 January 2018).
McNamee, Roger (2018), 'How to Fix Facebook – Before It Fixes Us', *Washington Monthly*, January/February/March, https://washingtonmonthly.com/magazine/january-february-march-2018/how-to-fix-facebook-before-it-fixes-us/ (accessed 9 January 2018).
Mbembe, Achille (2003), 'Necropolitics', *Popular Culture*, 15.1, 11–40.
Oppenheimer, J. Robert (2015), 'Now I Am Become Death...', *Atomic Archive*, http://www.atomicarchive.com/Movies/Movie8.shtml (accessed 9 January 2018).
Pessl, Marisha (2013), *Night Film*, London: Windmill.

Poole, Steven (2013), '*Night Film* by Marisha Pessl – Review', *The Guardian*, 5 September, https://www.theguardian.com/books/2013/sep/05/night-film-marisha-pessl-review (accessed 5 April 2018).

Shakespeare, Tom (2018), *Disability: The Basics*, Abingdon: Routledge.

Sheehan, Thomas (1988), 'Heidegger and the Nazis', *The New York Review of Books*, 16 June, http://www.nybooks.com/articles/1988/06/16/heidegger-and-the-nazis/ (accessed 9 January 2018).

Shelley, Mary (2012) [1818], *Frankenstein*, New York: Norton.

Turing, A. M. (1950), 'Computing Machinery and Intelligence,' *Mind*, 49, 433–60.

Vincent, James (2016), 'Twitter Taught Microsoft's AI Chatbot to Be a Racist Asshole in Less Than a Day', *The Verge*, 24 March, https://www.theverge.com/2016/3/24/11297050/tay-microsoft-chatbot-racist (accessed 9 January 2018).

Wolfe, Cary (2010), *What Is Posthumanism?*, Minneapolis: University of Minnesota Press.

Part IV

Ethnogothic

Chapter 16

South African Gothic
Rebecca Duncan

A Gothic influence is present in Anglophone Southern African fiction-writing from at least as early as the late nineteenth century. It is visible in colonial ghost stories and imperial adventure narratives, and – more complexly and subtly – in Olive Schreiner's famous anti-pastoral *Story of an African Farm* (1893). And yet, it is only recently that the term 'Gothic' has begun to gain traction in South African literary criticism.[1] In line with established accounts of the postcolonial Gothic, it has most often been invoked to identify in late twentieth- and early twenty-first-century South African literature what David Punter calls 'a logic of haunting' (2003: 193), although, as will become clear across this chapter, this spectral lexicon is currently being superseded by Gothic vocabularies of a different, more immediate kind. Nonetheless, Gothic *has* frequently been deployed by writers to imagine South African pasts in revenant terms. 'Gothic', Gerald Gaylard remarks, 'is a mode much suited to Southern Africa, given Southern Africa's history of social engineering. The Gothic [. . .] has helped to expose that which social engineering attempted to sweep under its carpet' (2008: 16).

Transitional Gothic

Gaylard's comments – and Punter's – are borne out by a number of South African fictions written around the final decades of the twentieth century, the most famous, perhaps, being Nadine Gordimer's *The Conservationist* (1974), in which the body of a black man refuses to stay buried in the earth of a white-owned farm. It is after 1994, however, that hauntings begin to proliferate in South African literature (Duncan 2018a). The year marks the fall of the National Party (NP) administration, to whose policy of racial apartheid Gaylard refers above and over whom the African National Congress (ANC) – leaders of the long struggle against oppression – triumphed in the country's first democratic election. The post-apartheid late twentieth century was also, significantly, the time of the Truth and Reconciliation Commission (TRC), the tribunal set up to witness the testimony of victims and perpetrators of gross human rights violations committed under the auspices of the apartheid state. Broadcast widely in national and international media, the TRC – Rita Barnard writes – ensured that 'confession was in the air' in South Africa (2012: 657), and from the late 1990s to the early 2000s South African literature registers this climate by 'insistently revisit[ing] [. . .] loci of memory – sites where the legacy of the past can still be traced' (657).

It is these sites that emerge as scenes of haunting in transitional South Africa's Gothic imaginaries: Shane Graham identifies spectres in post-TRC narratives as 'indicat[ing] the present absence of a past that has been erased [. . .] but which leaves marks of its erasure' (2011: 19–20). Ghosts in South African fiction of this period thus operate as a strategy for addressing what Sam Durrant calls 'the impossible task' facing postcolonial literatures widely: that 'of finding a mode of writing that [. . .] can bear witness to its own incapacity to recover [. . .] history' (2004: 6). As signs for what cannot be retrieved from colonial and apartheid pasts – for unspeakable trauma, for what has been erased or never recorded – Gothic hauntings function not only to interrogate sanitised accounts of social engineering, but also as a representational recourse in the ethical (re)articulation of a history of oppression. Here we might think, for example, of Marlene van Niekerk's *Triomf* (1999), which opens with the howls of ghost dogs from Sophiatown – the black settlement infamously bulldozed by the state to make way for white suburbia. We might turn, too, to Zoë Wicomb's monumental *David's Story* (2001), in which the haunting figure of the tortured Dulcie Oliphant appears – in the protagonist's own words – as a 'scream that echoes' through the narrative (134), or to several novels from the period by André Brink, *The Rights of Desire* (2000) in particular.

If South African fiction of the early 2000s deploys Gothic as a logic of haunting, then later writing is more resistant to this established rubric for the postcolonial Gothic. Around a decade into the new millennium, a shift becomes discernible away from spectral aesthetics. Recent South African fiction-writing has begun to engage the Gothic not so much for its capacity to represent an unspoken or unspeakable history, but rather as a lexicon of immediate violence. A turn to horror – and specifically a horror that is preoccupied with the materiality and perishability of the body – is visible in the corpus that Ronit Frenkel and Craig MacKenzie have called 'post-transitional' South African literature and which is characterised, in part, by its movement away from the 'ethical high-mindedness' of serious apartheid-era and transitional narratives and by a 'new willing[ness] to take risks' (2010: 4).

In this chapter, I explore the vividly risky vocabularies of post-transitional South African Gothic, with a particular view to locate the impulses animating this still-emerging mode. Building on arguments I have made elsewhere around horror in millennial South African (Duncan 2018a, 2018b), I turn here to the cutting edge of new speculative production – to work published in literary periodicals, to cinema and short-fiction from emerging voices – and read it alongside narratives and films by now relatively established authors and directors. In concluding, I suggest that a preoccupation with what Xavier Aldana Reyes calls 'body Gothic' – that is Gothic understood as a 'form of experience' (2014: 2) – is related in millennial South Africa to a particular phenomenology of violence that new narratives are seeking to mobilise in the service of critical agendas. In this sense, the shift from lexica of haunting to those of horror visible after the millennium registers a deeper shift that pertains to basic postcolonial assumptions about imperial formations of power: what is not dead, after all, cannot come back as a ghost.

Post-Apartheid South Africa and the Neoliberal Turn

Even as it exemplifies the audaciousness associated with post-transitional writing, post-millennial South African Gothic also emerges – as I will argue across this chapter – in response to material shifts within the post-apartheid nation, where, as John S. Saul and Patrick Bond have put it, 'the problem lies in just how "new" the new South Africa really is' (2014: 3). They go on:

> Against the undeniable drama of the transition from the formal structures of white minority rule that has occurred must be set the fact that South Africa today is a much more unequal society than during apartheid, one deeply stratified in class and gender terms, and also in racial terms ('class' still remaining so substantially 'raced' in the country). (3)

Across the second half of the twentieth century, the social and geographical divisions enforced by the NP (divisions built on earlier segregations instantiated under British colonial rule) deliberately produced radical inequality. Under the policy of apartheid, rights to movement, land, education, marriage and employment (to give only key examples) were allocated according to an artificial taxonomy of races, and poverty and its attendant vulnerabilities – including systemic vulnerability to labour coercion and exploitation, to disease, to violent environments – were equally distributed in racial terms. While all of this came to an official conclusion with the end of the racist state, the world instantiated by that administration has not been fully eradicated two-and-a-half decades after 1994. At the root of this durability, Saul and Bond also note, is the shift to macroeconomic neoliberalism that accompanied South Africa's transition from the system of apartheid (itself a species of hyperbolically racialised capitalism) to democracy.

The neoliberal imperative to 'maximise the reach and frequency of market transactions' (Harvey 2005: 3) takes hold globally from the 1970s as exhaustive privatisation and deregulation, and an expanding international division of labour. In South Africa – as elsewhere – this agenda has proved a wholly inadequate redress for the material inequalities cultivated and entrenched across the previous century. Indeed, as Saul and Bond note above, inequality has been compounded in many areas: structural unemployment amid deindustrialisation; AIDS and TB epidemics amid uneven access to healthcare; commercial development prioritised against a history of land dispossession; and fees that render higher education practically out of reach for many young South Africans. Realities such as these have led critics of the so-called 'new' South Africa to condemn 'what they consider the ineffectual, even unjust and undemocratic nature of the ANC government's response to the existence of deep-seated inequalities in the country' (Saul and Bond 2014: 3) – a response that has been delegitimised further in recent years by allegations of 'state capture' (or systemic corruption) across the highest levels of government. Events at the Lonmin platinum mine at Marikana, where in 2012 South African police killed thirty-four mineworkers striking over low pay, have cast an especially grim light on the allegiances and priorities of the post-apartheid state, as have the major student protests – #Rhodesmustfall and #Feesmustfall – that have rocked South Africa's higher education institutions since 2015. With their explicit calls for decolonisation, youth activists in particular have brought what is increasingly irrefutably South Africa's post-apartheid imperium to public attention.

It is here, with the rising sense of dissatisfaction and disillusionment animating recent protest movements, that we might come back to the Gothic lexicon. Indeed, in a short, sharply satirical creative piece, published in *The Johannesburg Review of Books* in 2017, cultural critic Bongani Madondo draws in part on a speculative vocabulary of corporeal unease precisely to imagine the overthrowing of a post-apartheid kleptocracy. 'A country's soul is captured by bloated elites', reads the prelude to 'The Return of the Afringers': '[i]ts heart – ripped by race mongers [. . .] There is no turning back' (Madondo 2017). Madondo's epigraph, the eponymous line from James Baldwin's 1963 book, elaborates: 'God gave Noah the rainbow sign, no more water, the fire next time!' (quoted in Madondo 2017). I will come back to 'Afringers' momentarily, but for now I would like to draw attention to another Gothic perspective on inequality and corruption in contemporary South Africa, one that deploys a species of body horror and blends this – as does Madondo's narrative, too – with a grim sense of humour.

In a particularly memorable scene from Charlie Human's *Apocalypse Now Now* (2013),[2] adolescent protagonist Baxter Zevcenko (recent initiate into Cape Town's seething occult underworld) finds himself at the 'Flesh Palace' (144): a nightclub, presided over by an enormous spider goddess, where, among other grisly spectacles, undead erotic dancers divest themselves of their flesh before a gawping audience. Hustled through these premises by a zombie strongman, Baxter spots 'familiar faces' in the crowd. Along with soap stars and middle-aged television personalities,

> [p]oliticians are delicately sucking the marrow out of dismembered pinkie fingers, and several members of the national cricket team sip congealed blood from Martini glasses. The Cape Town elite, it seems, are into zombie chic, gourmet cannibalism. Fucking poseurs. (148)

Gothic 'is always teetering on the edge of self-parody', write Avril Horner and Sue Zlosnik (2005: 12): its 'representation of extremes of feeling and experience' can be turned easily towards the comical representation of 'ludicrous excess' (11). And 'ludicrous excess' appears to be Human's intended effect in this scenario, which as it invokes laughter also clearly 'engage[s] critically with aspects of the contemporary world' (12). The extravagant lifestyles of South Africa's political class are refigured in this passage in absurdly grisly terms, which present post-apartheid power and privilege as both ridiculous and abhorrent. It is noteworthy, in this last respect, that the Flesh Palace is the base of operations for a corporate trafficking organisation, members of which are photographed – ominously *before* Baxter witnesses the cannibalistic fine-diners – herding 'a group of street people into a van' (Human 2013: 130).

In its engagement of vivisected and eating – indeed excessive – bodies, of images of gluttony, and intertwining elements of humour and disgust, Human's depiction of the Flesh Palace resonates with Mikhail Bakhtin's formative discourse on grotesque corporeality, which – located amid the 'festive suspension [. . .] of restrictions' (1984: 412) that characterises the feast-time of medieval carnival – designates those visions of the perforated, splayed, consuming or excreting body that, despite the possible visibility of this body's 'inner features' (318), are nonetheless presented as part of a comically irreverent, subversive engagement with the structures and personages of power. Where, for Bakhtin, the grotesque in the carnival context enables this kind of 'opposition to the official world and all its prohibitions' (412), Achille Mbembe has (not uncontentiously) argued that in the postcolony, the same possibility is foreclosed. For Mbembe, this is because the sign systems through which what he calls the postcolonial *commandement* has tended to articulate its power already themselves operate in grotesque registers of bodily excess – of feasting, for example, of extravagant state-funded revelry. To critique the *commandement* through grotesque mockery is thus, from this perspective, to participate in the cosmology of its authority. 'Those who laugh', Mbembe writes, 'are not necessarily bringing about the collapse of power, or even resisting it [. . .] [T]hey are simply bearing witness that the grotesque is no more foreign to officialdom than the common man [*sic*] is impervious to the charms of majesty' (2001: 110).

Mbembe's argument is censorious. It forms part of his wider insistence on a mode of postcolonial critique that moves beyond simplistic conceptions of resistance as binary opposition. And yet, even as his grotesque *is* critically mobilised, Human's aesthetic appears designed to make a point at least tangentially related to Mbembe's own: namely, that power is communicated at the influential echelons of post-apartheid society via a tendency to what Barnard, in her own analysis of grotesquery, calls 'South African excess' – 'an element of tasteless display', sometimes questionably defended (as she shows) at the level of political leadership (2004: 291). It is salient, in this respect too, that even as Human's deliberately ludicrous horror-writing prompts a humorous response, his novel's bodily grotesquery retains strong associative ties to the properly anxious symbology of the Gothic – from the menacing undead to threatening violence and unsavoury decay. In the Gothic, the aesthetics of the grotesque are – as Aldana Reyes writes – 'unredeemed by laughter' (2014: 4). Catherine Spooner, drawing on Bakhtin's own comments on the Gothic grotesque, writes similarly that this is 'sombre and sterile, and conveys terror rather than laughter' (2006: 68). In Human's narrative, the Gothic's sense of genuine unease is metonymically referenced amid wider provocations to laughter and is marshalled in critique of a contemporary South African elite. Envisioned via this almost self-consciously Gothic grotesque, power and privilege are thus ridiculed as they are equated to a proclivity for absurd excess, but – further – they are also presented in such a way that excess is exposed as chilling indifference and exploitative violence. The understated sadism of the celebrity, who 'raises his glass' as Baxter is manhandled to a gruesome fate (Human 2013: 148), offers one especially illuminating example here; the relation between the cannibal politerati and their victims provides another.

Similarly, Madondo's allegory represents the mechanics of inequality by invoking recognisably Gothic terms. In this tale there are 'slimy characters [...] at the nucleus of state institutions', themselves only 'networks of warring, looting, wheeling-and-dealing human vampires' (Madondo 2017). The metaphor of the vampire state (redolent of Marx's famous assessment of capital) weighs particularly heavily here, published as this story is amid the (ongoing) scandal around state capture in South Africa, but Gothic, as shorthand for violent malpractice, is once again coupled to an irreverent sense of humour. Indeed, on the twenty-fifth anniversary of its democracy, South Africa's mood is described by Madondo explicitly as 'carnival-esque' (2017) so that when the narrative presents its readers with eviscerated bodies, the horror of such images is knowingly tinted by the not-entirely-serious lens of the grotesque: in a still-segregated coastal city, unmistakably Cape Town, attacks on various forms of those 'human vampires' (including the 'rich and indifferent') leave victims 'strangled, sliced apart, clawed to death, their eyes gouged out' (Madondo 2017).

The laughing deathliness of the grotesque, Barnard reminds us, 'serves as a sign of a particular temporality – of the moment at which the old is making way for the new' (2004: 284), and in this sense it is significant that in Madondo's story, the fall of the existing order, the allegorical moment of revolution, is also the moment of lexical shift from the Gothic vocabulary of vampires to the carnival language of grotesque corporeality. A kind of ambivalent optimism emerges from this modulation: the grotesque operates as a productive mode in which to anticipate a fire (in Baldwin's sense) from the ashes of which there will rise something new.

Occult Inflections

In 2016, a short graphic narrative by South African artist Phumle April appeared in *The Chronic*, the subsidiary to the pan-African journal of culture and politics *Chimurenga*. This issue, which won the Nommo Award for graphic speculative fiction by Africans in 2017, is entitled 'The Corpse Exhibition', and April's contribution – appearing alongside pieces produced in various speculative modalities – demonstrates the thematics of horror that this heading suggests. The tale, 'Avions de Nuit', follows protagonist Skuta as he is abducted and enslaved by a cohort of sinister figures who eliminate his sentience by messily cutting out his tongue and driving a nail into his skull. The story leaves Skuta (now invisible to the living) mid-flight, ducking to avoid drones and commercial aeroplanes, and 'doing his masters' bidding from the back of an insane hairless [airborn] baboon' (2016: 45).

April's piece clearly articulates anxieties relating to work and employment. It thematises a dehumanising vulnerability to exploitation, articulating this as horrifically realised corporeal mutilation, and showing Skuta's plight to be rendered more violent still by that distressing state of mute invisibility that evokes (as in Human and Madondo) a systemically indifferent society. As it resonates with the aesthetics of body horror, 'Avions de Nuit' also – crucially – operates in the terminology of popular occult beliefs in actual circulation in contemporary South Africa: Skuta is the victim of '*igqwirha*', or witches, and his enforced transformation into a voiceless labouring body marks his becoming '*isithunzela*', a zombie.

Discourses around witchcraft and the toiling undead (along with a host of other occult figures and practices) have proliferated in South Africa over the last three decades. Since the fall of apartheid, Jean and John L. Comaroff write,

> [l]ong-standing notions of witchcraft [. . .] have come to embrace zombie-making, the brutal reduction of others [. . .] to instruments of production; to insensible beings stored, like tools, in sheds, cupboards, or oil drums at the homes of their creators [. . .] Thus do some build fortunes with the lifeblood of others. And as they do, they are held to destroy the job market. (2002: 787–8)

It is salient, then, that the zombie emerges with force in the midst of spiralling unemployment in South Africa, which takes hold just as the promises of long-awaited democracy were supposed to be materialising. The zombie is a response to these circumstances – to what the Comaroffs call 'liberation under neoliberal conditions' (785) – and, in the first instance, it functions as what Stephen Shapiro terms a 'catachrestic narrative' *explanation* of the persistent socio-economic unevenness that contours the neoliberalising post-apartheid nation (2008: 31). The zombie aetiologises wealth where it exists in the midst of joblessness and poverty, even as it rationalises joblessness itself. The pointed question is who would pay for labour with undead workers at their disposal?

At the same time, the zombie also bears witness to a particular experience: one in which old, oppressive patterns of life and work are breaking up, and where what succeeds these is neither wholly familiar from the past nor recognisable as the long-anticipated change for the better much-vaunted over the transition to democracy. 'In their silence', the Comaroffs write, zombies

> give voice to a sense of dread about the human costs of intensified capitalist production; about the loss of control over the terms in which people alienate their labor power; about the demise of a moral economy in which wage employment, however distant and exploitative [under apartheid], had 'always' been there. (2002: 798)

A world in which zombie-makers are abroad is a dangerous, profoundly bewildering place, and as it registers this sense of generalised disorientation and threat the figure of the zombie bares the deleterious effects of unfolding neoliberalisation. It is significant then that April's fictional deployment of *isithunzela* produces a similar effect. Skuta is jostled in international airspace by avatars of a neoliberal world order – of global mobility, cross-border surveillance and remote-controlled warfare. Voiceless and enslaved, he exposes a local South African experience of this planetary configuration that is characterised overwhelmingly by a vulnerability to violence.

April thus underscores the critical potential inherent in the occult figure of the zombie and mobilises this in the narrative to deliberately critical ends. And 'Avions de Nuit' is not alone in pursuing such a strategy. A number of recent South African fictions in different media compose a lexicon of often vividly corporeal horror from the anxious occult figures that have emerged in the post-apartheid nation, harnessing these in pursuit of an interrogative agenda. Lauren Beukes's *Zoo City* (2010) takes inspiration from a (again actually existing) post-apartheid trade in (human) organs for magical medicine (or *muti*). As I have shown elsewhere (Duncan 2018a), she presents this as the covert, grisly underside of the 'new' South Africa's neoliberal economy, the vivid violence of which is thus exposed. Organ harvesting returns in Human's *Apocalypse Now Now*, where – as we have seen – it is relocated in the corporate domain. It features too (albeit more problematically) in Neill Blomkamp's alien dystopia, *District 9* (2009), where it is a threat primarily to those relegated to states of extreme insecurity at the margins of a multinationalising post-apartheid society (Duncan 2018b). More recently, director Jerome Pikwane's *The Tokoloshe* (2018) deploys the figure of the infamously lascivious witch's familiar from which the film takes its title as part of a multilayered interrogation of persistent, racialised poverty in present-day South Africa, conditions handled by the movie as a disproportionate vulnerability – especially among women and children – to violence, abuse and disease.

This pattern of activating occult figures of catachresis in ways that maximise their tacitly interrogative potential is, the Warwick Research Collective (WReC) has suggested, widely discernible across 'irrealist' literary production from the frequently postcolonial (semi-)peripheries of the millennial world-system (Deckard et al. 2015: 51–2).[3] WReC follows Shapiro, who – writing outside his work with the collective – argues that Gothic, from its earliest iterations, registers the bewildering experience of socio-economic transformation in the context of the world economy. Gothic has thus proliferated, he notes, at those moments in the history of the capitalist world-system when one phase of accumulation gives way to another: periods when the shape of reality shifts to disorientating and widely injurious effect (Shapiro 2008: 30–1). As is the case with the magical threats that circulate in post-apartheid South Africa, it is thus possible to see in Gothic forms the suggestion of violences that are 'strongly felt but [as yet] inchoately understood' (31), and if in earlier narrative responses to upheaval, such loaded figures of fear 'functioned more on the level of the political unconscious as an expression of social anxieties', then in later fictions 'the aesthetic adaptation of [. . .] catachresis [. . .] is deliberate' (Deckard et al. 2015: 105). On this account, and as in April, Beukes and Human, contemporary Gothic figures are deployed *both* to register the texture of a violent reality and, in exposing that reality, to critique the historical conditions within which it is produced. Gothic in this way retains the aetiologising or explanatory function of catachrestic figures (like *isithunzela*, *muti*, the *tokoloshe*) but summons this function to the service of a particular socio-economic and political diagnostics (Duncan 2018a).

Figures of Ruination

Precisely *where* (or perhaps *when*) this visceral South African Gothic diagnostic locates the roots of post-millennial violence and anxiety is a complex question. Even as April situates Skuta's plight in the violent telescoping relation between rural South Africa and a neoliberal world order, the narrative also connects this millennial present to the longer history of racialised capitalism, of which apartheid is an especially fastidious example, and which is conjured in the text as histories of enslavement: the magical aircraft in which the doomed Skuta is transported also 'makes nightly flights across the Atlantic, carrying passengers into slavery' (April 2016: 40). Both Beukes and Blomkamp position their speculative figures of horror in a similar way: Beukes's villain and Blomkamp's kettled alien population signify both South Africa's colonial and apartheid-era segregations, and the multinationalising, deregulating post-apartheid present.

The same temporal ambivalence is discernible in Mandisi Nkomo's short story 'The Wild Dogs', which appears among other emerging (and established) voices in African horror-writing in the anthology *Lights Out: Resurrection* (Nkomo 2016). The tale, set in Cape Town in the throes of a mysteriously spread therianthropic plague, details the social effects of were-hyenaism – the afflicted are called 'Yenas' – as racism and unofficial segregation. For the majority of the tale, the narrative pointedly refuses to rule out the possibility that the disease (which transforms people into violent, anthropophagic human-hyena hybrids) is somehow connected to race. The contagion has 'skipped all the rich white areas', one protagonist tells the other, and, consequently, the populations of these suburbs have locked themselves away in fortified communities which – as the duo learn first-hand – 'don't let non-whites in anymore' (2016: 113). As it highlights the notoriously untransformed geography of Cape Town (designated 'the fortress city' by Meg Samuelson (2014: 813)), the figure of the Yena also generates an analogic relation between the contemporary South Africa in which the tale is located and the country under the NP administration. '*Die baas is sleg*' ('the boss is mean') remarks a black security guard to the central characters, using the racialised apartheid-era expression of rank to explain their rejection from the safe community (Nkomo 2016: 117). The past persists, the narrative appears to suggest: apartheid's legacy has outlived that regime's official demise.

And yet, the figure of the Yena is also more than a vestigial marker of history in the present. As circumstances in neoliberal, post-apartheid South Africa suggest with particular force, it seems reductive to imagine imperial power as anything less that actually unfolding. 'The challenge', writes Ann Laura Stoler in her illuminating assessment of post-millennial, postcolonial studies, 'is not to imagine "the postcolony" or the postcolonial imperium as replicas of earlier degradations or as the inadvertent inactive leftovers of more violent relations' (2013: 29). Instead, it is necessary at this juncture to attune critical focus to the living immediacy of 'imperial formations', which *overlay and compound* the structures and effects of earlier regimes, capitalising on these via strategies that include varied 'reappropriations, neglect and strategic and active positioning within the [...] present' (11). Such a perspective would not see the static 'ruins of empire' (the image around which Stoler's essay circles). Rather it would apprehend empire as a process, uncompleted in the present, of 'ruination': 'a violent verb' (7).

Nkomo's therianthropes have, by the end of the narrative, acquired precisely this sense of ongoing historical accretion. If few Yenas are white, this is not because – Nkomo writes – the spread of the disease has anything 'to do with race' (it turns out to be carried by rats) (2016: 124). It has instead, the narrative shows, to do with the effects of macro-economic neoliberalism as this has been implemented in the historical context of cultivated, racialised material inequality. Yena-ism is related to race, in other words, to the same extent that 'unacceptable poverty [. . .] a lack of access to sanitation, [and] healthcare' are related to race in post-apartheid South Africa (124). And Nkomo might just as well be writing here of the mysteriously 'animalled' pariahs in Beukes's *Zoo City* (2010: 74), bound to a creature-familiar for their crimes and rendered horrifically disposable as a result, or of the radically marginalised and brutally exploited extraterrestrials in Blomkamp's *District 9*. As critical images of ruination, Yenas and other avatars of unease figure the still-racialised condition of disproportionate precarity produced as the privatisations and deregulations of the millennial present overlay the structures and effects of the apartheid past. Their temporal ambivalence thus exceeds the haunting language of analogy – the sense that the present is somehow 'like' the past – and instead critically registers a sedimentation of older and newer systems of violence, skewering a mode of imperialism that is actively unfolding.

A Gothic Sensorium

If there is a diagnostic or aetiologising impulse in post-millennial South African Gothic then it is here, in this sedimented historical present, that these fictions locate the injurious realities they index – as Nkomo's Janus-like hyena-therianthropes demonstrate with particular clarity. And Yenas also significantly demonstrate the grotesque corporeal imaginary I emphasise above. Even as they perform brutal and grisly acts, their characterisation strongly suggests that their condition is equally lived as a painful, bodily corrosion. One of the affected is described, for example, as both 'stretched and [. . .] stunted, as if through medieval torture', with '[c]laws ripp[ing] unnaturally from her fingers', and skin like an 'unhealthy mosaic' (Nkomo 2016: 119). Thus, the Yena might critically figure ruination, but they also – like April's mutilated Skuta and the catachrestic figures of the popular occult more widely – suggest an *experience* of a ruining world, one that is disorientating and vividly violent. Writing into the context of ongoing imperialism, and outside his work with the WReC, Neil Lazarus has called for a postcolonial studies that takes seriously the 'phenomenological' dimension of literary production (2011: 79): the capacity of the writer for apprehending a 'sensorium' (Deckard et al. 2015: 12), for 'show[ing] us what it feels like to live on a given ground' (Lazarus 2011: 79). Across post-transitional South African writing, speculative narratives dealing in corporeal lexica appear to make a similar demand. Stepping away from the Gothic vocabularies of ghostly residues, authors are currently mining the resources of body horror for a language that encodes – returning to Lazarus, who draws on Raymond Williams – the 'structure of feeling' taking shape amid South Africa's accumulating, active imperial ruins (2011: 79).

And well they might. As Stoler shows, the rubrics within which postcolonial conditions have routinely been conceptualised – 'pervasive ones like "colonial legacy" and "colonial vestige"' – can 'do little to account for the contemporary force of imperial remains' (2013: 12). As they turn to what she calls 'the microecologies of matter and mind' (10), post-apartheid horror fictions locate themselves, in Williams's phrasing, 'at the very edge of semantic availability' (1977: 134). From this perspective, their heightened affectivity and insistence on corporeal immediacy bears on a 'social experience *in solution*', one that has yet to be '*precipitated*' into 'readily available' interpretive codes (134–5, emphasis in original). If we follow Williams further, we will see that creative production frequently offers 'the first indications that [. . .] a new structure is forming' (134), and this, on the evidence of texts considered here, appears a complex cocktail entailing, firstly, mounting rage at the post-apartheid imperium. In this respect, it seems important that Gothic aetiologies in post-transitional texts – their manipulation of horror to expose the roots of ruinous experience – distinguish millennial writers from the majority of authors engaging with the Gothic over South Africa's transitional period. If in *those* fictions Gothic, as haunting underscored alterity, signals the essential unknowability of history and of the Other, then in recent work its purpose is to excavate and make tangible the systemic foundations of lived precarity, insecurity and heightened risk. This operational shift in the aesthetics of fear suggests a much deeper transformation taking place at the level of what might be called postcolonial metaphysics: a changing apprehension of the nature and objectives of dissenting postcolonial thought. Gothic from millennial South Africa is registering this reorientation and is doing so in narratives animated by what Lazarus, writing of postcolonial fictions widely, calls a 'materialist spirit' (2011: 79).

Returning to structures of feeling: there is here, entangled with diligently directed and politicised anger, also a species of hopefulness. Why write out against the violence, after all – why name it and bring it into consciousness – if not in anticipation of something else? Perhaps Madondo's allegory encapsulates all of this most clearly in its sense of deathly renewal, in the horror-joy with which it conjures a fiery South African future.

Notes

1. See for example Gaylard (2008), Stobie (2008) and Shear (2006).
2. Emerging voices in South African literary criticism Esthie Hugo (2014) and Kamilini Govender (2018) have each also highlighted Human's Gothic poetics as responsive to post-millennial, post-apartheid South Africa.
3. The Warwick Research Collective is Sharae Deckard, Nicholas Lawrence, Neil Lazarus, Graeme Macdonald, Upamanyu Pablo Mukherjee, Benita Parry and Stephen Shapiro.

Film and Television

District 9 (Neill Blomkamp, USA/New Zealand, 2009)
The Tokoloshe (Jerome Pikwane, South Africa, 2018)

References

Aldana Reyes, Xavier (2014), *Body Gothic: Corporeal Transgression Contemporary Literature and Horror Film*, Cardiff: University of Wales Press.
April, Phumle (2016), 'Avions de Nuit', *Chimurenga Chronic: The Corpse Exhibition and Older Graphic Stories*, 3, 40–5.
Bakhtin, Mikhail (1984) [1965], *Rabelais and his World*, Helene Iswolky (trans.), Bloomington: Indiana University Press.
Barnard, Rita (2004), 'On Laughter, the Grotesque, and the South African Transition: Zakes Mda's *Ways of Dying*', *NOVEL: A Forum on Fiction*, 37.3, 277–302.
Barnard, Rita (2012), 'Rewriting the Nation', in David Attwell and Derek Attridge (eds), *The Cambridge History of South African Literature*, Cambridge: Cambridge University Press, pp. 652–67.
Beukes, Lauren (2010), *Zoo City*, Johannesburg: Jacana.
Comaroff, John L., and Jean Comaroff (2002), 'Alien-nation: Zombies, Immigrants and Millennial Capitalism', *South Atlantic Quarterly*, 101.4, 779–805.
Deckard, Sharae et al. (2015), *Combined and Uneven Development: Towards a New Theory of World-Literature*, Liverpool: Liverpool University Press.
Duncan, Rebecca (2018a), *South African Gothic: Anxiety and Creative Dissent*

in the Post-apartheid Imagination and Beyond, Cardiff: University of Wales Press.
— (2018b), 'From Cheap Labour to Surplus Humanity: World-Ecology and the Post-apartheid Speculative in Neill Blomkamp's *District 9*', *SFFTV*, 11.1, 45–72.
Durrant, Sam (2004), *Postcolonial Narrative and the Work of Mourning: J. M. Coetzee, Wilson Harris and Toni Morrison*, New York: SUNY Press.
Frenkel, Ronit, and Craig MacKenzie (2010), 'Conceptualizing Post-Transitional Literature in English', *English Studies in Africa*, 53.1, 1–10.
Gaylard, Gerald (2008), 'The Postcolonial Gothic: Time and Death in Southern African Literature', *Journal of Literary Studies*, 24.2, 1–18.
Govender, Kamilini (2018), 'Transformation and Children's Gothic Fiction in a South African Context', presented at International Gothic Association conference, Manchester, 31 July–3 August.
Graham, Shane (2011), *South African Literature after the Truth Commission: Mapping Loss*, Scottsville: University of KwaZulu-Natal Press.
Harvey, David (2005), *A Brief History of Neoliberalism*, Oxford: Oxford University Press.
Horner, Avril, and Sue Zlosnik (2005), *Gothic and the Comic Turn*, Basingstoke: Palgrave Macmillan.
Hugo, Esthie (2014), 'Sinister Surface: Contemporary South African Horror (on Stage and Off)', *Litnet*, https://www.litnet.co.za/sinister-surfaces-contemporary-south-african-horror-on-stage-and-off/ (accessed 6 October 2018).
Human, Charlie (2013), *Apocalypse Now Now*, London: Century.
Lazarus, Neil (2011), *The Postcolonial Unconscious*, Cambridge: Cambridge University Press.
Madondo, Bongani (2017), 'Return of the Afringers: An Allegory', *Johannesburg Review of Books*, https://johannesburgreviewofbooks.com/2017/12/06/fiction-issue-return-of-the-afringers-an-allegory-by-bongani-madondo/ (accessed 13 September 2018).
Mbembe, Achille (2001), *On the Postcolony*, Berkeley: University of California Press.
Nkomo, Mandisi (2016), 'The Wild Dogs', in Wole Talabi (ed.), *Lights Out: Resurrection*, The Naked Convos.
Punter, David (2003), 'Arundhati Roy and the House of History', in Andrew Smith and William Hughes (eds), *Empire and the Gothic: The Politics of Genre*, Basingstoke: Palgrave Macmillan, pp. 192–207.
Samuelson, Meg (2014), '(Un)lawful Subjects of Company: Reading Cape Town from Tavern of the Seas to Corporate City', *Interventions*, 16.6, 795–817.
Saul, John. S., and Patrick Bond (2014), *South Africa – The Present as History: From Mrs Ples to Mandela and Marikana*, Suffolk, UK: James Currey.
Shapiro, Stephen (2008), 'Transvaal, Transylvania: *Dracula*'s World-System and Gothic Periodicity', *Gothic Studies*, 10.1, 29–47.
Shear, Jack (2006), Haunted House, Haunted Nation: *Triomf* and the South African Postcolonial Gothic', *Journal of Literary Studies*, 22.1, 70–95.
Spooner, Catherine (2006), *Contemporary Gothic*, London: Reaktion.
Stobie, Cheryl (2008), 'Sisters and Spirits: The Postcolonial Gothic in Angelina N. Sithebe's *Holy Hill*', *Current Writing: Text and Reception in Southern Africa*, 20.2, 26–43.

Stoler, Ann Laura (2013), '"The Rot Remains": From Ruins to Ruination', in Ann Laura Stoler (ed.), *Imperial Debris: On Ruins and Ruination*, Durham, NC: Duke University Press, pp. 1–35.

Wicomb, Zoë (2001), *David's Story*, New York: The Feminist Press.

Williams, Raymond (1977), *Marxism and Literature*, Oxford: Oxford University Press.

Chapter 17

Asian Gothic
Katarzyna Ancuta

The global demand for Japanese millennial horror in the wake of the phenomenal success of films like *Ringu* (*Ring*, Hideo Nakata, 1998), *Ôdishon* (*Audition*, Takashi Miike, 1999) or *Batoru rowaiaru* (*Battle Royale*, Kinji Fukasaku, 2000) resulted in the promotion of Asian horror as a single marketable category. While encompassing strikingly different genres – from Japanese big monster *kaiju* movies, South Korean serial killer thrillers and Hong Kong cannibal exploitation, to Southeast Asian ghost comedies, Chinese supernatural romances and Bollywood horror musicals – this umbrella term was nevertheless accepted enthusiastically by both filmmakers and film distributors. Soon after, unsurprisingly, academic interest turned to Asian Gothic. Unlike Asian horror, however, Asian Gothic remains a contested label and a term that exists mostly in scholarly discourse.[1] In twenty-first-century Asia, 'Gothic' is still perceived as a foreign category and a denominator of paperback literature of questionable quality.

The authors who consciously relate to Gothic tend to openly acknowledge its Western heritage in their works. In his 'light' novel *Gosu* (*Goth*, 2002), Otsuichi for instance explains that

> Goth refers to a culture, a fashion, and a style [. . .] Goth is short for Gothic but has little connection with the European architectural style. It has much more to do with the Gothic horror novels popular in Victorian London, like *Frankenstein* or *Dracula*. (2015: 98)

Despite this lack of self-recognition, Gothic as a mode of expression is not unusual in Asian texts, which are rich in supernatural references.[2] The poetic violence of the Gothic mode and its propensity for the grotesque is often attractive to Asian authors working under authoritarian governments and battling censorship, as social and political criticism rarely invites repercussions when perceived as 'magical realism' or a ghost story.

Similar to its Western counterpart, Asian Gothic has roots in supernatural fiction. By the fourth century the ghost story was already an established literary genre in China. Ancient Sanskrit epics *Ramayana* and *Mahabharata* featured stories of gods, monsters and demons that continue to inspire contemporary texts throughout the region. Rejecting eighteenth-century Western Enlightenment philosophies and Eurocentric rationalism, Asian modernity embraced animistic practices to propagate the myth of Asian uniqueness; indeed, animism has been employed in the service of governments. Gerald Figal observes that the discourse on the *fushigi* (the mysterious, supernatural and fantastic) 'played fundamental roles in the constitution of modernity in Meiji Japan' (1999: 6) and was employed to counteract the assumption that Japan's modernisation was equivalent to Westernisation.

The 'supernatural' itself is of course an ambiguous term here, given that in the animistic context ghosts, spirits, monsters, demons, deities and immortals are all seen as perfectly 'natural' and co-existing with humans. Their existence reaffirms the balance of the universe and, while often not completely compatible with dominant religious doctrines, they flourish in popular beliefs. The unstable hybrid properties of the entities in question – perceived as simultaneously material and immaterial, anthropomorphic and animalistic, objects and events – make them hard to conceptualise in English. Shapeshifting animals can appear human, ghosts can turn into animals, and spirits can have tangible monstrous bodies but also possess people. Such figures continue to thrive in twenty-first-century films and fiction.

Given the wealth of material to cover, this chapter offers a rather selective survey of twenty-first-century Asian Gothic. Its main focus is the most prominent trend involving reconfigurations of Asian folklore and the ghost story. More specifically, this chapter investigates narratives dealing with individual and collective trauma centred on the figure of the vengeful ghost, texts which reclaim animism as an inherent part of Asian modernity, and Asian Gothic's interrogation of gender dynamics and empowered women.

The Rise of the Vengeful Ghost

By far the most dominant contemporary Asian Gothic theme widespread across the region is the return of the vengeful spirit. Frequently referencing local folklore and urban legends, vengeful spirits proliferate in twenty-first-century Asian cinemas that have always been partial to ghosts. As often the case in strongly patriarchal societies, most stories privilege the monstrous feminine; however, their female ghosts are simultaneously terrifying and evoke sympathy. In the stories, the monstrous feminine is a product of systemic patriarchal oppression – the female ghosts were often denied equal opportunities in life, abused, raped and/ or murdered by men.

Furthermore, in contemporary texts, these vengeful feminine spirits recall iconic Japanese *onryō*; Sadako Yamamura from *Ringu* and Kayako Saeki from *Ju-on* (*Ju-on: The Grudge*, Takashi Shimizu, 2002) illustrate modern iterations of the figure.[3] In Japanese folklore, the *onryō* are the spirits that died violent deaths and returned to take vengeance upon the living. Their visual representation, marked by the 'funereal white attire, long black hair, and pallid, staring visages' (McRoy 2015: 199), solidified in the Kabuki performances of the Edo period (1603–1868). While Sadako and Kayako complement this image with their idiosyncratic movements and other peculiarities, they are mostly remembered for the ease with which they infiltrate modern telecommunication technologies and their insatiable rage. Unlike their predecessors, these ghosts cannot be appeased, they do not aim to punish individual wrongdoers but rather 'have no specific enemy [. . .] challenging one and all' (Gerow 2002: 20). As such, their unquenchable rage indicts larger systemic behaviour and society as the ultimate culprit in their deaths.

The popularity of Sadako and Kayako resulted in a cornucopia of ghost movies across the region, many of which appropriated the image and modus operandi of the modern *onryō* to stylise a variety of locally-positioned vengeful spirits. Some were contrasted with the more benevolent members of the spirit world, like the ghost of the murdered Filipino maid set against the backdrop of the Chinese ancestral spirits returning to Singapore for the Hungry Ghost Festival in *The Maid* (Kelvin Tong, 2005). Others blended with Indigenous liminal beings like the Malay *pontianak* or the Indonesian *kuntilanak* (*Pontianak harum sundal malam* (*Pontianak*, Shuhaimi Baba, 2004), *Kuntilanak* (*The Chanting*, Rizal Mantovani, 2006)). Vengeful spirits found a fertile ground in Korean cinema known for its tendency to blend horror with melodrama, spinning sad tales of murdered lovers (*Pon* (*Phone*, Byeong-ki Ahn, 2002), *Geoul sokeuro* (*Into the Mirror*, Sung-ho Kim, 2003)), abused children (*Sinderella* (*Cinderella*, Man-dae Bong, 2006), *Gisaeng ryung* (*Ghastly*, Seok-jin Ko, 2011)) and bullied schoolgirls (*Bunshinsaba* (*Ouija Board*, Byeong-ki Ahn, 2004), *Sonyeogoedam* (*Mourning Grave*, In-chun Oh, 2014)). The horror of the vengeful female spirit has thus become a popular tool to engage various types of social turmoil.

The rise of South Korean films featuring vengeful spirits created through school bullying corroborates the findings of sociologists detailing the trauma of school violence. Sociologists describe bullying in South Korea in terms of 'collective ostracism, social exclusion (*jipdan ttadollim*) and/or peer harassment (*gipdan-gorophim*)' (Bax 2016: 94) rather than an action between individuals and link it to the alarmingly high suicide rate among young people (Min et al. 2015). Modern Korean Gothic films suggest such socialised abuse leads to haunting. In *Bunshinsaba* a bullied schoolgirl places a curse on her tormentors that invokes the rage of another schoolgirl murdered by the villagers in the past. Similarly, *Mourning Grave* introduces a ghost with a multiple personality disorder. Bullied and driven to suicide, Sae-he creates her vengeful ghost persona 'The Mask', which in turn possesses people to exact revenge on her classmates. Importantly, as much as such films seem to focus their horror on the cruelty of adolescents, they also reveal the ambivalence typical to twenty-first-century Korean cinema, which is torn between the nostalgic desire to return to the past when the country flourished under strong governmental control and the need to address the horrors of the authoritarian military regimes that have solidified into collective wounds that continue to afflict the nation.

Blending Thai 16mm cinema *nang phi* (ghost film) heritage with contemporary Japanese and Korean horror models, Thai vengeful ghosts like the *phi tai hong* (ghosts that died violent deaths) act as karmic forces punishing the sinners and balancing the universe. The much-celebrated final shot of *Shutter kot tit winyan* (*Shutter*, Banjong Pisantanakun and Parkpoom Wongpoom, 2004) particularly illustrates this kind of haunting as it reveals the ghost of Natre sitting on the shoulders of her former boyfriend, who orchestrated and photographed her rape, thus prompting her suicide. Natre's ghost represents the weight of karma and human responsibility for their own life, a recurring motif of many ghost movies made in predominantly Buddhist Thailand; but then, vengeful spirits seem capable of adapting to any religion. In Filipino films, they often function as the expression of Catholic guilt, as in *The Road* (Yam Laranas, 2011), where the killer shares his house with the ghosts of the women he murdered; in *Sigaw* (*The Echo*, Yam Laranas, 2004), where the ghost of an abused woman haunts her neighbours who ignore cases of marital violence; or in *Seklusyon* (*Seclusion*, Erik Matti, 2016), where ghosts appear as representations of sins committed by young deacons preparing to enter priesthood. The Taoist framework of *Geung si* (*Rigor Mortis*, Juno Mak, 2013) validates a Hong Kong tenement house as a space cohabited by the living and the dead and warns against the imbalance of *yin* and *yang* energies, exemplified by the vengeful twin spirits whose rage animates the corpse of an elderly tenant and turns him into a *jiangshi*, or 'hopping vampire'.

Collectively-oriented Asian vengeful spirits engage with social issues and channel the frustration of their audiences, who often see themselves becoming 'ghost-like' and insignificant under a globalised neoliberal economy. In *The Maid*, Esther's ghost highlights the exploitation of overseas Filipino workers in Singapore. The ghost of a Burmese maid murdered while guarding the property of an absent foreigner in *Laddaland* (Sophon Sakdaphsit, 2011) reflects the fate of her Thai neighbours locked in blind pursuit of social mobility and economic success, who become ghosts of themselves long before death reduces them to such. Ghosts haunt apartments, but equally haunting is the elusive dream of home ownership that can easily turn into nightmare. In *Tumbok* (Topel Lee, 2011), the landlord of a tenement in Manila is revealed to be a demon, while *Bhoot* (*Ghost*, Ram Gopal Varma, 2003) makes the case that, given the property prices in Mumbai, knowingly renting a haunted apartment and allowing your wife to get possessed may still be considered a valid alternative. Seemingly focused on the repetition and resolution of their personal traumas, vengeful ghosts seem acutely aware that they have larger socio-cultural roles to play, as each haunting is also a 'process that links an institution and an individual, a social structure and a subject, and history and a biography' (Gordon 2008: 19).

Haunted History, Gothic Present

In a region swarming with ghosts, these have multiple roles to play, channelling contemporary socio-cultural anxieties but also engaging with the continent's turbulent history and its colonial past. Emilie Cameron notices that 'ghostliness is a politicized state of being' (2008: 390) and 'a function of visibility [. . . where] the uncovering and exposure of the ghosts of the past is an emancipatory act' (390), but she also warns against reducing the Indigenous to the ghostly, as this puts colonial power structure back into place. While the ghosts in twenty-first-century Asian texts are part of the fabric of reality, their return is commonly linked with past trauma. Their return reminds us that '[t]he Gothic present can only be imagined in terms of an endless repetition of the same traumatic moment' (Juranovszky 2014: 3), where the possibility of healing is postponed or denied.

Shilpa Agarwal's novel *Haunting Bombay* (2005) invokes the ghost of a baby girl said to have drowned due to her nanny's negligence. Released from the confines of the locked bathroom, the ghost of Chakori feeds on water, travelling alongside dripping clotheslines that criss-cross the family bungalow. Chakori's death is eventually revealed to be a mercy killing performed by her grandmother upon learning that the baby was born a *hijra*, or a hermaphrodite: '[n]ot completely female, nor completely male, but somewhere in between, she had no rightful place, no rightful future in the Mittal bungalow' (Agarwal 2009: 349). Chakori was the Gothic Other even before she became a ghost. The book describes *hijras* as the unfortunates born with deformed genitals, ostracised, feared, expelled from the community and expected to 'make a living by playing on the dread and superstition they evoke in others' (77), as they are believed to possess 'supernatural powers which stem from their ability to be both man and woman and to be neither' (77). This, to Chakori's grandmother, was a fate worse than death.

Little Chakori highlights the fate of many figurative 'ghosts' that can be found in the marginalised citizens of contemporary India who are destined, whether by caste or gender or poverty, to be invisible and untouchable. Although the novel is set in the 1960s, not much has changed for Indian *hijras* in the twenty-first century, as they are still denied basic liberties and rights and 'remain not recognized as human, let alone a woman' (Khatri 2017: 387). A similar link between ghosts and undesirable social groups is made by Han Kang in *Sonyeon-i Onda* (*Human Acts*, 2014), a novel that describes the violent suppression of the Gwangju Uprising in May 1980 by the Korean military, which targeted mostly students and trade unions' members. The novel starts with the depiction of corpses, a poignant opening because, as Deborah Smith explains, '[p]iled up, reeking, unclaimed and thus unburied, they present both a logistical and an ontological dilemma' (2014: 2), since in Korean animist beliefs 'violence done to the body is a violation of the spirit/soul which animates it' (2).

The novel gives voice to several victims of the massacre, among them the ghost of a teenage boy killed by a sniper and forced to watch his body decompose and melt into the ground as it is crushed by the weight of the cadavers mounting on top of it. Released from its bondage when the corpses are finally set on fire, the spirit of the boy wonders where he is supposed to go next. Unable to locate either his sister or the soldier who killed him, he decides to search for his friend instead, only to hear the frantic scream of his friend's soul being 'shocked' from his body by bullets.

Ghosts have often been called upon as witnesses of cultural and historical trauma, as their appearance allows for the Gothic moment of repetition. Danel Olson maintains that by gradually gothicising trauma such texts are able to embody the carnage that used to be conceived of as 'unspeakable' (2016: 257). He argues that '[t]he arrival of ghosts is perhaps the greatest externalized trace to a concealed but corroding vault of traumatic memory' (258). Eka Kurniawan's novel *Cantik Itu Luka* (*Beauty Is a Wound*, 2002) is a commentary on tumultuous Indonesian history told from the perspective of an undead prostitute. Dewi Ayu rises from her grave to defend her family from the vengeful ghost of her ex-husband.

The novel is set in the town of Halimunda, where the spirits of the dead often play mischievous games and have to be chased away 'like other people shoo out a chicken that has wandered into the kitchen' (Kurniawan 2015: 326). Though a common appearance, not all of the ghosts are so amusing. The ghosts of massacred communists who were denied burial roam the streets of the city, causing car crashes and market fires, and haunting Shodancho, the man responsible for their deaths. There is also the vengeful ghost of Ma Gedik, the lover of Dewi Ayu's grandmother snatched from him by the Dutch master, who committed suicide after being forced to marry his lover's granddaughter. Ma Gedik's ghost is what Tabish Khair calls 'the ghost from the empire' (2009: 169) present in many colonial Gothic texts as 'a threat and a source of terror' (169), marginalised and abused while alive but drawing strength from years of hatred as a ghost. But Kurniawan's Halimunda is not simply a place where wounded memory materialises as ghosts, since ghosts have always been there. When the presence of ghosts is a facet of life it is not the appearance of ghosts that gothicises the trauma but rather the disturbance of the natural balance. Indeed, the fantastic grotesque in the novel offsets the brutal accounts of colonial excesses, Japanese war atrocities, the chaotic violence of the revolution and the extermination of communists, each of them raising their ghosts.

In the animistic context, liminal beings – spirits, ghosts, monsters or deities – are commonly imbued with agency and intellect; while seen as capricious they are also rational, as they negotiate and occasionally side with humans. In Sandi Tan's novel *The Black Isle* (2012), the ghosts swarming the fictional island that stands in for transmogrified Singapore are enlisted by the protagonist Cassandra to rise against the British and the Japanese invaders. Cassandra's supernatural sight that allows her to see ghosts is at first described as a burden. It is only after her encounter with the *pontianak* and embracing Indigenous Muslim magic that she realises their political potential. The *pontianak* is a liminal female entity native to the Malay Peninsula. Tan depicts her as a voracious monster:

> The girl wasn't helping Robin. She was gouging into his belly with long sharp nails. Blood sprayed everywhere. On the carpet, on the settee – all over her. She turned toward us and screeched, blood dripping from her gums. Her

teeth weren't teeth but little black fangs. Before we could move, she flew at us. (Tan 2012: 120)

Cassandra kills the *pontianak*, although she feels a certain affinity with the monster. The moment marks her transition from a Chinese immigrant to the 'native' of the Black Isle. After the war she teams up with an aspiring local politician to clean up the island of ghosts in the name of progress, but when the man, who eventually becomes the Prime Minister, intends to destroy the graveyard to lay tracks for the underground train system, Cassandra sides with the ghosts and allows them to claim his life instead. Unlike the foreign intruders, ghosts and spirits are indigenous to the island and will not be driven away. The Black Isle can prosper and progress only if it embraces its ghostly citizens as part of the multicultural fabric of the new nation.

Kurniawan and Tan enmesh their ghost tales in the larger historical narratives of colonialism, war, revolution and struggle for independence that form the background of Asian modernity. Yet the non-human world they describe is very much part of the everyday life in the region. In Uthis Haemamool's novel *Lap Lae, Kaeng Khoi* (*The Brotherhood of Kaeng Khoi*, 2009), ghosts and spirits function both as the markers of permanence and change. The story of Lap Lae and his dysfunctional family chronicles the development of Thailand since the 1940s, when his grandparents arrived from China as refugees until the 1990s, which marked the peak of the Thai economic boom before the 1997 Asian financial crisis. The grandparents work on the coconut plantation and the father works at a cement factory; both places are intimately connected with the gradual deforestation that characterises Thai modernisation. Deforestation, river regulation and massive urbanisation are often portrayed as causing imbalance in the spirit world traditionally associated with the forces of nature. As both animism and Buddhism privilege harmony, such discordance can be seen as deeply unsettling.

Unable to reconcile the conflicting worldviews of his superstitious mother and authoritarian father, Lap Lae projects his frustration onto his half-brother, Kaeng Khoi. The plot culminates in Lap Lae killing Kaeng Khoi and assimilating his identity in a symbolic act of renaming himself as his brother. The ending of the book, however, reveals that Kaeng Khoi died as a toddler and Lap Lae's narrative is an elaborate fabrication leaving us with several alternative explanations that suggest that the boy was possessed by the spirit of his brother, invaded by an angry forest spirit protesting human encroachment on the forest, or that he simply invented the 'ghost' to avoid taking responsibility for his life. The haunting in this case is not the return of the past but rather the embrace of a Gothic present where '[t]he everyday is like a ghost – secretive, ungraspable, yet with an acutely felt presence – and is itself beset by ghosts' (Blanco and Peeren 2010: xiii).

The persistence with which ghosts insert themselves into Asian narratives raises a valid question. If the repetitive return of these ghosts constitutes a Gothic moment, such encounters do not necessarily evoke dread and terror as the relationship between the living and the dead is more complicated in the animistic context. While ghosts are the returning dead, they are also part of the vast spirit realm the connection to which can be both disadvantageous and beneficial. This is particularly true in the case of women, whose culturally sanctioned spiritualism has both empowered them and led to their persecution.

Exorcising Ghosts, Empowering Women

If Asian female ghosts evoke both sympathy and terror, female shamans and witches are seen as simultaneously blasphemous and enlightened, transgressing against religion by asserting spiritual agency in the absence of legitimate access to male-centred official systems of worship. Their fate mirrors that of Asian goddesses, dethroned by their male companions but nevertheless profoundly influential. Female spirits and deities tend to embody the creative and destructive power of nature, therefore women are said to enjoy a special relationship with nature and the spirit world. Across Asia women are considered to have a weaker spiritual constitution which can be easily penetrated by spirits. Consequently, women are a likely target of demonic possession, particularly during illness, when they are menstruating and in childbirth. Indeed, abject substances associated with the female body, such as menses or placentas, are seen to both attract spirits and act as potent magical materials. Yet women's spiritual sensitivity makes them particularly powerful shamans and spiritual healers. However, Asian cultures worry over women's abuse of magic and warn that it can turn women into monsters. Such ambivalent ideals about women's spirituality means that women are denied full access to organised religion and its scriptures, but can attain spiritual agency as shamans and witches. Thus, the spiritual power of women is often seen as transgressive and subjugated by the patriarchal religious order.

Consequently, while the animistic framework does not impose a negative value judgement on women, witches, female spirits or other entities, they are likely to be re-classifed as corrupt or inherently evil in confrontation with dominant religious systems and the patriarchal social order.

This double framing persists in twenty-first-century Asian Gothic texts that oscillate between depictions of female shamanic power as a source of dread and the assumption that such power draws on the 'spiritual' aspect of being a woman. Female spiritualism has been explored in films across Asia. Apart from numerous *lung poh* or 'old dragon ladies' communicating with the dead in films out of Hong Kong, Singapore and Taiwan, they have featured as shinto priestesses (*Shikoku*, Shunichi Nagasaki, 1999) and spirit guardians (*Inugami*, Masato Harada, 2001) in Japanese productions, as shamans in Korea (*Toema: Munyeokul* (*The Chosen: Forbidden Cave*, Hwi Kim, 2015)), as healers in the Philippines (*The Healing*, Chito S. Roño, 2012) or as witches in Thailand (*Long Khong* (*Art of the Devil 2*, The Ronin Team, 2005)) and India (*Ek Thi Daayan*, Kannan Iyer, 2013). The effects of their mediumship vary. Some acquire superpowers and immortality, like the witch in *Ek Thi Daayan*, who is capable of self-reincarnation. Others have shapeshifting abilities, like the shamaness in *The Chosen: Forbidden Cave*, who becomes a snake-woman.

Films that portray shamanism as an alternative religion, where the shaman replaces a monk or a priest, do not always feature women in such roles. Yet in recent productions male spiritual authority frequently falters and female characters are not easily silenced. This is the case with *The Chosen: Forbidden Cave*, where the male shaman doubles as a respected psychiatrist. Confronted with the spirit of a powerful shamaness, however, he is unable to control her, even with the help of a Catholic priest. In *Gok-seong* (*The Wailing*, Hong-jin Na, 2016), a vengeful female spirit defeats two male mediums. The exorcist in the Thai film *P* (Paul Spurrier, 2005) dies emasculated by a female demonic entity. In both *The Chosen: Forbidden Cave* and *P*, evil is defeated through the selfless sacrifice of a woman, while *The Wailing* does not offer a resolution. Such films problematise the readings of female spirits or spiritualists as essentially evil and suggest that female spiritualism may be a source of strength and a method to counteract male domination.

The old Chinese custom of ghost marriage exemplifies female affinity with the spirit world and tests women's empathy by uniting the living with the dead. Although normally ghost weddings are symbolically arranged between two unmarried deceased people for the benefit of the spirits and their families (Schwartze 2010: 87), the betrothal of a living bride to a dead groom is more aligned with the Gothic sensibility. In Yangsze Choo's novel *The Ghost Bride* (2013), set in nineteenth-century Malaya, Li Lan accepts a marriage proposal from the mother of recently deceased Lim Tian Ching to escape poverty, as her father's opium habit effectively bankrupts her family. Although she expects to live comfortably as a widow in her in-laws' mansion, she finds herself drawn into the bureaucratic Chinese afterlife instead. She narrowly escapes with her life helped by a heavenly guardian, Er Lang, a fitting Gothic hero who also happens to be a dragon. The heroine of the Filipino film *The Ghost Bride* (Chito S. Roño, 2017) agrees to a similar contract to support her family and avoid marrying their exploitative landlord. She breaks her promise upon discovering that she is meant to be sacrificed to a demon instead.

Ghost marriage scenarios evoke early Gothic narratives that involved rescuing maidens from underground vaults and relied on help from daredevil male companions and sympathethic female ghosts. Occasionally, however, in the texts that conceive of their universe as the balance of complementary powers of *yin* and *yang*, death is described not as a punishment but rather a natural state for a woman. Natsuo Kirino's novel *Joshinki (The Goddess Chronicle*, 2008) is a retelling of a Japanese creation myth. Kirino's heroine, Namima, was born as a second daughter in a family of shamans. While her older sister is destined to serve as the High Priestess, Namima's duty is to be entombed alive as the Keeper of the Dead. Freed from the tomb by Mahito, a young man from a family shunned for his mother's inability to give birth to daughters, Namima escapes from the island only to be murdered by her lover upon giving birth to a baby girl, which he then presents to the islanders as his sister. Dead at sixteen, Namima finds herself in the underworld serving the Goddess of Creation, Izanami. Once the mother of Japan's islands, Izanami was betrayed by her husband, Izanaki, and trapped in the realm of the dead, where she rules over the deceased. Meanwhile Izanaki continued to roam the world making every woman he encountered his wife. Consumed by hatred, Izanami vowed to kill all the women her husband slept with and the two gods have been locked in a contest between life and death ever since.

Unable to understand the motive behind her murder, Namima is a mirror image of the goddess. Allowed to leave the underworld as a wasp, she kills her former lover Mahito in a fit of anger, seeing him happily married to her sister. But his death brings her no satisfaction, as Mahito's ghost has erased her from his memory. Unable to find release both women are consumed by pain. Asked why a goddess must suffer, Izanami replies '[b]ecause I am a *female* god' (Kirino 2012: 292). She thus joins a long list of Kirino's heroines who have the odds stacked against them at all times. While both Namima and Izanami grow bitter reminiscing over the injustices that befell them, they quickly resign themselves to their fate. Although men in the novel fear and resist death, the heroines find death neither disturbing nor painful; rather, their pain stems from betrayal at the hands of the men they once loved.

Conclusion

Although 'Gothic' remains a contested label in Asia, Gothic inclinations are fairly common in twenty-first-century Asian texts. By far the most predominant are various 'supernatural' texts that draw upon local folklore and urban legends, engage their ghosts and spirits as politically-charged cultural metaphors and position magic as a viable solution to one's problems. Many of these texts are female centred, as manifestations of the monstrous feminine tend to dominate collective nightmares in heavily patriarchal Asian societies. Yet the perceived affinity of women with the spirit world in Asian cultures complicates the positioning of women in Asian Gothic texts, as it makes them potentially amoral and capable of channelling both good and evil. This is evident in the overwhelmingly sympathetic portrayal of female monstrosities in Asian texts, decrying the lost innocence of wronged women turned by their circumstances into demons and vengeful spirits, and in the respect afforded to female healers and shamans increasingly depicted as equal in authority to male representatives of organised religions.

Gothic heroines have a long presence in Asian cultural texts, although their perception as monstrous and intrinsically evil is questionable. In the animistic context that many Asian cultures still relate to, the spiritual powers of women and female creatures are hardly ever subject to moral judgement and accepted as given. Equally fluid is the conceptualisation of ghosts in twenty-first-century Asian texts, negotiating Western metaphors of haunting, particularly eminent in postcolonial narratives, and Asian worldviews that see ghosts as part of the natural order. These differences effectively problematise definitions of Gothic that still adhere to Anglo-American standards, as they call into question Gothic's understanding of concepts such as 'death', 'ghost' or 'monster', frequently formulated in the context of Western philosophies and sciences. Twenty-first-century Asian Gothic may thus seem more a liminal category than a fixed genre but, ultimately, it is this liminality that makes it Gothic.

Notes

1. The versatility of the established Asian horror category makes it particularly difficult to make a case for cinematic Asian Gothic, and critics tend to use

these two labels interchangeably or opt for an examination of the Gothic elements in texts otherwise branded as horror.
2. Non-supernatural Asian Gothic texts are also in abundance, but they are not the topic of this chapter.
3. Created by Koji Suzuki, Sadako has appeared in five novels and seven Japanese movies to date (not counting manga and television series), has spawned one Korean and three American remakes, and has been crystallised into an instantly-recognisable pop-cultural reference. Shimizu's Kayako shot to fame in 2002. As of 2018, there have been nine *Ju-on* films, three American versions, seven novelisations by Ken Ohishi, two manga series and a video game. Kayako also appears on Instagram, where she posts pictures with her blue-faced son Toshio. Unsurprisingly, the fossilisation of Sadako and Kayako into horror icons has greatly simplified the characters, especially Sadako, reduced in Tsunomu Hanabusa's *Sadako 3D* (2012) to an insect-like monster with blue skin, grasshopper legs and sharp teeth, or forced to literally wrestle with Kayako over her victims in *Sadako vs. Kayako* (Kôji Shiraishi, 2016).

Film and Television

Bhoot (*Ghost*, Ram Gopal Varma, India, 2003)
Bunshinsaba (*Ouija Board*, Byeong-ki Ahn, South Korea, 2004)
Ek Thi Daayan (Kannan Iyer, India, 2013)
Geung si (*Rigor Mortis*, Juno Mak, Hong Kong, 2013)
Gok-seong (*The Wailing*, Hong-jin Na, South Korea, 2016)
Ju-on (*Ju-on: The Grudge*, Takashi Shimizu, Japan, 2002)
Laddaland (Sophon Sakdaphsit, Thailand, 2011)
P (Paul Spurrier, Thailand, 2005)
Ringu (*Ring*, Hideo Nakata, Japan, 1998)
Seklusyon (*Seclusion*, Erik Matti, Philippines, 2016)
Shutter kot tit winyan (*Shutter*, Banjong Pisantanakun and Parkpoom Wongpoom, Thailand, 2004)
Sigaw (*The Echo*, Yam Laranas, Philippines, 2004)
Sonyeogoedam (*Mourning Grave*, In-chun Oh, South Korea, 2014)
The Ghost Bride (Chito S. Roño, Philippines, 2017)
The Maid (Kelvin Tong, Singapore, 2005)
The Road (Yam Laranas, Philippines, 2011)
Toema: Munyeokul (*The Chosen: Forbidden Cave*, Hwi Kim, South Korea, 2015)
Tumbok (Topel Lee, Philippines, 2011)

References

Agarwal, Shilpa (2009), *Haunting Bombay*, New York: Soho.
Bax, Trent M. (2016), 'A Contemporary History of Bullying and Violence in South Korean Schools', *Asian Culture and History*, 8.2, 91–105.

Blanco, María del Pilar, and Esther Peeren (2010), *Popular Ghosts*, New York: Continuum.
Cameron, Emilie (2008), 'Indigenous Spectrality and the Politics of Postcolonial Ghost Stories', *Cultural Geographies*, 15.3, 383–93.
Choo, Yangsze (2013), *The Ghost Bride*, New York: William Morrow.
Figal, Gerald (1999), *Civilization and Monsters: Spirits of Modernity in Meiji Japan*, Durham, NC: Duke University Press.
Gerow, Aaron (2002), 'The Empty Return: Cicularity and Repetition in Recent Japanese Horror Films', *Minikomi*, 64.2, 19–24.
Gordon, Avery F. (2008), *Ghostly Matters*, Minneapolis: University of Minnesota Press.
Haemamool, Uthis (2012), *The Brotherhood of Kaeng Khoi*, Peter Montalbano (trans.), Bangkok: Amarin.
Juranovszky, Andrea (2014), 'Trauma Reenactment in the Gothic Loop: A Study on Structures of Circularity in Gothic Fiction', *Inquiries Journal/Student Pulse*, 6.5, 1–4.
Kang, Han (2014), *Human Acts*, Deborah Smith (trans.), London: Portobello Books.
Khair, Tabish (2009), *The Gothic, Postcolonialism and Otherness: Ghosts from Elsewhere*, London: Palgrave Macmillan.
Khatri, Sapna (2017), 'Hijras: The 21st Century Untouchables', *Washington University Global Studies Law Review*, 16.2, 387–410.
Kirino, Natsuo (2012), *The Goddess Chronicle*, Rebecca Copeland (trans.), Edinburgh: Canongate.
Kurniawan, Eka (2015), *Beauty Is a Wound*, Annie Tucker (trans.), London: Pushkin Press.
McRoy, Jay (2015), 'Spectral Remainders and Transcultural Hauntings: (Re)iterations of the *Onryō* in Japanese Horror Cinema', in Murray Leeder (ed.), *Cinematic Ghosts: Haunting and Spectrality from Silent Cinema to the Digital Era*, London: Bloomsbury, pp. 199–217.
Min, A., S. C. Park, E. Y. Jang, Y. C. Park, and J. Choi (2015), 'Variables Linking School Bullying and Suicidal Ideation in Middle School Students in South Korea', *Journal of Psychiatry*, 18.3, 1–7.
Olson, Danel (2016), '9/11 Gothic: Trauma, Mourning, and Spectrality in Novels from Don DeLillo, Jonathan Safran Foer, Lynne Sharon Schwartz, and Jess Walter'. Unpublished PhD dissertation, University of Stirling.
Otsuichi (2015), *Goth*, Jocelyne Allen (trans.), San Francisco: Haikasoru.
Schwartze, Lucas J. (2010), 'Grave Vows: A Cross-Cultural Examination of the Varying Forms of Ghost Marriage among Five Societies', *Nebraska Anthropologist*, 60, 82–95.
Smith, Deborah (2014), 'Introduction', in Han Kang (ed.), *Human Acts*, London: Portobello Books, pp. 1–5.
Suzuki, Koiji (2017), *S*, Greg Gencorello (trans.), New York: Vertical.
Tan, Sandi (2012), *The Black Isle*, New York: Grand Central Publishing.

Chapter 18

Latin American Gothic
Enrique Ajuria Ibarra

In order to understand Latin American Gothic in the twenty-first century, we must consider that the region's notion of the supernatural has broadened with the introduction of narrative forms and themes as a result of expanding global connections. This process accepts the incorporation of a wider range of elements that reveal an increasingly transnational cultural and artistic tradition. The most recognised Latin American filmmaker involved in this process is Guillermo del Toro. His fascination with the monstrous, the weird and the supernatural is not restricted to regional geographical boundaries; on the contrary, his films demonstrate an elaborate and detailed mixture of influences from around the world while still recognising local narrative forms of horror.[1] This has led Deborah Shaw to claim that he, along with Alejandro González Iñárritu and Alfonso Cuarón, is able to 'blur generic and national boundaries and create new hybrid formations' (2013: 7). Similarly, Dolores Tierney, Deborah Shaw and Ann Davies see del Toro 'negotiate very successfully between his own increasingly transnationalised national culture and that of an ever more globalized Hollywood' (2014: 2). The content of del Toro's work also prompts Ann Davies to claim that the explicit fluidity of his monsters demonstrates 'the difficulty of placing him within the national cinema of his home country Mexico', but discloses inevitable transnational exchanges (2014: 41). In short, del Toro's career has provided an international audience with a look at the Gothic in Latin America, but he should not be considered an isolated case. The turn of the century has led to an increased production of Gothic horror cinema in the region, with notable examples such as Juan Felipe Orozco's *Al final del espectro* (*At the End of the Spectra*, 2006), from Colombia; Rigoberto Castañeda's *KM 31: Kilómetro 31* (*KM 31*, 2007), from Mexico; Adrián García Bogliano's *Sudor frío* (*Cold Sweat*, 2010), from Argentina; Alejandro Hidalgo's *La casa del fin de los tiempos* (*The House at the End of Time*, 2013), from Venezuela;

and Guillermo Amoedo's *The Stranger* (2014), from Chile. Such artists reveal that Latin American Gothic is not a sign of Western literary or critical dominance, but rather the result of overlaps in the genre's elements and the region's inherently dark cultural concerns.

Thus, Latin American Gothic is not a recent phenomenon, but in the twenty-first century, the Gothic is accepted as a critical approach to the aesthetic movements that have dominated the region's literature and culture. In their ground-breaking edited collection *Latin American Gothic in Literature and Culture* (2018), Inés Ordiz and Sandra Casanova-Vizcaíno recognise that 'Latin American Gothic fiction has remained a marginalized form compared [. . .] to magical realist fiction' (2018: 1). Nevertheless, the Gothic today points to a different perspective that acknowledges how 'contemporary Latin American literature is inscribed within the fluctuating currents of world literature' (5). The Gothic is welcomed as a term that responds to globalisation, facilitates a retrospective critical revaluation of past works and allows for a more dynamic assessment of the fluid articulations that can be discerned between the Gothic, magic realism and the fantastic. Additionally, other studies have helped incorporate Latin American concepts into contemporary Gothic criticism, such as Tropical Gothic, which will be discussed later in this chapter.

Latin American Gothic, like global Gothic, 'constitutes a tangible reaction to the distress and anxiety of a globalised system that erupts within or from public cultures across the world' (Botting and Edwards 2013: 12). Furthermore, Fred Botting and Justin D. Edwards argue that the persistent presence of supernatural creatures across the world is not just the result of the ever-growing commercialised exchange of ideas and commodities in a more interconnected world. It is also evidence that 'despite huge variations in cultural-historical factors, spatial and temporal modes and the significances tied to locality and specificity, there are certain continuities and commonalities between imaginary supernatural, spectral and monstrous forms in fiction, film, fashion, media, music and culture' (12). Ultimately, these are varying manifestations and projections of 'otherness and fear' (12). The recognition of the fear of the Other materialises in local forms of monstrosity that still share features with other cultures and localities, feeding into the global exchange of tropes in art, literature and the media. It considers the Gothic not as the result of isolation and entrapment, but as a facilitator of cultural expressions of horror and terror that is constantly fluid, malleable and hybrid. Recent Gothic horror films, TV series and trending topics on social media help shed light into the dark recesses of terror and anxiety in Latin America.

Urban Monsters, Dark Secrets

In Latin America, terror, horror and the uncanny are reconsidered in narratives that develop isolation and social and political anxieties. Latin American filmmakers, like the ones mentioned above, focus on exploring and unearthing sources of fear and unease in their own nations. They reveal the hauntings arising from each country's historical past and present political situation even as the global exchange of economic and cultural products revitalises their appropriation of Gothic themes and tropes. Films like Jorge Michel Grau's *Somos lo que hay* (*We Are What We Are*, 2010), Gustavo Hernández's *La casa muda* (*The Silent House*, 2010) and Alejandro Brugués's *Juan de los muertos* (*Juan of the Dead*, 2011), all pay close attention to setting – old houses, engulfing urban conglomerations and isolated island nations – in order to disclose how characters open up and must face the monstrous fears that haunt them, whether individually or as members of a larger community.

Grau's film rejects supernatural horror in favour of a more gruesome and naturalistic account of global cosmopolitanism in Mexico City. The plot revolves around a family of cannibals whose father has just died and who are desperate to fulfil a ritual that is never explained. The two sons vie to become the new leader of the family, and their competition for power threatens to disintegrate the family. When they finally round up the victims for the ritual, they are discovered by two police officers. A shoot-out ensues where everyone dies except for the daughter, Sabina (Paulina Gaitán). As the sole survivor, she is the only one who will be able to perpetuate the ritual. This film addresses social and economic hardships within a family that is evidently isolated. The death of the father forces them to open their doors and go out into the world in order to provide for the family. Consequently, characters bound by ritualistic tradition are suddenly thrust into the modern global consumerism that governs Mexico City. Thus Paul Julian Smith interprets the film beyond 'the banality of cannibalism', positing that it also 'stands in to some extent for the cycle of violence, corruption and stasis that many Mexicans diagnose in their country' (2014: 153–4).

Grau's film grounds its associations with social fears by drawing away from the supernatural to focus on a mundane family with a taste for flesh and blood. The image of the dark, enclosed house of the family of cannibals evidently addresses issues of physical violence and kidnapping that result in violent death, a growing concern in Mexico over the past few years. Likewise, Smith acknowledges that the film amplifies monstrosity to a more social and realistic scale, and suggests that 'social exclusion, whether of gays or the destitute, is more of a monstrosity than cannibalism' (153). As such, *We Are What We Are* examines those who are marginalised in the urban scheme of cosmopolitanism. The domestic space, a traditional setting for Gothic horror, is also challenged by unavoidable change and different forms of monstrosity that infiltrate what should be local, familiar and secure. This approach towards the monstrous is picked up by Gustavo Subero, who convincingly demonstrates that Grau's film also focuses on gender-related power dynamics, mainly male machismo. Subero claims that the narrative is haunted by the dead father, who represents what he calls 'macho monstrosity' (2016: 78), an overwhelming spectral (and ideological) figure that controls family relationships and attitudes towards masculinity and femininity. Cannibalism as monstrosity is displaced as a form of resistance and action against the real, social threat of the patriarchy (83). In this sense, cannibalism is subverted; the marginalised display a resistance against male-centred power structures.

Hernández's *La casa muda* also addresses gender and monstrosity, particularly in the form of abusive male figures. In this film, Laura (Florencia Colucci) and her father Wilson (Gustavo Alonso) are hired by Néstor (Abel Tripaldi) to clean up an abandoned country house that he wants to sell. Inside, the sense of time is completely lost as all the windows are boarded up and the characters need to use electric torches to find their way around the dark rooms. When Laura is awakened by a strange sound coming from upstairs, Wilson tries to calm her down by investigating the commotion. But Wilson returns, and Laura must explore the rooms, eventually revealing that she had already been in this house, had been Néstor's lover, and that he and her own father had sexually abused her and had disposed of her child. The film hints at the secret of Laura's sexual abuse, but also suggests that Laura is mad. The story is set in real time and is told strictly from Laura's point of view. The use of hand-held cameras, point-of-view shots and long takes tricks the viewer into trusting Laura, but quick reflections on mirrors and clever tracking shots where Laura enters and exits the frame from the right and left side eventually disclose the possibility that her previous experience in the house resulted in a split identity: one that has chosen to forget the abuse from her father and his friend, and another that avenges herself. Hernández uses the trope of the haunted house to look at the haunted self and connect the origin of a monstrous feminine subject to an abusive macho behaviour that physically and mentally damages this young teenager.

Conversely, Brugués's Spanish-Cuban comedy-horror film *Juan of the Dead* addresses a man's national identity crisis, as the eponymous Juan

(Alexis Díaz de Villegas) and his friend Lázaro (Jorge Molina) face an inevitable zombie apocalypse in Havana. The film rightly addresses the tension between local political isolation and inevitable globalisation. In this case, the undead have been able to reach an island that has faced political and economic stagnation since the Cuban Revolution, thus eliciting within the characters actions and attitudes that flaunt Cuban idiosyncrasy. Gabriel Eljaiek-Rodríguez argues that Brugués's film takes the zombie figure as it has developed in the Western Gothic horror tradition back to its Caribbean origin, where 'it is re-tropicalised' (2015: 96). The zombie is thus re-appropriated to address the issues that ail the island nation. More than being just an allegory for the external threat of capitalism, Eljaiek-Rodríguez observes that the zombie may also symbolise the shortcomings of the communist regime in Cuba (98). This re-appropriation demonstrates that the film is very much aware of the zombie tradition that developed in cinema throughout the twentieth century and suggests that this monstrous figure is open to adaptability and relocation. What is most relevant about *Juan of the Dead* is that this monster may not be framed exclusively by the politics of Western neoliberalism. On the contrary, the film reveals that the impassivity and lack of vitality of the zombie can easily accommodate interpretations that return it to its Caribbean setting, with all its symbolic implications. Gothic horror is incorporated into local, political situations challenged by cultural figures that have circulated freely around the world. *Juan of the Dead* also discloses a reconsideration of Gothic from or in the tropics. Whereas the Gothic has been traditionally associated with dark and cold settings, the Gothic in Latin America encourages a display of horror and secrets that lie hidden in the dense vegetation, heat and humidity of the tropical regions, most particularly of the Caribbean and the rainforests of Brazil and Mexico.

Tropical Gothic

Tropical Gothic has its origins in Colombia, where filmmakers Luis Ospina and Carlos Mayolo coined the term to refer to the horror films they made during the 1980s. Mayolo defines it as 'a gothic structure in a tropical setting' (quoted in Edwards and Vasconcelos 2016: 1). Tropical Gothic rethinks the Gothic's flexibility and adaptability to explore monstrous and disturbing narratives situated in a location usually associated with sunlight, warmth and richness of natural resources. Justin D. Edwards and Sandra Guardini Vasconcelos recognise that the tropics are indeed a hotbed for the Gothic because of their historical, social and cultural baggage. They argue that 'the indigenous cultures that existed long before European invasion include their own ghosts, just as the violence of colonization engendered a haunted history often incorporated into the tropical Gothic text' (2016: 2). As such, Tropical Gothic is enshrined within a complex cultural and historical frame of reference that is born out of violence, acculturation and transculturation: European colonisers brought forth a mythical vision of the conquered lands that haunts the region under the guise of a colonial past and of more ancient systems of belief that are always in the process of being unearthed, recognised and remembered with detachment, fear and awe. For Juana Suárez, Tropical Gothic is not just a simple translocation of motifs, but rather 'a negotiation that generates a new hybridity' (2014: 24). It involves processes of appropriation and the recognition of the cultural construction of the tropics in colonialist terms. Tropical Gothic is an example of transculturation that ideally helps disclose cultural fears over social, political and even religious discourses in tropical zones around the world. In Latin America, it particularly attests to the region's plurality of landscapes and environments that may also provoke fear and anxiety towards subjects, as well as further developing the tension that exists between civilisation and nature in Latin American countries.

Such is the case of the Mexican TV series *Niño santo* (2011–14). The series is inspired by the life of José Fidencio Síntora Constantino, a local healer, or *curandero*, from Northern Mexico who became particularly famous during the 1920s and the 1930s – popularly known as Niño Fidencio because of his childish appearance.[2] Claudia Agostini argues that the popularity of Niño Fidencio was primarily due to the country's lack of efficient institutional medical care in the years that followed the Mexican Revolution (1910–20). Additionally, 'the massification [*sic*] and growing presence of mass media – such as newspapers, magazines and film' that publicised Fidencio's miracle work had a strong impact on the population of Mexico, and prompted massive pilgrimages to Espinazo, where he resided (Agostini 2018: 220, 228).

Niño santo explores faith when it stands against interventions of an institutionalised medical practice. The plot focuses on three young physicians, Lucía (Karla Souza), Damián (José María de Tavira) and Farca (Francisco de la Reguera), who visit the village of Agua Azul in the tropical region of southeastern Mexico during a vaccination campaign. Upon their arrival, they are neglected and rejected by the inhabitants who claim the medicine is poisonous. Lucía adamantly advocates inoculating the resisting townsfolk but manages to strike an agreement with the leaders of the village. After they leave Agua Azul, the physicians find their discarded medicine and discover that the village has a Niño santo, a 'curandero', or folk healer, who lives in the depths of the mangrove swamp and who can miraculously cure all ailments. El Niño (Gabino Rodríguez) possesses powers that are derived from the healer's belief that his soul must be transferred via blood transfusions to the body of a young woman who serves as his surrogate. Even though the three young physicians attempt to unravel the mystery of El Niño's power, all rational and scientific explanations utterly fail: Damián falls ill when he gets lost in the mangrove, is cured by El Niño and becomes another of his followers and defenders, while Lucía and Farca lose all professional credibility when they return to Mexico City and tell their story.

The shift of setting from Northern Mexico to a tropical area, away from urban and developed centres, helps foreground social and governmental neglect. *Niño santo* directly addresses issues of medical politics in a geographical setting that lacks effective health services. The isolation of Agua Azul prompted the development of a cult following that revolves around the idea of spiritual healing. Lucía, Damián and Farca are constantly challenged by the inexplicable supernatural healing abilities of El Niño, whose own identity is cemented by local rituals that elevate his status to that of a living saint. Agua Azul does not question the veracity of El Niño's powers and, subsequently, cuts off any contact with the rest of the world. El Niño's representatives exert absolute power over the other inhabitants, dictating the decisions that affect the village. By means of medical politics, a small group of people impose social politics; social control is affected by the ability of an individual to oversee and decide each inhabitant's life and death.

Faced with inexplicable supernatural acts of healing, the young physicians fall prey to El Niño and his protectors' political desires. Most importantly, Lucía is offered a deal to become the new vessel for El Niño's soul, alluding to the tense gender dynamics of a male-dominated culture that also revolves around healing and faith. The series mainly represents the clash between the legal imposition of institutionalised medical practice and the religiously-inclined folk healing that is exercised in Agua Azul. This clash recalls nineteenth-century Gothic medical narratives which reveal a tension between professional medical practitioners and domestic practices of healing whereby 'the practitioner becomes a shocking and dangerous figure whose professionalism is persistently held up to question' and even a source of horror due to their portrayal as avaricious monsters (Mandal and Waddington 2015: 47). The contemporary, tropical setting of *Niño santo* develops a similar encounter between two forms of medical practice that are simultaneously questioned and perceived as monstrous. Firstly, the young physicians are repudiated by the village, and, when they manage to vaccinate the people, all those inoculated faint and report various maladies. Secondly, the three physicians are appalled by the lack of sanitary conditions, thus claiming that El Niño's curative powers are a health threat. The conflict that develops here is similar to what Mandal and Waddington see in other Gothic fictions: a concern 'about the professional status of physicians' that provides them with 'power and authority' and that affects the 'doctor-patient relationship' (2015: 48). The isolation of Agua Azul discloses that these concerns, originating during the era of Niño Fidencio and the revolution, are still relevant today. In this sense, the presence of a 'niño santo' as a key character for the development of the conflicts pertaining to medical and political issues evinces the continuing lack of effective public measures to tend to the country's population.

The tropical setting in *Niño santo* is consequently not coincidental. It reveals folk-healing practices that should have been supplanted by modern medical practices but are nevertheless still relevant to a village that has seen a lack of effective assistance from a neglectful government. What is initially seen as a paradisiacal society where absolutely no one gets ill slowly discloses the control of the miraculous medical politics that are embodied in El Niño. The three physicians become bound in a moral and professional conflict that puts them to the test; scientific reason and religious faith turn into a monstrous struggle that reveals the unstable relations between those in power and the rest of society. The tropical haunting may not be spectral, but it nevertheless continues to reveal national issues that arise from a persistent lack of effective government support and the decisions made by those who have been left behind in the journey towards political, medical and institutional improvement. The Gothic in Latin America uses the tropics to manifest the region's peculiar development: the impending lack of full, universal well-being, which in turn reveals the terror and anxiety derived from failed social and political projects.

Reconfigured Origins

While particular settings and locations reconsider the adaptability of the Gothic in Latin America, the current exchange of virtual information that is facilitated in digital environments has also helped propagate hauntings beyond the region. Social networks provide renovated awareness of urban legends such as 'Charlie Charlie', which has been popularised online with the hashtag #CharlieCharlieChallenge. This is a game which involves the invocation of a spirit that uses pencils to answer any question that requires a simple affirmative or negative reply.³ As Charlie has passed on from one generation to the next, his origins have been forgotten to give way to an abstract, spectral entity whose origins are being affected by the exchange of digital information. Children from Mexico and Central America have played a variant of this game for several generations, and the game became a viral sensation over the past couple of years, with posts from young people playing or questioning its veracity on several visual social media. According to a report in *The Washington Post*, the game rose to popularity once again after a television report from the Dominican Republic sparked interest on Twitter, where it became viral in other Hispanic American countries and in the US (Dewey 2015). When spread digitally, a different experience of the game works through various communication channels, analogue or digital, affecting the memory of its origin(al) narrative.

The recent popularity of Charlie has not been re-established solely through word of mouth. This time, the haunting's revitalisation and re-entry into the everyday has also depended on its digital nature. Individuals involved in the challenge interact through images, videos, messages, comments and feedback that help propagate the haunting. The rules of the game have changed – the pencils work on their own without the need of a physical intervention, thus providing a new level of supernatural perception, as digital cameras record every slight movement the pencils may make. Charlie today also relies on the new forms of 'technologies of witnessing' that Linnie Blake and Xavier Aldana Reyes have brought to attention (2016: 6). The act is not performed with others; instead, it is performed for others to see, either simultaneously via live streaming, or later on as the video is posted on the web and shared. Witnesses do not require their physical presence but can attest to the veracity of the haunting with what is evidenced in online videos.

YouTube videos help propagate the legend of Charlie as a myth and further enhance the disturbing uncanniness that envelops the game. Like a lost manuscript unearthed from the sea of digital information, the legend acquires a new, open, dynamic sense through digital dissemination – Neal Kirk calls this 'networked spectrality' (2016: 55). Charlie's haunting evolves and adapts from its analogical urban legend to a fast-paced, highly visual digital phenomenon that crosses the borders of where it had been played regionally in different communities in Latin America, as it is appropriated by fascinated young people beyond the Spanish-speaking world.

These processes affect the value of the haunting, not just in its present experience, but also in the construction of its past. What the #CharlieCharlieChallenge reveals is that shared experience is prone to a new sense of social memory of the past: the ageless spirit of Charlie, the ghost that communicates when invoked, is put into question when several versions of an urban legend are combined, re-worked and shared. Following the rumours that Charlie was a real person, the Mexican newspaper *Excelsior* sought to debunk these claims and clarified that the game and its subsequent hashtag had spread only after spectators had watched the promotional videos for the Warner Bros. horror film *The Gallows* (2015), directed by Chris Lofing and Travis Cluff (see Anonymous 2015c). Another article also wanted to deny that Charlie was a Mexican boy who committed suicide or a pre-Hispanic pagan deity (Anonymous 2015b).[4] Whether real or fake, based on an urban legend or on a horror film, the fact is that the #CharlieCharlieChallenge demonstrates that the veracity of the legend is not at stake. Instead, the expanded possibilities of amalgamating fiction, legend and reality on a virtual platform that simultaneously plays with actual spectrality causes an uncanny effect.

We witness here a form of everyday popular haunting that builds itself in a complex, narrative way. The notion of past veracity, if there is actually any truth behind Charlie, is blurry at best. Charlie is Gothic not just because of how he is portrayed, but also because of how his past is idealised and how it affects our popular memory. Whenever a new narrative is embedded into the game, Charlie is redefined, much as his origin is. This is its Gothic vitality: like Piatti-Farnell and Beville claim, living Gothic offers a world perspective that not only shapes our everyday experience, but our sense of identity too (2014: 3). Charlie may not even possess a veritable past – his origin may be lost in the very practice of his invoking. Now that Charlie has entered the digital domain, he acquires a new capacity for haunting by whatever lies in the process of the movement of information. As the legend turns digital, it explores a complex cultural exchange that is the result of the open access to available information beyond the physical, geographical plain. This ghost thrives beyond the borders of space, as it discloses local re-appropriations based on generative games played across Latin America and a simultaneous uncanny, transnational vitality.

As the legend of Charlie infiltrates virtual networks of shared experience, it also determines the open and fluid movements of haunting spectrality that detach themselves from geopolitical locations. This urban legend is now able to reach out and be experienced by social media users across the globe, thus determining the extensive potential that new forms of visual and digital culture have in the reception, exchange and re-appropriation of the uncanny that moves across and beyond Latin America. Whether in film, television or on the internet, the growing awareness of the Gothic in the region is undeniable. Gothic criticism indeed focuses more on understanding the suitability of the term to address a wide range of works from the eighteenth to the twenty-first century, and it also proves that Latin American Gothic contributes to the Gothic's flexibility, whether by proposing new concepts, such as Tropical Gothic, or by reworking notions of terror, horror, anxiety or monstrosity. Latin American Gothic in the twenty-first century means not only an awareness of the term in a region that had rarely considered itself Gothic before. It is primarily, and most importantly, evidence of the expansion of the global connectivity that helps explore the Gothic in more heterogeneous and complex situations that enrich an already conscious and malleable fictional form.

Notes

1. *Cronos* (1994), del Toro's first feature-length film, is the only one he made in Mexico. From then on, all his films have been produced elsewhere. Del Toro still endorses film production in Mexico and encourages the restoration of films from Mexico's past (Tierney, Shaw and Davies 2014: 3–4). He has also produced Hispanic American films, such as the animated feature *The Book of Life* (2014), directed by Jorge R. Gutierrez.
2. A *curandero* is a person dedicated to 'the art of Mexican folk healing' (Torres and Sawyer 2014: 10), which involves elements of spiritualism and faith. The *curandero*'s credibility as a healer is based on their own daily spiritual practices. Fidencio's hometown, Espinazo, still thrives with *curanderos* who channel healing spirits and oversee the well-being of a marginalised population with little access to public health services (22–4).
3. This popular game of invocation and spiritual haunting 'has a long history as a schoolyard game in the Spanish-speaking world' (Dewey 2015). It follows a process very similar to that of the Ouija board. In the case of Charlie, the traditional game involves at least two people who hold pencils in each hand. The players face each other to make the ends of each pencil meet. When the pencils bend inwards, Charlie is answering 'yes', and when they bend outwards, Charlie is saying 'no'.
4. An article on *BBC Mundo* further argues that there is no evidence that the game refers to Mexican tradition or folklore, which puts the idea of a first origin of the legend into question too (Anonymous 2015a).

Film and Television

Al final del espectro (*At the End of the Spectra*, Juan Felipe Orozco, Colombia, 2006)
Juan de los muertos (*Juan of the Dead*, Alejandro Brugués, Spain/Cuba, 2011)
KM 31: Kilómetro 31 (*KM 31*, Rigoberto Castañeda, Mexico, 2007)

La casa del fin de los tiempos (*The House at the End of Time*, Alejandro Hidalgo, Venezuela, 2013)
La casa muda (*The Silent House*, Gustavo Hernández, Uruguay, 2010)
Niño santo (Canada Films/Once TV, Mexico, 2011–14)
Somos lo que hay (*We Are What We Are*, Jorge Michel Grau, Mexico, 2010)
Sudor frío (*Cold Sweat*, Adrián García Bogliano, Argentina, 2010)
The Book of Life (Jorge R. Gutierrez, USA, 2014)
The Stranger (Guillermo Amoedo, Chile, 2014)

References

Agostini, Claudia (2018), 'Ofertas médicas, curanderos y la opinión pública: El niño Fidencio en el México posrevolucionario', *Anuario Colombiano de Historia Social y de La Cultura*, 45.1, 215–43.
Anonymous (2015a), '#CharlieCharlieChallenge: El misterioso juego de los lápices que agita las redes', *BBC Mundo*, 26 May, http://www.bbc.com/mundo/noticias/2015/05/150526_charlie_charlie_challenge_gtg (accessed 30 April 2018).
Anonymous (2015b), '¿Qué pasa con el juego Charlie Charlie?', *Aztecaamerica.com*, 28 May, http://www.aztecaamerica.com/notas/ddc/206090/que-pasa-con-el-juego-charlie-charlie (accessed 30 April 2018).
Anonymous (2015c), 'Charlie Charlie no era un demonio, esta es la verdadera historia', *Excelsior*, 1 June, http://www.excelsior.com.mx/global/2015/06/01/1027130 (accessed 28 December 2017).
Blake, Linnie, and Xavier Aldana Reyes (2016), 'Introduction: Horror in the Digital Age', in Linnie Blake and Xavier Aldana Reyes (eds), *Digital Horror: Haunted Technologies, Network Panic and the Found Footage Phenomenon*, London and New York: I. B. Tauris, pp. 1–13.
Botting, Fred, and Justin D. Edwards (2013), 'Theorising Globalgothic', in Glennis Byron (ed.), *Globalgothic*, Manchester: Manchester University Press, pp. 11–24.
Casanova-Vizcaíno, Sandra, and Inés Ordiz (eds) (2018), *Latin American Gothic in Literature and Culture*, New York: Routledge.
Davies, Ann (2014), 'Guillermo del Toro's Monsters: Matter out of Place', in Ann Davies, Deborah Shaw, and Dolores Tierney (eds), *The Transnational Fantasies of Guillermo del Toro*, Basingstoke: Palgrave Macmillan, pp. 29–43.
Dewey, Caitlin (2015) 'The Complete, True Story of Charlie Charlie, the "Demonic" Teen Game Overtaking the Internet', *The Washington Post*, 26 May, https://www.washingtonpost.com/news/the-intersect/wp/2015/05/26/the-complete-true-story-of-charlie-charlie-the-demonic-teen-game-overtaking-the-internet/?noredirect=on&utm_term=.8f075667536c (accessed 30 April 2018).
Edwards, Justin D., and Sandra Guardini Vasconcelos (2016), 'Introduction: Tropicalizing Gothic', in Justin D. Edwards and Sandra Guardini Vasconcelos (eds), *Tropical Gothic in Literature and Culture: The Americas*, New York: Routledge, pp. 1–10.

Eljaiek-Rodríguez, Gabriel (2015), 'El retorno de los muertos vivientes (al Caribe): *Juan de los muertos* y los zombis en el cine cubano contemporáneo', *Hispanic Research Journal*, 16.1, 86–102.
Kirk, Neal (2016), 'Networked Spectrality: *In Memorium*, *Pulse*, and Beyond', in Linnie Blake and Xavier Aldana Reyes (eds), *Digital Horror: Haunted Technologies, Network Panic and the Found Footage Phenomenon*, London and New York: I. B. Tauris, pp. 54–65.
Mandal, Anthony, and Keir Waddington (2015) 'The Pathology of Common Life: "Domestic" Medicine as Gothic Disruption', *Gothic Studies*, 17.1, 43–60.
Ordiz, Inés, and Sandra Casanova-Vizcaíno (2018) 'Introduction: Latin America, the Caribbean, and the Persistence of the Gothic', in Sandra Casanova-Vizcaíno and Inés Ordiz (eds), *Latin American Gothic in Literature and Culture*, New York: Routledge, pp. 1–12.
Piatti-Farnell, Lorna, and Maria Beville (2014), 'Introduction: Living Gothic', in *The Gothic and the Everyday: Living Gothic*, Basingstoke: Palgrave Macmillan, pp. 1–12.
Shaw, Deborah (2013), *The Three Amigos: The Transnational Filmmaking of Guillermo Del Toro, Alejandro González Iñárritu and Alfonso Cuarón*, Manchester: Manchester University Press.
Smith, Paul Julian (2014), *Mexican Screen Fiction*, Cambridge: Polity Press.
Suárez, Juana (2014) 'Tropical Gothic: Cinematic Dislocations of the Caribbean Imaginary in South West Colombia', *Studies in Gothic Fiction*, 3.2, 24–37.
Subero, Gustavo (2016), *Gender and Sexuality in Latin American Horror Cinema: Embodiments of Evil*, Basingstoke: Palgrave Macmillan.
Tierney, Dolores, Deborah Shaw and Ann Davies (2014) 'Introduction', in Ann Davies, Deborah Shaw and Dolores Tierney (eds), *The Transnational Fantasies of Guillermo Del Toro*, Basingstoke: Palgrave Macmillan, pp. 1–8.
Torres, Eliseo 'Cheo', and Timothy L. Sawyer (2014), *Curandero: A Life in Mexican Folk Healing*, Albuquerque: University of New Mexico Press.

Chapter 19

Aboriginal Gothic
Katrin Althans

The Gothic has come a long way since its first appearance in *The Castle of Otranto* in 1764 and has undergone several important shifts since its introduction. Among the most important of these would rank its transition from genre to mode (and back) and the role it played in imperial projects. The Gothic has always maintained its subversive potential, although this is often undercut by its own eagerness to ultimately submit to rules of society. The major characteristics of Aboriginal Gothic focus on exactly those three transformative shifts: the Gothic's generic instability; its use in imperial, colonial and postcolonial contexts; and its subversive quality. By turning to these characteristics and at the same time acknowledging its own Indigenous heritage, Aboriginal Gothic realises its full transformative potential, as it appropriates the features of the Gothic novel proper as well as imperial and colonial developments of the Gothic. Aboriginal Gothic thus challenges colonial depictions of Australian Indigenous people and subverts the traditional Gothic in order to reclaim an Aboriginal cultural identity.

At this point, a brief look at the term Aboriginal Gothic itself is necessary. I will use the term Aboriginal to refer to the various nations of Australian Indigenous people only and will therefore limit my discussion of Aboriginal Gothic to Australian examples, although there are similar usages of the Gothic in cultural expressions of other Indigenous peoples from around the world. At the same time, the term does not differentiate between the many different Indigenous nations of Australia, as examples of Aboriginal Gothic can be found all over the country. However, Aboriginal Gothic has nothing to do with white authors' or filmmakers' appropriations of Aboriginal culture as exotic Gothic thrills, but instead describes a transformation of the European original at the hands of Aboriginal artists. As such, the term denotes both an Aboriginal qualification of the European literary tradition and Aboriginal cultural expressions which, however faintly, remind their audience of the Gothic. Yet it is important to keep in mind that what people with a Western European background understand as Gothic is unknown in Aboriginal culture, and monsters and gruesome events only serve as warnings, not as chills.

The term Aboriginal Gothic also runs the risk of maintaining the binaries of centre and periphery, of coloniser and colonised, as the point of reference remains the Gothic – which is charged with European worldviews and literary traditions. The transformative and liberating potential of Aboriginal Gothic then lies in its ability to challenge what has been written in the Gothic language of Europe by changing this point of reference. Rather than referring to a literary form only, Aboriginal Gothic responds to a variety of cultural phenomena. Therefore, I suggest understanding Aboriginal Gothic as engaging in transcultural dialogue with European cultural traditions, Aboriginal culture and identity as well as with contemporary anxieties of Aboriginal Australians. To be more precise, Aboriginal Gothic combines the European Gothic tradition, the colonial history of Australia, Aboriginal cultural traditions and the contemporary situation of Aboriginal people in Australia. In the hands of Aboriginal artists, those influences are usurped, appropriated and finally transformed into something I have come to refer to as Aboriginal Gothic.

Aboriginal Gothic in Context

Aboriginal Gothic writes back to both the Gothic tradition in Australia and to imperial and colonial Gothic in general. The figure of the Other, which looms large in any colonial Gothic project, and its recreation by non-European artists, plays an important role in Aboriginal Gothic. Australia literally was the 'other' side of the world, the antipodean version of Europe; Gerry Turcotte expressly links the Gothic to the colonial experience when he writes '[t]he Gothic [. . .] has from its inception dealt with fears and themes that are endemic in the colonial experience: isolation, entrapment, fear of pursuit and fear of the unknown' (2009: 18). After some initial hesitation, the literary Gothic was embraced as a means to express Australian identity pitted against villainous English authorities. The true monster of Australian Gothic fiction, however, was the white settlers' dark Other, Australian Indigenous people – 'Hell's worst fiends', as Charles Harpur wrote in his 'The Creek of the Four Graves' of 1845 (1998: 365, l. 194). This semiotic act of de-humanising Aboriginal Australians served to justify the colonial endeavour and established the Gothic as a disabling discourse of colonial power.

In postcolonial contexts, this relationship is challenged. As Fred

Botting suggests, monsters are no longer simply a sign of alterity, but rather bring to light and criticise the very act of othering (2014: 14). Postcolonial Gothic thus acts as a revisionist discourse which works on a counter-discursive level and allows for agency through appropriation. In Australia, issues in postcolonial Gothic and questions of the Other shifted significantly after 1992, the year the High Court handed down the Mabo decision, which granted Aboriginal people native title to land. In the wake of this decision, Australia's Gothic literature became haunted by the absent Aboriginal presence. As Sarah Ilott argues in this collection (see Chapter 1), however, postcolonial Gothic of the twenty-first century has moved from the haunting presence of the colonial past and the excavation of historical silences to new cultural others and to transnational renderings of the Gothic other. Due to Australia's status as debatably postcolonial – postcolonial in terms of gaining virtual independence from the UK, yet also being a settler colony with a fourth-world population and neo-colonial with regard to migrants and refugees – contemporary twenty-first-century Gothic in Australia addresses various concerns and issues simultaneously: the anxieties of white settlers, the quest for home and belonging of migrants, and the reclaiming of place and identity of Aboriginal people. In twenty-first-century manifestations of Aboriginal Gothic, issues of colonial history and their contemporary legacy therefore still play a key role.

The history of Aboriginal cultural expressions plays an equally important role. Aboriginal societies are oral cultures and there is a strong emphasis on stories and on matters concerning the authority of knowledge. Orally transmitted stories are much more than fairy tales, they form the complete body of law governing every aspect of Aboriginal life (Black 2011: 15). They may fall into categories of the 'secret-sacred' and their transmission is restricted by protocols of ownership.[1] Therefore, any transfer into different media necessarily involves a consideration of the impact of possible permanent storage (the written text, the recorded image), as secret-sacred knowledge might be disclosed to non-initiated people (van Toorn 2000: 20). Those oral origins and their adaptation to contemporary needs then pair up with the European tradition of the Gothic to produce a uniquely Aboriginal Gothic which challenges this European tradition and its strict narrative rules.

Particularly, the fact that the Gothic was originally produced in the form of novels needs to be kept in mind. Writing, and thus novels, is foreign to oral cultures, and the use of the Gothic by Aboriginal artists is as disabling as it is enabling. On the one hand, writers submit to a European genre, whereas on the other hand elements of oral storytelling may feature as means for transgressing the Gothic's generic boundaries and are part of the subversive potential of Aboriginal Gothic. One way of challenging classic Gothic patterns then is the use of TV/film and new media, as they are closer to oral traditions. Still, the development of Aboriginal literature is important for understanding the various ways in which Aboriginal Gothic dismembers traditional structures and presuppositions of the classical Gothic. The focus of the early beginnings of contemporary Aboriginal writing, though, was on political poetry and life writing, which already showed significant differences to Western styles of autobiography (van Toorn 2000: 36). In the case of fictional writing, '[m]any Aboriginal writings resist classification within conventional European genre systems', as van Toorn states (38). This considered, it seems that the Gothic, with its generic and modal instability, is more than suitable for appropriation by Indigenous Australian writers.

The Shapes of Aboriginal Gothic

There are several guises Aboriginal Gothic takes when engaging with its European counterpart, each struggling with both its literary predecessor and colonial history. What they have in common is that they all contest mechanisms of othering and that they strengthen Aboriginal cultural aspects. Firstly, there is what seems to be an imitation of the original European conventions of the Gothic; secondly, the roles of stock characters of colonial Gothic fiction are reversed in an act of resistance; thirdly, Gothic elements are used to assert and reclaim Indigenous identity; fourthly, trauma is personified in the form of ghosts returning to haunt; and fifthly, the Gothic is stripped of its fictional quality and assumes the form of Gothic realities.

Due to the relatively young history of Aboriginal writing in literary genres in general, it is no wonder the first pieces of Aboriginal Gothic emerged at the turn of the millennium. There are single exceptions, the novel *The Kadaitcha Sung* by Murri writer Sam Watson of 1990 and *Night Cries* and *beDevil*, two films by Tracey Moffatt of 1990 and 1993, respectively, but most examples of Aboriginal Gothic stem from the end of the twentieth and beginning of the twenty-first century.[2] No example of Aboriginal Gothic neatly falls into any single category I proposed earlier, but they contain elements of several at the same time. Furthermore, Aboriginal Gothic of the twenty-first century is characterised by an emerging sense of powerful interplay with the limitations of Gothic patterns in European discourse, thus demonstrating a developing self-confidence concerning cultural identity. This corresponds to an intensified awareness of the production and accessibility of different media as well as the potential they hold for Aboriginal storytelling.

Most cultural expressions of the Gothic by Aboriginal artists are written texts, a form which is closest to the Gothic original and its mechanisms, yet quite removed from Aboriginal traditions. Even though writing is by definition alien to oral cultures and in most cases is charged with a certain ideological precariousness as the colonial master's instrument of authority and administration, Aboriginal people have from the beginning used writing as a means of resistance, as Penny van Toorn argues (2000: 26). Therefore, turning to the Gothic is for Aboriginal artists a means of unlocking the subversive potential of the Gothic to give their anxieties a voice.

The most easily recognisable way Aboriginal artists make use of the Gothic is by imitating traditional Gothic conventions. Such imitations can be found in the short story 'The Little Red Man' (2011) by Raymond Gates, in which a classical Australian hitchhiking horror scenario meets the Aboriginal tale of the Yara Ma Tha Who, a being that somewhat resembles the vampire in its eating and reproductive behaviours. Although the setting is distinctively Australian – out in the bush – the story is infused with what the reader expects of the Gothic: there are strange sounds as well as chilling movements in a tree. Then there is the nocturnal gradual infection-like transformation of the male character which culminates in his being turned into a Yara Ma Tha Who, much like *Dracula*'s Lucy Westenra gradually transforms into a vampire as a result of the count's night-time visits to her bedchamber. Although Aboriginal, white Australian and European traditions seem to complement each other in order to create an alternate version of the classical vampire, in this case the evil is of Indigenous origins. Instead of being retold in its original form as a cautionary tale, the story of the Yara Ma Tha Who is revamped into a Gothic tale in which Aboriginal culture provides the Gothic-ness of the story. The Yara Ma Tha Who is not put into a cultural perspective, as it is denied its proper cultural meaning. Instead, it is transformed into a random Gothic monster familiar to Western readers.

Although 'Namorrodor' and 'The Curse', two Dreaming stories from Arnhem Land which feature the monstrous spirit being of Namorrodor, also make ample use of traditional Gothic elements, their imitation of European conventions is ambiguous.[3] They can be read as Aboriginal stories told in a Gothic fashion and relying on stock features, but they stay within an Aboriginal context and do not alter the cultural meaning of Namorrodor. Produced as part of a series of twelve animated films called *Dust Echoes* and originally also developed for an interactive website, they are by now only available in ABC's digibook format, which contains written explanations and short videos.[4] Both stories are easily recognised as Gothic: they are set during the night and feature eerie sounds, both naturally nocturnal and non-diegetic ghostly music as well as ritual singing. Namorrodor itself has all a Gothic monster needs: it is a man-eating beast from Aboriginal tradition with coal-black skin, huge claws, long sharp fangs and saliva dripping from its mouth. His reptile-like yellow eye features especially prominently in the visual rendering of the story through a number of close-ups. It is tempting to read such instances of Aboriginal Gothic as a mere replication of the European Gothic, yet the stories retain their original character as cautionary tales. They thus preserve their cultural integrity and do not lend themselves to being exploited as the source of an exotic Gothic.

One observes another overt reference to traditional Gothic when texts such as Mudrooroo's *The Undying* (1998) reverse the roles of Gothic hero and villain in an act of writing back. It is part of a trilogy which rewrites Mudrooroo's earlier work, Australian history and various Victorian texts. All three novels, *The Undying*, *Underground* (1999) and *The Promised Land* (2000), feature the Aboriginal character George and the white vampire Amelia, who feeds on Aboriginal blood. Blood here stands for identity, and by reversing the roles of bloodthirsty savage and damsel in distress, the trilogy comments on the effects of colonialism on Australia's Aboriginal inhabitants. George has been robbed of his Aboriginal (cultural) identity by Amelia and thus epitomises a loss of identity which featured prominently in Aboriginal writing at the turn of the century.

In the twenty-first century, such a reversal of traditional Gothic roles reveals the processes used for othering Aboriginal people and unmasks the Gothic nature of these processes. A case in point here is the recent ABC TV series *Cleverman* (2016–17), an Indigenous production created by Ryan Griffen. It visualises and features several stories and characters of the Dreaming, such as the titular Cleverman and the Hairypeople, mythological people known to many Aboriginal communities (Richards 2016). The titular Cleverman also is conceived as an Aboriginal superhero, with the show '[b]lending 60,000 years of culture with the superhero world', always respecting Aboriginal protocols (Griffen 2016). Thus, the show is firmly embedded in Indigenous cultural traditions and emphasises the communal aspect of Aboriginal storytelling in that the creation of the different mythological elements of the story depends very much on the narrative exchange with Elders and their permission to use the stories in particular ways (Griffen 2016). This community-based approach to the stories, which includes a strong participatory element, transgresses the structural binaries of the Gothic, which in its traditional manifestations relies on being separated from the story's action in order to scare the viewer. *Cleverman* is also a highly politicised series when it comes to the 'Hairies', a human-like species with different DNA who the government constructs as a threat to humans. They are confined to live in what is called 'the Zone', a ghetto run by the formerly state-run, now privatised, Containment Authority. Tellingly called 'sub-human' by the authorities and 'concerned citizens', the Hairies stand for the de-humanised Other of our time to whom human rights do not need to apply. This, on the one hand, recalls the treatment of Aboriginal people in white Australia and, on the other, refers to contemporary Australian migration policies with their privately-run detention facilities. The format of the TV series allows for a meticulous screening of the ways techniques of othering develop and come to a head. In the end, it begs the question of who really is human and who is a monstrous double.

Throughout the first season, Namorrodor is also a recurring threat to all members of society. It comes to earth in the very first episode and it remains an undiscernible and uncanny presence until the very last episode, in which it is killed by the Cleverman Koen's singing the right words and using a nulla nulla.[5] Namorrodor in *Cleverman* displays the same attributes it does in *Dust Echoes* and is brought to the screen in a recognisably Gothic way. There is, however, an important difference: in *Cleverman*, Namorrodor does not stay in an Aboriginal-only setting but enters a city world populated with a variety of different people. This use of Namorrodor recalls at first sight Gothic examples which exoticise the Indigenous Other and exploit its supposedly superstitious culture. Yet, here it is also an example of the third manifestation of Aboriginal Gothic, which is characterised by a reinvigorated Aboriginal cultural identity. For a Western audience, Namorrodor is an exotic foreign monster par excellence, but it plays a different role in Aboriginal tradition and becomes a vehicle for reclaiming and strengthening cultural identity. The fact that Namorrodor is read in Gothic terms is limited to non-Indigenous perceptions, whereas the Aboriginal perspective is one of respectful fear paired with cultural knowledge. In the end, Namorrodor in *Cleverman* is defeated with this cultural knowledge handed down through the generations. What is considered Gothic from a Western perspective is here re-appropriated and portrayed as an integral part of Aboriginal culture, which illustrates that Gothic instances are only Gothic from a Western point of view but do not feature as such from an Aboriginal Australian point of view. This also shows in an exorcism scene. In the Western cinematic tradition clearly connoted with evil, the exorcism in episode five of the first season of *Cleverman* serves as a means of healing, an understanding which is emphasised by the quiet and soothing atmosphere of the scene instead of the well-known gory and shrieking exorcisms of Western popular Gothic culture. What is introduced as an exotic version of a traditional Gothic trope is thus returned to its cultural origins.

A similar rendering of the Gothic is found in *Crocodile Dreaming* (2006), a short film directed by Dunghutti filmmaker Darlene Johnson. As the dreaming of their mother is disturbed and causes the death of two children by crocodiles, two estranged brothers have to pair up to return a missing stone to its proper resting place and eventually restore order. Again, the menacing sounds and whispers which accompany the opening credits introduce the Gothic scenery and continue throughout the opening scenes. The titular dreaming is also visualised in Gothic terms, for example by the muddy colours used when showing the crocodile swimming in the murky billabong and particularly by the gory water when it kills the children in slow motion. The visual eeriness is repeated when the two brothers retrieve the stone from the crocodile-infested waters: it is again the eye of the crocodile which is given visual prominence through a close-up shot, and it starts a fire which is both real and mystical. The dual nature of the fire is mirrored in the seemingly non-diegetic chilling sounds heard. Those sounds, however, are acoustic signs indicating the existence of Aboriginal cosmology within what Westerners refer to as reality – thus they have to be considered as diegetic sounds. *Crocodile Dreaming* is again an example of the two-faced nature of the Gothic in Aboriginal discourses. On the one hand, it uses well-known Gothic imagery and other cinematic means; on the other hand, it bestows them with different cultural meanings. Those instances are not meant to *work* in the same way as traditional Gothic does, they only *look* like the Gothic.

Other examples of how the Gothic is a tool to wrest Aboriginal cultural identity from the exoticising grip of its (neo-)colonial counterpart include Noongar author Kim Scott's short story 'Asleep' (2006), Murri writer Nicole Watson's novel *The Boundary* (2011), and the short film *Karroyul* (2015) directed by Ngarluma/Bunuba filmmaker Kelrick Martin and written by Kim Scott. Kim Scott's 'Asleep' introduces us to yet another scary Aboriginal monster, Naatj. Not much is revealed about this creature except for the fact that the white people in whose garden it appears are afraid, while a Noongar elder seems to recognise and accept it as part of his cultural tradition. This tradition, however, is not explained to either the couple or the audience, thus the story rejects an easy closure and submission to Western expectations. Equally resistant to closure is the ending of *The Boundary*. Gothic elements are employed in this literary negotiation of the Mabo decision in the form of a spirit being called Red Feathers, who takes bloody revenge for an unsuccessful native title claim. Not by coincidence Red Feathers reminds the audience of the titular hero of Sam Watson's *The Kadaitcha Sung*, a traditional avenger giving red feathers to his future victims. *The Boundary* can be read as a contemporary reworking and as a story passed on from father to daughter in an act of resistance to cultural annihilation. There is a similar insistence on the importance of keeping cultural identity alive in *Karroyul*. The female protagonist Kelly is, like Koen in *Cleverman*, not interested in her Indigenous heritage in the beginning. After a daylight introduction to both Aboriginal culture in the form of the wedge-tailed eagle, Waalitj, and the curlew, a death bird, and colonial history (Kelly and her uncle Geoff have driven to a massacre site), the scenery turns to distinctly Gothic night, with a heroine leaving the safety of the house she has been sleeping in. Her sleepwalk-like stroll through the bush and to the beach is filled with nocturnal sounds of various death birds and human whispers when she touches a tree. Unlike in conventional Gothic scenarios, however, she is not killed but rather returns from the bush connected to Aboriginal culture, no longer indifferent to her heritage. As in the case of *Cleverman*, the form of *Karroyul* is also of importance. Film is usually credited with continuing Aboriginal visual arts and storytelling due to its being a team-produced art form as well as being a means to counter the ethnographic and cinematographic gaze of the white filmmaker. Yet, Indigenous filmmaking still very much depends on white production processes and funding (Althans 2010: 134–7). *Cleverman* involves an 80 per cent Indigenous cast as well as a number of high-profile Indigenous people in its production. This makes it and other recent films realised by Indigenous filmmakers an important tool for reclaiming authority over the content and the way Indigenous stories are told on screen, thus allowing for Indigenous protocols to be followed.

In Australian Aboriginal Gothic of the twenty-first century, the fourth category, in which trauma and ghosts abound, is still very much present. The uncanniness of the Australian situation, of white settlers' fears of Aboriginal people returning to claim their land, is literally made visible in Darren Siwes's night-time series of photographs *Just Is* (2004): using long exposure, he captures the ghostly presence of colonial history in the form of shadowy figures standing in front of deserted buildings. Those buildings shown in the photographs are examples of Federation architecture, whereas the ghost-like Aboriginal figures are wearing contemporary clothing. This way, Siwes situates the remnants of the colonial past in the present and solidifies them while at the same time reducing the actual Aboriginal presence to nothing but spectres. His photographs are thus a visual comment on the unsettledness of contemporary Australia, which is still very much concerned with its colonial legacy and the uncanny return of the repressed. There is also Kamilaroi writer Vivienne Cleven's novel *Her Sister's Eye* (2002), as well as Warramungu director Beck Cole's short film *Plains Empty* (2005), both of which let the colonial past return to express the traumatic experiences of colonisation. In *Her Sister's Eye*, set in the small country town of Mundra, the personal trauma of a single person, Raymond Gee/Archie Corella, who witnessed the murder of his little sister at the hands of the town's white patriarch, has become a communal trauma. Although Raymond's trauma proves too burdensome for a single person to bear, the passing on of his story through storytelling turns it into memory that heals the whole Aboriginal community of Mundra.

The DVD cover prepares the audience to expect a conventional ghost story in *Plains Empty*, an expectation which is then met by the cinematography and storyline of the movie. The film tells the familiar story of a soul with unfinished business, yet it differs from Western folklore in that the ghost of a little Aboriginal girl does not want to take revenge. Instead, she wants recognition and to be literally laid to rest properly, as she disappeared while searching for her master's dog. This shows the extent to which Aboriginal people were denied their humanity (think of *Cleverman*'s Hairies), as her white master cared enough for the dog, but not for the Aboriginal girl when she went missing. She literally resurfaces from her grave in an abandoned mineshaft, and through the protagonist setting her ghost free the ghosts of the colonial past are acknowledged and exorcised. Another example of Aboriginal Gothic can be found in Waanyi author Alexis Wright's novel *The Swan Book* (2013), which features various interconnected strands of the Gothic such as Ecogothic and the female Gothic tradition, but also elements of haunting and ghosts of the past. The ghosts which haunt the pages of *The Swan Book*, however, are multilayered and ambiguous and not limited to the traumas of the colonial past. Rather, they are a sign of the ongoing trauma surrounding white and Aboriginal relations in Australia.

A different take on the classical ghost story is offered by Warwick Thornton's film *The Darkside* (2013), which is accompanied by a website project and smartphone app called *The Otherside* (2013). For the film, Thornton collected a number of stories telling of actual encounters with ghosts and had the interviews re-enacted by actors alongside instances of the original audio illustrated with edited pictures. The film is an example of the way Aboriginal (maban) reality intersects with the Western concept of rational reality and the extent to which ghosts are part of everyday life.[6] Here, it is not the colonial past with its trauma haunting later generations, but rather the ghosts of family reconnecting with the living, thus giving comfort instead of being scary, much like the healing exorcism performed in *Cleverman*. It is, however, the cross-media project *The Otherside* which completely challenges Gothic assumptions in more than one structural aspect and emphasises the incongruity of the Gothic with Aboriginal culture. *The Otherside* is a project completely dependent on community involvement, as it requires storytellers to share their stories online. Its purpose is 'to create a living archive of Indigenous ghost stories' in order to 'further [the] indigenous heritage of storytelling' (*The Otherside*). This interactive aspect is even extended with the help of the smartphone app and its augmented reality which allows the ghosts to step into your bedroom. Here, the oral and participatory character of Aboriginal storytelling is given a prominent place and reworks Gothic narrative structures which reject any interactivity. The situation is mutually exclusive, it seems: Aboriginal storytelling cannot accommodate the Gothic and the Gothic cannot exercise its full power in an Aboriginal storytelling setting. By combining the Gothic with storytelling, however, *The Otherside* creates a framework for a new understanding of the Gothic, one which frees itself from any narrative constraints.

A similar adjustment of Gothic framing can be found in the fifth shape taken by the Aboriginal Gothic: the direct depiction of the Gothic realities of Aboriginal existence. In *Her Sister's Eye*, for example, the repressed memories of a gruesome reality are too much to bear for Raymond and are no longer removed to some far-off place, time and culture. Kim Scott's most recent novel *Taboo* (2017) works with the same idea of Gothic realities. In referencing parts of his earlier novel *Benang* (1999), which can also be read in Gothic terms, Scott returns to the massacre site of Kepalup and turns to other issues of violence as well. There are overt Gothic references in the beginning, in their apparentness emphasising the fictional quality of the Gothic which pales in the face of the actual horrors experienced by Aboriginal people: '[e]xcept this is no fairy tale, it is drawn from real life' (Scott 2017: 8). This goes hand in hand with yet another variation of Aboriginal Gothic, one which engages with the very concept. Aboriginal people are introduced as the undead and zombies in the very first lines of *Taboo*, an image rejected straight away as being conjured up by a white audience. The ideas developed as driving Aboriginal Gothic are then ironically dismantled: '[w]e thought to tell a story with such momentum [. . .] There must be at least one brave and resilient character at its centre (one of us), and the story will speak of magic in an empirical age; of how our dead will return, transformed, to support us again and from within' (Scott 2017: 7).

The many guises in which Aboriginal Gothic appears in the twenty-first century shows that it has left early examples of revisionist Gothic behind and is becoming a more refined and self-confident discourse of cultural identity. Its development is symptomatic of Aboriginal cultural expressions in general, as it refuses to remain caught in binary oppositions and instead focuses on Aboriginal culture. Aboriginal Gothic renegotiates the very meaning of the Gothic in Indigenous contexts by emphasising an Indigenous perspective. It turns to classical patterns of the Gothic (both in terms of content and form) only to deconstruct and transform them and to thwart a Western audience's expectations. Especially the incorporation of Aboriginal forms of storytelling has created new ways of dealing with the Gothic tradition while still voicing contemporary anxieties. There is only one preoccupation of the original European Gothic with which Aboriginal Gothic is not able to come to terms: the idea of wronged heritage and land taken away.

Notes

1. The term 'secret-sacred' describes matters which are kept from public knowledge and are only disclosed to those members of a community who are entitled to know about them.
2. Wherever possible, I will use the name of the particular group an artist identifies with instead of using the general term 'Aboriginal'.
3. What has been translated into English as 'Dreaming' tries to capture an Aboriginal concept which has many meanings: (the time of) creation, knowledge, law, a state of being, animal ancestors and so on.
4. The website offered the opportunity to move from background information to story and back at a click, and also illustrated the locale each story belongs to by positioning the click area in the air, the water and under or above the surface of the earth. In its current form, there are only the stories and study guides left, arranged chapter-wise, although clickable in random order, and thus submitting to a Western narrative linearity.
5. A nulla nulla is a traditional club used by Aboriginal people for hunting.
6. Like magical realism in a general postcolonial context, the term maban reality denotes a specific Aboriginal version of reality that differs from the European understanding of reality.

Film and Television

Cleverman (ABC, 2016–)
Crocodile Dreaming (Darlene Johnson, Australia, 2006)
Karroyul (Kelrick Martin, Australia, 2015)

Plains Empty (Beck Cole, Australia, 2005)
The Darkside (Warwick Thornton, Australia, 2013)

Webpages

Dust Echoes (2007), ABC, http://splash.abc.net.au/home#!/digibook/2570774/dust-echoes (accessed 5 January 2018).
The Otherside (2013), www.theothersideproject.com (accessed 10 October 2017).

References

Althans, Katrin (2010), *Darkness Subverted: Aboriginal Gothic in Black Australian Literature and Film*, Göttingen: Bonn University Press.
Black, C. F. (2011), *The Land Is the Source of the Law: A Dialogic Encounter with Indigenous Jurisprudence*, London: Routledge.
Botting, Fred (2014), *Gothic*, 2nd edn, London: Routledge.
Cleven, Vivienne (2002), *Her Sister's Eye*, St. Lucia: University of Queensland Press.
Gates, Raymond (2011), 'The Little Red Man', in Russell B. Farr (ed.), *Dead Red Heart: Australian Vampire Stories*, Greenwood: Ticeronda Publications, pp. 379–95.
Griffen, Ryan (2016), 'We Need More Aboriginal Superheroes, So I Created Cleverman for My Son', *The Guardian*, 27 May, https://www.theguardian.com/tv-and-radio/2016/may/27/i-created-cleverman-for-my-son-because-we-need-more-aboriginal-superheroes (accessed 5 January 2018).
Harpur, Charles (1998) [1845/1853], 'The Creek of the Four Graves', in John Leonard (ed.), *Australian Verse: An Oxford Anthology*, Oxford: Oxford University Press, pp. 361–9.
Richards, Tim (2016), 'ABC TV's Gripping Indigenous Superhero Series Cleverman to Premiere', *The Age*, 24 May, https://www.theage.com.au/entertainment/tv-and-radio/m28cover2-20160524-gp2e90.html (accessed 5 March 2018).
Scott, Kim (1999), *Benang: From the Heart*, Freemantle: Freemantle Arts Centre Press.
— (2006), 'Asleep', in Robert Drewe (ed.), *The Best Australian Stories 2006*, Melbourne: Black Inc., pp. 304–13.
— (2017), *Taboo*, Sydney: Picador.
Siwes, Darren (2004), *Just Is*, http://gagprojects.com/index.php/artists/darren-siwes/just-is-2004/ (accessed 5 January 2018).
Turcotte, Gerry (2009), *Peripheral Fear: Transformations of the Gothic in Canadian and Australian Fiction*, Brussels: Peter Lang.
van Toorn, Penny (2000), 'Indigenous Texts and Narratives', in Elizabeth Webby (ed.), *The Cambridge Companion to Australian Literature*, Cambridge: Cambridge University Press.

Chapter 20

Black Diasporic Gothic
Maisha Wester

Milton, the middle-class black protagonist of Edgar Mittelholzer's 1955 novel *My Bones and My Flute*, is tasked with a seemingly simple duty: to write the story of the mysterious haunting plaguing him and his friends – to create 'a Ghost Story in the Old-fashioned Manner', as the novel's subtitle proclaims. Milton's introduction documents his anxiety about getting the form and genre correct, and calls readers to question whose tradition he acknowledges in trying to pen an 'old-fashioned ghost story'. The question is one which plagued the novel's author to his dying moment and which confronts twenty-first-century black artists, trying to relay their narratives through the Gothic genre that has historically marginalised racial minorities and colonial subjects. In answering this question, modern Black Diaspora artists such as Nalo Hopkinson, Jeremy Love and Jordan Peele introduce new monsters – antagonists which often blend figures from African and Caribbean folk belief with Western compulsions – to better encapsulate the horrors of racial subjugation and construction, and the insidious terror of Western regimes.

The rise of new monsters in Black Diasporic texts reveals the problem of trying to revise the coding for traditional monsters which were largely popularised in nineteenth-century Europe. The problems such authors face is starkly similar to the problem of Creole, a form in which modern black subjects write resistance to colonial domination by adapting the dominator's language. Critics debating the problem of Creolised languages – a form whose concerns and methods are strikingly similar to those in the Black Diasporic Gothic – note that, although such blended forms are sites of resistance, they are also 'the end of resistance. In spite of the many African elements [. . .] that have gone into Caribbean Creoles, the Creoles retain a European base, however convoluted and contested' (Khair 2002: 124). Consequently, Khair concludes that while writers such as Derek Walcott and David Dabydeen prove brilliant in their use of Creole languages, they remain captured within the Western Imperial systems and are

> read as part of English-language literature courses and by an English-language reading public. Often the African/Asian/Native American element is weak enough for the work to be legible to non-Creole readers who only know the European 'parent' language, and without much more use of a reference source than most literature demands anyway. (125)

Such languages and forms, built as they are upon colonial cultures, risk failing to assault and dismantle the unity and ideologies of the colonising cultures at their base. While Creolised English languages may forcefully adapt the English to the needs of black cultures, Creole forms also risk rendering English, and the systems and ideologies represented therein, ultimately coherent. Thus, Maryse Conde, a twentieth-century black writer who parodies the Gothic, anxiously declares 'I fear that Creole might become a prison in which the Caribbean writers run the risk of being jailed' (quoted in Smith 2002: 13).

Black Gothic Beginnings

Black Diasporic Gothic can trace its origins back to the nineteenth century at the height of the Gothic's appearance. As white authors metaphorise discourses of racial difference in the genre and politicians applied the genre's tropes to actual (enslaved) minorities, defining minorities as monstrous and thus unfit for an equal place in society, black writers began to appropriate the genre to describe the real horrors of existence within racially oppressive and enslaving societies. Formerly enslaved writers, such as Mary Prince, necessarily slipped into the genre in describing the torture and imprisonment inherent within slavery while others, such as Frederick Douglass and Harriet Jacobs, astutely deployed tropes of haunting and living burial to describe the tormenting spectre of a seemingly unattainable freedom. In the late mid-nineteenth century, Hannah Crafts penned her highly fictionalised slave narrative *The Bondswoman's Narrative*, a novel which explicitly appropriates and speaks back to Gothic texts such as Horace Walpole's *The Castle of Otranto* (1764).

Black use of the Gothic continued well into the twentieth century as realist writers such as Richard Wright modelled *Native Son*'s (1940) protagonist Bigger Thomas on James Whales's film rendition of *Frankenstein* (1931) while also responding to the racist elements of Edgar Allan Poe's story 'The Black Cat' (1843). Maryse Conde's *I, Tituba, Black Witch of*

Salem (1986) proved a mock-Gothic fictional autobiography of a figure blamed as the source of a moment of profound horror in US history. The text protests white determination to create monsters out of victims, decrying the vicious nature of white 'virtue' while also borrowing from traditional Gothic texts like Nathaniel Hawthorne's *The Scarlet Letter* (1850). Even black theorists such as W. E. B. Du Bois and Frantz Fanon turned to the Gothic in theorising the complex psychosis arising from experiencing daily racism. Du Bois's theory of double consciousness adapts the split consciousness experienced by the character Spencer Brydon in Henry James's story 'The Jolly Corner' (Smethurst 2001: 30). Similarly, Fanon describes the terror of being captured in tropes of monstrosity, and the horror of being helplessly aware amidst the process that changes him from a man into a 'thing'. In each case, black authors around the globe recognise the ways the genre proves the dominant method for discussing race and inadvertently defining their reality. Consequently, while the Gothic is weighted with tropes and discourses used to dehumanise minority bodies, black writers acknowledge that they cannot ignore such mechanisations. Rather they must confront the genre if they are to escape imprisonment within its conventions, manifested both in fiction and in a social reality which insists on reading them through the Gothic.

Some twenty-first-century black artists attempt to escape imprisonment within a racially loaded genre by adding layers and meanings to traditional Gothic monsters. Phyll Perry's *Stigmata* (1999), Brandon Massey's *Dark Corner* (2004) and Tananarive Due's *Good House* (2004), to name just a few, illustrate such efforts. Massey's novel particularly exemplifies black determination to remake the vampire into a modern creature decrying racist history and assaults. His vampire Diallo was an African warrior and prince who, captured by his enemies, was sold to white slavers and shipped to America. A witness to the horrific conditions of slavery, he refuses to be broken and disdains those blacks who eventually submit and fully become 'slave'. Transformed into a vampire by his black lover Lisha, Diallo declares war on the Southern slave owners and those slaves who refuse to resist. In addition to loading his vampire with a history of racist oppression, Massey also uses Diallo to embody racist violence in the late twentieth century. Diallo is named after Amadou Diallo, a Guinean immigrant who, unarmed, was killed by plain-clothes police officers when they shot him over forty-one times on 4 February 1999 in New York. Likewise, vampire Diallo's son Kyle is named after the lawyer who represented the victim's family in the civil trial. Loaded with such history and referents, Diallo's rage proves understandable. However, in light of the vampire's century-long popularity,

Massey cannot utterly erase the monster's previous significations. Thus, even his vampire is haunted by Vlad Țepeș, the inspiration for Bram Stoker's *Dracula* (1897). As such, Diallo recalls the threat of conquest and reverse colonisation offered by Stoker's vampire.

A problem of the appropriation exemplified in *Dark Corner* is its failure to defamiliarise Western readers and reposition them outside of those discourses. Theorists such as Edouard Glissant significantly envision radical Creolised forms which destabilise their bases and dismantle constructions of Black Diasporic population as mere composites of Indigenous and colonising cultures, with the indigene responsible for adapting to and utilising the colonising culture. Rather Glissant, in *Antillanité* (1981), argues for languages and forms which are 'a cross-cultural process' of 'unceasing transformation' (quoted in Smith 2002: 14), equally incorporating and recognising the diverse aspect of the 'Créolistes' identity in a constant exchange. A number of twenty-first-century Black Gothic texts accomplish Glissant's radical vision by producing texts which defamiliarise (white) Western Gothic readers by switching paradigms, thus removing them from the traditional language of the genre's discourses and tropes, and introducing monsters from black folk traditions, rather than reinventing traditional monsters from the European Gothic. In doing so, black authors realise the subversive potential of the genre.[1]

In shifting the ground under readers' feet, to paraphrase Hopkinson in her interview 'Fantastic Alternatives', twenty-first-century black writers construct radical texts which destabilise and disrupt problematic norms by smuggling in non-Western concepts and figures. The new Gothic monsters force readers to acquaint themselves with black folk myths and thus to acknowledge and grapple with the ways the cultures of these myths have been silenced and destroyed to become the ghosts of Western culture. Equally important is how the use of these figures points to the presence of a cultural past; they are the very chronicle which colonisers denied existed in order to argue against black humanity on the premises that people of African descent lacked a recorded history predating European contact. Consequently, in using monsters from the African Diasporic folk tradition, black writers 'refuse the violence in which the West dominates' (Okpala 2004: 151). Rather, their introduction of black folk figures proves a Creolisation that changes the style of the Western narrative.

Throughout the short story collection *Skin Folk* (2001), Nalo Hopkinson's use of Caribbean figures and beliefs to revise Western fairy tales stages an exemplary assault on Western dominance, producing texts which critique submission to Western ideals. In stories such as 'The

Glass Bottle Trick', Hopkinson rewrites European myths such as the French story of Bluebeard without merely replicating the structure and content of the narratives. Rather, she borrows characters to render the stories' general anxieties global while imbuing the myths with the horror of (internalised) racial oppression. Thus, while Bluebeard murders his wives for disobedience, in 'The Glass Bottle Trick' Samuel murders his wives because they get pregnant with 'his beautiful black babies' (Hopkinson 2001: 98).

A handsome man, Samuel thinks himself ugly because of his dark skin. Spiritually ugly, the story defines Samuel's hideousness as a consequence of his allegiance to white bourgeois ideals. For instance, he insists Beatrice perform a modern version of True Womanhood, sacrificing her vision of a career in order to be a perfect housewife. Samuel virtually imprisons Beatrice within the home, worrying his wife might get 'too brown' and disdaining the way the sun 'brought out the sepia and cinnamon in her blood, overpowered the milk and honey' because such rich, lovely brownness would prevent him from continuing to 'pretend she was white. He loved her pale skin' (93–4). In Hopkinson's story, the horrors of patriarchal dominance are not the sole concern; rather patriarchal dominance enables the propagation of colourism in monstrous ways.

'The Glass Bottle Trick' makes a number of important changes to the original myth, including the introduction of the bottle tree. The concept of the bottle tree, according to Hopkinson, originates in West Africa and crossed the Atlantic with slavery (Simpson 2005: 103). Retelling a French myth with a figure which signifies the Atlantic slave trade, Hopkinson links Samuel's internalisation of Western standards with ancestral enslavement and violence. Further, Hopkinson updates the African myth with meanings specific to the Caribbean. As Beatrice explains, you must have a bottle tree with blue bottles to capture and cool duppy spirits 'so [they] won't come at you in hot anger for being dead' (Hopkinson 2001: 86). The 'coolness' of the bottle connects to the 'coolness' of the house, which Samuel keeps frigid in order to preserve the corpses of his former wives. Thus, the glass bottle tree is made to signify upon Beatrice's entrapment in the house, a place where her 'spirit' is cooled to a ghost of its former self.

In the original tale, the spectral wives only foreshadow the heroine's fate. In Hopkinson's narrative, however, the wives are not mere corpses or even ghosts: they are duppies, corrupted, restless, unhappy spirits that bring trouble to the living. According to Jamaican folktales, every person's soul is composed of a good half which immediately travels to Africa/heaven at the moment of death, and a bad or earthly half which lingers with the corpse for three days after death and, without ritualistic precautions, becomes a duppy. The tree's presence in the French story, retold as a Caribbean narrative of racial self-hatred, in connection to the duppy wives suggests that the 'hotness' of the spirit and its transformation into a duppy has more to do with the ways in which black souls are imprisoned by destructive Western ideals. The 'earthly' half, the text suggests, only becomes bad when 'earthly' signifies a specific type of materiality and ideology. Consequently, unlike the original myth, Beatrice's salvation is unclear; uncertain the duppies will spare her, the truth is that Beatrice is already on her way to becoming a duppy herself.

Monsters from the Folk

Hopkinson's story 'Greedy Choke Puppy' reveals the anxiety of adopting Western ideals by positioning the African and West Indian figure of the soucouyant at the story's heart and refusing to mark her as innately monstrous.[2] Although the soucouyant is traditionally defined as a witch who sheds her skin at night to roam the region as a ball of fire, seeking young people and children from whom to drain their life, Jacky's friend Carmen marks the soucouyant as a figure of envy rather than horror. She remarks to Jacky, an actual soucouyant, 'I always wondered what it would be like to take your skin off, leave your worries behind, and fly so free' (Hopkinson 2001: 172). Jacky, in the form of a fireball, confirms the freedom Carmen envisions, thinking '*Oh God, I does be so free like this! Hide the skin under the bed, and fly out the jalousie window. The night air cool, and I flying so high [...] I could feel them, skin-bag people, breathing out their life*' (177, italics in original). Notable in both women's comments is the emphasis on freedom from the skin, rather than freedom from body, in specific connection to freedom from worries. In light of Afro-Caribbean history and modern experience, the emphasis on skin alludes to the horror of entrapment within a racialised system where blackness signified non-human beasts of burden at worse and non-citizen alienated colonial subject at best. Thus, Jacky mourns '*The skin only confining me. I could feel it [...] binding me up inside it. Sometimes I does just feel to take it off and never put it back on again*' (177, italics in original).

The story repeatedly contrasts folk wisdom with textual scholarship, identified primarily with Western ideology. Jacky, a graduate student of folklore, encounters an entry which attempts to familiarise the soucouyant by insistently connecting the figure to Europe:

> SOUCOUYANT/OL' HIGUE (Trinidad/Guyana)
> Caribbean equivalent of the vampire myth. See also 'Azeman.'
> 'Soucouyant,' or 'blood-sucker,' derives from the French verb 'sucer,' to suck. 'Ol' Higue' is the Guyanese creole expression for an old hag, or witch woman. The soucouyant is usually an old, evil-tempered woman who removes her skin at night, hides it, and then changes into a ball of fire. (Hopkinson 2001: 173, bold in original)

The entry gets elements of the figure wrong; Jacky is by no means 'an old, evil-tempered woman'. The mistakes suggest that African Diasporic folk figures escape containment within Western regimes of knowledge, which can only access a portion of black experience. The entry continues, rationalising the origin of the soucouyant as a means of explaining the mortality rates for infants through a patriarchal framework which envied women their longer lives (178). Yet the explanation is self-contradicting, arguing at once that women tended to die in childbirth, that they lived longer than men and that life in primitive eras of superstition was both hard and brief. The entry's contradictions and its organisation – it is interrupted by a description of Jacky feeding on an infant – implies that the figure of the soucouyant and the black cultural reality to which it speaks cannot be captured and explained through Western accounts.

The horror of the soucouyant is not innate to her but stems from her alignment with certain ideologies, specifically Western notions of beauty and age. Jacky enunciates her recognition of her soucouyant nature specifically in connection to the experience of youthful attractiveness versus aging as loss. She starts to feel old, '[*l*]*ike something wither-up* [. . .] *dead and dry*' (170; italics in original), until one night, feeling her skin ablaze, she snatches off her nightgown to find that her skin goes with it. Hopkinson's use of the figure proves notably womanist given that Jacky

> spouts forth a sexist ideology that demands to be challenged [. . .] She preys on children, not because this behaviour is necessary for her survival but out of vanity. She constantly laments growing older, not because it brings her closer to death and a time when she will not be able to fly free but because she is no longer able to attract male attention. (Anatol 2004: 45)

Though Anatol critiques the evil seemingly innate in Hopkinson's soucouyant, the story posits that such evil is garnered through ascription to Western materialist ideology, given that the grandmother is also a soucouyant. The generational difference between grandmother and granddaughter (and even the deceased mother) alludes to differences in relationship and access to white Western ideals. Indeed, Jacky's anxiety about remaining beautiful 'voices the socially sanctioned belief that women's worth is determined exclusively by male desire', and leads her to objectify herself as a '"something" rather than someone' (45). Notably, objectification characterises the history of Western racial and colonial encounter.

In contrast, the story's title alludes to the ways in which black folk culture can save blacks from modern oppression. The story's beginning alludes to this dynamic as Jacky, researching Caribbean folklore for her thesis, comments 'you did right about that part' (169) in connection to the details of her grandmother's description of La Diablese, implying that her grandmother's version alone does not warrant belief but requires scholarly validation of its details. Granny challenges Jacky's determination to privilege Western forms and knowledge by constantly interrupting Jacky's account of her 'research'. Of course, nothing of Jacky's research provides illumination into her existence or salvation. Rather, Jacky's grandmother fully enunciates the title and thus offers a remedy, warning '[g]reedy puppy does choke. You mother did always taste straight from the hot stove, too. I was forever telling she to take time [. . .] Love will come. But take time. Love your studies, look out for your friends-them. Love your old Granny' (Hopkinson 2001: 175–6). She continues this explanation just before she kills her gluttonous granddaughter, mourning '[w]hen we lives empty, the hunger does turn to blood hunger. But it have plenty other kinds of loving, Jacky. Ain't I been telling you so? Love your work. Love people close to you. Love your life [. . .] Don't be greedy' (180–1). The story thus argues that privileging communal connection and love, in contrast to the Western idealisation of material consumption, is salvation. Only the shared love of community offers fulfilment; consumption only breeds more emptiness and, ultimately, destruction.

Helen Oyeyimi likewise uses the figure of the soucouyant and relocates the African Diasporic monster within the heart of Britain in *White Is for Witching* (2009). In doing so Oyeyimi speaks to the complex question of identity, belonging and the function of blacks within British nation(ality). The metaphor of the soucouyant provides an interesting solution to the threats presented within the text. On the one hand, the monster – and the anxiety over the possibility of becoming her – helps articulate the complex horrors of the nation in its assimilating drives and use of women as co-conspiring oppressors. Further, 'using [the] soucouyant myth to describe the heroine Miranda's vampirism thus employs the colonial mythos in a different way, as it reflects the consumptive nature of the empire back to itself' (King 2013: 68) in a manner which the metaphor of the vampire cannot as a product and reiteration of proper 'Englishness'. The soucouyant, as an immigrating monster, alludes to the minority's ability to recognise and properly name the denied and invisible politics of the nation state.

In reading the British nation through the black folk monster, the text reveals the latent horrors of imperial domination, which are typically recast as anxieties about reverse colonisation in traditional Gothic texts such as Bram Stoker's *Dracula*. Ore, Miranda's black girlfriend, defines three notable things about the soucouyant which also hold true for Britain. First, though the soucouyant seems more lonely than bad, her seemingly pathetic nature is a trick 'so you couldn't decide if she was a monster' (Oyeyemi 2009: 137). Further, the soucouyant consumes because she 'is not content with her self' (144). And finally, she poses a double threat, 'there is the danger of meeting her, and the danger of becoming her' (144). Oyeyemi's migrating monster reveals the truths at the heart of British nation, buried beneath the cultural obsession over 'Englishness'. First, the nation feigns qualities which make it attractive and less threatening as part of its 'trick'. Second, the nation, discontent with itself, has always depended upon the consumption of racial bodies for sustenance. Third, the true terror of migrating into Englishness is not the threat of its denial, but the possibility of becoming it. And lastly, the only way to defeat such monsters is by fighting them from the inside out, given that the only way to defeat a soucouyant, according to Ore, is to rub the inside of her skin with salt and pepper. Ore's insights into the soucouyant prove invaluable and emphasise the revolutionary potential of Afro-Diasporic myths in rearticulating the Western nation. But most intriguing is the question Ore ponders about the soucouyant given the place of such nations in a global age: '[d]oes the nightmare of her belong to everyone, or just to me?' (144).

In Jeremy Love's graphic novels *Bayou* (2009–10, volumes 1 and 2), the horror of Jim Crow whiteness is accompanied by fiends grown out of the grotesque racist figures productive and illustrative of white violence. Love derives each monster from specific racist tropes and figures destructive to African American life and psychology. The heroine Lee travels through the Mississippi Bayou accompanied by the seemingly monstrous embodiment of the bayou, a giant greenish black man named Bayou. Although Lee marks the bayou as innately gruesome – a locale where young black boys like Billy are brutally beaten and lynched – the novels insist that the region's monstrosity is not inherent.[3] Like the giant Bayou, it is misread and is actually a place which births blackness. Notably, Bayou mourns that the region's faceless white master holds his black children captive, and he longs for the day when he sees them free again. In contrast to Bayou, the overly visible but misrecognised figure, the dominating fiend haunting the novels is the faceless, Confederateuniformed white master who controls all of the other horrors of the region. Each supernatural embodiment of racist ideology appears at the master's call to do his bidding. His dominating power in addition to his omnipresence returns attention to the true horror which initiates the novels' action: the threat of an amorphous, powerful, unchallenged white (lynch) mob and people's passivity in the face of such injustice, given the Sheriff's comment that he will not protect Lee's father if it means risking himself or standing against other whites.

A number of new monsters roam *Bayou*, figures which may be familiar to blacks and/or Southerners, but which would be fairly alien to most other readers. Love's association of figures such as Stagolee and Uncle Remus with the demonic compels readers to investigate and re-evaluate seemingly known characters whose popularity in blues music and Southern folklore belies their terrible significations. Stagolee is one of the nicknames for 'Stag' Lee Shelton, a dashing black man who became notorious after murdering his friend William Lyons in 1895 after Lyons supposedly 'took' Shelton's Stetson as his prize in a card game. In several songs about the crime, Lyons pleads for his life, noting that he has a wife and child waiting for him. Shelton came to epitomise the 'bad man' trope common to blues lyrics. However, Love's novels emphasise the terror of Shelton's crime as he is turned into a shapeshifting demon happy to work for a white master if it means he gets to kill people, primarily other African Americans. As such, Love's depiction of Stag clarifies his persona, refusing to praise Stags's rejection of social mandate and re-centering upon his wickedness in his betrayal of his friend and people. Equally important, Love's recreation of Stagolee as the demonic enforcer for the white master also marks the figure's appearance in popular music as a tool of racist assault and betrayal.

Bayou likewise marks Uncle Remus, another notable figure of Southern folklore, as a vicious force. The creation of Joel Chandler Harris, Remus was the racist version of Charles W. Chesnutt's trickster storyteller Uncle Julius in 'The Goophered Grapevine' (1887). Revealed in volume 2 of *Bayou* as a gigantic evil chicken, the novel connects Remus to another figure, the Doodang, a gargantuan creature from Harris's 'The Story of the Doodang' (1910).[4] Remus narrates the tale to a young black child who proves discontent, much like the monstrous Doodang of Remus's story. The tale's moral, which is to be content with your lot and not reach for more, directs the black child to stay in his social place. Notably, in *Bayou*, Doodang guards prisoners without physical force, keeping them jailed without bars or chains. Similarly, once Remus assumes the form of the giant demon chicken, he destroys the embodiment of black resistance and survival. Remus, in this light, proves a horrifying force in the lives of African Americans as his stories warp Chesnutt's invaluable narratives of black resistance, psychologically imprisoning black children instead.

A final but equally important threat which appears in *Bayou* appropriates the anti-black caricature of the golliwog. Originating in Florence Upton's book series *The Adventures of Two Dutch Dolls* (1895), golliwogs have jet black skin, large white-rimmed eyes, red or white clown lips and wild, frizzy hair. It began as a hybrid of a dwarf-sized minstrel and an animal, and was often depicted with paws in the place of hands and feet (Dunk 2009). Indeed, the Steiff Company mass-produced several versions, including one which 'looked like a wooly haired gorilla' (Pilgrim 2012). Particularly popular in Europe, the golliwog appears on a variety of items such as postcards, jam jars, clocks, pottery and even sheet music. In addition to the explicitly problematic nature of its depiction, its name likewise recalls the racist epithet 'wog', a British slur for dark-skinned people of colour. As recently as 2009, consumers argued that the golliwog was a harmless lovable icon, despite its racist overtones, because the original texts reveal that the black gnome-creature is good and brave (Pilgrim 2012).

Unsurprisingly, Love indicts arguments supporting the Golliwog as 'harmless', emphasising its hideous appearance and augmenting its already explicitly racist elements, such as the wild hair and large red lips, elements easily traceable to twentieth-century minstrelsy. More importantly, he puns upon the notion of the figure's haplessness as a traitorous possum approaches the Golliwog with a plan to betray Bayou and Lee for a reward. The Golliwog, huge and ominous, leers grotesquely at the possum before consuming the creature whole in order to capture the other two and claim the reward for itself. Furthermore, in a climactic moment, Lee lays trapped beneath the Golliwog, gazing into its rolling eyes as drool runs from its lips and its gnarled claws reach for her. The scene puts the child in confrontation with the supposedly 'child-like' icon to reveal the absurdity of attempting to dismiss the (ideological) violence implicit in the Golliwog.

Black Nightmares, White Suburbs

Jordan Peele's hugely successful *Get Out* (2017) illustrates monsters who, while not from any black folkloric tradition, destabilise via their origins in African Americans experiences of racial oppression. As such, the film is layered with meanings requiring either intimate knowledge of African American history or an extensive investigation into the socio-historical experiences of this population, if one is to decipher the text. Peele's film literalises the notion of consumption which bell hooks defines in the chapter 'Eating the Other' in *Black Looks* (1992), where hooks connects cultural appropriation to colonisation and commodification. Eating the Other, as a theory, emphasises the abjection and consequences of a cultural appropriation which utterly disconnects the cultural product from its body of origin, rendering that body so much detritus and waste.[5] Thus, the film's quip '[a] mind is a terrible thing to waste' is particularly loaded. In this case, the white mind must be salvaged by consuming the black body, whose psyche is considered 'waste'.

Inspired in part by George Romero's *Night of the Living Dead* (1968) as well as *The Stepford Wives* (1975), *Get Out* reintroduces Romero's anxieties about hyper-consumptive whiteness, replacing the white zombies with white suburbanites who evaluate and (ap)praise the protagonist Chris for his physical abilities. Zombie and suburbanite seek to equally 'eat' their respective black heroes, rejecting their humanity and agency as so much shit. The white Armitage family and their neighbours are likewise grotesque through their engagement of practices recalling racist stereotype. For instance, one woman explicitly discusses the supposed sexual virility of black men, while a male grasps Chris's arm, remarking upon his strength and presumed athletic abilities. Furthermore, the neighbourhood 'Bingo game' recreates the experience of the slave auction block. Although the scene seems absurdist, the encounters and grotesque behaviours of the white neighbours speak to interactions that are all too familiar to many twenty-first-century African Americans. Indeed, Daniel Kaluuya, the actor playing Chris, expressed similar remarks, wondering why Chris would stay for so long. Notably, the film anticipates black audiences' reactions from the beginning; the lyrics to the title song, sung in Swahili, translate to 'Brother, run! Listen to the elders. Listen to the truth. Run away! Save yourself.'

More importantly, the film's reference to, and pun upon, Du Bois's notion of double consciousness marks the black body as a second locale of monstrosity because of the erasure it suffers at white hands. One of the most tragic and horrifying revelations in the film is not the misdeeds of the white suburbanites, rendered overtly grotesque and bizarre, but the moments in which black subjects reclaim their voices and speak from their possessed bodies, such as when Andre (Lakeith Stanfield) snaps to consciousness and when Walter (Marcus Henderson) commits suicide. Such moments reveal the complex horror of blackness in modern America: to live in a body historically defined and possessed by whiteness through literal ownership and through psychological manipulation – via promises of citizenship and access to 'the American Dream' in exchange for allegiance and submission – from which black subjects struggle to articulate their experience, consumption and betrayal. Significantly the film is rife with references to materials and ideologies used to lure blacks into submission by offering the hope of success and equality. One such object is Missy's (Catherine Keener) china tea cup and silver spoon, which she uses to literally hypnotise and subdue Chris in several encounters; another such 'object' is Missy's daughter and Chris's girlfriend Rose (Allison Williams). Thus, as monstrous as the privileged white villains prove, the film is populated with African Americans, such as the dismissive police captain, who have essentially been possessed by whiteness and made into modern overseers. In a film without supernatural monsters, horror is complexly relocated within black bodies at very specific moments, alluding to how blacks have been historically marked as monstrous in social discourses and (Gothic) fictions while clarifying the moments when blacks actually become monstrous – the moment when they become Stepford blacks.

As the Black Diasporic writers above reveal, the Gothic's emphasis on grotesque figures as radical tropes which destabilise the normative and defamiliarise readers makes it perhaps the most suitable mode to stage disruptive narratives. Yet, modifying traditional Gothic monsters from European folk traditions is not the method of creating texts that introduce subversive strangeness. Familiar monsters are so overloaded with meaning that it is nearly impossible to escape re-instituting the very racial and classist ideals already encoded within their texts. Rather, as the artists discussed above reveal, one has to force the Western reader out of their region entirely by introducing monsters from the African Diaspora, creatures with histories that record the horror of physical and cultural theft even as they demand recognition of a pre-encounter cultural history. Only alien figures such as these can record the complex meaning and questions of twenty-first-century black existence, lives which are still rife with actual horrors.

Notes

1. As Nalo Hopkinson explains, '[i]t's the nature of the genre [fantasy and horror] to allow one to step outside the box and examine what's in it and think about what might be excluded and why' (Simpson 2005: 108–9).
2. Western television shows such as *Sleepy Hollow* illustrate the difficulty of appropriating such monsters outside of their context. In season three's episode 'This Red Lady from Caribee' (2015) the show depicts a figure it

calls a soucouyant but which, as a kind of hive, bug woman, bears almost no resemblance to the actual figure. The show's hive monster in many ways illustrates the mythical figure's successful eluding of Western grasp.
3. Billy is Love's reimagining of Emmett Till.
4. The Doodang is an amalgamation of creatures who nonetheless envies the abilities of other smaller beasts, such as fish and birds, despite his awesome stature. His discontentment with his lot in life leads to his death.
5. Such consumption proves another type of abject encounter in which the positive aspects of the Other are re-incorporated into the dominant white body even as the Other are made to signify all the horrors of whiteness. 'Eating the Other' means consuming the spectacle of horrors projected from the self onto an abject body as well as the desirable aspects of that Other body which are then relocated within the abjecting subject.

Film and Television

Get Out (Jordan Peele, USA, 2017)

References

Anatol, Giselle Liza (2004), 'A Feminist Reading of Soucouyants in Nalo Hopkinson's "Brown Girl in the Ring" and "Skin Folk"', *Mosaic*, 37.3, 33–50.

Dunk, Marcus (2009), 'How the Golliwog Went from Innocent Children's Hero to Symbol of Bitter Controversy', *Mail Online*, 5 February, http://www.dailymail.co.uk/news/article-1136016/How-golliwog-went-innocent-childrens-hero-symbol-bitter-controversy.html (accessed 9 December 2017).

hooks, bell (1992), 'Eating the Other', in *Black Looks: Race and Representation*, New York: South End Press, pp. 21–40.

Hopkinson, Nalo (2001), *Skin Folk*, New York: Hatchett Books.

Khair, Tabish (2002), '"Correct(ing) Images from the Inside": Reading the Limits of Erna Brodber's Myal', *Journal of Commonwealth Literature*, 37.1, 121–31.

King, Amy K. (2013), 'The Spectral Queerness of White Supremacy: Helen Oyeyemi's *White Is for Witching*', in Lisa B. Kröger and Melanie Anderson (eds), *Ghostly and the Ghosted in Literature and Film: Spectral Identities*, Newark: University of Delaware, pp. 59–73.

Love, Jeremy (2009), *Bayou*, vol. 1, New York: DC Comics.

— (2010), *Bayou*, vol. 2, New York: DC Comics.

Massey, Brandon (2004), *Dark Corner*, New York: Kensington Books.

Mittelhozer, Edgar (1951), *My Bones and My Flute*, London: Peepal Tree.

Okpala, Jude Chudi (2004), 'Deterritorialization, Black British Writers, and the Case of Ben Okri', in Victoria R. Arana and Lauri Ramey (eds), *Black British Writing*, New York: Palgrave, pp. 146–59.

Oyeyimi, Helen (2009), *White Is for Witching*, New York: Nan A. Talese.

Pilgrim, David (2012), 'The Golliwog Caricature', *The Jim Crow Museum of Racist Memorabilia*, https://ferris.edu/jimcrow/golliwog/ (accessed 9 December 2017).

Simpson, Hyacinth M. (2005), 'Fantastic Alternatives: Journeys into the Imagination: A Conversation with Nalo Hopkinson', *Journal of West Indian Literature*, 12.1/2, 96–112.

Smethurst, James (2001), 'Invented by Horror: The Gothic and African American Literary Ideology in *Native Son*', *African American Review*, 35.1, 29–40.

Smith, Heather (2002), '"Roots beyond Roots": Heteroglossia and Feminist Creolization in *Myal* and *Crossing the Mangrove*', *Small Axe*, 12, 1–24.

Notes on Contributors

Enrique Ajuria Ibarra is Assistant Professor at Universidad de las Américas Puebla, Mexico. He has previously published several articles and book chapters on Mexican horror cinema. He is the editor of the peer-reviewed online journal *Studies in Gothic Fiction* and is currently preparing a book on the relationship between movement, Gothic and the horror film.

Xavier Aldana Reyes is a Reader in English Literature and Film at Manchester Metropolitan University and a founder member of the Manchester Centre for Gothic Studies. He is the author of *Spanish Gothic* (2017), *Horror Film and Affect* (2016) and *Body Gothic* (2014), and the editor of *Horror: A Literary History* (2016). Xavier is chief editor of the Horror Studies book series run by the University of Wales Press.

Katrin Althans is a Senior Lecturer at Heinrich Heine University, Düsseldorf, Germany. She is currently writing her second book on 'The Stories of Refugees: The Narrative Authority of the Law'. Her publications include the monograph *Darkness Subverted: Aboriginal Gothic in Black Australian Literature and Film* (2010) as well as several articles on Australian Indigenous literature, the Gothic, video games and refugees in literature.

Katarzyna Ancuta is a Lecturer at KMITL in Bangkok, Thailand. Her research interests oscillate around the interdisciplinary contexts of contemporary Gothic/Horror, currently with a strong Asian focus. Her recent publications include contributions to *A New Companion to the Gothic* (2012), *Globalgothic* (2013) and *The Cambridge Companion to the Modern Gothic* (2014), as well as two co-edited special journal issues on Thai (2014) and Southeast Asian (2015) horror film.

Linnie Blake is founder and Head of the Manchester Centre for Gothic Studies and Reader in Gothic Literature and Film at Manchester Metropolitan University. She is author of *The Wounds of Nations* (2008). She has published widely on numerous aspects of Gothic and Horror literature and film, most recently co-editing the collections *Neoliberal Gothic* (2017) and *Digital Horror* (2015) with Agnieszka Soltysik Monnet and Xavier Aldana Reyes, respectively.

Joseph Crawford is a Senior Lecturer in English Literature at the University of Exeter. He is the author of three academic monographs – *Raising Milton's Ghost* (2011), *Gothic Fiction and the Invention of Terrorism* (2013) and *The Twilight of the Gothic* (2014). He is currently researching nineteenth-century poetry and insanity.

Sharae Deckard is a Lecturer in World Literature at University College Dublin. She is author of *Paradise Discourse, Imperialism, and Globalization: Exploited Edens* (2010) and co-author with the Warwick Research Collective of *Combined and Uneven Development: Towards a New Theory of World-Literature* (2015). She has published multiple essays on Ecogothic in the context of Caribbean, South Asian and post-Soviet literature.

Rebecca Duncan teaches in the Division of Literature and Languages at the University of Stirling, where she is affiliated to the International Centre for Gothic Studies. She is the author of *South African Gothic: Anxiety and Creative Dissent in the Post-Apartheid Imagination and Beyond* (2018). She is also co-editor of *Fantastika Journal,* and the author of articles and book chapters in the fields of postcolonial, eco-critical and Gothic studies.

Kaja Franck was awarded her PhD at the University of Hertfordshire in 2017. Her thesis explored the literary werewolf as an Ecogothic monster, concentrating on the relationship between wilderness, wolves and werewolves, and on how language is used to demarcate animal alterity. She is a post-doctoral researcher on the 'Open Graves, Open Minds' research project and has published on the depiction of wolves and werewolves in *Dracula* and Young Adult fiction.

Sam George is Senior Lecturer at the University of Hertfordshire and the Convenor of the popular 'Open Graves, Open Minds' project. She has published widely on natural history, vampire literature, children raised by wolves and contemporary werewolf myths. The edited collection

In the Company of Wolves and a special issue of *Gothic Studies* on 'Wolves, Werewolves and Wilderness' are forthcoming in 2019. Sam is leading an AHRC-funded project on literature and folklore and completing a monograph on the cultural history of the shadow.

Anya Heise-von der Lippe is Assistant Lecturer with the Chair of Anglophone Literatures at the University of Tübingen, Germany. Her research focuses on Gothic bodies in postmodern and contemporary texts, particularly on the parallels between monstrous corporeality and monstrous textuality. She is the editor of the collection *Posthuman Gothic* (2017) and co-editor (with Russell West-Pavlov) of *Literaturwissenschaften in der Krise* (2018).

Sarah Ilott is Senior Lecturer in English Literature and Film at Manchester Metropolitan University. Sarah is a postcolonial scholar specialising in genre fiction and film, particularly comedy and the Gothic. She is author of *New Postcolonial British Genres: Shifting the Boundaries* (2015) and co-editor of *Telling It Slant: Critical Approaches to Helen Oyeyemi* (2017), *New Directions in Diaspora Studies: Cultural and Literary Approaches* (2018) and *Comedy and the Politics of Representation: Mocking the Weak* (2018).

Murray Leeder is an Adjunct Assistant Professor at the University of Calgary. He is the author of *Horror Film: A Critical Introduction* (2018), *The Modern Supernatural and the Beginnings of Cinema* (2017) and *Halloween* (2014), as well as the editor of *Cinematic Ghosts: Haunting and Spectrality from Silent Cinema to the Digital Era* (2015) and *ReFocus: The Films of William Castle* (2018).

Bernice M. Murphy is Lecturer in Popular Literature at the School of English, Trinity College Dublin. Her books include *The Suburban Gothic in American Popular Culture* (2009), *The Rural Gothic: Backwoods Horror and Terror in the Wilderness* (2013), *The Highway Horror Film* (2014) and the essay collection *Lost Souls of Horror and the Gothic* (2016, co-edited with Elizabeth McCarthy). She has also published the textbook *Key Concepts in Popular Fiction* (2017) and co-edited (with Stephen Matterson) *Twenty-First-Century Popular Fiction* (2017).

Claire Nally is a Senior Lecturer in Twentieth-Century English Literature at Northumbria University, and researches Irish studies, neo-Victorianism, gender and subcultures. She is the author of *Envisioning Ireland: W. B. Yeats's Occult Nationalism* (2009) and *Selling Ireland*

(2012, with John Strachan). She has co-edited a volume on Yeats and two volumes on gender, as well as the library series 'Gender and Popular Culture' for I. B. Tauris (with Angela Smith). She has written widely on subcultures, and her most recent work looks at the development of steampunk in literature, film, music and fashion.

Sorcha Ní Fhlainn is Senior Lecturer in Film Studies and American Studies and a founder member of the Manchester Centre for Gothic Studies. She is Reviews Editor for *Gothic Studies*, the journal of the International Gothic Association, and editor of *Open Screens: The Journal of the British Association of Film, Television and Screen Studies* (Ubiquity Press/Open Library of Humanities). Recent and forthcoming books include *Clive Barker: Dark Imaginer* (2017), *Postmodern Vampires* (2019) and a monograph and special edition of *Gothic Studies* on the long 1980s.

Andrew J. Owens is a Lecturer in the Department of Cinematic Arts at the University of Iowa. His work has appeared in *Feminist Media Studies* and *Television & New Media* and is forthcoming in *New Review of Film and Television Studies*. His book, *Desire After Dark: Contemporary Queer Cultures and Occultly Marvelous Media*, is forthcoming from Indiana University Press.

Carl H. Sederholm is Professor of Interdisciplinary Humanities at Brigham Young University and Chair of the Department of Comparative Arts and Letters. He is also the editor of *The Journal of American Culture*. He is co-editor (with Jeffrey Andrew Weinstock) of *The Age of Lovecraft* (2016), co-editor (with Dennis Perry) of *Adapting Poe: Re-Imaginings in Popular Culture* (2012) and the co-author (also with Dennis Perry) of *Poe, the 'House of Usher,' and the American Gothic* (2009).

Catherine Spooner is Professor of Literature and Culture at Lancaster University. She has published widely on Gothic in literature, film and popular culture, including the books *Fashioning Gothic Bodies* (2004), *Contemporary Gothic* (2006) and *Post-Millennial Gothic: Comedy Romance and the Rise of Happy Gothic* (2017). She was co-president of the International Gothic Association from 2013–17.

Maisha Wester is an Associate Professor at Indiana University and author of *African American Gothic: Screams from Shadowed Places* (2012). She was a 2017–18 Fulbright Scholar at the University of Sheffield. Her research interests include racial representation in Gothic literature and horror films, Black Diasporic Gothic literature and the socio-political deployment of Gothic tropes in racial discourses.

Gina Wisker is Professor of Contemporary Literature and Higher Education at the University of Brighton, ex-chair of the contemporary women's writing association and author of *Horror* (2005), *Margaret Atwood: An Introduction to Critical Views of Her Fiction* (2012) and *Contemporary Women's Gothic Fiction* (2016).

Index

Works in languages other than English are listed with the original title first followed by the English title. Notes are indicated by page number followed by note number.

#CharlieCharlieChallenge (online game), 270–2

28 Days Later (film), 92
28 Weeks Later (film), 93
30 Days of Night (film), 113
4chan (internet forum), 78, 79, 81

Abbott, Stacey, 38, 98, 103, 104
Abbott and Costello Meet Frankenstein (film), 190, 192
abjection, 12, 13
   Black Diasporic Gothic, 300, 302n5
   Muslims, 25–6, 27
   women, 50, 54, 257
   zombies, 89, 91, 95
Abney Park (band), 203, 207, 213–14
Aboriginal Gothic, 276–87
Abrahamson, Lenny, 137
Addams Family, The (television series), 199
Addiction, The (film), 107
adolescence, werewolves and, 151
Adventures of Two Dutch Dolls, The (Upton), 299
Afterlife (television series), 135
Agarwal, Shilpa, 253
ageing: Black Diasporic Gothic, 295
Agostini, Claudio, 268
Ajvide Lindqvist, John, 98, 109–10
Al final del espectro / At the End of the Spectra (film), 263
Albigenses, The (Maturin), 145
Aldana Reyes, Xavier, 161, 235, 238, 271

Alex (Lemaitre), 121
Alfaya, J. F., 215
Alien: Resurrection (film), 227–8
alienation: horror genre, 39
alt.folklore, 73, 74
alt.horror, 72
Always Watching (film), 82
Ambergris (city, VanderMeer), 167–9
Amenábar, Alejandro, 137
American Horror Story: Murder House (film), 140
American Psycho (Ellis), 126
American Psycho (film), 126
American Werewolf in London, An (film), 147
America's Got Talent (television series), 189–90
Amirpour, Ana Lily, 110
anarchism: steampunk, 208, 209
Anatol, Giselle Liza, 28–9, 295
Andrianova, Anastassiya, 153
Angel (television series), 107, 108
animism, 9, 176, 250, 254, 255, 256, 257–8, 260
Anita Blake: Vampire Hunter (Hamilton), 107
anonymity: online content, 81–2, 83
Antillanité (Glissant), 292
Anubis Gates, The (Powers), 205
apartheid, 233–6, 241, 242–3, 244
apocalypse
   vampires, 113
   zombies, 67, 90–1, 92, 93, 95, 113, 267

Apocalypse Now Now (Human), 237, 238–9, 241
Appropriate Adult (television drama), 125
April, Phumle, 239, 240, 241, 242
Argentina: Gothic cinema, 263
Armitt, Lucie, 196
Armstrong, Kelley, 153
art cinema, world: ghosts, 138–40
artificial intelligence, 226, 227–8
arts and crafts: steampunk, 211
Ashamoil, 169
Ashcroft, Bill, 19
Ashdown, Matthew, 178–9, 180
Asian Gothic, 249–61
Asian supernatural cinema, 133–4, 139, 141n2
Aslam, Nadeen, 26
'Asleep' (Scott), 283
Asma, Stephen, 146
Assayas, Olivier, 138–9
Asylum Steampunk Festival, The, 207, 209
Atwood, Margaret, 19, 212
Auerbach, Nina, 103
August Eschenburg (Millhauser), 53
Australia: Aboriginal Gothic, 276–87
Aventures extraordinaires d'Adèle Blanc-Sec, Les / The Extraordinary Adventures of Adèle Blanc-Sec (film), 211
'Avions de Nuit' (April), 239–40, 241, 242
Awakening, The (film), 135

Bad Seed, The (March), 122
Badham, John, 105
Bakhtin, Mikhail, 197, 237–8
Balderston, John, 103
Ball, Alan, 108, 111
Banyard, Geof, 209
Barclay, Robert, 175–6, 185
Baring-Gould, Sabine, 145
Barlow, Toby, 149
Barnard, Rita, 238, 239
Barnes, Jennifer Lynn, 146
Barns, Laurie (character), 134
Bates, Norman (character), 127
Bates Motel (television series), 127
Batoru rowaiaru / Battle Royale (film), 249
Bax, Trent M., 252
Bayou (Love), 297–9
Beattie, James, 196

Beauty, The (graphic novel series), 224
Beckinsdale, Kate, 148
beDevil (film), 279
Being Human (television series), 154–5
Ben Drowned (online media), 77, 80
Benang (Scott), 286
Benshoff, Harry, 35
Bethel, Brian, 73
Beukes, Lauren, 121, 241, 242–3, 244
Beyond Black (Mantel), 137
Bhoot / Ghost (film), 253
Bieber, Justin, 207
Bierce, Ambrose, 181
biopics, serial killer, 123–6
biotechnology, 62–3, 67, 68
Birdcage Walk (Dunmore), 51–2, 58
Bishop, K. J., 161, 165, 169
Bitten (Armstrong), 153
Black, Holly, 54
Black Diasporic Gothic, 289–302
Black-Eyed Kids, 73, 84n2
Black Isle, The (Tan), 255–6
Black Looks (hooks), 300
Black Mirror (television series), 218–19, 220–1, 223–4
Blackwood, Algernon, 171
Blade (film), 107
Blade II (film), 112
Blair Witch Project, The (film), 73
Blake, Linnie, 90, 271
Blanco, María del Pilar, 131, 256–7
Blaylock, James P., 205
Bloch, Robert, 117
blogs, 76, 77, 95
Blomkamp, Neill, 241, 242–3, 244
Blood & Chocolate (film), 152
Blood & Chocolate (Klause), 151
Bloody Mary, 73, 84n2
Blumhouse Pictures, 138
body *see* corporeal, the
Bolton, Micheal Sean, 220
Bond, Patrick, 235, 236
Bondswoman's Narrative, The (Crafts), 290
Bones (television series), 120
Bongcheon-Dong Ghost, The (webcomic), 79–80
Book of Life, The (film), 273n1
Book of Werewolves, The (Baring-Gould), 145
border Gothic, 23–4
Boscovich, Desirina, 212
Botting, Fred, 164, 192, 195, 221, 264, 277–8

Boundary, The (Watson), 283–4
Bourgault du Coudray, Chantal, 152
Brabon, Ben, 47
Brady, Ian, 125
Braidotti, Rosi, 50, 225, 226
Bram Stoker's Dracula (film), 105, 114, 191
Brand upon the Brain! (film), 139
Brantlinger, Patrick, 19
Breaking Dawn (Meyer), 154
Breathers (Browne), 96, 194, 198
Bride That Time Forgot, The (Magrs), 198
Briggs, Patricia, 153
Brink, André, 234
Britain: Black Diasporic Gothic, 296–7
Brite, Poppy Z., 107
British nationalism, 23–4, 30
British Film Institute, 2
British Library, 2
Brontë, Charlotte, 19, 20
Brooks, Max, 67, 92
Brotherhood, The (film), 39
Brown, Charles Brockden, 3
Brown, Robert, 207
Browne, S. G., 96, 194
Browning, Tod, 103
Bú sàn / Goodbye, Dragon Inn (film), 139
Buchbinder, David, 126
Buell, Lawrence, 182
Buffy the Vampire Slayer (television series), 55, 56, 57, 106, 107, 108, 190–1
Bulloff, Libby, 214
bullying, school: South Korea, 251–2
Bulwer-Lytton, Edward, 132
Bunny Game, The (film), 121–2
Bunshinsaba / Ouija Board (film), 251, 252
Bunting, John, 124–5
Burton, Tim, 190, 191, 197
Butler, Gerald, 113–14
Butler, Judith, 54
Byron, Glennis, 9–10, 11–12, 118–19
Byzantium (film), 110

'Call of Cthulhu, The' (Lovecraft), 163, 179
Cameron, Emilie, 253
camp, 198
Campion, Jane, 19
Canadian Gothic (Sugars), 29–30
Canal, The (film), 135

'Candle Cove' (online media), 78, 82
cannibals: Latin American Gothic, 265
Cantik Itu Luka / Beauty Is a Wound (Kurniawan), 255
capitalism
  Ecogothic, 174–5, 180, 183–4
  racialised, 242–4
  serial killers and, 126
  vampires and, 61
  see also neoliberalism
Captain Robert, 207
Carey, M. R., 92–3
Caribbean Ecogothic, 176–80
Carnahan, Michael, 67–8
carnival, 197, 198, 237–8, 239
Carriger, Gail, 210
Carroll, Emily, 80
Carroll, Noël, 192
Carter, Angela, 49, 53–4
Casa del fin de los tiempos, La / The House at the End of Time (film), 263
Casa muda, La / The Silent House (film), 265, 266
Casanova-Vizcaíno, Sandra, 264
Casefile (podcast), 125
Castle of Otranto, The (Walpole), 132, 164, 190, 290
catachresis, 242
Catastrophone Orchestra and Arts Collective, The, 208
Chakushin Ari / One Missed Call (film), 133
change, economic and social, 7–9
Channel Zero (television series), 82
chap-hop, 214
Chaplin, Susan, 107
Chariandy, David, 29
Charlie Charlie, 270–2, 273nn3–4
Chesnutt, Charles W., 298–9
Chess, Shira, 78
chick lit, 48, 56–7, 58
Chile: Gothic cinema, 263
Chimurenga (journal), 239
Choo, Yangsze, 258
Chronic, The (journal), 239
Cisco, Michael, 165
City of Lost Children, The (film), 211–12
City of Mirrors, The (Cronin), 63
City of Saints and Madmen (VanderMeer), 161, 165, 167–9
Cleven, Vivienne, 285

Cleverman (television series), 281–3, 284
Coetzee, J. M., 19
Cohen, Jeffrey Jerome, 192
Coldest Girl in Coldtown, The (Black), 54, 57
Cole, Beck, 285
Colichman, Paul, 36, 39–40
Colin (film), 98
Colombia: Gothic cinema, 267
colonial violence, 19, 21, 22, 23, 24, 25, 30
colonialism: Australia, 276–7, 279–80, 281, 283, 284–6, 287
Comaroff, Jean, 240, 241
Comaroff, John L., 240, 241
comedy, Gothic, 189–201
commandement, postcolonial, 238
Company of Wolves, The (film), 147
Conde, Maryse, 290–1
Conjuring, The (film), 138
Conrad, Joseph, 19, 20
Conservationist, The (Gordimer), 233
conspiracy theories, 73–4
Cooper, Melinda, 62
Coppola, Francis Ford, 105, 114, 191
Cornwell, Patricia, 120
corporeal, the, 174
   posthuman Gothic, 218
   South African Gothic, 235, 236–8, 239, 240, 241, 244, 245
Corpse Bride (film), 190–1, 197–8
corset, the: steampunk, 205–6
Cowards Bend the Knee (film), 139
Crafts, Hannah, 290
'Creek of the Four Graves, The' (Harpur), 277
'Creepypasta' (website), 78
Creole, 289–90, 292
crime, true, 123–6
Crime Feed (podcast), 125
Criminal Minds (television series), 119
Crimson Peak (film), 122, 138
Crocodile Dreaming (film), 283
Cronin, Justin, 63, 64, 112
Cronos (film), 273n1
Cruise, Tom, 107
CSI: Crime Scene Investigation – Las Vegas (television series), 120
Cuarón, Alfonso, 263
Cuba: Gothic cinema, 266–7
cultural context: Gothic, 7–14
curanderos, 268–9, 273n2
Curtis, Dan, 104–5

cyberpunk, 218
'Cyborg Manifesto, A' (Haraway), 226
cyborgs, 53, 55, 58, 218, 219, 222, 226, 228
   postfeminist Gothic, 53, 54, 58

Dabydeen, David, 289–90
Dacre, Charlotte, 10
Dahmer (film), 123–4
dandies, 193
Danielewski, Mark Z., 221
Dante's Cove (television series), 35, 36–41, 44
Danuta Walters, Suzanne, 38, 40–1
Darby, Rhys, 199, 200
Dark Corner (Massey), 291–2
Dark Horse, The (Sedgwick), 146
Dark Shadows (television series), 37, 42, 43, 104–5
Darkside, The (film), 285–6
Darwin, Charles, 146
Datamancer, 211
David, Charlie, 33, 37, 38
David's Story (Wicomb), 234
Davies, Ann, 263
Davis, Emily S., 12
Dawn of the Dead (film), 89–90
Day of the Dead (film), 91
Daybreakers (film), 113
Dead Father, The (film), 139
Deane, Hamilton, 103
Death Proof (film), 121–2
DeCoteau, David, 39
del Toro, Benicio, 147
del Toro, Guillermo, 122, 137, 138, 263, 273n1
dementia, 29
Derrida, Jacques, 131, 140, 141, 192, 228
Desperate Housewives (television series), 199
Detroit, 62, 112
Dexter (Lindsay), 126–7
Dexter (television series), 126–7
Diallo, 291–2
Diary of the Dead (film), 95
Dick, Philip K., 218
Difference Engine, The (Gibson and Sterling), 205, 209–10
difference, cultural *see* otherness
digital Gothic, 8–9, 72–84, 270–2
Dionaea House, The (online media), 76, 77
Dirge, Roman, 196

Disembodied Spirit, The (exhibition), 135
District 9 (Blomkamp), 241, 242–3, 244
diversity: postfeminist Gothic, 52, 53, 55
Do Androids Dream of Electric Sheep? (Dick), 218
Doctor Geof, 209
Dr Grymm, 211
Dog Soldiers (film), 148
domesticity: Gothic comedy, 198–200
Doodang, The, 298, 302n4
Doty, Alexander, 34–5, 43
double consciousness, 291, 300
Douglas, John, 120
Douglass, Frederick, 290
Dracula
   Gothic comedy, 192
   race issues, 10–11
Dracula (film, 1931), 103
Dracula (film, 1979), 105
Dracula (Stoker), 4, 10–11, 19, 102, 145
   Black Diasporic Gothic and, 292, 297
   Ecogothic and, 177
   Goths and, 214
   postcolonial Gothic and, 23–4
Dracula (TV film), 105
Dracula 2000 (film), 113–14
Dracula Tape, The (Saberhagen), 105
Dracula Untold (film), 114
'Dradin, In Love' (VanderMeer), 168
Dreaming, the, 280, 281, 287n2
Du Bois, W. E. B., 291, 300
Duchess of Malfi (Webster), 145
Due, Tananarive, 137, 291
Duncan, Glen, 149, 194
Dunmore, Helen, 51–2, 58
duppies, 57, 176, 179, 293–4
Durrant, Sam, 234
Dust Echoes (films), 280–1, 282
Dworkin, Andrea, 54
Dyer, Richard, 128

Ecogothic, 53, 148, 155, 174–86
ecology, werewolves and, 144, 156
ecophobia, 174, 176, 182
Ed Gein (film), 123
Edward Scissorhands (film), 190
Edwards, Justin D., 264, 267–8
Ek Thi Daayan / There Was a Witch (film), 258
Eljaiek-Rodríguez, Gabriel, 267

Elliott, Kamilla, 190
Ellis, Bret Easton, 126
Ellis, Markman, 89
Enemy, The (Higson), 92
English Ghost Story, An (Newman), 137
'Englishness', 296–7
Enlightenment, the, opposition to, 7, 12, 118, 189
environmental violence, 181–4
equality
   neoliberal Gothic, 60, 61, 65–6, 67
   postcolonial Gothic, 30
   postfeminist Gothic, 47, 48–9, 50, 51, 52–3, 54, 56, 58
   South Africa, 235–6, 239, 244
   vampires, 65–6, 67, 111
   zombies, 67
Espinazo del diablo, El / The Devil's Backbone (film), 137–8
essentialism, biological: werewolves, 153, 154
Estok, Simon, 174
Etched City, The (Bishop), 161, 165, 169–70
Ethnogothic, 10, 11–13
Evans, Luke, 114
'evil': lack of innateness, 6
Evil Dead, The (film), 190
Ex Machina (film), 219, 221, 226–7, 228
Excelsior (newspaper), 272
excess
   Ecogothic, 174, 182
   Gothic, and, 6, 12, 109, 118, 237–8
   Gothic, and the weird, 165
   South African Gothic, 237, 238
exhibitions, 2
Experimental Film (Files), 222
Eyes of My Mother, The (film), 127

Fall, The (television series), 120–1
Fallout 4 (video game), 176, 184–5
family
   Gothic comedy, 191, 194, 198–9, 200
   postfeminist Gothic, 55–6, 57
   serial killer narratives, 118, 122–3, 127
   vampires, 55–6, 111
Fanon, Frantz, 291
Far Harbor (video game), 184–5
Farmiga, Vera, 127
FBI: serial killer Gothic, 118, 119, 120

fear, 264
    Aboriginal Gothic, 277, 282, 284
    Asian Gothic, 254, 259–60
    digital Gothic, 79, 81–2
    Ecogothic, 174, 177, 179–80
    Gothic comedy, 191, 192, 195
    Latin American Gothic, 265, 268
    New Weird, 163, 164
    postcolonial Gothic, 19, 25, 26
    postfeminist Gothic, 52
    posthuman Gothic, 218, 220–1, 227, 228
    South African Gothic, 242, 245
    werewolves, 146, 148, 150
    zombies, 92, 95, 97, 98, 99, 100
Fear the Walking Dead (television series), 93–4
FeardotCom (film), 134
Fearless Vampire Killers, The (film), 104
Feed (Grant), 94–5
female ghosts, 133–4
female serial killers, 118, 120, 121, 124, 125, 127–8
female werewolves, 144, 146, 147, 151–2, 153
females
    Asian Gothic monsters, 250–2, 253, 255–6, 257, 260
    posthuman Gothic, 219, 225–6, 228
    see also women
feminism
    postfeminism and, 48–50, 52, 53, 56–7, 58
    steampunk, 209, 212–13
    vampires, 110
Feral Nights (Smith), 154
Fidencio, Niño, 268, 270
Fifty Shades of Gray (James), 49
Figal, Gerald, 250
Files, Gemma, 222
Finch-Field, Ian, 211
Fincher, David, 120, 124
Fireproof (Jha), 26–7
Fires I Started, The (album, Unwoman), 212–13
first wave Gothic, 4, 14n5
Fisher, Mark, 90, 163
Flanagan, Mike, 138
Flight of the Conchords, The (television series), 199
Flower Smith, Kirby, 145
folk healing, 269, 270, 273n2
folklore
    Asian Gothic, 250, 251, 260

Black Diasporic Gothic, 28, 30, 176, 289, 292–9
Ecogothic, 176, 180, 185, 186
modern, 73, 119
serial killer narratives, 118, 119
werewolves, 144, 147
zombies, 89, 100
Following, The (television series), 120
Forever Knight (television series), 106
fossils, time and, 171
Foucault, Michel, 194
Found (film), 122
found footage horror, 73, 74–5, 81, 134, 136, 140
Frankenstein: Gothic comedy, 192, 195
Frankenstein (film), 195, 290
Frankenstein (Shelley), 4, 10, 42, 218, 228
Freud, Sigmund, 146
Fright Night (film), 106
From Dusk Till Dawn (film), 107
Frostbiten / Frostbite (film), 113
Frye, Northrop, 195
Fukurai, Tomokichi, 133
Funny Games (film), 121–2

Gacy (film), 123
Gallows, The (film), 272
Gandillon family, 145
Gashlycrumb Tinies, The (Gorey), 196
Gates, Raymond, 280
gay vs queer: television shows, 35, 37
Gaylard, Gerald, 233
Gein, Ed, 117, 127
gender stereotyping: posthuman Gothic, 219
Gender Trouble (Butler), 54
Generation Dead (Waters), 97
Genz, Stéphanie, 47
Geoul sokeuro / Into the Mirror (film), 251
Get Out (film), 299–302
Geung si / Rigor Mortis (film), 252
Ghost Bride, The (Choo), 258–9
Ghost Bride, The (film), 259
Ghost Dance (film), 140, 141
Ghost Hunters (television series), 136
ghost-hunting television shows, 136
Ghost in the Shell (film), 219, 226, 228
ghost marriage, 258–9
Ghost Story, A (film), 139
Ghost Story for Christmas, A (television series), 136
Ghost Whisperer (television series), 135

Ghostbusters (film), 190
ghosts, 131–41
 Aboriginal Gothic, 279, 284–5, 285–6
 Asian Gothic, 250–7, 258–9, 260
 classic, 136–8
 postcolonial Gothic, 27–8
 South African Gothic, 233, 234, 235, 245
Gibson, William, 205, 209–10, 218
Gidam / Epitaph (film), 138
Gilgamesh, 145
Ginger Snaps trilogy (films), 147
Girl Walks Home Alone at Night, A (film), 110
Girl with All the Gifts, The (Carey), 92–3
Gisaeng ryung / Ghastly (film), 251
'Glass Bottle Trick, The' (Hopkinson), 57, 292–3
Glissant, Edouard, 292
'Glitch Gothic', 134, 140
globalisation, Gothic and, 8–14
God of Small Things, The (Roy), 21, 28
Goddu, Teresa, 22
Gok-seong / The Wailing (film), 258
Goldacre, Ben, 68
golliwogs, 299
González Iñárritu, Alejandro, 263
Good House (Due), 291
Good Marriage, A (film), 122
Good Me, Bad Me (Land), 128
Goodman, Tim, 42–3
'Goophered Grapevine, The' (Chesnutt), 298
Gordimer, Nadine, 233
Gordon, Avery F., 253
Gorey, Edward, 196
Gosu / Goth (Otsuichi), 249
Goth Girl (television series), 190–1
goth subculture, steampunk and, 203, 204, 206–7, 208, 213–15
Gothic, definitions of, 1–7, 14n3
Gothic and the Comic Turn (Horner and Zlosnik), 190, 192–3
Gothic Studies, 2
Graham, Shane, 234
Grant, Mira, 94–5
Grave Encounters (films), 136
Graves, Oliver, 189–90, 191
Great Tea Referendum, 209
'Greedy Choke Puppy' (Hopkinson), 294
Grenier, Jean, 145

Griffen, Ryan, 281
Griffiths, Gareth, 19
Grifter, The (online video), 76, 79
grotesque, the
 Asian Gothic, 249, 255
 Black Diasporic Gothic, 297, 300, 301
 Gothic comedy, 192, 197
 New Weird, 166–7
 South African Gothic, 237–8, 239, 244
Guantanamo Bay, 66
gynoids, 225, 226–7, 228

Habila, Helen, 175–6, 182
Habit (film), 107
Haemamool, Uthis, 256
Haggerty, George, 35
Haiti: zombies, 89
Halimunda, 255
Hall, Elaine J., 48
Halperin, Victor, 89–90
Hamilton, Laurell K., 107
Hammer Horror, 104
Hampshire, Jo, 203
Han, Kang, 254
Handmaid's Tale, The (Atwood), 212
Hannibal (television series), 118, 126–7
Hanteringen avodöda / Handling the Undead (Lindqvist), 98
Haraway, Donna, 226
Hardwicke, Catherine, 152
Harman, Graham, 164
Harpur, Charles, 277
Harris, Charlaine, 57, 65, 108, 111, 154
Harris, Joel Chandler, 298
Harris, Thomas, 117, 119
Harron, Mary, 126
Harvey, Jonathan, 169
'Haunted and the Haunters, The' (Bulwer-Lytton), 132
'haunted video games', 80
Haunting, A (television series), 136
Haunting, The (film), 136
Haunting Bombay (Agarwal), 253–4
Haunting in Connecticut, The (film), 135
Haunting of Hill House, The (Jackson), 138
Haunting of Hill House, The (Netflix series), 138
Hauntings (art installation), 139
Hawthorne, Nathaniel, 3, 291
Hayles, N. Katherine, 222

Healing, The (film), 258
Hebdige, Dick, 204
Heilman, Robert B., 34
Heintz, Andy, 213
Heise-von der Lippe, Anya, 53
Heisserer, Eric, 76, 82
Hell House LLC (film), 136
Hemlock Grove (Netflix series), 62, 63
Henry: Portrait of a Serial Killer (film), 127
Her Sister's Eye (Cleven), 285, 286
Herbrechter, Stephan, 228
Here! (television channel), 35, 36–41
hermaphrodites, 254
Herzog, Werner, 105
heterotopias, monster, 194–5, 198, 199
Highmore, Freddie, 127
Higson, Charlie, 92
hijras, 254
Hindley, Myra, 125
Historical Study of the Werewolf in Literature, An (Flower Smith), 145
Ho, Elizabeth, 205
Hodkinson, Paul, 208
Hoffmann, Heinrich, 196
'Holders, The' (website), 78
Hong Kong: Gothic cinema, 252
Honogurai Mizu no soko Kara / Dark Water (film), 133
hooks, bell, 300
Hopkins, Anthony, 147
Hopkinson, Nalo, 49, 57, 292–3, 294–5, 296, 301n1
Horner, Avril, 190, 192–3, 237
horror genre
  gay community, 39
  South Africa, 234–5, 237
Hosadu, Manoru, 146
Hotel Transylvania (films), 195–6, 198
Hôtel Transylvania (Yarbro), 105
Hounds of Love, The (film), 124
House of Leaves (Danielewski), 221
Housman, Clemence, 146
Howling, The (film), 147
Howling, The: Reborn (film), 147–8
Huggan, Graham, 185
Hughes, Bill, 151
Hughes, Kathryn, 156
Hughes, William, 20
Hugo (film), 211–12
Human, Charlie, 237, 238–9, 241
human/animal link: werewolves, 146, 148–9, 150, 151, 152, 153, 156
human/nature dualism, 174–5

human/non-human: posthuman Gothic, 218–28
Hunger, The (Strieber), 106
Hurley, Kelly, 146
hybridisation of Gothic, 5
hybridity
  New Weird, the, 167
  postfeminist Gothic, 53
  soucouyant, 29
  tropical Gothic, 268
  werewolves, 146, 149
hyperlinks, 75–6
hypertext: posthuman Gothic, 218, 221, 222

I Am Legend (film), 112–13
I Am Legend (Matheson), 91, 103–4, 112–13
I, Tituba, Black Witch of Salem (Conde), 290–1
I, Zombie (film), 91
identity: Black Diasporic Gothic, 292, 296–7
I'm Buffy and You're History (Pender), 56
imperial Gothic, 19–20, 21–2, 23
imperialism, present-day: South African Gothic, 243–4, 245
In the Flesh (television series), 66, 68, 96–7
India
  Gothic cinema, 253, 258
  Gothic fiction, 253–4
  Hindu nationalism, 26–7
Indifference Engine, The (album, Professor Elemental), 214
Indonesia: Gothic fiction, 255
Infernal Devices (Jeter), 205, 209–10
Innkeepers, The (film), 140
Innocents, The (film), 136
Insidious (films), 138, 140
'interface series' (subreddit), 83
International Gothic Association, 2
internet, Gothic and the, 8–9, 72–84, 270–2
Interview with the Vampire (film), 107, 110
Interview with the Vampire (Rice), 105, 110, 113, 191
Inugami (film), 258
Irma Vep (film), 107
irrationality: Gothic, 34, 118
irrealism: postcolonial Gothic, 22–3, 24, 27, 242

Irvin, Sam, 39, 40
isithunzela, 240, 241, 242
Islamophobia, 25–7
Island of Doctor Geof, The, 209
isolated spaces, 38
isolation, vampires and, 109–10, 112
iZombie (television series), 99

'J-Horror', 133–4
Jackson, Shelley, 218
Jackson, Shirley, 138
Jacobs, Harriet, 290
Jagose, Annamarie, 34
Jamaica: plantation Gothic, 175–6, 177–80
James, E. L., 49
James, Henry, 4, 291
Japan
   cuteness, 197
   fushigi, 250
   ghosts, 133–4
   Gothic cinema, 258
   Gothic fiction, 259–60
   nationalism, 10
   onryō, 251
Jarchow, Stephen P., 36
Jarmusch, Jim, 62, 112
Jenkins, Patty, 124
Jenkins, Philip, 119
Jeter, K. W., 204, 205, 209–10
Jha, Raj Kamal, 26–7
Jinks, Catherine, 194
Johannesburg Review of Books, The (journal), 236–7
Johnson, Darlene, 283
Joplin's Ghost (Due), 137
Jordan, Neil, 107, 110
Joshinki / The Goddess Chronicle (Kirino), 259–60
Jowett, Lorna, 38
Juan de los muertos / Juan of the Dead (film), 265, 266–7
Ju-on / The Grudge (films), 133, 251, 261n3
Juranovsky, Andrea, 253
'Just a Lark' (McTair), 175–6, 177–80
Just Is (Siwes), 284–5

Kadaitcha Song, The (Watson), 279, 284
Kairo (film), 77–8, 134
Kalix MacRinnalch (Millar), 151
Kaluuya, Daniel, 300
Karroyul (film), 283, 284

Kato, 206
Kaveney, Roz, 152
Kayako Saeki, 251, 261n3
Keep, Christopher, 222
Kerr, Elizabeth, 7–8
Keyhole (film), 139
Khair, Tabish, 26, 255, 289–90
Kiernan, Caitlín, 165, 170–1
Kind Worth Killing, The (Swanson), 128
Kinsella, Sharon, 197
Kinski, Klaus, 105
Kirino, Natsuo, 259
Kirkman, Robert, 92
Klause, Annette Curtis, 151, 152
Klein, Naomi, 66, 68
KM 31: Kilómetro 31 / KM31 (film), 263
Knowledge of Angels (Paton Walsh), 146
Knudsen, Eric, 81, 82–3
Kohnen, Matthew, 98
Korea, South
   Gothic cinema, 251–2, 258
   Gothic fiction, 254
Kristeva, Julia, 54
Kuntilanak / The Chanting (film), 251
Kurniawan, Eka, 255, 256
Kurosawa, Kiyoshi, 133–4

Laddaland (film), 253
Lafferty, Andrea, 40
lagahoo, 176
Lair, The (television series), 41
Land, Ali, 128
Land of the Dead (film), 67
Langan, John, 223
Langdon St. Ives (book series, Blaylock), 205
Lap Lae, Kaeng Khoi / Brotherhood of Kaeng Khoi, The (Haemamool), 256–7
Last Man on Earth, The (film), 91
Last Werewolf, The (Duncan), 149, 194
Låt den rätte komma in / Let the Right One In (film), 33, 109–10
Latin American Gothic, 263–73
Lawn, Jennifer, 27–8
Lazarus, Neil, 244–5
League of Extraordinary Gentlemen, The (book series, Moore), 210
League of Extraordinary Gentlemen, The (film), 211

League of Gentlemen, The (television series), 192–3, 198
Lecter, Hannibal (character), 117–18, 126
Lemaitre, Pierre, 121
Lemony Snicket's A Series of Unfortunate Events (film), 190–1
Lenore (Dirge), 196
lesbian love, 50–1, 52, 58
lesbian vampires, 52
Let Me In (film), 110
Let the Right One In (Lindqvist), 109–10
Levine, Stuart, 36
Lewis, Matthew, 10, 118
Lights Out: Resurrection (Nkomo), 243
liminality
  posthuman Gothic, 218
  werewolves, 144, 146, 149, 151
Lindsay, Jeff, 126
Lirette, Christopher, 182
'Little Red Man, The' (Gates), 280
Little Red Riding Hood, 152, 206
Little Stranger, The (film), 137
Little Stranger, The (Waters), 51, 56, 137
Logan, John, 42, 43
London Labour and the London Poor (Mayhew), 210
Long Khong / Art of the Devil 2 (film), 258
Longford (television drama), 125
Lonmin platinum mine, 236
Lost Boys, The (film), 106
Lost Horizons (album, Abney Park), 213–14
Lost Souls (Brite), 107
Louisiana, 181–2
Love, Jeremy, 297, 299
Lovecraft, H. P., 161, 162–3, 164–5, 171–2, 177, 178, 179–80, 184
Lovely Bones, The (Sebold), 50, 122
'Loves of Lady Purple, The' (Carter), 54, 57
Lowe, Alice, 127–8
Lowery, David, 139
Löwy, Michael, 22
Luckhurst, Roger, 162, 178
Lugosi, Bela, 103, 114, 192
Lung Bunmi Raluek Chat / Uncle Boonmee Who Can Recall His Past Lives (film), 139
lung poh, 258
lycanthropy see werewolves

McBrien, Justin, 183
McDermid, Val, 120, 121
McGuire, Ann Elizabeth, 126
machinery
  posthuman Gothic, 218, 220, 221
  steampunk, 211, 213
machismo: Latin American Gothic, 266
McLennon, Leigh, 152
McNamee, Roger, 223
McRobbie, Angela, 48, 56
McTair, Roger, 175–6, 177, 178–9, 180
Mad Monster Party? (film), 194–6
Maddin, Guy, 139, 140
Madondo, Bongani, 236–7, 239, 246
magazines, crime, 123
magic realism, Latin American Gothic and, 264
Magrs, Paul, 198
Mahabharata, 250
Maid, The (film), 251, 253
male Gothic, 118–19
Mama (film), 138
Mandal, Anthony, 269, 270
Mantel, Hilary, 137
Maps for Lost Lovers (Aslam), 26
Marble Hornets (YouTube channel), 75, 78, 81, 82
Marion, Isaac, 61, 97
Marshall Islands, 185–6
Marsocci, Joey, 211
Martin (film), 105
Martin, Kelrick, 283
Martin, Robert K., 7
Marx, Karl, 61, 63
masculinity: *What We Do in the Shadows* (film), 199–200
Masquerade, The (video game), 107
Massey, Brandon, 291–2
Master Detective (magazine), 123
materialism: postcolonial Gothic, 22, 30
Matheson, Richard, 103
Maturin, Charles, 145, 164
Mayhew, Henry, 210
Mayolo, Carlos, 267
Mbembe, Achille, 225, 238
media
  feminism and, 48
  state sponsored: zombie fiction, 94–5
medical politics: Mexico, 268–70
Medium (television series), 135
Meļaļ (Barclay), 175–6, 185

Melmoth the Wanderer (Maturin), 164
Memnoch the Devil (Rice), 107
Men That Will Not Be Blamed For Nothing, The (band), 208–9, 213, 214
Mercy Thompson (Briggs), 153–4
Mereana Mordegard Glesgorv (online media), 79
Metamorphoses (Ovid), 145
Mexico
    Gothic cinema, 263, 265, 273n1
    Gothic television, 268–70
Meyer, Stephenie, 110, 111, 114, 150, 154
Midnight's Children (Rushdie), 20
Miéville, China, 161, 163–4, 165, 166
Mikkelsen, Mads, 118
Mikkelson, Barbara, 73–4
Mikkelson, David, 73–4
Millar, Martin, 151
Millhauser, Steven, 53
Mindhunter (Netflix series), 120
Mirrors (film), 140
Misrach, Robert, 181
Mitchell, Dominic, 68
Mitchell, W. J. T., 171
Mittelholzer, Edgar, 289
Moffatt, Tracey, 279
Monk, The (Lewis), 118, 164
Monster (Jenkins), 124
monstrosity, 5–6, 14nn8–9, 264
    Aboriginal Gothic, 276–8, 280, 281, 282, 283
    Asian Gothic, 250–2, 253, 255–6, 257, 260
    Black Diasporic Gothic, 289, 290, 291–2, 293, 294, 296–8, 299, 300–2
    imperial Gothic, 20
    Latin American Gothic, 265–6, 267, 269, 273
    plantation Gothic, 176–7
    posthuman Gothic, 218, 219, 220, 221, 223, 224, 227, 228
    werewolves, 144, 145, 146, 147–50
    zombies, 99–100
Moore, Alan, 175, 210
Moore, Jason W., 180
'Moors Murders', 125
Morant Bay, 179, 180
Morey, Peter, 25
Morlock Night (Jeter), 210
Most Haunted (television series), 136
Mr. B The Gentleman Rhymer, 214

Mudrooroo, 281
Muggleton, David, 204, 207–8
Mumler, William, 135
Munsters, The (television series), 199
Murnau, F. W., 102
music, steampunk, 204, 207, 208–9, 212–14
Muslims, othering of, 25–7
My Bones and My Flute (Mittelholzer), 289
My Favourite Murder (podcast), 125
My Winnipeg (film), 139
Myrick, Daniel, 73
Mysteries of Udolpho, The (Radcliffe), 164
Mysterious Explorations of Jasper Morello, The (film), 212
Mythology Entertainment, 82–3

Nadja (film), 107
Nagy, Richard, 211
Namorrodor, 280–1, 282
nationalism
    British, 23–4, 30
    Indian, 26–7
    Japanese, 10
    postcolonial Gothic and, 23
Native Son (Wright), 290
nature *see* Ecogothic
Near Dark (film), 106
Necromancer (Gibson), 218
Necronomicon (Lovecraft), 178
necropolitics: posthuman Gothic, 225
Needles, Sharon, 190–1
Negra, Diane, 48, 210
Neoliberal Gothic, 8, 60–70
neoliberal vampires, 62–6, 113
neoliberal zombies, 66–8, 90, 97
neoliberalism
    Asia, 253
    South Africa, 236, 240–1, 242–4
NES Godzilla (online media), 80
Never the Bride (Magrs), 198
New Crobuzon (city, Miéville), 166
New Orleans, 63
New Weird, The, 161–72
New Weird, The (VanderMeer and VanderMeer), 161
New Zealand, 199
Newgate Calendar, 123, 126
Newman, Kim, 137
Niblett, Michael, 177–8, 181–2
Niger Delta, 182–4
Night Cries (film), 279

Night Film (Pessl), 221–2
Night of the Living Dead (film), 89, 300
Nightmare on Elm Street, A (film), 133
Nights at the Circus (Carter), 54
Niño santo (television series), 268–70
Nixon, Rob, 182
Nkomo, Mandisi, 243–4
Nosferatu (film), 102–3
Nosferatu: Phantom der Nacht / Nosferatu The Vampyre (film), 105
'NoSleep' (subreddit), 78
'Note from Dr. V to Dr. Simpkin, A' (VanderMeer), 168–9
nuclear irradiation: Ecogothic, 184–6

obeah, 176, 177, 178–9, 180
objectification: Black Diasporic Gothic, 295–6
Ōdishon / Audition (film), 249
Oil on Water (Habila), 175–6, 182–4
oil: Ecogothic, 181–4
Okorafor, Nnedi, 24–5
Old Stinker, 155
Oldman, Gary, 105, 114
Olivier, Marc, 134, 140
Oloff, Kerstin, 175
Olson, Danel, 254–5
On the Origin of Species (Darwin), 146
O'Neill, Andrew, 213
Only Lovers Left Alive (film), 62, 112
onryō, 251
oral culture: Aboriginal Gothic, 278–9, 280
Ordiz, Inés, 264
Orfanato, El / The Orphanage (film), 138, 140
Originals, The (television series), 61
Ospina, Luis, 267
otherness, 264
    Aboriginal Gothic, 277–8, 279, 282, 286
    Asian Gothic, 254
    Black Diasporic Gothic, 300, 302n5
    Gothic comedy, 191–5, 200–1
    Gothic fiction, 26
    imperial Gothic, 20
    posthuman Gothic, 218, 219, 220, 224, 225, 226
    vampires, 103, 107
    werewolves, 144, 147, 148–9, 150, 151, 152–3, 154, 155
    young adult novels, 152
    zombies, 96–100

Others, The (film), 137, 140
Otherside, The (website project/app), 285, 286
Otsuichi, 249
Oyeyemi, Helen, 23–4, 29, 30, 296–7

P (film), 258
pandemics, 91–5, 104
Paranormal Activity (franchise), 136, 140
paranormal romance, 108, 144, 150, 151–2, 153, 198
Parasol Protectorate book series (Carriger), 210
Passage, The (Cronin), 63–4, 66, 112
Patchwork Girl (Jackson), 218
Paton Walsh, Jill, 146
patriarchy
    Asian Gothic, 250–1, 257–60
    Black Diasporic Gothic, 293
    Latin American Gothic, 266
PATRIOT Act, 65, 69n4
Paul, William, 190
Paying Guests, The (Waters), 49, 50–1, 56–7, 58
Pearce, Jackson, 152
Peele, Jordan, 299, 300
Peeren, Esther, 131, 256–7
Pender, Patricia, 56
'Penny Bloods', 123
Penny Dreadful (television series), 35, 41–4, 149–50, 194
Percy, Benjamin, 148, 149
Perdido Street Station (Miéville), 161, 165–7
Perfect Medium, The (exhibition), 135
performativity: postfeminist Gothic, 53, 54–5, 57, 58
Perry, Phyll, 291
Perschon, Mike, 210
Personal Shopper (film), 138–9
Pesce, Nicolas, 127
Pessl, Marisha, 221–2
Petrochemical America (Misrach and Orff), 181
Petronius, Gaius, 145
pharmacology, corporatised, 62–3, 68, 97
Philippines: Gothic cinema, 252, 253, 258, 259
Piano, The (film), 19
Picart, Caroline Joan (Kay) S., 124
Picture of Dorian Gray, The (Wilde), 193

Pikwane, Jerome, 241
Pizolatto, Nic, 120
place, significance of, 3
Plains Empty (film), 285
plantation Gothic, 176–80, 181
Playback (film), 135
podcasts: serial killers, 125–6
Poe, Edgar Allan, 120, 163, 176, 177, 290
Polanski, Roman, 104
politics: Latin American Gothic, 265, 267, 268, 269–70
Poltergeist (film), 133
Pon / Phone (film), 251
pontianak, 251, 255–6
Pontianak harum sundal malam / Pontianak (film), 251
Poole, Steven, 222
postcolonialism, Gothic and, 9–14, 19–30, 176–80, 185–6
  Aboriginals, 276, 277–8, 284–6, 287
  Asia, 253, 255, 256, 260
  Black Diaspora, 289–90
  South Africa, 233, 234, 235, 238, 242, 243, 244–5
  tropical regions, 267–8
postfeminism: steampunk, 210
postfeminist Gothic, 47–58
posthuman, postfeminist Gothic and the, 53
posthuman Gothic, 218–28
Postmortem (Cornwell), 120
Powers, Tim, 205
Prevenge (film), 127–8
Price, Marc, 98
Priest (film), 113
Priest, Hannah, 111
Prince, Mary, 290
Prince Lestat (Rice), 112
procedurals: serial killer narratives, 119–21
Procter, James, 19–20
Professor Elemental, 214
Profiler (television series), 119
progress, Gothic and, 7–8
Promised Land, The (Mudrooroo), 281
psychical research and ghosts, 135
Psycho (Bloch), 117
Psycho (film), 117
psychoanalysis: werewolves, 146
Pulse (film), 134
punk, steampunk and, 208, 211, 213
Punter, David, 53, 118–19, 233

Queen of the Damned (Rice), 106
queer Gothic, 33–44
  vampires, 33, 39, 41, 42, 44, 106
queer theory, 34–5, 43
Quiet Ones, The (film), 135

racial difference, Gothic and, 10–11
Radcliffe, Ann, 132, 164
Rader, Dennis, 122
Raised by Wolves (Barnes), 146
Ramayana, 250
rational societies, the supernatural and, 131–2
'Raven, The' (Poe), 177
Real Crime (magazine), 123
real-time updates, 75
reality, the weird and, 163–4, 165, 166, 167, 168–9, 171–2
Red Dragon (Harris), 117–18, 121
Red Moon (Percy), 148–9
Reddit, 78, 83
Reformed Vampire Support Group, The (Jinks), 194
Regent Entertainment Group, 36, 39
Reichs, Kathy, 120
Remus, Uncle, 298–9
Resident Evil (film), 92
'Return of the Afringers, The' (Madondo), 236–7, 239, 246
Return of the Living Dead (film), 91
Returned, The (television series), 98–9
Revenants, Les / The Returned (television series), 98–9
Reynold, G. W. M., 145
Rhys, Jean, 19
Rice, Anne, 105, 106, 107, 113, 114, 150, 191
Rich, Adrienne, 53
Richardson-Brown, James, 203, 215
Rights of Desire, The (Brink), 234
Rigney, Todd, 122
Ring, The (film), 133, 221
Ring Virus, The (film), 133
Rings (film), 135
Ringu / Ring (Suzuki), 133
Ringu / Ring (film), 77, 79, 133, 221, 249, 251
Rivers, Jonathan (character), 135
Road, The (film), 252
Road Games (film), 121–2
Robinson, Kim Stanley, 208
Roček, Miriam, 209
'rom zom coms', 97

romance
  vampire/human, 108–9, 110–11
  whimsical macabre, 197–8
  zombie/human, 97–8
romanticism: steampunk, 210, 211
Romero, George A., 67, 89–90, 91, 105, 300
Roy, Arundhati, 21, 26
Ruby Gloom (television series), 196
Rudd, Alison, 21
Rule, Anne, 123
Rushdie, Salman, 20–1, 22

Saberhagen, Fred, 105
Sadako Yamamura, 251, 261n3
Saga of the Swamp Thing (Moore), 175
Sage, Victor, 175
Salupo Rodriguez, Marnie, 48
Sánchez, Eduardo, 73
Sandinistas, 66, 69n5
Santa Clarita Diet (television series), 99, 199, 201
Satanic Verses, The (Rushdie), 20–1
Satrapi, Marjane, 127
Satyricon (Petronius), 145
Saul, John S., 235, 236
Savoy, Eric, 7
Scarlet Letter, The (Hawthorne), 291
Schecter, Harold, 123
Schlozman, Steven C., 92
Schmid, David, 123, 124, 126, 128
Schreck, Max, 102, 114
Schreiner, Olive, 233
science fiction, steampunk and, 205, 210–11, 214, 215
Scotland: werewolves, 148
Scott, Kim, 283, 286
'SCP Foundation, The' (website), 78
Seances (online media), 139–40
Sebold, Alice, 50, 122
Sedgwick, Eve Kosofsky, 34
Sedgwick, Marcus, 146
See No Evil (television drama), 125
Seklusyon / Seclusion (film), 252
Serial (podcast), 125
Serial Killer Podcast, The (podcast), 125
Serial Killer Quarterly (e-magazine), 123
serial killers, 117–29
Serial Killers (podcast), 125
Sesame Street (television series), 196
sex
  Here! (television channel), 39–40, 41
  Penny Dreadful (television series), 43

sexual abuse, 124–5, 128, 251, 252, 266
sexual violence: serial killers, 118–19
sexualities in Gothic, 33–4, 35, 38, 43, 44, 106
sexuality: vampires, 108–9
'Shadow over Innsmouth, The' (Lovecraft), 184
shamans: women, 257–8, 259, 260
Shame (Rushdie), 20
Shan, Darren, 99
shapeshifters, 151, 153–4, 176, 177, 250, 258, 298
Shapiro, Stephen, 242
Sharp Teeth (Barlow), 149
Shaw, Deborah, 263
Shelley, Mary, 4, 10, 42, 218, 228
Shelton, 'Stag' Lee, 298
Sherlock Holmes (film), 211
Shikoku (film), 258
Shining Girls, The (Beukes), 121
Shutter kot tit winyan / Shutter (film), 252
Shyamalan, M. Night, 137
Sigaw / The Echo (film), 252
Silence of the Lambs, The (film), 124
Silence of the Lambs, The (Harris), 117
Simpson, Philip L., 117–18, 124, 128
Sinderella / Cinderella (film), 251
Singapore
  Gothic cinema, 251, 253
  Gothic fiction, 255–6
Sinister (film), 135, 138
Sisters Red (Pearce), 152
Siwes, Darren, 284–5
Sixth Sense, The (Shyamalan), 137
Skin Folk (Hopkinson), 292–4
Skuse, C. J., 128
Sleepy Hollow (television series), 301n2
Slender Man (film), 82–3
Slenderman, 77, 80–3
Smile Dog (online media), 77, 79
Smith, Andrew, 20
Smith, Angela, 19–20
Smith, Deborah, 254
Smith, Leitich, 154
Smith, Paul Julian, 265–6
Smo, Jill, 56
snopes.com, 73–4
Snowtown (film), 124–5
social media
  Latin American Gothic, 270–2
  posthuman Gothic, 223–4
socio-ecology, 175–6

socio-political work, Gothic, 7–14
Some Like It Hot (film), 195
Something Awful (internet forum), 78, 81
Something Borrowed (Magrs), 198
Somos lo que hay / We Are What We Are (film), 265–6
Sontag, Susan, 198
Sonyeogoedam / Mourning Grave (film), 251, 252
Sonyeon-i Onda / Human Acts (Han), 254
soucouyant, 28–30, 176, 294–5, 296–7, 301n2
Soucouyant (Chariandy), 29
Soulless (Carriger), 210
South African Gothic, 233–46
Southern Vampire Mysteries, The (Harris), 57, 65, 108, 111, 154
Spearey, Susan, 20
spectacular subcultures, 204
Spectral (film), 225
spirit photography, 135–6
spiritualism and ghosts, 135
spirituality, female: Asian Gothic, 257–60
Spooner, Catherine, 204, 238
Stagolee, 298
Stake Land (film), 113
state, the: zombie fiction, 94–5
Static (film), 140
steamgoth, 215
steampunk, 203–15
  aesthetics, 204–8, 211, 212, 213, 214
  music, 204, 207, 208–9, 212–14
  politics, 205, 206, 208–9, 210, 212–13, 215
Steampunk Couture, 206
Steampunk Emma Goldman, 209
Steampunk Journal, The, 207
Steampunk Magazine, The, 205, 208–9, 214
Steampunk'd (television show), 206
Steele, Valerie, 206
Stepford Wives, The (film), 300
Sterling, Bruce, 205, 209–10, 211
Stevenson, Robert Louis, 4
Stiefvater, Maggie, 151
Stigmata (Perry), 291
Stoker, Bram, 4, 19, 20, 102, 145
  Black Diasporic Gothic and, 292, 297
  Ecogothic and, 176, 177
  Goths and, 214
  postcolonial Gothic and, 23–4

Stoler, Ann Laura, 243, 245
Story of an African Farm (Schreiner), 233
'Story of the Doodang, The' (Harris), 298
Stott, Andrew, 193–4
Strain, The (television series), 64, 66
Strange, Glenn, 192
'Strange Case of X, The' (VanderMeer), 168–9
Stranger, The (film), 263
Stranger Beside Me, A (Rule), 123
Strieber, Whitley, 106
Struwwelpeter (Hoffmann), 196
Suárez, Juana, 268
subcultures, nature of, 207–8
Subero, Gustavo, 266
suburban Gothic
  Black Diasporic, 300
  comedy, 192, 199
  serial killers, 122–3
  vampires, 115
  zombies, 90
Suchîmubôi / Steamboy (film), 211–12
Sudor frío / Cold Sweat (film), 263
sugar Gothic, 177–80, 181–2
Sugars, Cynthia, 29–30
supernatural, the, 264
  Asian Gothic, 249–50, 254, 260
  Latin American Gothic, 263
  rational societies and, 131–2
Supernatural Horror in Fiction (Lovecraft), 163, 164
surfaces: *Ex Machina* (film), 226–7
Surfacing (Attwood), 19
Suzuki, Koji, 133
Swainston, Steph, 161
Swan Book, The (Wright), 285
Swanson, Peter, 128
Sweetpea (Skuse), 128
swine flu, 62–3
Sword and Scale (podcast), 125
Sydeian, Captain, 203
sympathetic monsters
  Asian Gothic, 250–1, 257, 259, 260
  Gothic comedy, 191–2, 193–4, 198
  vampires, 104, 105, 106
  werewolves, 144, 146, 148, 149–55
  zombies, 91, 95–9

Taboo (Scott), 286
Tale of the Body Thief, The (Rice), 107
Tan, Sandi, 255–6

Tangiers, 112
Tasker, Yvonne, 48
'technoghosts', 133
technology
  ghosts and, 131–2, 133–5, 139–40
  posthuman Gothic, 218–28
  steampunk, 204, 205, 211, 213
Ted Bundy (film), 123
Ted the Caver (website), 74–6
Teen Wolf (film), 147
Teen Wolf (television series), 153
teenage vampires, 106
telesthesia, 175, 180, 183
television: queer Gothic, 35–44
Texas Chain Saw Massacre, The (film), 117
Thailand
  Gothic cinema, 252, 253, 258
  Gothic fiction, 256–7
therianthropes, 243–4
Theron, Charlize, 124
Thornton, Sarah, 207
Thornton, Warwick, 285
Threshold (Kiernan), 165, 170–2
Tierney, Dorothy, 263
Tiffin, Helen, 19, 185
Time Machine, The (Wells), 210
Todorov, Tzvetan, 132
Toema: Munyeokul / The Chosen: Forbidden Cave (film), 258
Tokoloshe, The (Pikwane), 241
Toro, Guillermo del, 137
trauma: ghosts, 253, 254–5
TribeTwelve (vlog), 77, 78
Triomf (van Niekerk), 234
Trolljegeren/Trollhunter (film), 190–1
tropical Gothic, 267–70, 273
Truax, Thomas, 213
True Blood (television series), 65, 97, 107, 108–10, 111, 113, 213
True Crime Garage (podcast), 125
True Detective (magazine), 123
True Detective (television series), 120, 176, 181–2, 183
Truth and Reconciliation Commission (South Africa), 234
Tsai Ming-liang, 139
Tumblr, 83
Tumbok (film), 253
Turcotte, Gerry, 277
Tuskegee syphilis experiments, 66
Twelve, The (Cronin), 63
Twilight (Meyer), 110–12, 150–1, 154

Twilight (television series), 48, 55–7, 61, 111–12
Tyree, J. M., 107–8

Ultraviolet (television series), 107
Underground (Mudrooroo), 281
Underworld (films), 148
Undying, The (Mudrooroo), 281
Unfriended (film), 134
United Kingdom: neoliberalism, 69
United States
  neoliberalism, 68–9
  racism, 297–9
Universal Studios, 103, 192
Unwoman, 208–9, 212–13
Upton, Florence, 299
urban fantasies, 152
urban legends
  Asian Gothic, 250, 260
  digital, 72–8, 270, 271–2
  werewolves, 144
urban monsters: Latin American Gothic, 265–7
Uruguay: Gothic cinema, 266
usenet, 72, 73, 84n1
utopianism: steampunk, 208

Vacancy (film), 121–2
'Vampire Bat, The' (Walrond), 177
'Vampire Chronicles' (Rice), 105, 107, 112
Vampire Diaries, The (television series), 61
Vampire Hunter D (video game), 107
Vampire Lestat, The (Rice), 106
vampires, 102–15, 177
  assimilation, 111–12
  Black Diasporic Gothic, 291–2, 296–7
  capitalism, 61
  domesticity, 199–200
  history, 102
  neoliberal, 62–6, 113
  otherness, 103, 107
  postfeminist Gothic, 52, 53, 55
  queer Gothic, 33, 39, 41, 42, 44, 106
  sexuality, 108–9, 177
  sympathetic, 191
  viral, 103–4, 106, 112–13
Vampires (film), 107
Van Niekerk, Marlene, 234
van Toorn, Penny, 279, 280
VanderMeer, Ann, 161–2, 164

VanderMeer, Jeff, 161–2, 164, 165, 167, 169, 205
Vasconcelos, Sandra Guardini, 267–8
Venezuela: Gothic cinema, 263
victim-focused narratives: serial killer narratives, 121–3
Victorian period,
 'Gothic cusp', 3
 Gothic revival, 132
 steampunk and, 205, 206, 208, 210, 213, 214–15
violence
 Aboriginal Gothic, 286
 Asian Gothic, 249, 251–2, 254–5
 Black Diasporic Gothic, 291, 292, 293, 297, 299
 colonial, 19, 21, 22, 23, 24, 25, 30
 environmental, 174, 175–6, 177, 178, 180, 181, 182–3, 185–6
 Latin American Gothic, 265, 268
 serial killers, 119, 120–1, 122, 126
 South African Gothic, 234, 235–6, 238–40, 241, 242–4, 245–6
 vampires, 105, 108, 109, 110
 werewolves, 146, 147, 148, 149–50, 155
violence against women, 48–9, 50, 51–2, 54, 57, 58, 120–1, 126
viral infection, 224
 digital, 77, 79, 80, 81, 82, 223–4
viral vampires, 103–4, 106, 112–13
viral zombies, 91–5, 99, 104
vlogs, 75, 77, 78, 81
Voices, The (film), 127, 128
Volk, Stephen, 135
Voltaire, 61
Volver (film), 140

Waddington, Keir, 269, 270
Wagner, the Wehr-Wolf (Reynold), 145
Waiting for the Barbarians (Coetzee), 19
Walcott, Derek, 289–90
Walking Dead, The (Kirkman), 92, 94
Walpole, Horace, 132, 190, 290
Walrond, Eric, 177
War on Terror, 65
Warm Bodies (Marion), 61, 97, 98
Warwick Research Collective (WReC), 22, 242
Washington Post, The (newspaper), 271
Wasting Away (film), 98
Waters, Daniel, 97
Waters, Sarah, 49, 50–1, 56–7, 58, 137

Watson, Nicole, 283
Watson, Sam, 279, 284
Waugh, Thomas, 40
weaponry: steampunk, 206–7, 211
webcomics, 79–80
Webster, John, 145
Weerasethakul, Apichatpong, 139
Weese, Katherine, 53
Weinstock, Jeffrey Andrew, 131, 164–5
weird, early, 163
Weird Tales (magazine), 163
Welcome to Night Vale (podcast), 83
Wells, H. G., 205, 210
were-hyenas, 243–4
Were-Wolf, The (Housman), 146
werewolf trials, 145
werewolves, 144–56
 domesticity, 199–200
 liminality, 144, 146, 149, 151
 monstrous, 144, 145, 146, 147–50
 sympathetic, 146, 148, 150–5
West, Fred, 125
West, Rose, 125
Westworld (television series), 219, 221, 225–6, 228
What We Do in the Shadows (film), 114, 199–200
Wheatley, Helen, 199
whimsical macabre, 196–8
Whitby, 198, 203, 207, 214
Whitby Gothic Weekend (WGW), 203, 206–7
Whitby Steampunk Weekend, 207
White Is for Witching (Oyeyemi), 23–4, 29, 30, 296–7
White Noise (film), 135
White Zombie (film), 89–90
whiteness: Black Diasporic Gothic, 297, 300–1, 302n5
Whitney, Sarah, 50
Who Fears Death (Okorafor), 24–5
Wicomb, Zoë, 234
Wide Sargasso Sea (Rhys), 19
'Wild Dogs, The' (Nkomo), 243–4
Wild Wild West (film), 211
Wilde, Oscar, 43, 193
Williams, Alison, 136
Williams, Raymond, 245
'Willows, The' (Blackwood), 171
Wire in the Blood (television series), 120
Wisconsin stabbing (2014), 82
witchcraft: South African Gothic, 240, 241

witnessing, technologies of, 271
wolf children, 146
Wolf Children (film), 146
Wolf Creek (film), 121–2
Wolf Gift Chronicles, The (Rice), 150
Wolf Man, The (film), 147, 149–50
Wolfblood (television series), 155
Wolfe, Cary, 220
Wolfman, The (film), 147
wolves, 146, 148, 149, 153, 155–6; *see also* werewolves
Wolves of Mercy Falls (Stiefvater), 151
women
  Asian Gothic, 250–2, 253, 255–6, 257–60
  Black Diasporic Gothic, 293–7
  objectification: male Gothic, 118–19, 120–1
  see also females
Wood, Robin, 35
World War Z (Brooks), 67, 68, 92
World War Z (film), 67–8
Wournos, Aileen, 124
Wright, Alexis, 285
Wright, Richard, 290

X-Files, The (television series), 106–7

Yamamura, Sadako (ghost), 133–4
Yaqin, Amina, 25
Yara Ma Tha Who, 280
Yarbro, Chelsea Quinn, 105
Year of Our War, The (Swainston), 161
Yenas, 243–4
Yorkshire: werewolves, 155
Young Adult Gothic fiction, 55, 144, 150, 152, 153, 154, 194
YouTube, 77, 78, 81

Z Nation (television series), 93
'Zalgo' (meme), 80
Zlosnik, Sue, 190, 192–3, 237
Zodiac (film), 120, 124
Zom-B (Shan), 99–100
zombi, 176
Zombie Autopsies, The (Scholzman), 92
zombie-human hybrids, 92, 93
zombies, 89–100
  Aboriginal Gothic, 286
  Latin American Gothic, 267
  neoliberal, 66–8, 90, 97
  otherness, 96–100, 194
  South African Gothic, 237, 240–1
  sympathetic, 95–100, 194
  viral, 91–5, 99, 104
Zoo City (Beukes), 241, 242–3, 244

EU representative:
Easy Access System Europe
Mustamäe tee 50, 10621 Tallinn, Estonia
Gpsr.requests@easproject.com

www.ingramcontent.com/pod-product-compliance
Lightning Source LLC
Chambersburg PA
CBHW070014010526
44117CB00011B/1564